Series Editors:
Steven F. Warren, Ph.D.
Marc E. Fey, Ph.D.

D0905161

Dual Language Development
and Disorders

Also in the *Communication and Language Intervention Series:*

Interventions for Speech Sound Disorders in Children
edited by A. Lynn Williams, Ph.D.,
Sharynne McLeod, Ph.D.,
and Rebecca J. McCauley, Ph.D.

*Speech and Language Development and Intervention
in Down Syndrome and Fragile X Syndrome*
edited by Joanne E. Roberts, Ph.D.,
Robin S. Chapman, Ph.D.,
and Steven F. Warren, Ph.D.

Clinical Decision Making in Developmental Language Disorders
edited by Alan G. Kamhi, Ph.D.,
Julie J. Masterson, Ph.D.,
and Kenn Apel, Ph.D.

Communication
and Language
Intervention
Series

Dual Language Development and Disorders

A Handbook on Bilingualism and Second Language Learning

Second Edition

by

Johanne Paradis, Ph.D.
Associate Professor
Department of Linguistics
University of Alberta
Edmonton, Canada

Fred Genesee, Ph.D.
Professor
Department of Psychology
McGill University
Montreal, Canada

Martha B. Crago, Ph.D.
Vice President of Research and
Professor
Dalhousie University
Halifax, Canada

·P A U L·H·
BROOKES
PUBLISHING Cᵒ ®

Baltimore • London • Sydney

Paul H. Brookes Publishing Co.
Post Office Box 10624
Baltimore, Maryland 21285-0624
USA

www.brookespublishing.com

Typeset by Aptara, Inc., Falls Church, Virginia.
Manufactured in the United States of America by
Sheridan Books, Inc., Chelsea, Michigan.

The individuals described in this book are composites or real people whose situations are masked and are based on the authors' experiences. In all instances, names and identifying details have been changed to protect confidentiality.

Library of Congress Cataloging-in-Publication Data

Dual language development and disorders : a handbook on bilingualism and second language learning /
by Johanne Paradis, Fred Genesee, and Martha B. Crago.—2nd ed.
      p.   cm.
   Includes index.
   ISBN-13: 978-1-59857-058-8
   ISBN-10: 1-59857-058-7
   I. Paradis, Johanne.   II. Genesee, Fred.   III. Crago, Martha B., 1945–
   P115.2.G458   2010
   404'.2083—dc22   2010037839

British Library Cataloguing in Publication data are available from the British Library.

2019   2018   2017   2016   2015
10   9   8   7   6   4   3

Contents

Series Preface vii

Editorial Advisory Board ix

About the Authors xi

Foreword   *Laurence B. Leonard* xiii

Acknowledgments xv

Section I: Foundations

1   Introduction 3
2   The Language–Culture Connection 27
3   The Language–Cognition Connection 38

**Section II: Understanding Bilingual and Second
Language Development**

4   Language Development in Simultaneous
     Bilingual Children 59
5   Code-Mixing in Bilingual Development 88
6   Second Language Development in Children 109
7   Language Development in Internationally
     Adopted Children 146
8   Schooling in a Second Language 164

Section III: Dual Language and Disorders

9   Language Impairment in Dual Language Children 199
10   Reading Impairment in Dual Language Children 234

Glossary 263

Index 275

Series Preface

The purpose of the *Communication and Language Intervention Series is* to provide meaningful foundations for the application of sound intervention designs to enhance the development of communication skills across the life span. We are endeavoring to achieve this purpose by providing readers with presentations of state-of-the-art theory, research, and practice.

In selecting topics, editors, and authors, we are not attempting to limit the contents of this series to viewpoints with which we agree or that we find most promising. We are assisted in our efforts to develop the series by an editorial advisory board consisting of prominent scholars representative of the range of issues and perspectives to be incorporated in the series.

Well-conceived theory and research on development and intervention are vitally important for researchers, educators, and clinicians committed to the development of optimal approaches to communication and language intervention. The content of each volume reflects our view of the symbiotic relationship between intervention and research: Demonstrations of what may work in intervention should lead to analysis of promising discoveries and insights from developmental work that may in turn fuel further refinement by intervention researchers. We trust that the careful reader will find much that is of great value in this volume.

An inherent goal of this series is to enhance the long-term development of the field by systematically furthering the dissemination of theoretically and empirically based scholarship and research. We promise the reader an opportunity to participate in the development of this field through debates and discussions that occur throughout the pages of the *Communication and Language Intervention Series*.

Editorial Advisory Board

About the Authors

Johanne Paradis, Ph.D., Associate Professor, Department of Linguistics, University of Alberta, 4–46 Assiniboia Hall, Edmonton, Alberta T6G 2E7, Canada

Dr. Paradis's education background includes linguistics, language education, psychology, and communication disorders. In addition to her professional experience as a university professor, she taught English as a second language to adults and children for 10 years. Dr. Paradis has published numerous articles and chapters in scientific journals and books on bilingual and second language children, with both typical language development and language impairment. She has also communicated her research findings through workshops and seminars to elementary school teachers, special educators, and speech-language pathologists in Canada and the United States. Dr. Paradis has researched the language development of French–English bilingual children, with typical development and with language impairment, from the toddler years to the elementary school years. One focus of this research has been to identify the similarities and differences between bilingual children and their monolingual peers, in order to better inform the expectations of educational and clinical professionals who deal with these children. Another focus of this research on bilinguals has been to understand theoretical concerns such as, "Can children acquire two languages the same way as they can acquire one?" and "Are children with language impairment capable of becoming bilingual?" Dr. Paradis has also carried out extensive research on children from minority language backgrounds learning English as a second language, with typical development and with impairment. This research has been aimed at documenting how these children approach native-speaker competence, what unique language development profiles they display, the factors explaining why some individual children learn English faster than others, and what language measures best differentiate English second language children with typical development from those with impairment. Dr. Paradis is currently developing a web site—the Child English Second Language Centre—which consists of resources to assist in more effective assessment and identification of language impairment in dual language children.

Fred Genesee, Ph.D., Professor, Department of Psychology, McGill University, Stewart Biological Sciences Building, 1205 Doctor Penfield Avenue, Montreal, Quebec H3A 1B1, Canada

Dr. Genesee's education background in is psychology. He is the author of nine books and numerous articles in scientific, professional, and popular journals and publications. He has carried out extensive research on alternative approaches to bilingual education, including second/foreign language immersion programs for language majority students and alternative forms of bilingual education for language minority students. This work has systematically documented the longitudinal language development (oral and written) and academic achievement of students educated through two languages—their home language and another language. He is currently conducting research on individual differences in reading and language development in second language immersion programs in order to identify predictors of risk for reading and/or language disability in second language learners and the overlap in reading and language disability in such learners. He has consulted with policy groups in Canada, Estonia, Germany, Hong Kong, Italy, Japan, Latvia, Russia, Spain, and the United States on issues related to second language teaching and learning in school-age learners. Dr. Genesee is also interested in basic issues related to language learning, representation, and use in bilingual children. His work in this domain focuses on simultaneous acquisition of two languages during early infancy and childhood; his specific interests include language representation (lexical and syntactic) in early stages of bilingual acquisition, transfer in bilingual development, structural and functional characteristics of child bilingual code-mixing, and communication skills in young bilingual children. Collectively, this work seeks to extend our understanding of the limits of the human faculty for language acquisition, which, to date, has been based primarily on studies of monolingual acquisition. Dr. Genesee's most recent research interests also include internationally adopted children. This research focuses on the short- and long-term language development of adoptees from China and on what this development can tell us about the effects of very early delays in exposure to a language on its acquisition.

Martha B. Crago, Ph.D., Vice President (Research) and Professor, Dalhousie University, 1144 Belmont on the Arm, Halifax, Nova Scotia B3H 1J3, Canada

Dr. Crago has an education background in anthropology and communication disorders from McGill University. Prior to becoming a professor in communication sciences and disorders at McGill, she worked as a speech-language pathologist. At present, Dr. Crago is the Vice President of Research at Dalhousie University. She has published numerous articles on language acquisition and socialization. Her research has focused on cross-linguistic and cross-cultural studies of the acquisition of Inuktitut, French, English, and Arabic across a variety of learners, including bilingual children as well as children with language impairments. Dr. Crago is Editor of the journal *Applied Psycholinguistics,* published by Cambridge University Press. She is also Vice President of the International Association of Child Language. As a university administrator, Dr. Crago has served on and presided over many national and international committees and boards pertaining to research, international affairs, and graduate studies.

Foreword

Parents, educators, and speech-language pathologists often pose rather fundamental questions concerning dual language development and disorders. These questions deal with the language(s) that should be used with a child at home, at school, or in therapy. The answers to these important questions can be found within the pages of this volume. However, they will be heavily tailored to the particular circumstances in which children find themselves. These circumstances influence not only the type of support needed to assist children in learning their new language, but also how best to ensure the children's maintenance or continued acquisition of their first language.

The authors begin to address these questions by identifying some of the critical factors that influence a child's particular circumstances. These include whether the child can be considered a simultaneous (or near-simultaneous) bilingual child, or is acquiring a second language after learning a first language, and whether the child's first language can be considered a majority or minority language. Although these distinctions allow for a division into quadrants (e.g., learning a second language after having learned a first, minority language), the authors make clear that there is a spectrum of varying degrees on which a child's particular circumstances can be placed. To assist readers with the range of circumstances, the authors introduce us to various hypothetical children whose backgrounds reflect realistic language-learning situations, including the increasingly common situation of international adoption in which the child is learning a "second first language."

The practical contributions of this volume are very clear. The authors not only raise important educational and clinical issues, but even also provide numerous examples of letters from parents, teachers, and speech-language pathologists that remind us that these issues are central to the personal and professional lives of many individuals in society. However, the authors also do an excellent job of providing readers with the scientific basis for many of their ideas. To be sure, the authors have a particular point of view. However, they endeavor to cover all sides of each issue, and make it clear when their suggestions are based on only limited evidence.

This is the second edition of this very successful volume. Each chapter has been updated, and new chapters appear on very important issues. One of these concerns the language development of internationally adopted children. As might be expected, the authors take great care in spelling out the different circumstances that can affect the language acquisition process in these children. The age of the children at adoption, the degree to which their physical and emotional needs were met, and their nutritional history are all important factors, along with the degree and type of language stimulation they received prior to joining their new family.

Another new chapter deals with the reading abilities of dual language learners. Difficulties with reading can arise for two distinct reasons. First, of course, children might have a reading disability even in their first language. However, it is also possible that reading difficulties surface because children are learning to read for the first time in what is their second language, at a point when their command of the second language is still quite limited. The authors discuss the many factors that must be considered in each of these cases.

The things that I have learned from this volume have been numerous, important, and, in some cases, even surprising. For example, prior to reading this work, I would not have expected that code-mixing can be an indication of language sophistication, that children with language impairments are no more language impaired when learning two languages than when learning one, and that developmental errors unrelated to language transfer can be abundant as children are acquiring a second language. No doubt other readers will discover surprising and informative facts within these pages.

Above all, what I most appreciate about this book is that the authors have gone beyond laudable but simplistic calls for cultural sensitivity and the need to consider the child as an individual. They have actually shown us how sensitivity and attention to individual circumstances can be translated into action in many different kinds of developmental, educational, and therapeutic situations. For the authors' efforts to provide us with these valuable details, I am grateful.

Laurence B. Leonard
Purdue University

Acknowledgments

We would like to thank the following people (in alphabetical order) for helpful comments on earlier versions of this volume: Naomi Holobow (Montreal), Leila Ranta (University of Alberta), Mabel Rice (University of Kansas), Gail Venable (San Francisco), and Lydia White (McGill University).

We would also like to acknowledge the generous support we have received from the following granting agencies that have funded our research on bilingual and second language learners: the Social Sciences and Humanities Research Council of Canada (Ottawa), the Hospital for Sick Children's Foundation (Toronto), the Canadian Language and Literacy Research Network (University of Western Ontario), the Alberta Heritage Foundation for Medical Research (Edmonton), the Alberta Centre for Child, Family & Community Research (Calgary), and the Kativik School Board (Montreal).

We dedicate the second edition of Dual Language Development and Disorders *to Wallace (Wally) E. Lambert (1922–2009). Wally was a professor in the Department of Psychology at McGill University for 36 years and a pioneer in the field of child bilingual research. Wally was a mentor to all of us, and his research has affected the lives of parents, educators, clinicians, and other researchers around the world.*

SECTION I

Foundations

CHAPTER 1

Introduction

Children come in all shapes and sizes. They differ in myriad ways that delight, puzzle, and challenge their caregivers. These differences make children unique individuals and make parenting a challenge and a joy. For educators, doctors, speech-language pathologists, psychologists, and other adults who provide professional support to children, consideration of these differences is a responsibility that can be particularly challenging when the sources of a child's differences are not part of their professional background. In this book, we focus on children who, in addition to having the differences that all children embody, are different linguistically and culturally. They are *dual language learners*—preschool and school-age children who have been learning two languages simultaneously from infancy or who are in the process of learning a second language after the first language has been established.

Simultaneous acquisition of two languages or learning a second language after a first language has been learned does not in itself make children exceptional or unusual; there are probably as many dual language children in the world as monolingual children (Tucker, 1998). But learning two languages during infancy and childhood introduces variation in children's experiences that add to their individual differences. Dual language children are often treated as if they are different, especially in communities where monolingual children are treated as the norm. The bias toward monolingual children is reinforced by the preponderance of research and theory on monolingual acquisition and the relative paucity of work on bilingual and second language learning children. The overall objective of this book is to provide a critical overview of the research on bilingual and second language learning in children and, in so doing, to *uncover* how dual language children can be different, and—most important—to show how differences in the case of dual language children is not a synonym or a euphemism for *deficits* or *disorders*. Our perspective is that there is more than one healthy and normal path to learning language(s) in child-hood and that dual language learning leads to differences that need to be both better understood and respected (Genesee, 2003). We believe that knowing two or more languages and being able to use them appropriately and effectively is a personal, social, professional, and societal asset.

This book focuses on the typical features of language and literacy development in dual language children of various types (see discussion in the next section, Who Are Dual Language Children?). The book also focuses on the developmental characteristics of dual language children who have language or reading impairments, and on considerations for assessment and intervention practices with these children. Appropriate identification of language and reading impairment in dual language children and determining intervention strategies and educational programming for dual language children affected with disorders are key concerns. Our overall goal is to present a comprehensive and up-to-date synthesis of what we know about typical and impaired bilingual and second language acquisition for professionals who work with children and for parents of these children, so that they are better able to make informed decisions on issues ranging from language choice in the home and school to determining the presence of a clinically significant developmental delay or disorder.

Our primary audience consists of speech-language pathologists who are on the front line in caring for the language development of children with reading or language disorders. But our audience also includes caregivers, early childhood educators, special education professionals (including reading specialists), and school teachers with simultaneous bilingual children or second language learners in their child care centers or classrooms, teacher educators who educate teachers who work with these children, and pediatricians and community health care professionals who may be consulted on the status of these children. Last but not least, parents of bilingual and second language children are also part of our intended audience, because parents have the utmost interest in knowing what we know about dual language development. Parent concern is often the starting point of the referral process, and parents must ultimately interpret the advice given by professionals and must make important decisions on behalf of their children.

Because our audience is broad and varied with respect to its formal background in research, theory, and clinical practice, we have sought to be as nontechnical as possible; however, when technicalities are important, we have not avoided them. Key concepts are discussed in detail in the text or in boxes throughout the book, and emphasized terms are defined in a glossary at the end of the book to aid readers who are less familiar with some of the terms that we use.

Our background is in research on dual language learning in preschool and school-age children. We are also educators who bring specific interests and experience to the book. Johanne Paradis started her professional career as a teacher of English as a second language. She subsequently earned a doctoral degree in psychology and pursued postdoctoral studies in communication disorders. All of her research has focused on dual language children, both typically developing children and children with impairment, including both preschool and school-age children. Paradis's research has covered topics such as the development of French and English when acquired simultaneously, the development of English acquired as a second language by minority children, and the sources of individual differences in that process. Paradis's research has also focused on the linguistic characteristics of language impairment in French–English bilingual children, and most recently, in learners of English as a second language. The primary goal of Paradis's research with second language learners who are typically developing and those with language impairment has been to develop methods for differentiating between them effectively in an assessment context. Paradis has conducted numerous seminars and workshops on child bilingualism, learning of a second language by children, and considerations for language assessment to local and national groups of speech–language pathologists and educators in the United States and Canada.

Fred Genesee's educational background is in psychology. He has conducted extensive research on the effectiveness of immersion and bilingual forms of education for language majority and language minority students. His research has also focused on the language development of children acquiring two languages simultaneously during the preschool years. He is interested in identifying typical patterns of language development in simultaneous bilingual children with a view to discovering the capacity of the brain for language learning. Most recently, his research has focused on the early language development of internationally adopted children and on reading development and reading impairment in children learning a second language. He has authored and edited a number of professional books for educators working with bilingual and second language learners.

Martha B. Crago worked for a number of years as a speech-language pathologist and was responsible for clinical training in speech-language pathology at McGill University before obtaining her doctorate in communication sciences and disorders at McGill University. Her research interests have focused on language development and cultural identity, as well as on the cross-linguistic nature of acquisition by children with typical language development and those with language impairment. She has worked with children from mainstream Canadian populations in the South, as well as with children from the indigenous Inuit community in the North.

WHO ARE DUAL LANGUAGE CHILDREN?

We use the terms *dual language children* and *dual language learners* generically throughout this book to refer to a diverse group of language learners. Before proceeding, we describe who these learners are and why they need to be considered as distinct groups at times. For our purposes in this book, dual language children can differ from one another in two important respects: 1) whether they are members of a majority ethnolinguistic community or a minority ethnolinguistic community and 2) whether they have learned two languages simultaneously from infancy or have learned a second language after their first language was established. There are differences among children within each of the four broad categories created by these intersecting characteristics, but these are the main categories that we refer to throughout the book.

A **majority ethnolinguistic community** is a community of individuals who speak the language spoken by most of the members of the larger community and/or are members of the ethnic or cultural group to which most members of the community belong. The community may be as large as a country, or it may be a state or province within a country or some smaller unit. The majority language and culture usually have special recognition as the official language and culture of the community. In other cases, the language and culture are regarded unofficially as the high-status language and culture in the community. The **majority language** is the language used by most newspapers and other media, in the courts, and by political bodies in the community. Examples are Anglo-Americans in the United States, English Canadians in Canada, and native German speakers in Germany. We also use the term **majority group** synonymously. A **minority ethnolinguistic community** is a community made up of individuals who speak a **minority language** and who belong to a minority culture within the larger community. The language and culture may be in the demographic minority; may have relatively low social, economic, and political power; or both. Examples are Spanish speakers or individuals of Hispanic background in the United States, speakers of Inuktitut or Cantonese in Canada, speakers of Navajo in the United States, and Turkish speakers in The Netherlands and Germany. We also use the term **minority group** synonymously.

The majority–minority distinction is not binary but reflects end points along a continuum. For instance, some minority linguistic communities are more of a minority than others. The Spanish-speaking minority community in California is closer to the middle of the continuum than the Korean-speaking community there, because the sheer number of Spanish speakers in California confers on them a certain status and power that Koreans, who are much fewer in number, lack. The status of a language can differ according to the region in which speakers of the language live; for example, in Canada as a whole, French speakers are a minority ethnolinguistic community, but in the province of Quebec, French speakers are the majority community. Because French is an official language of the country, even in the regions of the country where speakers of French are clearly a minority numerically, they enjoy a higher status than other minority ethnolinguistic communities, due to access to French-language schooling and government services (by law), French language media, and government-funded cultural centers and events. Similarly, the status of Spanish speakers varies considerably in the United States, from southern Florida and Texas (where it is relatively high) to the Midwest or Northwest (where it is relatively low). However, Spanish is not an official language of the United States and is frequently associated with newcomer communities and thus does not have the status of French in Canada, regardless of the number of speakers in a region.

The majority–minority group distinction could be important in predicting children's language outcomes. For example, the size and status of the speech community can determine a child's opportunities for frequent, varied, and rich input in a particular language. It could also differentially affect motivation to maintain that language and attitudes toward the ethnolinguistic community or communities of origin. Effectively, the more in the minority a language and culture, the more vulnerable they can be to erosion and loss as children grow older. This is discussed in more detail in Chapters 4 and 6.

When we refer to **simultaneous bilingual children,** we mean children who are exposed to, and given opportunities to learn, two languages from birth or shortly after. Ideally, simultaneous bilingual children are exposed to both languages fairly regularly from the outset, but this seldom means they are exposed to each language equally, and we discuss the implications of unequal exposure in Chapters 4 and 5 in particular. When we refer to **second language learners,** we mean children who have already made significant progress toward acquisition of one language when they begin the acquisition of a second language. These children are also often referred to as **sequential** or **successive bilinguals.** There is no definitive point in development that demarcates bilingual from second language acquisition. Many researchers have accepted the cutoff to be 3 years of age. There are two reasons for this. First, a first language can be well established in terms of vocabulary and grammar at that point, and thus effects of already knowing and speaking one language and being neurocognitively more mature can be visible in the learning of the second language (see Chapter 6). This effect is less obvious if an additional language is introduced to a child's environment at the age of, for example, 14 months. Second, broadly speaking, all children who begin to learn two languages early in life are expected to be fluent speakers of both languages later in life. However, there is some emerging evidence that subtle differences in outcomes arise in a language when learning does not begin at birth, or before 3 or 4 years of age (see Chapters 6 and 7).

Whether children are simultaneous bilinguals or second language learners could be important when assessing how much progress children have made in their languages. By definition, in a group of dual language learners the same age, the simultaneous bilinguals would have had more experience with both their languages than the second language learners would have had with their second language. Children could be expected to be more advanced in a language when they have had more experience learning it. In addition, simultaneous bilinguals are exposed to both languages very early in life, and as mentioned previously, the age at which children are first exposed to a language might have long-term consequences. Finally, the distinction between simultaneous bilinguals and second language learners could signal differences in the contexts where each language is used. Most commonly, simultaneous bilinguals acquire two languages in the home, and second language learners often have a separate home and school and community language.

Using the majority–minority group, and bilingual–second language learner distinctions, we can consider dual language children to comprise four broad subgroups:

1. Children from a majority ethnolinguistic group who have learned or are learning two majority languages simultaneously from birth or at least before 3 years of age.
2. Children from a majority ethnolinguistic group who have learned or are learning a second language after their first language was established. The second language could be a minority or majority language of the community.
3. Children from a minority ethnolinguistic group who have learned or are learning two languages simultaneously from birth, or at least before 3 years of age. One language could be a majority language.
4. Children from a minority ethnolinguistic group who have learned or are learning a second language after their first language was established. The second language is typically the majority language and the language of schooling.

In order to put personal faces on these types of dual language children, we provide more details in the next section about each group by reference to individual fictional children who have the primary characteristics of their subgroup and who differ from each other in ways that could be important to educators and clinicians. We refer to these children throughout the book to illustrate the characteristics and concepts we discuss in each chapter. The subgroups of dual language learners and the children who exemplify them are presented in Figure 1.1. Note that we have placed a dotted line between the categories to illustrate that there are no definitive boundaries between them. In Chapter 7 of this book, we also discuss the language development of **internationally adopted (IA) children.** These are children who have been adopted by families that speak a language that differs from the one experienced by the children prior to adoption; for example, children

	Majority group	Minority group
Simultaneous bilinguals	Both languages widely spoken/ high status *James*	One or both languages not widely spoken/not high status *Bistra* *Gabriela*
Second language learners/sequential bilinguals	First language is widely spoken/ high status Education through the second language/may be majority or minority language of the community *Samantha* *Trevor*	First language is not widely spoken/not high status Education through the second language/majority language of the community or wider region *Luis* *Bonnie* *Faisal* *Pauloosie*

Figure 1.1.   Types of dual language learners.

who were born and raised in China for 1 year but are adopted by English-speaking families in Canada or the United States. The fictional case we include in the next section is a girl who was adopted from Russia and was thus exposed to Russian before beginning to learn English as her "second first language." These children are unique dual language learners because they discontinue learning their first, or birth, language once they are adopted and are exposed to the language of their adoptive families. They are of particular interest in this book because they are often thought to be at risk for delays or disorders in their language development. There are a number of reasons for this: 1) they often experience social and physical deprivation preadoption; 2) termination of acquisition of the birth language could undermine the neurocognitive foundations for learning the new language, according to some theories of language acquisition; and 3) their exposure to the new language is delayed, albeit well within the classic critical period for second language learning. All of these issues are discussed further in Chapter 7.

IA children are difficult to classify using conventional terminology or our own scheme, described earlier and illustrated in Figure 1.1. They differ from simultaneous bilinguals, because—although many learn the adopted language within the first year or two of life—they discontinue acquiring the birth language and are delayed in starting to learn the new language. They differ from typical second language learners who continue to acquire and use their first language. Research on IA children is not sufficient at this time to determine with certainty whether their language acquisition resembles that of children who learn an additional language from birth, such as simultaneous bilinguals, or that of second language learners. Thus, they are a unique type of dual language learner. In any case, and as in the case of other dual language learners discussed in this book, it is important to have a solid scientific understanding of IA children's language development in order to establish appropriate expectations of what is typical for such learners, to identify whether individual children are making appropriate progress, and to ascertain whether individual children need additional support and what kind of support they need. In short, understanding the language development of IA children and the factors that influence it are critical for providing them with learning environments and supports that foster their language competence as much as possible.

PROFILES OF SIMULTANEOUS BILINGUAL CHILDREN

James

James lives in Montreal, the largest city in the French-speaking province of Quebec in Canada. His mother is French Canadian and although she speaks English and French fluently, she uses only (or primarily) French with James and has done so since he was born 5 years ago. James's father is English Canadian and is functionally bilingual in English and French, but he uses only (or primarily) English with James. James's parents decided to speak their respective native languages to him so that he will grow up bilingual. In effect, James has two first languages—he is a simultaneous bilingual child. James hears and uses both French and English on a daily basis at home. He also uses both languages outside the home with schoolmates and friends of his family, some who speak only English or only French and some who speak both. His French is a little stronger than his English, because his family lives in a neighborhood of Montreal that is predominantly French-speaking and because he speaks French in kindergarten, but James is functionally proficient in both languages. James is a majority group simultaneous bilingual child because he is growing up in a family that is part of Quebec's two dominant cultural groups—English and French. This means not only that there is strong support for both his languages in the family, but also that both have widespread utility in the community at large—in stores, with friends, at the movies, and eventually in the job market. James's parents have the choice to send him to an English medium school or a French medium school, or even to a French **immersion program** designed for English-speaking children to learn through the medium of French. They have chosen a French medium school but intend to enroll him in English-language summer day camps.

A number of children around the world resemble James; they are children of parents from the majority group who learn two first languages. In James's case, he is learning his two languages from his parents. In other cases, the sources of language input might be different—from grandparents or child care workers. Box 1.1 shows an excerpt from the *New York Times* (2002) about English-speaking parents who are choosing to employ Spanish-speaking au pairs (nannies) who take care of the children while the parents are at work; by entrusting the care of their children to Spanish-speaking child care providers, these parents are seeking to give their children the opportunity to learn Spanish along with English. Psycholinguistically speaking, simultaneous bilingual children such as James are robust language learners who are likely to acquire full proficiency in both languages, because the environment in which they live supports the learning of additional languages with no cost to either language.

Bistra

Bistra is 4 years old and lives in Iowa. Her parents are both graduate students completing their doctoral degrees in the same Slavic Studies department, which is where they met. Bistra's father, an American, is a native speaker of English and a proficient second language speaker of Russian, and knows some Bulgarian. Bistra's mother is a Bulgarian who immigrated to

---

BOX 1.1

The New York Times

September 19, 2002

"Hello Mommy, Hola Nanny: Immigrant Baby Sitters Double as Language Teachers"
—by Mireya Navarro

When Daniel Etkin first spoke, he said words like "mommy" and "vacuum," perhaps not what his daddy most wanted to hear but a reflection of his fascination with the vacuum cleaner.

But Daniel's first words also included "agua" (water) and "bonito" (pretty), taught to him by the Salvadoran nanny who has been at his side since he was a week old.

The nanny, Morena Lopez, does not speak English and his parents are not fluent in Spanish, so at the tender age of 2, Daniel is the only person in the household with the facility to communicate between them. And as with many other children in New York City and other areas with large immigrant populations, the nanny in Daniel's case not only feeds him and watches after him but has become his language instructor.

The rising demand for nanny services by working parents over the last decades and the niche that new immigrants have found in such work have combined to make nannies de facto language teachers to children of English-speaking parents. That trend, along with many children whose immigrant parents speak other languages, has given higher visibility to a cultural phenomenon in many playgrounds: the bilingual toddler. (p. B1)

---

the United States. She is a fluent second language speaker of both English and Russian as well as a native speaker of Bulgarian. Bistra's mother has spoken to her exclusively in Bulgarian from birth, and her father uses exclusively English with her. The parents speak to each other in English or sometimes in Russian. Bistra attends a child care center where only English is spoken. Like James, Bistra is a simultaneous bilingual child, because she has been exposed to two languages consistently since birth. But, unlike James, one of her two languages is not widely spoken outside her home, so she could be considered a member of a minority ethnolinguistic community of Bulgarian speakers in the United States.

Bistra's mother considers it a high priority for her daughter to speak and eventually read and write Bulgarian fluently; however, achieving this goal will be a challenge. There is no Bulgarian-speaking community in Bistra's city, so aside from her family and a few of her parents' friends, Bistra has no exposure to Bulgarian, and in particular, she has no opportunity on a day-to-day basis to use Bulgarian with peers. In addition, Bistra's child care center uses English, and her schooling will be in English. Even at 4 years of age, she speaks English more proficiently than she speaks Bulgarian, and sometimes she switches to English when speaking with her mother.

Maintaining the **heritage language,** or the language of the country of origin, is often a struggle for many immigrant and refugee families. Children such as Bistra may go through a stage in which they refuse to speak the minority language and insist on using only English, even with people with whom they have used their heritage language most of the time. Some children will lose most or all of their fluency in their heritage language once they attend school. Sometimes it is impossible for parents to find resources such as cultural events or books and videos or DVDs in the heritage language in order to give their children a broad and rich range of experience with the language. But the more parents persist in speaking the heritage language, and the more contexts they expose their children to in which that language is used, including traveling back to the country of origin, the more likely it is that their children will retain an ability to speak that language after school entry. It is especially important to give minority language children opportunities to interact with other children the same age in the heritage language to promote full, native-like fluency in it. Bistra is a simultaneous bilingual child at age 4, but whether she will become a fully proficient bilingual adult is not entirely certain. We discuss the issue of loss of the heritage language in Chapters 4 and 6.

Gabriela

Gabriela is 6 years old, and, like Bistra and James, she is a simultaneous bilingual child, because she has been exposed to both Spanish and English from birth. Gabriela was born in the New York City area, as were both of her parents, and her family still lives near New York City. Her mother is a nurse, and her father works for an insurance company. Gabriela's grandparents on both her mother's and her father's sides moved to New York from Puerto Rico when they were young adults. Gabriela's parents and grandparents all speak both Spanish and English in the home and in the community, although they try to speak more Spanish than English in the home. Gabriela lives in a neighborhood where there are many families of Puerto Rican heritage, so she is exposed to Spanish not just in the context of her family but also at local businesses, in church, and with other children on the playgrounds and at school. She attended an English child care facility before kindergarten, but is now in first grade at a Spanish–English bilingual school where Spanish is taught until third grade. More details about language and academic development in bilingual programs are given in Chapter 8.

Gabriela is unusual among bilingual children in that she is a third-generation immigrant, yet she still speaks the heritage language. Many second-generation immigrants lose their heritage language. Gabriela's family has managed to maintain Spanish because of their pride in their heritage and their belief in the importance of passing on that heritage. In addition, Puerto Ricans in New York City can easily travel back and forth between Puerto Rico and the United States. As a result, Spanish is a prevalent minority language in New York City, and Gabriela's family lives in an entire community in which Spanish is used every day. She has already traveled to Puerto Rico twice for extended holidays.

Unlike James and Bistra, Gabriela is exposed to English and Spanish from both her parents, so neither parent is associated with only one language and both parents speak Spanish and English fluently. For some families raising simultaneous bilingual children, it is difficult to maintain the child's bilingualism if one parent is monolingual. For example, Bistra's father speaks some Bulgarian, but not well enough to have an extensive conversation with his daughter. In contrast, Gabriela can speak either English or Spanish freely with both parents. Because Gabriela's parents speak both English and Spanish, they sometimes mix words from the two languages together in one conversation, even within one sentence. This phenomenon, called *code-mixing,* is common in bilingual communities across the globe. Details about how code-mixing works and how bilingual children code-mix are in Chapter 5.

It might seem that Gabriela is growing up in a similar environment to that of James; however, in Figure 1.1 we considered her a minority simultaneous bilingual child such as Bistra. This is because even though Spanish is widely spoken in New York and in many regions of the United States, it does not have the same high status that French does in Canada. However, even though Gabriela is a minority bilingual child, because Spanish is widely spoken in her community and she will grow up with many opportunities to use Spanish, she has a good chance of maintaining her bilingualism throughout her life. Contrasting Bistra's and Gabriela's situations exemplifies another point made previously: that the concept of minority language is on a continuum. Some languages are much more in the minority than others, and this can affect children's exposure to and attitudes toward those languages, and can in turn affect their chances of becoming bilingual adults. The language development of simultaneous bilingual children such as James, Bistra, and Gabriela in the preschool and early school-age years is examined in detail in Chapter 4.

PROFILES OF SECOND LANGUAGE LEARNERS

Samantha

Samantha is 7 years old and lives in Tucson, Arizona. Samantha's parents are both monolingual English speakers; consequently, Samantha learned and used English in the home during her preschool years. Samantha's parents, however, decided to send her to a Spanish-speaking child care center when she was 3 years old and then to a Spanish immersion program when she turned 5 so that she could become bilingual. They felt that it would be good for her to be bilingual in Spanish and English, because there is a large Hispanic community in the southwestern United States as well as in other regions of the country, and because Spanish is one of the most widely spoken languages in the world. Knowing Spanish would afford Samantha opportunities for travel and professional work on a global scale.

Like James, Samantha is also considered a majority group dual language learner, because her family and the community in which they live are members of the majority ethnolinguistic group. As a result, Samantha also has all of the linguistic and cultural advantages of being part of a high-status ethnolinguistic group. There is no question of her losing her English, even if she has extensive exposure to Spanish in preschool and later in elementary school. She has intensive exposure to English and mainstream American culture at home and in the community, and she will undoubtedly learn the values and orientations of that group at the same time as she learns Spanish and some of the cultural ways and values of Spanish-speaking cultural groups in her community. As discussed in Chapter 8, immersion programs in a second language typically offer language arts instruction and even some context classes in English; exact proportions of English versus second language instruction vary with different programs. Therefore, Samantha will receive academic instruction in English at school, alongside Spanish.

In contrast to James, Samantha is a second language learner, for the obvious reason that she began acquiring her second language after her first language had been established. Samantha is a fortunate second language learner, because with a little bit of effort on her parents' part, she has access to many native Spanish speakers, including adults and children, and this will greatly enhance her probabilities of acquiring full functional proficiency in Spanish. Other second language learners are not so fortunate, because there are few or no native speakers of the second language in the community. For example, some children in the state of Oregon begin to learn Japanese at 5 years of age, when they start their primary schooling in one of the Japanese immersion programs in that state. Because all of the other children in the Japanese immersion program are native English speakers and there is no sizable Japanese-speaking population in Oregon, the Japanese immersion students have relatively little access to native speaker models; thus, they have a much greater challenge in acquiring full proficiency in Japanese. In response to this challenge, the Japanese immersion schools have arranged for exchange visits with schools in Japan so that the immersion children can spend part of their summer vacation living with Japanese families. Many parents around the world are choosing to send their children to second language immersion schools so that they will become functionally proficient in two languages (see Christian & Genesee, 2001, and Johnson & Swain, 1997, for case studies of such programs).

Trevor

Trevor is 6 years old. He was born in a small suburban community north of Chicago. Trevor's parents are both native-born Americans who speak English. Trevor's father works for a large pharmaceutical company that has extensive international business dealings, and he was relocated to Berlin, Germany, 2 years ago to head up the European office. Trevor had not yet started school in America when they moved. Trevor's parents could have sent him to the American International School in Berlin, where English is used to teach other American and English-speaking children of relocated parents, but they decided to send him to a German public school so that he could learn German and socialize with other children from Germany. Trevor found the first 6 months of schooling in German difficult because of his lack of competence in German, so his parents arranged for him to have a German language tutor who helped him learn German and keep up with his schoolwork. In addition, Trevor's teachers met with his parents and developed an individualized program of instruction for him so that he had time to learn German before he was exposed to the same curriculum of studies as native German-speaking students. The transition to the all-German school—although a challenge for Trevor—went smoothly, because he had a number of advantages that helped him adapt. First, he was already well on his way to learning to read and write in English when he entered the German school, because he had advanced emergent literacy skills. This is common among children in families of professional parents who read and write frequently for work and during their leisure time. Most children who can read and write in one language make the transition to reading and writing in another language relatively easily. Above all else, Trevor was highly motivated to learn German in order to fit in and make friends with his German-speaking classmates.

Although German has become Trevor's primary language in school and outside school when he is with his friends, English continues to be a dominant force in his life; indeed, there is no question of Trevor giving up his English as he learns German. Although Trevor is learning German as a second language in Germany and is surrounded by the German language all day—every day—he is considered to be a member of a majority ethnolinguistic group because of the status of English in his family and internationally. Also, Trevor and his family belong to an expatriate community, which is distinct from an immigrant community in that the members of the community are usually in the host country temporarily and will eventually move back to their country of origin. Trevor, in the same way as Samantha, has a lot of advantages that help him become bilingual. Children such as Trevor who are in expatriate families whose home language is a major international language such as English, are examples of additive bilingualism (see Chapter 3).

Luis

Luis is an example of a second language learner from a minority group. Luis is 6 years old and lives in California with his parents, both of whom speak Spanish and very little English. They are migrant workers who maintain contact with family and friends in Mexico but spend most of their time living and working in the United States. Luis was born in the United States but grew up speaking only Spanish until he started school. Luis's first real contact with English came when he started kindergarten in a rural school in southern California. All of Luis's teachers speak only English, and all of their instruction is in English. Luis is faced with a triple challenge: to learn English for purposes of schooling, to keep up with his schoolwork in English, and to begin to integrate into the larger Anglo-American culture. Because Luis has grown up in a Spanish-speaking, largely Mexican enclave in California, he is most comfortable and competent in cultural contexts that are Mexican in orientation. In fact, he has some difficulty knowing exactly how to behave with monolingual English-speaking children, because their cultural norms for interacting with one another and with adults are different. The educational challenges faced by Luis and children like him are considerable, not simply because his education is entirely in English, but also because his parents' literacy skills in Spanish are not well developed, and as a result, they do not read and write well in either English or Spanish. This means that Luis has not had the benefits of family literacy, unlike many children from more socioeconomically advantaged homes, who have plenty of books at home, are read to at home, and observe their parents reading and writing for both work-related and personal reasons. Research shows that family literacy facilitates children's acquisition of literacy skills in school (Goldenberg, 2003).

Despite his lack of full functional proficiency in English, Luis is often referred to by teachers and educational authorities as "bilingual." This is misleading, because in fact he was really monolingual in Spanish upon school entry. The situation is even more complicated because in reality there is no single way to classify all Hispanic American children; the homes and communities in which they live are incredibly diverse. The same is true for children of Asian and Southeast Asian backgrounds. Of particular importance to our concerns in this book is that not all children of Hispanic background necessarily speak Spanish or are bilingual, even though there is a tendency to label all such children as bilingual. Many children of Hispanic background, but not all, come to school speaking only Spanish (such as Luis); some come to school speaking only English; and some come to school speaking both (such as Gabriela). Those who speak only Spanish at school entry will learn English only once they have begun schooling. Thus, some children of Hispanic background would fall into the simultaneous bilingual learner group, whereas others would be considered second language learners. Information about the language learning background of minority children such as Luis is important for educators and other professionals to obtain because there are some different patterns of development and different challenges for simultaneous bilingual children versus second language learners. Because of these differences, we discuss language development in simultaneous bilinguals and second language learners in separate chapters (see Chapters 4 and 6).

Bonnie

Bonnie is 8 years old and was born in Taiwan. Her parents are both speakers of Mandarin (Chinese), and the family immigrated to Vancouver, Canada, when Bonnie was 4½ years old. Both of her parents are professionals with well-paying jobs in the private sector, and unlike many immigrant families, they both spoke English reasonably well before arriving in Canada, although Bonnie did not. She is a second language learner like Samantha, because her first language, Mandarin, was well established before she began learning her second language, English. When Bonnie began kindergarten after having been in Canada a few months, she spoke very little English; however, she already had emergent literacy skills in Chinese, which helped her acquire comparable skills in English.

Bonnie belongs to a minority ethnolinguistic community, as does Bistra, but Mandarin is much more available to her than Bulgarian is to Bistra. Vancouver is a large, cosmopolitan city on the west coast of Canada with a substantial Asian community. Bonnie's parents rarely socialize with non-Chinese people, so she has a great deal of social contact with adults and other children her own age who speak the heritage language. Her parents rent videos and DVDs in Mandarin, buy Chinese newspapers, and plan to hire a Chinese-speaking private tutor to teach Bonnie piano lessons. In spite of being competent English speakers, Bonnie's parents choose to speak Mandarin exclusively, or nearly exclusively, at home. In Vancouver, there are numerous restaurants, and even entire shopping centers, where mainly Mandarin and Cantonese are spoken and the signs are in Chinese. In addition, Bonnie attends a weekend school so that she can develop her literacy in Chinese. Thus, even though English is the majority language, there is every reason to believe that Bonnie will grow up to be bilingual in both Mandarin and English. Bonnie is fortunate because knowing these two languages fluently will maximize her educational and professional choices.

Not all minority second language learners are as fortunate as Bonnie. Many immigrant families do not have easy access to other speakers and resources in their language and do not enjoy the kind of social status that Chinese Canadians and Chinese Americans have in cities such as Vancouver and San Francisco, respectively. As mentioned previously for simultaneous bilingual children in a minority group (such as Bistra), without strong support outside the home, many minority second language children lose their ability to speak their first language. Moreover, in contrast to Bonnie's parents, many immigrant and refugee parents struggle to earn a living, work several jobs at the same time, and cope with difficult issues of integration into their new communities. These challenges all add to the complexity of raising children and supporting their education. Luis's parents, and the parents of the next profiled child, Faisal, are examples of newcomers who are facing these challenges.

Faisal

Faisal was born in a refugee camp near the border of Kenya and Somalia. His family fled the violence and poverty of the ongoing civil war in their home country, Somalia, and lived for 2 years in the camp before coming to Edmonton, Canada, as refugees. Faisal, his parents, and his five older brothers and sisters live in a three-bedroom apartment in the northeast area of the city in a neighborhood of low socioeconomic status. After a brief period taking government-sponsored English second language courses, Faisal's father started working as a taxi driver. When Faisal first started school, his mother began working in a chicken-processing plant. Some members of Faisal's extended family have died as a result of the war, and the children in his family witnessed violence—sometimes fatal violence—on a regular basis in the refugee camp. Faisal's parents have had very little schooling, and their children had even less when they arrived in Canada. The adjustments and struggles that Faisal and his family have had to make are often difficult for Canadians who are native-born and mainstream to comprehend. Everything from coping with winter to food shopping in supermarkets is unfamiliar to them. The war, displacement, and migration have taken a toll on their mental health as well. Faisal is in first grade and finished 1 year of kindergarten in Canada. He is approximately 6 years old. His Canadian documents list his birthday as January 1, because his actual birth date is unknown. Faisal was very uncertain about how to behave and what to do during his first days at school because he had never seen or been in a classroom before. Faisal is aware that none of the teachers at school look, dress, or act as Somalis do. However, three quarters of the children in his class are from newcomer families from Africa, Southeast Asia, the Indian subcontinent, and the Middle East. Two of his classmates are Somali.

Similar to Luis, Faisal is a minority second language learner from a low socioeconomic background who faces challenges in school beyond simply learning the majority language. But unlike Luis, he does not belong to a relatively large minority community, and his family suffered traumatic experiences before their migration to the host country. Faisal lives in a linguistically and culturally diverse community of mainly newcomers, with some Canadians of European origin and some aboriginal Canadians. English is the common language for all. At home, Faisal's parents often do not have time to interact much with the children, because they work long hours in shifts. Faisal's oldest sister, Aliyah, is often responsible for the other children, and for handling communication in English with financial, government, and educational institutions. The children in the family now speak mostly English with each other. Because of his community and family situation, Faisal is even more at risk for losing his first language than Luis is. Also, because of the family's past and present struggles, Faisal might be in need of extra support and understanding from educators and other professionals.

Pauloosie

Pauloosie is an 8-year-old Inuk boy who lives in a small community (populated by 500 Inuit residents and 15 non-Inuit residents) in Northern Quebec (Nunavik), Canada. He is the fourth child in a family of six children. Both of his parents and all of his siblings speak Inuktitut as their first language. Although Inuktitut is the language of his home and of the community, many people in his settlement, including Pauloosie's parents and all of his nuclear and extended family members, speak some English. Two of his brothers have received second language schooling in French; they speak Inuktitut, French, and whatever English they have picked up from watching television and overhearing English-language interactions with people who are non-Inuit and who live in or visit the settlement.

Pauloosie's community is many hundreds of miles and a prohibitively expensive airplane ride from the cities of southern Canada. He is not likely to go to a non–Inuit community unless he becomes very ill and needs medical services or until he goes to postsecondary school. There are, however, numerous television channels available that broadcast in English and French. In comparison, there is only one television channel that broadcasts in Inuktitut.

Pauloosie attends a school in which he was taught in Inuktitut exclusively in kindergarten, first grade, and second grade. As a result, not only is he a fluent native speaker of Inuktitut, but he can also read and write it. This year, he entered third grade. His family had to decide whether he would be educated in French or in English. They chose English for Pauloosie, because they knew the third-grade English teacher and liked her teaching style. From this year until the end of secondary school, Pauloosie will have only 1 hour of instruction each day on the Inuktitut language, the Inuit culture, or the Inuit religion.

Pauloosie, like many of his classmates, finds third grade an unsettling year. For the first time, he has a non–Inuit teacher. In fact, this is Pauloosie's first sustained contact with an adult who is not an Inuk. This is also the first time that Pauloosie has had to speak English on a regular basis and for a number of hours each day. His teacher is in her second year of teaching. Her teacher education program had no courses in second language or multicultural education. Pauloosie has been surprised by many things in these first weeks at school. In his previous classes, he was never asked to speak alone in front of others, to raise his hand when called on by his Inuit teachers, or to look a teacher in the eye. He and his classmates answered together as a group, shared their work, and often copied the work of the smartest girl in class to learn from her. These ways of learning were considered appropriate by his Inuit teachers, but his third-grade teacher wants all of his work done alone. He was surprised when she called what he considered to be sharing work with others *cheating* or *copying*. Pauloosie finds it uncomfortable to be called on and to have his answers to the teacher's seemingly incessant questions evaluated. He feels ashamed, even if he knows the correct answer, and he misses the comfort of answering as one voice in a group of other children's voices. Pauloosie, like the other children in his community, has the special challenge of encountering another culture and language for the first time in school at age 8.

PROFILE OF AN INTERNATIONALLY ADOPTED CHILD

Kristina

Kristina is 5 years old and lives in Chapel Hill, North Carolina. She was born in Russia, and her name at birth was Tatiana, which is now one of her middle names. Kristina is a special dual language learner; she is learning English as a second first language and has discontinued learning her birth language, Russian. Kristina's adopted parents are both professionals—one is a lawyer and the other is a university professor—and have been married for 15 years, but were not able to have a child of their own. It took them about 5 years from making the initial decision to adopt to bringing Kristina home with them from the orphanage in Russia. Like many IA children, Kristina's family has a high socioeconomic status, and she benefits from a home environment in which she receives a great deal of attention and support as an only child of two highly educated parents. These benefits are important for her, because the conditions in the orphanage in which she was previously raised from birth were not optimal; for example, there were few caregivers for the large number of children. Kristina entered the orphanage at about age 2 and was adopted at the age of 30 months.

After she first arrived in the United States, her parents arranged for her to have a complete medical examination and a developmental assessment. Like many IA children from Eastern Europe, Kristina displayed some physical delays and medical problems. More specifically, at the time she was first examined, at almost 3 years of age, her head circumference was smaller than expected for her age and her body weight and length were also less than normal for her age group. She also had some gastrointestinal problems like other IA children from orphanages with suboptimal resources. It was not clear how much Russian Kristina learned before being adopted, because the orphanage personnel were reluctant to talk about her language abilities when Kristina's parents inquired. However, Kristina appeared to have lost any knowledge of Russian within several months of adoption; Kristina's parents had a friend who tried speaking Russian to her when she was approximately 3½ years old, and she did not appear to understand anything he said. This is not uncommon for IA children.

Within a year or so of living in her new home, Kristina's medical problems were resolved and her body weight and length improved considerably, although her head circumference continued to be of some concern. Kristina was slow to produce her first words in English and her vocabulary development was not as fast as her parents had expected, but her parents were happy with the progress she made at learning English over the first 2 years after adoption. At the time she started preschool, when she was 4 years old, her comprehension of English was good and her expressive language was fluent and easy to understand. After a year in the preschool program, Kristina made even more progress, possibly as a result of the additional stimulation in language she got from the other children and her preschool teachers.

WHAT IS (SPECIFIC) LANGUAGE IMPAIRMENT?

This book addresses dual language development in children with typical development as well as in children with language disorders. Developmental disorders are those that children are born with, in contrast to acquired disorders that can arise from environmental factors such as accidents causing neurological trauma or disease. Broadly speaking, developmental language impairment typically consists of delay in the onset of speaking; that is, delay in achievement of milestones such as first words and sentences, followed by protracted difficulties and delays extending to the school-age years in mastering vocabulary, grammar, and cognitively integrated aspects of language use, such as narratives. There are a number of reasons why children might have difficulty learning language. Language impairment can arise as one affected area among others in neurodevelopmental syndromes such as autism spectrum disorder (ASD) or Down syndrome. Language impairment can also be exhibited by children with moderate hearing loss, because they are trying to learn oral language with insufficient auditory input. The particular developmental disorder that concerns us most in this book is **specific language impairment (SLI).** A variety of other terms have been used to describe SLI, including *childhood aphasia, dysphasia,* and most recently *primary language impairment.* What distinguishes SLI from other developmental or acquired disorders is that children's difficulties are centered in learning language itself, rather than language learning difficulties being a consequence of other factors such as severe cognitive disabilities or frank neurological damage. However, there is debate about whether some mild, nonclinically significant cognitive deficits are also a component of SLI (Leonard, 1998).

There are two reasons we focus mainly on SLI when considering dual language learners and oral language disorders. The first reason is that most of the research on dual language learners who have developmental disorders has included children with SLI. Thus, there is an emergent body of knowledge that enables us to make recommendations for evidence-based practice. The second reason has to do with assessment and identification of delay and disorders in dual language children. Because other neurodevelopmental and acquired disorders can be diagnosed in part on the basis of inclusionary factors outside of language itself, the potential for over- and underidentification with dual language children is less acute when dealing with these kinds of disorders than it is for SLI. We discuss this issue in detail in Chapter 9. In spite of our focus on SLI, it is important to point out that many of the considerations and recommendations we make concerning language assessments with dual language children, as well as our advice to parents about language choice in the home and at school, could apply to all dual language children who have been referred for assessment or are being monitored, regardless of the suspected source of their language-learning difficulty. Where there is pertinent information available on dual language children with developmental disorders other than SLI, we have included this information in the book. We use both the broader term *language impairment* as well as the more particular term *SLI* throughout the book as appropriate.

SLI affects approximately 7% of 5-year-olds in North America (Leonard, 1998; Tomblin et al., 1997). The incidence of the disorder depends to some degree on how it is defined and the criteria for diagnosis, which vary across regions and countries. SLI is a developmental disorder that is defined mainly by exclusionary criteria. Children with SLI have typical hearing levels, and their nonverbal intelligence is within or above the normal range. They are not children with pervasive developmental delay or any apparent neurological damage, such as epilepsy or traumatic brain injury. They do not have social and emotional disorders like those exhibited by children with ASDs. In short, these children experience typical development in every area but one: learning to speak and use language. Thus, the main inclusionary criteria for identifying SLI is that a child falls short of age-expected performance on an oral language test battery.

The onset of language is delayed in children with SLI, as mentioned previously. They may have problems both speaking and understanding language that is spoken to them. Furthermore, particular aspects of language development cause them special difficulty. Some of these difficulties give their language certain properties that are similar to those of language spoken by children about 2 years younger; other difficulties cause more profound delays in their language development. In general, children with SLI have consistently smaller vocabularies and produce shorter sentences than children with typical development, even in the early years of elementary school (Rice, 2003; Rice, Redmond, & Hoffman, 2006). As they grow older, speaking and understanding complex sentences can be problematic for them (Leonard, 1998). It is important for us to point out that children with SLI are a heterogeneous group, and the profile of what aspect of language is most difficult for one child can be different from that of another child, even though they are both affected with SLI. Overall, the language of children with SLI improves with time and with treatment. Some children's linguistic abilities even develop into the typical range for their age, although usually at the lower bound of that range. Others never resolve all of their grammatical difficulties, even into adulthood. One study showed that 60% of children with SLI at 5½ years old continued to have language learning disabilities at 15 years of age (Stothard, Snowling, Bishop, Chipchase, & Kaplan, 1998; see also Botting, Simkin, & Conti-Ramsden, 2006). Specifically, Rice, Hoffman, and Wexler (2009) have found that the deficits in the grammatical knowledge of children diagnosed with SLI at the age of 4 or 5 diminish but never completely resolve by the teenage years.

Research on SLI in English and in other languages has shown consistently that children with SLI have prominent problems in mastering the specifics of the grammar of their language. By *prominent,* we mean that their difficulties with specific aspects of grammar often go beyond a general 2-year delay in language development typically found for vocabulary size, narrative skills, or even general grammatical abilities such as sentence length (Leonard, 1998; Rice, 2003). This is true regardless of which language they speak; however, the specific grammatical forms that cause them the most difficulty vary across languages. For instance, English-speaking children with SLI have particular problems with the auxiliary verbs and suffixes that indicate the tense of the verb (Rice & Wexler, 1996). For example, they may say, "He go to school every day" instead of "He goes to school every day," or "He going to school now" instead of "He is going to school now." They make errors with the suffix /s/ on the verb *go,* even if they are able to use a similar /s/ sound to mark the plural or the possessive form, as in *the boy's shirts.* Our own work with French-speaking children with SLI has shown us that children speaking that language often omit object pronouns (*le, la, les* = *him, her, [it], them*), which in French are positioned before the verb in the middle of a sentence, as in "*Elle la mange*"/"She is eating it" (Paradis, 2007; Paradis, Crago, & Genesee, 2005/2006). It is interesting that they do not have the same problem with the same words *le, la,* and *les* when they are used as definite articles before a noun. English-speaking children with SLI do not have difficulties with object pronouns (Paradis, 2007; Paradis et al., 2005/2006).

Children with SLI often have trouble with reading. By second grade, approximately 42% of children with SLI have reading disabilities. This has been shown to persist into fourth grade, when research has shown that approximately 33% of children with SLI continue to have reading difficulties (Catts, Fey, Tomblin, & Zhang, 2002). The reading and writing problems of children with SLI can affect their performance in other school subjects. For instance, word problems in math are difficult for children with SLI due to the complexity of language used. Researchers are still investigating whether there is a common underlying cause of SLI and reading impairment, but no conclusive evidence has been found to date (Catts, Adolf, Hogan, & Ellis Weismer, 2005). Children who have SLI sometimes display signs of attentional limitations, or even clinically significant conditions such as attention-deficit/hyperactivity disorder, or ADHD (Cohen et al., 2000; Finneran, Francis, & Leonard, 2009). The potential for overlap between SLI and reading or attentional difficulties often causes children with SLI to be labeled rather imprecisely as learning disabled (LD) once they are in school. (See the following section for more discussion on overlap between language and reading difficulties in school-age children.)

No one is sure what specific neurocognitive deficits are caused by SLI. However, there is consensus that SLI is a developmental disorder, not an acquired disorder (Leonard, 1998). As do some other developmental disorders, SLI affects boys more than girls (Leonard, 1998). Also, SLI has been found to occur among populations of children who speak any language that has been studied to date, showing that SLI is inherent to the affected child and not to the language type (Leonard, 1998). There is evidence for frequent occurrence of SLI within certain families and between twins, suggesting an inherited genetic component (Bishop, Adams, & Norbury, 2006; Crago & Gopnik, 1994; Rice, 2007). The precise location of genetic disruptions that result in the expression of SLI in individuals is still under investigation (Rice, 2007; Rice, Smith, & Gayán, 2009). Over the years, a number of theories have been posited about the nature of the deficits caused by SLI. Some theories tend to assume deficits lie in the neurocognitive structures used to build a representation for language in particular; other theories assume deficits lie in more fundamental and general perceptual and cognitive mechanisms implicated in language learning and use (e.g., Leonard, 1998; Leonard et al., 2007; Rice, 2004, 2007). To date, this theoretical debate has not been resolved.

WHAT IS READING IMPAIRMENT?

We also discuss reading acquisition in dual language learners and, in particular, issues concerning difficulties learning to read in a second language. We have added this topic to the second edition of our book because competence in reading is critical for success in school and later on in life. We also consider reading because there is often a link between language and **reading impairment,** so children with SLI often also exhibit difficulties learning to read, as noted in the preceding section. However, not all children with SLI have difficulty learning to read and not all children with reading impairment have language learning difficulties. Understanding the extent to which and how language and reading impairment overlap or are distinct is important for accurate identification of school-age children who are suspected of having learning disabilities and for providing them with appropriate support. Research indicates that intervention is more effective the more it is fine tuned to the specific learning challenges that children face (Scanlon, Gelzheiser, Vellutino, Schatschneider, & Sweeney, 2008). To the extent that school children are often identified simply as having learning disabilities and provided with general support, their specific impairments are less likely to be resolved. We believe that it is critical that the specific learning difficulties of dual language learners be identified in order to provide them with the appropriate support.

As in our treatment of children with SLI, we are concerned with children who have reading impairments that are developmental and not acquired. That is, our concern is with children who have great difficulty learning to read accurately and fluently despite normal intelligence and visual–auditory abilities, adequate learning opportunities, and the absence of neurological and psychological problems. In this sense, we are concerned primarily with *specific* reading impairment. Thus, for an identification of reading impairment to be made, certain exclusionary factors must first be ruled out. Dual language students could have difficulty learning to read a second language for reasons that do not implicate impairment as defined earlier; for example, insufficient or incomplete acquisition of oral aspects of the second language that underpin reading acquisition, limited or nonexistent prior experiences with literacy in the home or community, poor mental or physical health as a result of trauma associated with migration from the home country to the new country, and so forth. We discuss these issues in greater detail in Chapter 10. Individuals with reading impairment can improve in their ability to read accurately and fluently with appropriate additional support, but the gap between their level of reading performance and that of individuals without reading impairment usually persists into adulthood despite intervention (Shaywitz et al., 1999).

Diverse terms have been used to refer to difficulty learning to read, including *dyslexia, specific developmental dyslexia,* and *specific reading disability/impairment.* The most common term is *dyslexia.* **Dyslexia** is usually used to refer to problems in learning to decode words. For example, the National Institute of Child Health and Human Development (1997) defines dyslexia as "a specific language-based disorder of constitutional origin characterized by difficulties in single word decoding, usually reflecting insufficient phonological processing abilities". However, there are reasons for adopting a conceptualization of reading impairment that goes beyond word reading. First, there is more to reading than decoding single words. In the long run, decoding is simply the first step to learning to read text-length material for comprehension. One of the earliest and still most widely cited theories of reading, the Simple View of Reading, has long recognized comprehension as central with decoding and other language-related skills serving critical roles in achieving accurate and fluent comprehension skills (Gough & Tunmer, 1986). In school, students read to learn; thus, being able to read and comprehend complex genres of written language fluently and accurately is essential for attaining grade-level competence in academic subjects, such as science, history, and mathematics. A second reason for adopting a broader conceptualization of reading impairment comes from a growing body of research indicating that there are significant differences between learning to decode and learning to comprehend text.

More specifically, it appears that although word decoding relies primarily on phonological processing of the units of sound that make up words and that link oral to written language, reading comprehension also entails higher order language skills (August & Shanahan, 2006; Bishop & Snowling, 2004; Catts et al., 2005; Genesee, Lindholm-Leary, Saunders, & Christian, 2006). Moreover, students learning to read in either a first or second language can have difficulties with reading comprehension that do not include problems in decoding but seem to be related to higher order language skills, such as semantics or grammar (Bishop & Snowling, 2004; Catts et al., 2005; Erdos, Genesee, Savage, & Haigh, 2009). Fluent and accurate reading comprehension depends on an additional set of skills that goes beyond decoding. Thus, we need to consider deficits in reading comprehension as well as decoding if we are to have a complete understanding of reading impairment. The question arises as to whether the language skills implicated in reading comprehension impairment are also implicated in SLI, and if so, to what extent. This is important for intervention. If SLI overlaps with impairment in reading comprehension, then intervention for children with reading impairment should include elements of intervention that are suitable for children with SLI. These issues are discussed further in Chapter 10.

For all of these reasons, we use the term *reading impairment* to encompass the diverse manifestations of difficulty that children have learning to read, including difficulty decoding single words and difficulty reading sentence- and text-length written language for meaning and with fluency. We use the term *dyslexia* when we discuss studies that use this term to refer to word-level reading impairment. We do not discuss impairment linked to writing and spelling, although these are associated with reading impairment. Lack of space makes it impossible to cover all aspects of literacy in this book. More information on the characteristics of reading acquisition generally, and reading impairment in particular, is provided in Chapter 10.

It is estimated that reading impairment affects between 5% and 20% of the school-age population (Shaywitz & Shaywitz, 2005). Variation in prevalence rates is due to different methods of calculating them and different criteria for determining impairment. The precise cause of reading impairment is not well understood yet, and it may well be that there is more than one cause. The specific cause might differ depending on the nature of the impairment—word level or text level. For example, on the one hand, it is widely thought that impairment in decoding words is related to poor phonological processing skills. On the other hand, it is beginning to appear that multiple causes might be associated with impairment in reading comprehension, although our understanding of impairment with reading comprehension is very incomplete at present. Impairment in reading comprehension could be linked to poor decoding skills in some learners, but to poor language-related skills, such as grammatical competence, in others. This is an important current issue among researchers, and there is no consensus on the answer. Even with respect to dyslexia, the most intensively studied form of reading impairment, there is little understanding of why some children have such poor phonological processing skills that they have trouble learning to decode and other children have phonological processing skills that allow them to learn to decode without difficulty. Neuroimaging studies indicate that children with and without dyslexia differ with respect to the underlying neurocognitive processes that they engage in while reading, especially with respect to phonological processing (Shaywitz & Shaywitz, 2005), but there is insufficient evidence at present to explicate why these differences exist.

ORGANIZATION OF THE BOOK

This book is organized into three sections that are in turn broken down into chapters, each with a specific focus. Section I: Foundations includes Chapters 1–3. Here in Chapter 1, we define dual language learners and offer definitions of SLI and reading impairment. In this chapter, we also seek to put faces on dual language learners so that readers have the same reference points as we do. In Chapter 2, we discuss the language–culture connection; that is, the process that links language learning with becoming a member of a cultural group or groups. This developmental process shapes the lives of all children and is especially important in the case of dual language learners, because they often have exposure to more than one culture and must learn to live in and mediate between these cultures. Interacting with multiple cultures has important implications for our understanding of dual language learners' language acquisition and ultimate language use. We continue to consider the foundations of language learning in Chapter 3 by examining the language–cognition connection. In Chapter 3, we also consider both the cognitive prerequisites and the cognitive consequences of dual language learning. More specifically, we consider whether infants and children have cognitive abilities that limit language learning to one language at a time or whether they are equally capable of learning two languages. We also examine whether the acquisition of additional languages, simultaneously or in succession, affects cognitive development—for better or for worse.

Section II: Understanding Bilingual and Second Language Development consists of Chapters 4–8. In this section, we discuss specific aspects of dual language learning in detail. In Chapter 4, we review current research and theory concerning the preschool and school-age language development of children who acquire two languages simultaneously during infancy, such as in our earlier discussion of James, Bistra, and Gabriela. The emphasis in this chapter is on the typical patterns of language development in children raised bilingually and the aspects in which they are similar and different to those of children raised monolingually. Chapter 5 continues the focus on this group of learners by discussing an aspect of simultaneous bilingual acquisition called code-mixing, which is often controversial and poorly understood, yet very important for our understanding of children who grow up with two languages. Chapter 6 addresses issues in second language development in children, with a special focus on children from minority backgrounds, such as Luis, Bonnie, and Faisal, who are often referred to as *English language learners* (ELLs), *English-as-an-additional-language* (EAL) children, or *English-as-a-second-language* (ESL) children in English-dominant countries. Chapter 6 includes information on patterns and rates of second language acquisition; in particular, how long it takes for these children to become like native-speakers and what factors influence how quickly children learn a second language. Chapter 7 focuses on information about the initial and long-term language development of IA children such as Kristina, who can be considered "second first-language learners." Chapter 8 discusses schooling in a second language. Here we extend the scope of our discussion to include children who are exposed to two or more languages in the context of schooling. These may be children who come to school speaking the majority societal language, such as Samantha, or who speak a minority language, such as Luis, Bonnie, and Faisal. For the former group, dual language learning is usually a choice, whereas for the latter, it is a necessity. Language- and education-related issues—in particular, reading development and achievement—are discussed. Finally, Chapters 4–8 include a Key Points and Implications section at the end to draw readers' attention to information in the chapter that is of particular relevance to parents, educators, and clinicians.

The final section of the book, Section III: Dual Language and Disorders, includes Chapter 9, which focuses on oral language, and Chapter 10, which focuses on reading; the content in these chapters is aimed primarily at professionals such as speech-language pathologists, special educators, and psychologists. In these chapters, we provide information on the characteristics of language and reading impairments in dual language learners, present considerations for assessment with dual language children suspected of being affected with a language or reading disorder, and also discuss strategies for developing more effective assessment and intervention practices with these children.

REFERENCES

August, D., & Shanahan, T. (Eds.). (2006). Developing literacy in second language learners. *Report of the National Literacy Panel on Language-Minority Children and Youth.* Mahwah, NJ: Lawrence Erlbaum Associates.

Bishop, D.V.M., Adams, C.V., & Norbury, C.F. (2006). Distinct genetic influences on grammar and phonological short-term memory deficits: Evidence from 6-year-old twins. *Genes, Brain and Behavior, 5,* 158–169.

Bishop, D.V.M., & Snowling, M. (2004). Developmental dyslexia and specific language impairment: Same or different? *Psychological Bulletin, 130,* 858–888.

Botting, N., Simkin, Z., & Conti-Ramsden, G. (2006). Associated reading skills in children with a history of specific language impairment. *Reading and Writing, 19,* 77–98.

Catts, H., Adolf, S., Hogan, T., & Ellis Weismer, S. (2005). Are specific language impairment and dyslexia distinct disorders? *Journal of Speech, Language, and Hearing Research, 48,* 1378–1396.

Catts, H.W., Fey, M.E., Tomblin, B., & Zhang, X. (2002). A longitudinal investigation of reading outcomes in children with language impairment. *Journal of Speech, Language, and Hearing Research, 45,* 1142–1157.

Christian, D., & Genesee, F. (Eds.). (2001). *Bilingual education.* Alexandria, VA: Teachers of English to Speakers of Other Languages.

Cohen, N., Vallance, D., Barwick, M., Im, N., Menna, R., Horodezky, N., et al. (2000). The interface between ADHD and language impairment: An examination of language, achievement, and cognitive processing. *Journal of Child Psychology and Psychiatry, 41,* 353–362.

Crago, M.B., & Gopnik, M. (1994). From families to phenotypes: Theoretical and clinical implications of research into the genetic basis of specific language impairment. In S.F. Warren & J. Reichle (Series Eds.), & R.V. Watkins & M.L. Rice (Vol. Eds.), *Communication and language intervention series: Vol. 4. Specific language impairments in children* (pp. 35–51). Baltimore: Paul H. Brookes Publishing Co.

Erdos, C., Genesee, F., Savage, R., & Haigh, C. (2009). *Predicting risk for oral and written language learning difficulties in students educated in a second language.* Unpublished manuscript, Department of Psychology, McGill University.

Finneran, D., Francis, A., & Leonard, L. (2009). Sustained attention in children with specific language impairment. *Journal of Speech, Language, and Hearing Research, 52,* 915–929.

Genesee, F. (2003). Rethinking bilingual acquisition. In J.M. de Waele (Ed.), *Bilingualism: Challenges and directions for future research* (pp. 158–182). Clevedon, England: Multilingual Matters.

Genesee, F., Lindholm-Leary, K., Saunders, W., & Christian, D. (Eds.). (2006). *Educating English language learners.* New York: Cambridge University Press.

Goldenberg, C. (2003). Making schools work for low-income families in the 21st century. In S.B. Neuman & D.K. Dickinson (Eds.), *Handbook of early literacy research* (pp. 211–231). New York: Guilford Press.

Gough, P.B., & Tunmer, W.E. (1986). Decoding, reading and reading disability. *Remedial and Special Education 77,* 6–10.

Johnson, R.K., & Swain, M. (1997). *Immersion education: International perspectives.* New York: Cambridge University Press.

Leonard, L. (1998). *Children with specific language impairment.* Cambridge, MA: The MIT Press.

Leonard, L., Ellis Weismer, S., Miller, C.A., Francis, D., Tomblin, B., & Kail, R. (2007). Speed of processing, working memory, and language impairment in children. *Journal of Speech, Language, and Hearing Research, 50,* 408–428.

National Institute of Child Health and Human Development. (1997). *A synthesis of the research on reading.* Retrieved May 19, 2010, from http://www.nrrf.org/synthesis_research.htm on May 19, 2010.

Navarro, M. (2002, September 19). Hello mommy, hola nanny: Immigrant baby sitters double as language teachers. *The New York Times,* p. B1.

Paradis, J. (2007). Bilingual children with SLI: Theoretical and applied issues. *Applied Psycholinguistics, 28,* 551–564.

Paradis, J., Crago, M., & Genesee, F. (2005–2006). Domain-specific versus domain-general theories of the deficit in SLI: Object pronoun acquisition by French-English bilingual children. *Language Acquisition, 13,* 33–62.

Rice, M.L. (2003). A unified model of specific and general language delay: Grammatical tense as a clinical marker of unexpected variation. In Y. Levy & J. Schaeffer (Eds.), *Language competence across populations: Towards a definition of specific language impairment* (pp. 63–94). Mahwah, NJ: Lawrence Erlbaum Associates.

Rice, M.L. (2004). Growth models of developmental language disorders. In M.L. Rice & S. Warren (Eds.), *Developmental language disorders: From phenotypes to etiologies.* (pp. 207–240). Mahwah, NJ: Lawrence Erlbaum Associates.

Rice, M.L. (2007). Children with specific language impairment: Bridging the genetic and developmental perspectives. In E. Hoff & M. Shatz (Eds.), *Handbook of language development* (pp. 411–431). Oxford, England: Blackwell.

Rice, M.L., Hoffman, L., & Wexler, K. (2009). Judgments of omitted *BE* and *DO* in questions as extended finiteness clinical markers of SLI to fifteen years: A study of growth and asymptote. *Journal of Speech, Language, and Hearing Research, 52,* 1417–1433.

Rice, M.L., Redmond, S., & Hoffman, L. (2006). Mean length of utterance in children with specific language impairment and in younger control children shows concurrent validity and stable and parallel growth trajectories. *Journal of Speech, Language, and Hearing Research, 49,* 793–808.

Rice, M.L., Smith, S., & Gayán, J. (2009). Convergent genetic linkage and associations to language, speech and reading measures in families of probands with specific language impairment. *Journal of Neurodevelopmental Disorders* [online publication]. doi:10.1007/s11689-009-9031-x

Rice, M., & Wexler, K. (1996). Toward tense as a clinical marker of specific language impairment in English-speaking children. *Journal of Speech, Language, and Hearing Research, 39,* 1236–1257.

Scanlon, D.M., Gelzheiser, L.M., Vellutino, F.R., Schatschneider, C., & Sweeney, J.M. (2008). Reducing the incidence of early reading difficulties: Professional development for classroom teachers vs. direct interventions for children. *Learning and Individual Differences, 18,* 346–359.

Shaywitz, S.E., Fletcher, J.M., Holahan, J.M., Schneider, A.E., Marchione, K.E., Stuebing, K.K., Francis, D.J., Pugh, K.R., & Shaywitz, B.A.. (1999). Persistence of dyslexia: The Connecticut longitudinal study at adolescence. *Pediatrics, 104,* 1351–1359.

Shaywitz, S.E., & Shaywitz, B.A. (2005). Dyslexia (specific reading disability). *Biological Psychiatry, 57,* 1301–1309.

Stothard, S.E., Snowling, M.J., Bishop, D.V.M., Chipchase, B.B., & Kaplan, C.A. (1998). Language-impaired preschoolers: A follow-up into adolescence. *Journal of Speech, Language, and Hearing Research, 41,* 407–418.

Tomblin, J.B., Records, N.L., Buckwalter, P., Zhang, X., Smith, E., & O'Brien, M. (1997). The prevalence of specific language impairment in kindergarten children. *Journal of Speech, Language, and Hearing Research, 40,* 1245–1260.

Tucker, G.R. (1998). A global perspective on multilingualism and multilingual education. In J. Cenoz & F. Genesee (Eds.), *Beyond bilingualism: Multilingualism and multilingual education* (pp. 3–15). Clevedon, England: Multilingual Matters.

CHAPTER 2

The Language–Culture Connection

C hildren who speak two languages are exposed to two cultures. These cultures, like
languages, may be relatively similar to or different from one another. Children
who are learning the languages of two very different cultures have a double
learning task. They have to learn not only both of their languages, but also how to use
each language in culturally appropriate ways. Children are brought up to become members of their cultural group in part by the way the people of their culture interact and use
language with them. They learn their cultural norms by observing and being exposed to
the behaviors of the people who live with them, talk to them, parent them, and educate
them. Language plays a central role in all of these socialization experiences. Children are
also sometimes directly instructed in the culturally appropriate means of interacting and
speaking: for example, when children are told that they should wait their turn before talking. The idea that culture and language are interwoven in the upbringing of a child has
been called **language socialization** (see Box 2.1). Children are socialized into their culture through language, and, in turn, cultural patterning socializes children in how and
with whom to use the language or languages they are learning. In this chapter, we introduce the reader to some of the cross-cultural differences in language socialization that
have been documented and discuss the outcomes for language socialization patterns
when cultures are in contact, including the changes that emerge in the cultures through
such contact. Our broad goal is to raise the awareness of professionals who deal with children from the nonmainstream culture about how many cultural and language-based practices in the classroom and in the clinic might conflict with the practices the children have
been raised with.

BOX 2.1

The study of *language socialization* has as its goal the understanding of how children become competent members of their social groups and the role language has in this process. Language socialization, therefore, concerns two major areas: socialization *through* the use of language and socialization to the use of language (Schieffelin, 1990).

LANGUAGE SOCIALIZATION ACROSS CULTURES

Think for a moment about the dominant North American culture. Parents from this culture treat their children as conversational partners from birth (Ochs & Schieffelin, 1984). Tiny infants' cries and burps are interpreted as conversational turns; it is not uncommon for mainstream North American parents to respond to such bodily noises by saying such things as "Oh, sweetie, listen to you. You are just so hungry. Mommy will give you some milk." Parents from the mainstream North American culture eagerly await their children's first words, attributing meaning to even early approximations of words. Parents label objects for children, then quiz them by asking the child to point to or name objects. Later, when the children in this culture can speak in words and small sentences, parents and relatives frequently address questions to them and ask children to recount events that have happened to them, including events where the adult has been present. In doing so, they are requesting that children display their ability to talk. Children's verbal displays are greeted with enthusiasm by adults and older children. Many mainstream, middle-class adults believe that practicing and displaying talk in this way will help children become better talkers. Furthermore, young children are explicitly taught to use politeness words such as *thank you* and *please*. For instance, before giving her child something, a mother from a middle-class, mainstream cultural background may ask the child to say "the magic word" (i.e., *please*).

In addition, children from mainstream North American culture are exposed to literacy activities well before they are expected to be able to read. In this way, these children are being prepared to participate in their culture's valued educational practice of reading. Even before children are 1 year old, parents show them books at bedtime, labeling pictures or reading stories in simple language. Parents often ask small children to point to pictures in the book. Later, they ask children questions about the story as they read it aloud. These particular language socialization practices will seem like ordinary, expected, typical behaviors to many of our readers who will consider them desirable ways to raise a child. They are, in fact, ways that socialize children to fit into the norms of the middle-class, mainstream North American culture. However, people from cultures with different belief systems and socialization practices may find these norms and behaviors peculiar and even untoward. In striking contrast to our description of the language socialization practices of the middle class, mainstream North American culture are behaviors that Martha Crago and colleagues learned about through their research in certain Canadian First Nation and Inuit homes (Crago, Annahatak, & Ninguruvik, 2009). We will use this contrast throughout this chapter as an example of just how different some cultures can be even though they reside in the same country. The Inuit people who live in the north of Canada inhabit small, remote villages. Until recently, they were a hunting and gathering society, where people lived nomadically, inhabiting tents and igloos. Traditionally, extended families lived together, with multiple generations interacting with each other on a daily basis. Although much has changed in their society, children in many homes of the eastern Arctic still grow up speaking Inuktitut.

Babies are carried on their mothers' backs in the pouch of a long wool parka called an *Amautik*. Typically, Inuit mothers do not converse with their babies. Instead, the children look out of their mothers' parkas, overseeing and overhearing their mothers' interactions with older children and adults. They become adept lookers and listeners. Inuit mothers address their babies using a rhyming, cadenced, affectionate talk. They do not interpret their babies' early vocalizations and bodily noises as talk and do not respond to them verbally. When their children are toddlers, Inuit parents do not often address the children directly. Instead, the children's needs are met silently, without requests for display, labeling, frequent questioning, or rehearsals of politeness terms. Book reading with young children is infrequent, and parents may actually frown on school-age children who read extensively, because these children are sitting quietly instead of developing their physical prowess. Children learn many skills simply by watching the behavior of a competent member of the culture. Girls learn to sew boots and parkas by watching their mothers and older relatives. Boys learn how to hunt from their fathers and other men. Children are not expected to converse with adults or to interrupt adult conversations. Instead, they are expected to play and talk with their peers.

It is easy to see why English- or French-speaking people from the Canadian mainstream cultures find Inuit socialization patterns strange and vice versa. The silence of Inuit interaction patterns can be disquieting for people from other cultures. However, Inuit find the talkative ways in which non-Inuit interact equally unsettling. An Inuk woman once said that white people must really hate their food, because "they talk so much while eating." This is just one indication of the different values that Inuit place on this way of talking. Minnie Aodla Freeman (1978) has described a number of other ways that she, as an Inuk woman, found non-Inuit Canadians strange in her book *Life Among the Qallunaat*.

Each of these cultures brings their children up in accordance with certain beliefs, using very different patterns of language socialization. Inuit, for instance, believe it is demeaning for an adult to sit on the floor and play with children or to talk with children as though they were adults. Inuit do not believe children have "reason" or *isuma* until they are about 5 years of age. Therefore, they consider it strange to engage in conversation with an "unreasonable" child, who does not have experience with life. Talking with children is left to other children. Children are oriented to interact with other children and not with adults. Inuit believe that children learn language by overhearing it and comprehending it. Listening to adults is emphasized more than speaking with adults. Similarly, activities that strengthen the body and teach children about the physical world are valued more than activities that prepare children for literacy. In contrast, middle-class North American parents believe that children learn to talk by talking. They also believe that children should be talked to directly and should engage with adults in conversation and play. Individual accomplishment is valued, and display of an individual's ability is applauded in the mainstream culture. In her two books, Barbara Rogoff has shown that parents' ways of guiding their children toward the accomplishment of culturally specified goals can vary widely (Rogoff, 1990, 2003).

Whom a child talks with, who talks to a child, what to talk about, when to talk about it, and in what ways to talk about it can and do differ across cultures. Such differences correspond to different sets of underlying beliefs. A number of researchers have also found that literacy practices vary across cultures—all of them with successful outcomes, yet all of them different and corresponding to different cultures' shared belief systems (Heath, 1983; Lewis, 2001; Schecter & Bayley, 2002; Strauss & Quinn, 1997; Torres-Guzman, 1998).

On the other hand, certain aspects of language socialization can overlap between one culture and another. A study of Chinese Canadian mothers' beliefs about **child-directed talk** revealed that this cultural group held beliefs that were both quite different from and at the same time similar to the beliefs held by mainstream Canadian mothers (Johnston & Wong, 2002). The Chinese Canadian mothers believed that teaching rather than playing with their children was the more appropriate way to help their children learn new words. The Chinese Canadian mothers were less likely than the mainstream Canadian mothers to prompt their children to tell about nonshared events, and they did not permit the intrusion of children into adult conversations, particularly with adults who were not family members. Yet this study, like others before it, found that no one culture is totally unique. Despite their marked dissimilarities, the Chinese Canadian and mainstream Canadian groups of mothers in this study had a number of beliefs about certain aspects of parent–child communication in common. For instance, they both believed that babbling could be interpreted as meaningful communication, and they also both reported that children understand words before they speak.

Similarities of language socialization practices have been pointed out for other cultural groups. Vasquez, Pease-Alvarez, and Shannon (1994) studied Mexicano homes in California, where they found that certain interaction patterns occurring in Mexicano homes were similar to those found in mainstream American homes. For instance, in both Mexicano and mainstream North American homes, mothers would scaffold their children's talk with what are called **contingent queries:** questions that promote a conversation. For example, a Mexican American mother, like a mainstream North American mother, might ask her child, "What did you do in school today?" Furthermore, within the Mexican American group itself, there was variation in how various parents socialized their children to use language.

These findings indicate that cultures are not monolithic, with totally unique and singular social practices, and that although cultures can be quite different from one another, they often share some social practices. The similarities and differences in cultural beliefs lead to similarities and differences in language socialization practices and cultural membership. Integral to this process is language itself, complete with its semantic meanings, grammatical and prosodic structures, and patterns of social interaction. When children learn more than one language, whether from birth or later, they are being socialized into more than one culture through their language.

CULTURES IN CONTACT

What happens when children are exposed to different cultural ways through multiple languages? What if they are exposed to two languages with two different cultural patterns? What happens when different cultures come in contact with each other in children's homes and schools? These questions have relevance to educational and clinical intervention practice with children. Many children around the world have parents who come from two different cultures and speak different languages. Children will also come into contact with pediatricians, child care workers, school teachers, or speech-language pathologists from different cultures who speak different languages. As people interact across their different languages and cultures—whether at home, in schools, or at clinics—certain dynamics influence the patterns of their interaction.

In many bilingual, bicultural homes, there are social forces such as gender and power differentials that influence language use and the participants' sense of cultural membership. For example, we found that in homes where two parents speak different languages (e.g., Inuktitut and English), there is likely to be a power differential (Crago, Chen, & Genesee, 1998). The more politically powerful culture, of course, is the mainstream culture. This means that there can often be pressure on the minority culture parent to adopt the languages and socialization patterns of the dominant culture. For instance, an Inuk mother is likely to speak to her children in English in the presence of their English-speaking, mainstream father.

Power differentials are particularly noteworthy in educational and medical environments, where a doctor or teacher has an evident power status in relation to minority language children. The situation is aggravated when such professionals have not been educated about the many forms that language socialization can take. In the example presented in Box 2.2, we once again draw on our experience in Northern Canadian Inuit communities to describe what can result from misunderstandings and power differentials

---

BOX 2.2

Language Socialization Differences in the Classroom

When Inuit teachers who teach in Inuktitut in the early elementary grades ask a question of their class of Inuit children, they do not expect the children to raise their hands, and they do not choose children to respond. They expect any or all of the children to volunteer an answer if they wish to. Often several children reply at the same time.

After 2 years of being taught in Inuktitut by Inuit teachers, Inuit children in Northern Quebec switch into second language third-grade classes taught by middle-class southern Canadian teachers. Picture the first day that one of these teachers asks a question of the class. She expects hands to go up and children to wait to be called on. Instead, a number of Inuit children simply call out the answer. This behavior appears rude and uncivilized to a mainstream teacher. Mainstream teachers consequently struggle with changing the children's behavior and persist in calling on individual students to display their knowledge in front of the class. If the child who is responding is wrong, the teachers will negatively evaluate his response.

Inuit children find it very hard to give individual responses and very humiliating to be evaluated, either negatively or positively, in front of their peers, because they have been brought up in a culture where people believe that peer-group interaction and collaboration are more valued behaviors than individual displays of competence.

(Crago, Eriks-Brophy, Pesco, & McAlpine, 1997; Eriks-Brophy & Crago, 2003), but it is important to point out that similar examples of cultural disconnect in school settings are also true for many children from newcomer—that is, immigrant and refugee—families in North America as well.

Most mainstream North American teachers who come to Inuit communities believe that they know what is appropriate classroom behavior for themselves and their students. The behaviors they expect are, unfortunately, premised on the cultural patterns of their own culture. These are not, as we have described earlier in this chapter, the beliefs and patterns of the Inuit culture. It is easy to see from the example in Box 2.2 how different the teachers' beliefs are and how uncomfortable these differences can become for both the children and their teachers; however, it is important to be aware that the teachers from the mainstream culture have the power to evaluate and, in the worst-case scenario, to punish the children whose language-use patterns they find unusual. Recall that Pauloosie, a child profiled in Chapter 1, experienced cultural as well as linguistic transitions in third grade when English became the language of the classroom and the teacher was no longer a member of his own cultural community. The educational history of the native people in North America and elsewhere in the world is filled with devastating examples of the deleterious effects of a lack of respect for cultural and linguistic differences that become ensnared in power differentials. Similar dynamics have been played out in numerous classrooms where there are newcomer children around the world with equally unfortunate educational and social consequences. When teachers do not understand the particular cultural patterns of their students, there are likely to be less than successful outcomes. Shirley Brice Heath described the different educational abilities of children from Cantonese families and those from Hispanic backgrounds in the United States (1986). The Hispanic children she studied were particularly good at collaborative work with their peers and at speculating on hypotheses. Their Cantonese counterparts performed better in teacher-led lessons and were particularly proficient at answering precisely and accurately. These different abilities were directly related to the language socialization practices of the children's different cultural groups. Clearly, teaching strategies that stressed collaborative work were not as comfortable or as successful for Cantonese children, and those that stressed teacher-led lessons were not as comfortable or as successful with the Hispanic children.

It is important for teachers from the mainstream culture to learn about and be aware of the various abilities that have been instilled in their students through their families' particular language socialization practices and culturally based values. Ignorance of these different patterns will reduce teachers' effectiveness and children's learning. In contrast, educational programs that build on the cultural bases established in the children's homes can be more successful for both the teachers and the learners. Finally, it is important to point out that some newcomer children, such as Faisal, who was profiled in Chapter 1, have limited or no prior experience with school or a broader school culture, before entering a mainstream North American classroom, because of the absence of educational opportunities in their home country and because of premigration experiences such as living in a refugee camp.

In many instances, when children learn two languages, they also learn about membership in the two cultures that go with their languages. When the two cultures are premised on very different beliefs, the contact between them is not always easy, and indeed, has the potential to become exceptionally difficult, with the threat that the minority culture will be overwhelmed by the dominant culture. Practitioners who are responsible for the care of dual language children need to be aware of the fragility and importance of certain cultures' practices and their susceptibility to domination and disappearance. Because of the interwoven nature of language and culture, dual language children are particularly at risk for both cultural and linguistic identity displacement. This sort of displacement takes place as children who straddle two very different cultures negotiate their dual identities across time and across a complex set of dynamics in what Nancy Hornberger (2007) named their "language socialization trajectory." In fact, it is easy to imagine that there are what Leisy Wyman (2009) referred to as "tipping" points, in which one of a child's languages will give way to the other. Cultural identity can "tip" and give way just as a child's language can and does. We discuss more about this "tipping" or "shifting" from the minority to the majority language that is often experienced by minority first language children in Chapter 4 and particularly in Chapter 6.

Erasing a child's language or cultural patterns of language use is a great loss for the child. Children's identities and senses of self are inextricably linked to the language they speak and the cultures into which they have been socialized. They are, even at an early age, speakers of their languages and members of their cultures. Language and culture are essential to children's identities. All of the affectionate talk and interpersonal communication of their childhoods and family life are embedded in their languages and cultures. Many North American immigrants have lost their language and cultural patterns of interaction within one generation. Lily Wong Fillmore (1996), the child of Chinese immigrants, has eloquently described the sense of loss that she and other Chinese immigrants felt when they could not communicate with family members and the sense of shame they felt about their culture's practices. She has pointed out the irony that North America is a continent of immigrants, but at the same time, North America, as a whole, has been particularly disrespectful of cultural and linguistic diversity.

Despite all the warnings we have just given, there is a dilemma that we need to bring to our readers attention. A preeminent American researcher, Anne Fernald (2009), has demonstrated that early language-processing skills in children from infancy to the preschool years predict long-term language acquisition and schooling outcomes. One of the factors she found to have enhanced these long-term skills is what she describes as the quality of child-directed speech. Fernald's contention is that language addressed to children not only guides vocabulary growth, but also enhances the ability for children to process language as it is spoken to them. In fact, she has suggested that what she refers to as "verbal exercise" could be crucial for the development of understanding, with important consequences for language learning (Fernald, 2009). Following her suggestion, however, raises complications for homes where parents do not have the same patterns of child-directed speech that are found in mainstream middle-class homes. If by "verbal exercise" she means bathing the child in language spoken directly by parents to children, one has to wonder how Inuit children become such proficient speakers of Inuktitut in a culture where parents do not address speech directly to their children nearly as often as often as parents do in mainstream middle-class homes. Fernald's work has important implications for languages and cultures in contact and raises some fundamental issues about what creates "quality" interactions in the language socialization of children from various cultures. In particular, the potential link between culturally specific early language socialization practices and success in the North American education system needs to be explored further to find out how much early language socialization patterns, versus other factors, contribute to educational outcomes.

CHANGING PATTERNS OF LANGUAGE AND CULTURE

Despite the potential for problematic results, new and positive forms of diversity can evolve from the contact between languages and cultures. In some bilingual, bicultural homes, children learn the cultural ways of both their parents. In certain instances, language and culture separate from each other, creating a new and different combination of behaviors. There are, for instance, a number of mixed marriages in Inuit communities. In these homes, Clair Chen (1997) reported that Inuit parents read aloud to their toddlers in much the same manner that English-speaking parents from the mainstream culture do. The only difference is that the Inuit parents read the story in Inuktitut. Changes such as this indicate that the Inuit culture is evolving and language socialization patterns are changing. Literacy skills are becoming increasingly important to the Inuit, now that schooling is a customary part of their children's lives.

A recent study of Puerto Rican mothers by Carol Hammer and her colleagues (Hammer, Rodriquez, Lawrence, & Miccio, 2007) documented cultural change and evolution in the beliefs and practices of these mothers after they lived in the U.S. mainland. Of the two groups of mothers that they studied, those whose children were raised bilingually from birth (HEC) and those who were exposed to English only at school age (SEC), the HEC group read to their children and taught them literacy-related skills more often than the SEC mothers did. This study showed that the HEC mothers included new mainland school-related cultural practices while maintaining certain practices of their own home culture.

Cultural change has also been documented in various immigrant populations. One language socialization researcher, Elinor Ochs, first studied Samoans' ways of talking with their children in Samoa (1988). A number of years later, she and a colleague (Ochs & Izquierdo, 2009) studied Samoans who had moved to the United States and discovered that they were now socializing their children with a mixture of traditional Samoan and recently acquired American interactional patterns.

There can also be a distinctive richness to the complex dynamics of bilingual and bicultural children's lives. In their study of Mexican American homes, Vasquez and her colleagues (1994) described how young children become linguistic interpreters and cultural brokers for their communities, translating and explaining mainstream North American institutions and practices to adults in their community. These children's skills in juggling multiple roles, languages, and cultures are remarkable. They develop skills and knowledge that children from mainstream English-dominant communities have limited access to because of their relative cultural and linguistic isolation. Recall from Chapter 1 that the older sister of Faisal assumed many adult-like responsibilities, such as communication with government institutions, due to her English skills, which were superior to those of her parents.

Sometimes children who live in close contact with other cultures will mix their cultural patterns, much as they code-mix their languages (see Chapter 5). In doing so, they create a new identity out of their new, mixed patterns of language use and cultural practices. Ben Rampton (1995) has described what he called **language crossing** in a school in London. Teenagers of British, Punjabi, Caribbean, and Bengali descent shared expressions in each other's languages, creating a striking multiethnic way of interacting and talking. This kind of friendly trading and crossing of language boundaries served to strengthen the boys' friendships and created a set of peer group interactions and new shared identities that reflected the multicultural diversity of these boys' lives.

Winnie Mucherah (2008) found that certain family patterns helped immigrant children to maintain their heritage languages while they learned a second language at school. These included exposure to native language media, visits to the native country, and speaking with other heritage language speakers. Conversely, other familial situations—ones in which the native language had a negative stigma or where one of the parents did not speak the heritage language—limited the retention of the native language. More details on the issue of maintaining the first language of minority children are presented in Chapter 6.

The power and impact of social institutions and family practices on children's cultures and languages serves as a reminder that any intervention with children, whether medical or educational, needs to take into account cultural and linguistic differences. In addition to finding ways to assess dual language children in their two languages, interventionists need to have culturally sensitive diagnostic procedures and interview techniques. Not only are there culturally varying attitudes to developmental delays and disorders, but there are also culturally varying norms for who talks to whom about what. Without realizing it, professionals working with dual language learners who are suspected of language or reading impairment may set up testing and diagnostic routines that violate certain cultural norms.

For instance, Martha Crago attempted to have Inuit adults elicit samples of Inuit children's language. At first glance, it seemed appropriate to us to have fluent speakers talk with the children in Inuktitut; however, we had made one very significant oversight in setting up this procedure. Inuit children are not accustomed to, or comfortable with, talking to adults. The end result was that the language samples collected by the teachers contained very limited language and were terribly misleading. Later, we remembered the pioneering work of William Labov (1972), who, by altering the circumstances in which he had African American children talk, elicited very different kinds of language. His landmark work showed that social settings and adult interlocutors have a profound influence on the language that children use. This led us to elicit language from Inuit children by putting them in a room with interesting things to play with, such as furry puppies and ugly fish. Talking with other children was comfortable and customary for them. They used vocabulary and grammatical structures that were much more complex than they had used when talking with Inuit teachers.

To give another example, when Johanne Paradis and colleagues were developing a parent questionnaire on the first language development of minority language children to be used for assessment, we ran across numerous barriers in obtaining information from parents about family history of language and learning disabilities. These barriers included the following: 1) dispreference for disclosing information about any disabilities in the family, often because of shame; 2) sociocultural differences in whether a developmental anomaly such as language delay would ever be diagnosed or treated; and 3) circumstances such as political instability, war, displacement, or economic hardships: these often prevented family members from going to or finishing schooling and/or interfered with parents' ability to recollect whether (relatively) minor developmental issues existed among family members, such as late talking or difficulties learning to read (Paradis, Emmerzael, & Sorenson Duncan, in press). Consequently, even though family history is known to be associated with many language and learning disorders, and family history information could play an important role in diagnostics, getting a sense of the presence or absence of positive family history for a child is not always straightforward in multicultural contexts.

Time and attention need to be given to developing intervention strategies that do not contravene children's or their parent's cultural norms. Intervention with children with language impairment is a language-based activity. Because language is rooted in culture, it is also a culture-based activity. We can remember mistakenly asking Inuit parents to sit on the floor to play and talk with their children with language impairment. We also requested that Inuit mothers keep diaries about their children's vocabulary, never stopping to realize that many homes did not have pencils and paper in them. One of us mused that asking such things of Inuit mothers was like asking parents like ourselves *not* to read stories to our children. It would be hard for us to do that, because it is such an ingrained pattern in our homes. In the same way, culturally inappropriate requests in nonmainstream homes are not likely to be met, and moreover, they reveal an insensitivity that will erode the clinical relationship. Inappropriate intervention practices suggest to parents and children that their cultural ways are not suitable and are not valued. In the long run, these sorts of requests can create confusion and even feelings of shame and insufficiency. They disrupt natural parent-children interactions, and over time, they risk contributing to cultural loss.

Pediatricians, nurses, child care workers, teachers, speech-language pathologists, second language specialists, and other professionals who work with dual language learners need to be aware of the connection between linguistic and cultural competencies, because it is susceptible to disruption. This connection has incredible importance; the link between children's languages and cultures helps the world maintain one if its greatest riches—the diversity of its peoples.

SUMMARY

This chapter describes how different cultures socialize their children in terms of language use and language interaction. Cultures in contact may often misunderstand each other's norms for language socialization, which can lead to misunderstandings and, in the case of children, to unfortunate educational and clinical outcomes. Nonetheless, cultures in contact influence each other and evolve. Children in multicultural environments have even found ways to share their cultural interaction patterns, thereby erasing the strength of the boundaries that can exist between them. To be successful and respectful, language education and language intervention need to take the cultural patterns of socialization into consideration.

REFERENCES

Chen, C. (1997). *Language use and language socialization in bilingual homes in Inuit communities.* Unpublished master's thesis, McGill University, Montreal, Canada.

Crago, M., Annahatak, B., & Ninguruvik,L. (2009). Changing patterns of language socialization in Inuit homes. In P. Singh (Ed.), *Indigenous identity and activism* (pp. 154–175). Delhi: Shipra.

Crago, M., Chen, C., & Genesee, F. (1998). Power and deference: Decision making in bilingual Inuit homes. *Journal of Just and Caring Education, 4*(1), 78–95.

Crago, M., Eriks-Brophy, A., Pesco, D., & McAlpine, L. (1997). Culturally-based miscommunication in class-room interaction. *Language, Speech, and Hearing Services in the Schools, 28*(3), 245–254.

Eriks-Brophy, A.E., & Crago, M. (2003). Variation in instructional discourse features: Cultural or linguistic?: Evidence from Inuit and non-Inuit teachers of Nunavik. *Anthropology and Education Quarterly, 34*(4), 1–25.

Fernald, A. (2009, November). *Developing fluency in understanding: How it matters.* Keynote address, Boston University Conference on Language Development, Boston.

Freeman, M.A. (1978). *Life Among the Qallunaat.* Edmonton, Alberta, Canada: Hurtig.

Hammer, C.S., Rodriquez, B.L., Lawrence, F.L., & Miccio, A.W. (2007). Puerto Rican mothers' beliefs and home literacy practices. *Language, Speech, and Hearing in the Schools, 38,* 216–224.

Heath, S.B. (1983). *Ways with words.* New York: Cambridge University Press.

Heath, S.B. (1986). Sociocultural contexts of language development. In *Beyond language: Social and cultural factors in schooling language minority children* (pp. 143–186). Los Angeles: Evaluation, Dissemination and Assessment Center.

Hornberger, N. (2007). Biliteracy, transnationalism, multimodality, and identity: Trajectories across time and space. *Linguistics and Education, 18,* 325–334.

Johnston, J., & Wong, M.-Y.A. (2002). Cultural differences in beliefs and practices concerning talk to children. *Journal of Speech, Language, and Hearing Research, 45,* 916–926.

Labov, W. (1972). *Language in the inner city: Studies in the Black Vernacular English.* Philadelphia: University of Pennsylvania Press.

Lewis, C. (2001). *Literacy practices as social acts.* Mahwah, NJ: Lawrence Erlbaum Associates.

Mucherah, W. (2008). Immigrants' perceptions of their native language: Challenges to actual use and maintenance. *Journal of Language, Identity, and Education, 7,* 188–205.

Ochs, E. (1988). Culture and language development: Language acquisition and language socialization in a Samoan village. Cambridge, England: Cambridge University Press.

Ochs, E., & Izquierdo, C. (2009). Responsibility in childhood: Three developmental trajectories. *Ethos, 37*(4), 391–413.

Ochs, E., & Schieffelin, B.B. (1984). Language acquisition and socialization: Three developmental stories and their implications. In R.A. Schweder & R.A. LeVine (Eds.), *Culture theory: Essays on mind, self, and emotion* (pp. 276–322). New York: Harper & Row.

Paradis, J., Emmerzael, K., & Sorenson Duncan, T. (in press). Assessment of English language learners: Using parent report on first language development. *Journal of Communication Disorders.*

Rampton, B. (1995). Language crossing and the problematisation of ethnicity and socialization. *Pragmatics, 5*(4), 485–513.

Rogoff, B. (1990). *Apprenticeship in thinking: Cognitive development in social context.* Oxford, England: Oxford University Press.

Rogoff, B. (2003). *The cultural nature of human development.* New York: Oxford University Press.

Schecter, S.R., & Bayley, R. (2002). *Language as cultural practice; Mexicanos en el Norte.* Mahwah, NJ: Lawrence Erlbaum Associates.

Schieffelin, B.B. (1990). *The give and take of everyday life.* New York: Cambridge University Press.

Strauss, C., & Quinn, N. (1997). *A cognitive theory of cultural meaning.* Cambridge, England: Cambridge University Press.

Torres-Guzman, M. (1998). Language, culture and literacy in Puerto Rican communities. In B. Perez (Ed.), *Sociocultural contexts of language and literacy* (pp. 99–121). Mahwah, NJ: Lawrence Erlbaum Associates.

Vasquez, O.A., Pease-Alvarez, L., & Shannon, S.M. (1994). *Pushing boundaries: Language and culture in a Mexicano community.* New York: Cambridge University Press.

Wong Fillmore, L. (1996). What happens when languages are lost? An essay on language assimilation and cultural identity. In D. Slobin, J. Gerhardt, A. Kyratzis, & J. Guo (Eds.), *Social interaction, social context, and language: Essays in honor of Susan Ervin-Tripp* (pp. 435–446). Mahwah, NJ: Lawrence Erlbaum Associates.

Wyman, L. (2009). Youth, linguistic ecology, and language endangerment: A Yupik example. *Journal of Language, Identity, and Education, 8,* 335–349.

CHAPTER 3

The Language–Cognition Connection

In this chapter, we explore links between language and cognition and their implications for understanding dual language development and disorders. The links between language and cognition are complex and multidirectional. There has been a rich history of research exploring these links, including such eminent theoreticians as Jean Piaget, Benjamin Whorf, Jerome Bruner, and Lev Vygotsky. Clearly, it is unnecessary to consider all of this research in detail because our objectives are more limited than researchers who seek to map the relationship between language and cognition in complete theoretical detail. Rather, we focus on those aspects of language and cognition that are related to the clinical, education, and general development of dual language learners. Two primary developmental links between language and cognition that we explore are 1) the cognitive foundations of language acquisition and use and 2) the consequences of dual language learning for cognitive development, including schooling. We organize our discussion of these topics around two general questions:

1. Do infants and children have cognitive limitations that make dual language learning burdensome?

2. Does dual language learning influence cognitive development?

These two questions can be thought of as two sides of the same coin: one side views cognitive capacity as setting limits on language development, and the other views language development as limiting or expanding the cognitive or intellectual capacities of the child. Both have been the subject of some controversy among researchers and theoreticians, and both are often of concern to parents, educators, and other professionals who care for dual language learners. We explain and present evidence about each of these controversies in the sections that follow.

Before proceeding, it is useful to provide a definition of cognition. Laura Berk, in her book *Child Development,* stated that "cognition refers to the inner processes and products of the mind that lead to 'knowing.' It includes all mental activity—attending, remembering, symbolizing, categorizing, planning, reasoning, problem solving, creating and fantasizing" (2003, p. 218).

WHY IS THE LINK BETWEEN LANGUAGE AND COGNITION IMPORTANT?

Why is it important to examine the developmental relationship between language and cognition? At first, this could seem like a largely academic issue of interest to theoreticians and researchers, not parents or professionals concerned with dual language children. There are a number of reasons why these issues are of some importance for professionals and parents who care for dual language learners. First, there is the matter of expectations. Professionals, parents, and others who are in a role where they can influence the course of children's language development—and whether they learn two languages instead of one—must have a solid, scientifically grounded understanding of the capacity of infants and young children for language learning. They need to understand whether infants and children have the capacity to learn two languages simultaneously or successively to the same extent as one language, or whether there are cognitive limitations to infants' or children's capacity to learn more than one language.

The belief that dual language learning exceeds infants' or children's typical developmental capacities could bias people to interpret the behaviors of dual language learners that differ from monolingual learners as signs of impairment, when in fact they might simply reflect individual differences or typical development for dual language learners. For example, some children are faster language learners than others. This is equally true of dual language learners. A parent or professional who believes that dual language learning is burdensome might interpret the language development of a slow dual language learner as a sign of impairment due to dual language learning rather than as simply a sign of a particular child's aptitude for language acquisition. It is not uncommon for language specialists to claim that learning two languages is ill-advised in the case of children with a language learning difficulty, and that parents should therefore use only one language in the home or that the child should not attend a bilingual school program. In Chapter 5, we consider in detail a specific aspect of dual language learning (code-mixing) that is typical among bilingual individuals but often misinterpreted by professionals and parents who are not familiar with the scientific literature on this topic. In Chapter 9, we review in depth research findings on dual language children who also have specific language impairment, demonstrating that learning an additional language is within the grasp of children affected by language disorder in certain circumstances.

Second, speech-language pathologists and educators with a solid understanding of the cognitive foundations of dual language learning can provide advice to concerned parents or other professionals, such a doctors, when asked whether children with cognitive challenges such as Down syndrome (DS) should or should not be encouraged to learn more than one language. Evidence that dual language learning exceeds the cognitive capacity of children could justify recommendations to limit children who experience difficulty to one language or to successive instead of simultaneous dual language learning; however, such recommendations may not be warranted. We regularly hear from parents and professionals who believe that a child's cognitive abilities set limits to language development and thus that dual language exposure should be curtailed for children with cognitive challenges. Decisions about whether dual language learning is possible have serious lifelong repercussions for some children, especially those who need to know more than one language to interact with family members and others in the community at the present time and in the future. Many adults with cognitive disabilities need to communicate with caregivers, family members, educators, and health care professionals—who may not all speak the same language.

Finally, an understanding of the links between language and cognition can help parents and professionals identify appropriate language outcomes for dual language learners with cognitive disabilities. In particular, understanding the nature of a child's cognitive capacities—especially those that might be manifest in the child's language behavior—helps clinicians set realistic expectations about the outcomes of remediation. In a related vein, professionals who understand the relationship between language and cognitive development may be better able to design intervention programs to match each child's cognitive abilities in order to accommodate individual differences in language learning ability. Language embodies children's thoughts and ways of thinking, and it is important that individual differences in these regards be considered when designing intervention programs and when evaluating the progress of children with language impairment following intervention.

IS DUAL LANGUAGE LEARNING BURDENSOME FOR INFANTS AND CHILDREN?

Are infants and children cognitively equipped to learn two languages, either simultaneously or successively, without costs to their ultimate language competence or their general or academic development? The fact that humans possess the cognitive capacity to learn one language without difficulty is easy for people to accept. In contrast, early dual language acquisition by preschool and young school-age children is often seen as problematic and is thought to challenge developing children. Writers for newspapers and magazines often describe the uncertain, problematic aspects of the learning phase of bilingualism (see Box 3.1).

BOX 3.1

Los Angeles Times

October 7, 2002

Judy Foreman

Kids who grow up in bilingual homes may be slower to speak than other kids, but once they've learned both languages, they appear to have a number of intellectual advantages (p. S.1).

Although Foreman acknowledged the positive attributes of later bilingualism, she claimed there are negative effects of early bilingualism (i.e., bilingual children learn language slower than monolingual children). In this chapter, we demonstrate that such claims about negative effects are not supported by the research evidence.

Scientists are also susceptible to such pessimistic thinking. For example, in an early influential theory, Macnamara (1966) argued that language acquisition in bilingual children is like an old-fashioned balance scale, with development in each language represented by each pan on the balance. According to Macnamara, as proficiency in one language increases, proficiency in the other falls behind. Such pessimistic views of bilingualism conceptualize the child's underlying cognitive capacity for language learning as a balloon that can contain only so much air; when the balloon expands as a result of acquisition of one language, acquisition of the other language is limited by the remaining space. Too much air (or too many languages) will burst the balloon. We refer to these views of dual language learning as the **limited capacity hypothesis** because these views argue that dual language acquisition is problematic because the language faculty has a limited capacity.

In the following sections, we discuss two aspects of this issue: 1) the innate capacity of infants to acquire two languages at the same time and 2) the relationship between dual language learning and cognitive development.

Are There Innate Limitations to Simultaneous Dual Language Learning?

The limited capacity hypothesis raises important fundamental questions about the innate ability of the human language faculty—are infants biologically predisposed to acquire only one language, and if so, as a consequence, does simultaneous dual language exposure and acquisition entail certain costs, in either cognitive or linguistic development? A more optimistic view is that infants possess the biological ability to acquire two languages without jeopardizing their development. The metaphor of a computer is useful here. A computer is an electronic device that has enormous processing capacity that is commonly referred to as *hardware*. The hardware of a computer relies on the help of programs called *software* to perform many complex functions, such as word processing, e-mail, viewing videos, and so forth. People purchase software to load into their computers in order to perform the desired tasks or functions. Infants' brains are like computer hardware because they have vast amounts of processing capacity, and infant development is like purchasing additional software that relies on the brain's hardware to perform functions.

The question is: Can the brain support the acquisition of only one language comfortably, or, like a computer, can a number of languages be learned (i.e., installed on the computer) without exceeding the processing capacity of the brain? The complete answer to this question is the subject of the entire book. In the next section, we focus on research that pertains to the earliest stages of language acquisition—evidence from infants and toddlers.

Speech Perception in Preverbal Infants   New research methods have made it possible to study language development even before children produce their first words. These methods examine young learners' perception of speech and language because they are not yet producing language. The findings from this research are important because they tell us what capacities children are born with that help them learn language and how early in development these capacities are functional. Most of this research has examined monolingual infants. There is much less such research on young dual language learners, but there is a growing body of research on these infants as well. Comparing the findings from monolingual infants with that from dual language learning infants can tell us whether both are using the same learning mechanisms and whether they result in the same patterns of development. One might imagine that the complexity of learning two different language systems could result in delayed development and in somewhat different patterns; what then do these delays and differences mean? Although we still have much to learn about this exciting and critical period in language acquisition, we think that the evidence supports an optimistic view of dual language learning.

The evidence on children who are monolingual indicates that children are born with remarkable processing capacities that allow them to begin the task of learning language very early in development. To quote Boysson-Bardies, "We now know that not only is the brain of the baby not empty, but in a certain sense it is fuller than that of the most brilliant scientist" (1999, p. 13). A brief and simplified view of some key studies follows, but see Chapter 1–3 in Golinkoff and Hirsh-Pasek (1999) for a nontechnical discussion of this work and Gerken (2007) for a more technical review. The evidence from studies on dual language learning infants so far indicates that they use the same capacities for language learning that have been identified in monolingual children, and that this results in patterns of development that are the same in some respects and different in others in comparison to monolingual infants.

Within 24 hours of birth, newborns prefer to listen to their mothers' voice more than another woman's voice (DeCasper & Fifer, 1980). Infants show that they prefer their mother's voice by visually fixating longer on an image (like a bull's-eye) that has the mother's voice coming from it than an image with an unfamiliar woman's voice. Preference for the mother's voice is not demonstrated if the voice samples are played backward, suggesting that the infants' preference is tied to perception of the rhythmic or prosodic features of language and not to the specific sounds that make up the language. **Prosody** refers to the intonational contours of language—the changes in pitch and stress that occur during talking. Prosody is a likely cue to early discrimination of dual language input because different languages have different prosodic characteristics. That neonates show such preferences so early after birth using prosodic features of language makes sense because prenatal infants are capable of detecting this kind of acoustic input while in the womb, and thus their responses in these experimental situations probably reflect prenatal experiences with language that they remember.

Indeed, there is empirical evidence that infants' impressive auditory discriminatory and memory capacities for language-related input after birth are based on language experiences in utero. More specifically, DeCasper and Spence (1986) found that fetuses who were read prose passages by their mothers on a daily basis 6 weeks prior to birth demonstrated a preference for these passages after birth in comparison to new passages. The infants demonstrated a preference for the previously heard passages even when they were read by another female, indicating that it was not simply familiarity with the mother's voice but rather the acoustic properties of the speech signal that the infants were responding to. By monitoring changes in fetal heart rates, these researchers also noted that fetuses in the 37th week of gestation distinguished between familiar and new poems following previous exposure to the familiar poem. These findings are important because they confirm that infants have the innate capacity to detect, discriminate between, and remember certain aspects of linguistic input and that these capacities are functional very early in development, even prenatally. This also means that dual language learners can benefit from these innate capacities, also prenatally. Time is important for dual language learning because infants must begin early if they are to analyze and make sense of dual language input.

Research on the postnatal speech perception abilities of infants has shown that newborn monolingual infants can differentiate between their native language and a "foreign language" shortly after birth if the languages belong to different rhythmic groups (e.g., French and Russian), and that they can differentiate between languages within the same rhythmic group (e.g., Spanish and Catalan) by 4½ months of age (Bosch & Sebastián-Gallés, 2001; see Polka, Rvachew, & Mattock, 2007, for a review). The ability to distinguish between languages early in development is an important foundation for building separate linguistic systems. Indeed, with respect to dual language learning infants, Bosch and Sebastián-Gallés (2001) found that 4-month-old infants exposed to both Spanish and Catalan had similar language differentiation abilities, indicating that reduced exposure to each language did not delay the emergence of this ability in these learners (see Sebastián-Gallés & Bosch, 2005, for a review of these studies). At the same time, their results suggested that the dual language infants used a different strategy than the monolingual infants. When latency to orientation was measured, the monolingual infants oriented more rapidly to the native language, whereas the bilingual Spanish–Catalan infants oriented more rapidly to the nonnative or unfamiliar language.

Additional evidence that newborns are prepared for dual language learning comes from research on infants' perception of the individual sounds that make up human language, for example, [b], [d], and [a]; these are referred to as **phonetic segments**. Extensive research on this topic has shown that infants begin life with the ability to discriminate many consonant and vowel sounds found in the world's languages, regardless of their experience with specific languages. The acoustic differences between some consonant and vowel sounds can be very subtle, yet these small differences can be **phonemic** in a language, which means that these differences change the meaning of a word. For example, [l] and [r] in English are phonemic because *lot* and *rot* are different words with different meanings. The segments [l] and [r], however, are not phonemic in Japanese; they are two acoustic variations on one phoneme, and there are no words in Japanese that contrast in meaning based only on the difference between [l] and [r]. Findings that infants can distinguish most contrasts that are phonemic in the world's languages from birth—regardless of whether they have had exposure to a language that uses those contrasts—is an important ability for dual language learners because it means that they have the capacity to discriminate many of the sound segments they need to construct two languages prior to extensive experience with any language.

Experience does matter, however. Researchers have found that infants' ability to discriminate speech sounds becomes language-specific during the second half of the first year of life. This means that they continue to discriminate contrasts that are phonemic in their native language after this age, but cannot discriminate contrasts that are not phonemic, indicating that their language experiences during the first 6–12 months of life reshape their speech-perceptual abilities to be tuned to the language, or languages, they are exposed to. Monolingual infants perceive language-specific vowel contrasts by 6 to 8 months of age (Bosch & Sebastián-Gallés, 2003; Kuhl, Williams, Lacerda, Stevens, & Lindblom, 1992), but consonant contrasts somewhat later, by 10 to 12 months of age (Werker & Tees, 1984). Simultaneous dual language learners go through a similar reorganization in speech perception at roughly the same ages as their monolingual peers (Burns, Yoshida, Hill, & Werker, 2007; Vihman, Thierry, Lum, Keren-Portnoy, & Martin, 2007).

The robustness of the timing of this reorganization in the face of dual language exposure constitutes further evidence that human infants have the capacity for dual language learning. Details on infants' development of dual speech perception systems, and how they compare with that of monolinguals, are given in Chapter 4.

Early Language Development Milestones

Another way to determine whether dual language learning is burdensome is to examine when simultaneous bilingual children achieve significant early linguistic milestones in their speech production. If human infants are not prepared to acquire two languages simultaneously, then one would expect significant delays in early milestones. For example, infants exposed to two languages might show differences with monolinguals in the emergence and time course of babbling, first words, and first word combinations (sentences). These kinds of milestones have been studied extensively in monolingual children (see Golinkoff & Hirsh-Pasek, 1999, for a nontechnical review). Unfortunately, there is no normative database on simultaneous bilingual children; however, large-sample studies have been conducted with Spanish–English bilingual infants and toddlers in the United States, which permit some generalizations to be made about early milestones in dual language learners. Collecting a large normative database on dual language learners would not be easy. Bilingual children differ considerably from one another in multiple ways that might affect their development, possibly in more ways than monolingual children. For example, bilingual children are rarely exposed to both languages equally. Their exposure to one or both languages might be disrupted for short periods of time, due to changes in where they are living, and this could alter their language development. We discuss in detail the impact of such factors and others in Chapters 4 and 6. Because bilingual children have more factors influencing individual differences in language development, the task of deciding whether an individual bilingual child's development is within the normative timeframe of monolingual children is a challenge, and should be approached with caution.

Starting with the early stages of verbal development, Kim Oller and his colleagues in Miami examined canonical babbling in a group of Spanish–English infants (Oller, Eilers, Urbano, & Cobo-Lewis, 1997). *Babbling* is the first stage of productive language development when infants vocalize language-like sounds. Oller and his colleagues examined 73 infants (monolingual and bilingual) longitudinally from 4 months of age to 1½ years of age. They found that the onset of canonical babbling for the bilingual infants did not differ significantly from that of the monolingual infants, and likewise, that specific infraphonological features that they examined (i.e., canonical babbling ratio, full vowel ratio, volubility) emerged at the same time for the bilingual and monolingual infants. Similarly, Maneva and Genesee (2002) reported that French–English bilingual infants exhibited variegated babbling that resembled that of monolingual French and monolingual English infants of the same age.

Studies that have examined lexical development in infants and toddlers report the following: bilingual children produce their first words at about the same age as monolingual children, 12–13 months on average (Genesee, 2003; Patterson & Pearson, 2004); bilingual children's rates of early vocabulary acquisition generally fall within the range reported for same-age monolinguals, as long as both languages are considered together for bilinguals (Conboy & Thal, 2006; Pearson, Fernández, & Oller, 1993); and the distribution of lexical categories (e.g., nouns, verbs, function words like prepositions, articles) in the early vocabularies of bilingual children is similar to that observed in monolingual children the same age or at the same vocabulary size (Conboy & Thal, 2006; Marchman, Martínez-Sussmann & Dale, 2004; Nicoladis, 2001). Petitto and her colleagues reported that first words, first two-word combinations, and the acquisition of the first 50 words occurred within the same age range for three bilingual children they studied as has been reported for monolingual children (Petitto, Katerelos, Levy, Gauna, Tetreault, & Ferraro, 2001). The children that Petitto and her colleagues studied were hearing children who were learning French oral language and sign language simultaneously (*langue des signes québécoises,* or LSQ; that is, "Quebec sign language"). Their findings suggest that early milestones emerge at the same time even in bimodal bilingual children.

Finally, longitudinal studies of small groups of Spanish–English and French–English bilingual children found that early word combinations emerged within the same general timeframe as that found for monolinguals, which is approximately between 1½ and 2 years of age (Padilla & Liebman, 1975; Paradis & Genesee, 1996). More recent research with larger sample sizes has also shown that Spanish–English bilingual children in the United States begin to produce word combinations in both or at least one of their languages in the same age range as monolinguals (Conboy & Thal, 2006; Marchman et al., 2004). Furthermore, Barbara Conboy, Virginia Marchman, and their colleagues found that associations between growth in vocabulary size and emergence of word combinations in bilingual toddlers within each language parallel what has been reported for monolingual toddlers (Conboy & Thal, 2006; Marchman et al., 2004).

In sum, research evidence indicates that bilingual acquisition is not necessarily burdensome. Bilingual children achieve critical milestones, like babbling, onset of first words and first word combinations within the same time frame as typically developing monolingual children, and the characteristics of their early vocabularies and sentences parallel those of monolingual children. These findings suggest that whether children are exposed to one language or two during infancy and the toddler years, the timing of language development and the mechanisms underlying it are the same. However, these findings do not mean that simultaneous bilingual children parallel monolinguals in every respect. In particular, rates of vocabulary and grammatical development within each of their languages is sensitive to how much exposure they have to each and can be a key source of difference with their monolingual peers beyond consideration of achieving the basic milestones. More detailed comparisons between rates of development of simultaneous bilingual and monolingual children in the preschool and school-age years are given in Chapter 4. Practically speaking, what is important about this examination of early milestones and dual language exposure is that significant delays in meeting these milestones are often an early sign that a child has a language disorder. Understanding that dual language exposure itself does not cause delay in the onset of these milestones—in at least one of a bilingual's two languages—is important for parents, speech-language pathologists, and other health care practitioners dealing with preschool children.

What Is the Relationship Between General Intelligence and Dual Language Learning?

In this section, we consider another aspect of the language–cognition connection related to children's capacity for dual language learning: the link between general intelligence and second language learning. By general intelligence, we mean the kinds of intellectual skills that are evident to parents and others in children's day-to-day behavior and in school: their abilities to think analytically, to learn new skills and knowledge, to solve problems, and to be creative. These kinds of skills are generally thought to be critical for success in school. They are measured by IQ tests or other tests of general ability, such as the *Peabody Picture Vocabulary Test–Third Edition* (Dunn & Dunn, 1997) and *Raven's Coloured Progressive Matrices Test* (Raven, 1965). These conceptualizations of intelligence are controversial and even objectionable to some people. However, this notion of intelligence is widely held and has significant influence on many people's thinking and decision making. For example, many parents are reluctant to enroll their children in bilingual school programs if they think that they are intellectually challenged. Speech-language pathologists often assess children's level of general intelligence in order to better understand the nature of their suspected language impairment. Children who show typical levels of general intelligence but poor language skills are thought to have language-specific problems. Thus, because of its practical importance, we include a discussion of general intelligence and its relationship to dual language learning here.

The link between general intelligence and dual language learning has been investigated most extensively in the case of second language learners (like Samantha, Trevor, and Bonnie from Chapter 1) and primarily second language learners of school age (see Chapter 8). One of the reasons for this focus stems from the fact that there are many tests of general intelligence for school-age children but relatively few for preschoolers. Moreover, tests for school-age children have better long-term predictive validity than those for preschoolers; in fact, the latter are notoriously unreliable. Tests of general intelligence for infants (and thus for simultaneous dual language learners) are virtually nonexistent because of the psychometric problems in defining and assessing this form of intelligence among such young children. In any case, there has been a focus on the link between general intelligence and bilingualism in school-age children because parents and educators are often concerned that children of below-average intelligence are not able to learn a second language successfully and that they are hampered if they are educated through the medium of a second language. This has spawned applied research to address this concern. What does this research tell us?

General intelligence is usually correlated with those aspects of language proficiency that are linked to reading and writing, so even monolingual children who score high on tests of general intelligence also usually score relatively high on tests that assess reading, writing, and spelling skills, for example. This pattern of correlations is to be expected because tests of general intelligence are usually validated against children's school grades, which in turn are heavily influenced by their reading and writing skills. The same pattern of correlations has been found in second language learners (see Genesee, 1976, 1987). That is, children who score high on tests of general intelligence also tend to score relatively high on tests of reading and writing in the second language. However—and this is of particular importance to this book—children with relatively low levels of general intelligence are not differentially challenged in learning their first language as a result of learning a second language. This has been documented by showing that students with low levels of general intelligence who are participating in second language or foreign language immersion programs score at the same level as comparable students with low levels of intelligence in native language programs on standardized tests of reading, writing, and spelling administered in their native language. At the same time, students with below-average intelligence participating in immersion programs can acquire reading and writing skills in the second language to the extent one would expect given their general intellectual abilities. The literacy skills of below-average intelligence students are not as advanced as those of their average or above-average peers in immersion, but they are impressive. We discuss these findings in greater detail in Chapter 8.

When it comes to acquisition of oral language skills in a second language, the picture is different. Correlations between measures of general intelligence and measures of speaking and listening comprehension in the second language are typically quite low, especially among elementary school-age children (Genesee, 1987). Low correlations in this case indicate that general intelligence is not necessarily a significant predictor of proficiency in second language speaking and listening comprehension. This is most likely if the tests assess speaking and listening skills of the type that are common in most face-to-face social conversations. It is less likely to be true when assessing oral and listening skills related to academic tasks, such as comprehending a science lecture or giving an oral science report. Genesee (1976) found few differences among elementary school immersion students with below-average, average, and above-average levels of general intelligence in their oral second language skills; this work is discussed in more detail in Chapter 8.

The differential effects of intelligence on different kinds of language learning (spoken versus written language) may be due, in part, to the importance of other factors. In particular, one might expect children's motivation to fit in and communicate orally with peers who speak the second language to have a powerful influence on their acquisition of that language. Indeed, most young children, regardless of their general intellectual ability, are successful in acquiring a second language if surrounded by same-age peers who speak the language, given sufficient exposure to the language. However, some children may take longer to learn a second language than others, perhaps because they have poor aptitude for language learning, or, in the case of immigrant and especially refugee children, they may have had traumatic premigration experiences or deprivation in terms of food and shelter that impede their sociocultural adaptation. From practical and clinical perspectives, it is important to examine the social and personal circumstances surrounding a child having difficulty learning a second language when trying to understand the source of the child's difficulty. In Chapter 6, we examine more carefully the rate at which young children learn a second language, as well as the numerous factors influencing how quickly, or slowly, they learn.

Children with Severe Cognitive Challenges   Questions still remain although research clearly indicates that children with typical capacities for learning—and even children with non–clinically low levels of ability—usually do not experience difficulty acquiring two languages. How well can children with severe cognitive challenges, such as DS or Williams syndrome, learn a second language? How well can children with severe sensory or perceptual difficulties, such as hearing or visual impairment, learn a second language? Except for children with DS, we know of no systematic research on such children.

Elizabeth Kay-Raining Bird and her colleagues in Canada have studied children with DS who were learning French and English simultaneously (Kay-Raining Bird, Cleave, Trudeau, Thordardottir, Sutton, & Thorpe, 2005; see also Feltman & Kay-Raining Bird, 2008). The bilingual children with DS were compared with typically developing children who were also learning English and French simultaneously and with children who were learning only English as well as with monolingual English-learning children with DS. All groups of children were comparable with respect to mental age, a usual control when conducting research on children with DS, and they varied in age from 30.5 months (the typically developing monolingual children) to 85.5 months (the bilingual children with DS). The bilingual children were either English-dominant or balanced, and the researchers refer to English as the L1, even though the children were acquiring both simultaneously. They had a number of important findings:

a. The bilingual children with DS exhibited the same profile of language abilities as monolingual children with DS; namely, strengths in receptive language and weaknesses in expressive language, especially morphosyntax.

b. There were no significant differences between the two groups with DS on any of the measures of English language ability, indicating that bilingualism was "not detrimental to the dominant language development of children with DS, at least when they experience intensive, ongoing, and consistent exposure to both languages" (Kay-Raining Bird et al., 2005, p. 195).

c. The children with DS and dual language exposure were becoming bilingual, as indicated by their good performance relative to the bilingual comparison group without DS on measures of French language ability.

d. There was wide individual variation among the bilingual children with DS in their acquisition of French; much of this variation may have been due to language input (Feltman & Kay-Raining Bird, 2008).

The conclusion that these researchers arrived at is given in Box 3.2. With respect to children who face other cognitive and/or sensoriperceptual challenges, we can only conjecture how well they would do if exposed to two languages simultaneously or to a second language after the first language has been acquired. Based on everything else we know about language acquisition, we believe that such children are capable of acquiring some proficiency in a second language, but we cannot assert with any precision how successful they would be and in what domains. The answers to these questions might be quite different for simultaneous exposure versus sequential exposure, especially if second

---

BOX 3.2

Children with Down Syndrome and Bilingual Development

The current study, though finding evidence for language impairment in children with Down syndrome, found no evidence suggesting a detrimental effect of bilingualism. Thus, the findings do not support restricting language input to a single language. Instead, our results suggest that children with Down syndrome can be successful in acquiring two languages and that bilingual children perform in their dominant language (in this case, English) at least as well as their monolingual counterparts with Down syndrome matched for developmental level. (Kay-Raining Bird et al., 2005, p. 197).

language learning takes place primarily in school. The success of children who learn a second language in school can be influenced by pedagogical factors, and these factors—along with the cognitive challenges that some children face—can impede second language acquisition. An elementary school teacher with 25 (or more) students can have difficulty providing the kind of intensive, individualized attention that a student with a cognitive or sensoriperceptual problem would need to learn to his or her full potential. In contrast, the success of preschool simultaneous bilingual learners is dependent primarily on their own inherent abilities, although the learning environment in the home is also important. From everything we know about language learning in natural contexts, these abilities, even when compromised by cognitive disabilities, are considerable. All things considered, we suspect that children with severe cognitive or sensoriperceptual challenges are likely to experience more success with dual language learning if they are preschool age and have extensive language exposure outside school than similar children whose second language learning is dependent on school experiences; however, we caution that this speculation is not based on systematic empirical evidence.

DOES DUAL LANGUAGE LEARNING INFLUENCE COGNITIVE DEVELOPMENT?

Theoreticians and laypersons alike have long been fascinated with the possibility that bilingual children are different from monolingual children in ways that go beyond knowing two languages. More specifically, some people think that bilingualism is a threat to the child's typical social, cognitive, and personality development. We saw the same view expressed about the linguistic consequences of learning two languages. There is no significant theoretical reason to believe that learning, knowing, or using two languages should jeopardize children's development, yet this fear is harbored by some people.

This fear does have some empirical support, although the evidence is flawed in many cases. For example, in an early review of research on bilingualism and personality, Diebold (1968) concluded that bilingualism leads to emotional maladjustment and, in particular, to psychodynamic conflict (such as, in the extreme case, schizophrenia). Closer to the issue at hand, a number of early researchers also reported that bilingual children exhibited lower levels of verbal intelligence and/or general intellectual ability (Arsenian, 1945; Darcy, 1946; Macnamara, 1966). Closer examination of these early studies, however, reveals that many of them had serious methodological shortcomings. In some cases, the performance of bilingual children was compared with that of monolingual children, but the two groups were not from the same socioeconomic stratum. The bilingual children were often from lower socioeconomic backgrounds and on those grounds alone would be expected to perform worse on the standardized tests used to assess their abilities. In addition, the bilingual children's level of proficiency in the language of the tests was not always controlled, so some of the children were evaluated using tests in their weaker language. As a result, their performance on tests that were supposed to measure intelligence was really a reflection of their level of second language proficiency.

Most important, many of the bilingual children in these early studies were living in **subtractive bilingual environments,** a term coined by McGill University psychologist Wallace Lambert (1977). Subtractive bilingualism occurs when acquisition of the majority language comes at the cost of loss of the native language. The prototypical case of a subtractive bilingual environment is that of immigrant children or the children and grandchildren of immigrants (like Bonnie, Gabriela, Luis, or Faisal). Such children are often expected to learn the dominant language of the wider community and to give up their native language. In fact, it is widely believed that the best way for immigrant children to learn the majority language is to abandon their home language, or what is sometimes called the heritage language, altogether—although this attitude is changing. In fact, the parents of immigrant children are often encouraged to use only the majority language in the home during the preschool years as a way of facilitating the child's integration into majority language schools (see Chapter 6).

Immigrant children are not the only children subjected to subtractive bilingual environments. Children who speak an indigenous language in a community that is otherwise dominated by another language also often experience subtractive bilingualism; native Inuktitut-speaking children in Canada (like Pauloosie) or Navajo-speaking children in the United States are examples of such cases. Other cases include the children of migrant workers who continue to learn and use the language of their national origin but live in communities (full time or part time) where another language is the majority language; children of Turkish descent in Germany or children of Mexican descent (like Luis) in the United States are examples. Bistra might have experienced a subtractive bilingual learning environment, except that her parents are going to great trouble to promote the acquisition and use of both her mother's language (Bulgarian) and her father's language (English).

In contrast, **additive bilingual environments** are contexts in which there is substantial support for children to maintain their native language as they acquire an additional language. Children like Samantha or Trevor, for example, are expected to continue to learn English at the same time as they learn Spanish and German, respectively. There is no suggestion that they should give up their native language for their second language. Dual language children from majority ethnolinguistic groups often enjoy the benefits of living in additive bilingual environments. Additive bilingualism supports dual cultural identities so that children can identify with and enjoy the cultures connected with both of the languages they are learning. They are not made to feel that they have to be a member of only one cultural group.

There was a significant turn of events in the history of research on the cognitive consequences of bilingualism in the early 1960s with research by Elizabeth Peal and Wallace Lambert of McGill University. Peal and Lambert (1962) corrected many of the methodological weaknesses of earlier work. They compared the performance of English–French bilingual children who were fully proficient in both languages with that of monolingual English- and French-speaking children from the same socioeconomic backgrounds and with the same level of education. What is particularly important about the Peal and Lambert study, and many subsequent studies, is that they have studied bilingual children, like James, who were raised in additive bilingual environments; for example, in Montreal, Canada. In contrast to previous studies, the study by Peal and Lambert found that the bilingual students they tested exhibited a number of cognitive advantages in comparison to their monolingual comparison group. More specifically, they found evidence that the bilingual students had a greater number of independent cognitive strategies at their disposal and exhibited greater flexibility in the use of these strategies to solve problems.

With stronger methodological controls, many studies since Peal and Lambert's landmark study have reported advantages for bilingual children in comparison to monolingual children on a variety of cognitive tasks (see Bialystok, 2001, and Kovacs, 2007, for reviews). Among the studies that have found a bilingual superiority, it has often been found that bilingual children are advantaged on tasks that called for **metalinguistic awareness.** Metalinguistic awareness is the ability to reflect on and manipulate the elements of language independently of their communicative use. There are numerous types of metalinguistic tasks, from those that focus on the sounds of language, to words, to grammar, and to language use itself. For example, the child might be asked to identify whether specific words (e.g., *if, cat*) are words or to identify which words have the same final, medial, or initial sound (e.g., *bat, boss, car*). A child might be asked to say what sound is left if the first sound is removed from a word (e.g., remove the first sound from "*cat*"). Awareness of these aspects of language is not particularly important when using language for most day-to-day communicative purposes; however, it is important when it comes to acquiring reading and writing. There is a strong positive correlation between learners' metalinguistic skills, especially in phonology, and the acquisition of reading and writing (National Reading Panel, 2000). Good readers and writers are aware of the structural properties of the language and of how the language functions as a system for communication.

Some of the most significant advances in our understanding of the cognitive consequences of bilingualism come from the laboratory of Ellen Bialystok of York University in Toronto. Bialystok (2001) has provided compelling evidence that there is a bilingual advantage when selective attention is required so that misleading information is inhibited in favor of relevant information in the performance of some cognitive tasks. Her research has focused on highly proficient bilinguals who use their two languages regularly, suggesting that low levels of bilingual proficiency or use are insufficient to engender these advantages. Collectively, the cognitive advantages that bilinguals experience are referred to as *executive control functions* and include the activation, selection, inhibition, and organization of information during, for example, problem solving or planning. Bialystok has argued that these cognitive advantages are related to the selective attention and inhibition that bilinguals exercise in the acquisition and use of two languages so as to avoid interference between their two language systems (see Chapter 7 in Bialystok, 2001, for more details). In other words, the selective attention and inhibition that is entailed in fluent bilingualism has a corollary effect on nonlanguage functions. Kovacs and Mehler (2009) similarly found that 7-month-old infants who were exposed to two languages since birth exhibited enhanced cognitive control abilities in comparison to matched monolingual infants.

The cognitive advantages associated with dual language input and learning are not restricted to children. Bialystok and her colleagues have found that they are also evident in adults who are bilingual and between 60 and 88 years of age (Bialystok, Craik, Klein, & Viswanathan, 2004). Moreover, in support of the theory that proficient bilingualism is a form of mental exercise that enhances executive control functions, Bialystok, Craik, and Freedman (2007) found that the onset of dementia was delayed by 4 years in the case of bilinguals in comparison to monolingual patients with the same clinical diagnosis.

It is important to point out that even some methodologically sound studies have failed to find a difference between bilingual children and monolingual children (see, e.g., Cummins, 1976; Rosenblum & Pinker, 1983). Thus, contrary to the simplistic notion that bilingualism confers unconditionally positive or negative cognitive consequences,

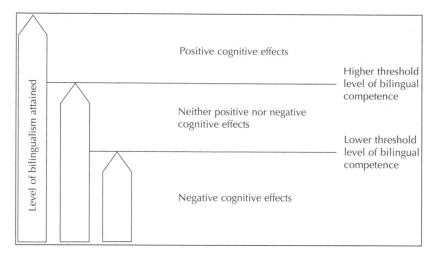

Figure 3.1.   Cognitive effects of bilingual competence.

contemporary research has demonstrated a variety of outcomes—some showing a bilingual advantage, some a monolingual advantage, and some no differences between monolingual and bilingual children. We should not be surprised that bilingualism can be associated with different patterns of outcomes. Children become bilingual for very different reasons and under very different circumstances—some that might favor bilingual children, others that might favor monolingual children, and still others that might result in comparable patterns of cognitive ability. Jim Cummins, from the Ontario Institute for Studies in Education at the University of Toronto, recognized this important point in the formulation of his threshold hypothesis. According to Cummins (2000), the cognitive consequences of bilingualism are dependent, in part, on the levels of language proficiency that bilingual children attain in their two languages; see Figure 3.1 for a schematic representation of this hypothesis. Cognitive advantages among bilingual children are usually associated with advanced levels of bilingual proficiency, whereas cognitive disadvantages (or relatively lower levels of cognitive ability, relative to monolingual children) are often associated with low levels of bilingual proficiency. Bilingual proficiency that falls between these two thresholds is likely to result in neither an advantage nor a disadvantage. Cummins has attributed these differential effects to the quality of the bilingual children's interactions with their learning environment. Children with low levels of proficiency in one or the other of their two languages could experience lowered levels of cognitive ability, as demonstrated in their ability to solve problems, critically analyze information, or identify alternative points of view, because they experience impoverished interactions with their learning environment. In contrast, children with advanced levels of bilingual proficiency are likely to experience enriched cognitive abilities as a result of enhanced metalinguistic awareness or attentional abilities of the type identified by Bialystok. The findings reported by Kovacs and Mehler (2009) in their study of 7-month-old infants who were exposed to two languages since birth, described earlier, suggests that early exposure to two languages confers an advantage that presumably is maintained later in life if acquisition of both languages continues and leads to high levels of proficiency. Indeed, the highly proficient bilinguals, children and adults, examined by Bialystok and colleagues all had had early exposure to both languages.

Taken together, these findings on language and cognitive development are important for a number of reasons:

1. They indicate unequivocally that the pessimistic view of bilingualism is not valid.

2. They indicate that the cognitive consequences of bilingualism may be positive, negative, or null, depending on the level of proficiency of the bilingual child. This makes eminent sense in view of the widely varied circumstances in which children learn two languages.

3. Parents, educators, and clinicians should consider the cognitive advantages that can result from learning and using two languages early in development when making decisions about raising and educating children bilingually, and not consider only the possibility of cognitive disadvantages, as has often been the case in the past.

4. Most important, parents, educators, and health care professionals are advised to aim for advanced levels of bilingual proficiency for individual children in order to ensure that they benefit from all of the advantages of being bilingual. An early start in exposing children to two languages is more likely to lead to high levels of proficiency and the cognitive advantages discussed in this section.

In short, children should be fully supported in their acquisition of two languages from early in development, and the decision to raise a child bilingually should be made only if the sustained, enriched, and consistent bilingual experiences that are necessary to achieve advanced bilingual proficiency can be provided.

SUMMARY

There are two sides to the language–cognition connection. One considers the cognitive capacity of infants and children for dual language learning, whereas the other considers the cognitive consequences of dual language learning. With respect to the cognitive capacity for dual language learning, there is no scientific evidence that infants' language learning ability is limited to one language. On the contrary, research on prenatal and preverbal infants suggests that they have innate capacities that allow them to learn two languages without significant costs to the development of either language, provided that they receive consistent and adequate exposure to both languages on a continuous basis. Viewed from the perspective of general intelligence, research has shown that general intelligence is often correlated with second language proficiency in domains related to reading and writing in a first and second language, but not necessarily to oral language development. Factors influencing oral language development are explored in detail in Chapter 6.

The cognitive consequences of dual language learning can be varied and probably depend on the circumstances of acquisition. In particular, whether the learning environment supports additive or subtractive bilingualism and, thus, whether the child achieves advanced bilingual proficiency can have important consequences for both language learning and cognitive outcomes. In Chapter 8, we will see that the same is true when it comes to bilingual schooling. Positive cognitive consequences are more likely to result from additive bilingual environments in which the child achieves advanced levels of language proficiency as a result of early dual language exposure. Negative consequences are more likely to result in subtractive environments in which the child's proficiency in one or both languages is limited. The latter is particularly true if the child is being educated through the medium of the second language. Dual language children should be provided with support—affective and linguistic—to learn both languages fully, and in so doing, to benefit from both positive linguistic and cognitive consequences.

REFERENCES

Arsenian, S. (1945). Bilingualism in the post-war world. *Psychological Bulletin, 42,* 65–85.

Berk, L. (2003). *Child development.* Toronto: Pearson Education Canada.

Bialystok, E. (2001). *Bilingualism in development: Language, literacy, and cognition.* New York: Cambridge University Press.

Bialystok, E., Craik, F.I.M., & Freedman, M. (2007). Bilingualism as protection against the onset of symptoms of dementia. *Neuropsychologia, 45,* 459–464.

Bialystok, E., Craik, F.I.M., Klein, R., & Viswanathan, M. (2004). Bilingualism, aging, and cognitive control. *Psychology and Aging, 19,* 290–303.

Bosch, L., & Sebastián-Gallés, N. (2001). Early language differentiation in bilingual infants. In J. Cenoz & F. Genesee (Eds.), *Trends in bilingual acquisition* (pp. 71–94). Amsterdam: John Benjamins.

Bosch, L., & Sebastián-Gallés, N. (2003). Simultaneous bilingualism and the perception of language-specific vowel contrast in the first year of life. *Language and Speech, 46,* 217–243.

Boysson-Bardies, B. (1999). *How language comes to children.* Cambridge, MA: The MIT Press.

Burns, T.C., Yoshida, K.A., Hill, K., & Werker, J. (2007). The development of phonetic representation in bilingual and monolingual infants. *Applied Psycholinguistics, 28,* 455–474.

Conboy, B.T., & Thal, D.J. (2006). Ties between the lexicon and grammar: Cross-sectional and longitudinal studies of bilingual toddlers. *Child Development, 77*(3), 712–735.

Cummins, J. (1976). The influence of bilingualism on cognitive growth: A synthesis of research findings and explanatory hypotheses. *Working Papers on Bilingualism, 9,* 1–43.

Cummins, J. (2000). Language, power and pedagogy: *Bilingual children in the crossfire.* Clevedon, England: Multilingual Matters.

Darcy, N. (1946). The effect of bilingualism upon the measurement of the intelligence of children of pre-school age. *Journal of Educational Psychology, 37,* 21–44.

DeCasper, A.J., & Fifer, W.P. (1980). Of human bonding: Newborns prefer their mothers' voices. *Science, 208,* 1174–1176.

DeCasper, A.J., & Spence, M.J. (1986). Prenatal maternal speech influences newborns' perceptions of speech sounds. *Infant Behavior and Development, 9,* 133–150.

Diebold, A.R. (1968). The consequences of early bilingualism in cognitive and personality formation. In E. Norbeck, D. Price-Williams, & W.M. McCord (Eds.), *The study of personality: An interdisciplinary appraisal* (pp. 218–245). New York: Holt, Rinehart & Winston.

Dunn, L.M., & Dunn, L.M. (1997). *Peabody Picture Vocabulary Test–Third Edition (PPVT-III).* Circle Pines, MN: American Guidance Service.

Feltman, K., & Kay-Raining Bird, E. (2008). Language learning in four bilingual children with Down syndrome: A detailed analysis of vocabulary and morphosyntax. *Canadian Journal of Speech-Language Pathology and Audiology, 32,* 6–20.

Foreman, J. (2002, October 7). Health sense: The evidence speaks well of bilingualism's effect on kids. *The Los Angeles Times,* p. S1.

Genesee, F. (1976). The role of intelligence in second language learning. *Language Learning, 26,* 267–280.

Genesee, F. (1987). *Learning through two languages: Studies of immersion and bilingual education.* Rowley, MA: Newbury House.

Genesee, F. (2003). Rethinking bilingual acquisition. In J.M. deWaele (Ed.), *Bilingualism: Challenges and directions for future research* (pp. 158–182). Clevedon, England: Multilingual Matters.

Gerken, L.A. (2007). Acquiring linguistic structure. In E. Hoff & M. Shatz (Eds), *Blackwell handbook of language development* (pp. 173–190). Malden, MA: Blackwell.

Golinkoff, R., & Hirsh-Pasek, K. (1999). *How babies talk.* New York: Dutton/Penguin Putnam.

Kay-Raining Bird, E., Cleave, P., Trudeau, N., Thodardottir, E., Sutton, A., & Thorpe, A. (2005). The language abilities of bilingual children with Down syndrome. *American Journal of Speech-Language Pathology, 14,* 187–199.

Kovacs, A.M. (2007). Beyond language: Childhood bilingualism enhances high-level cognitive functions. In I. Kecskes & L. Albertazzi (Eds.), *Cognitive aspects of bilingualism* (pp. 301–323). Dordrecht, The Netherlands: Springer.

Kovacs, A.M., & J. Mehler, J. (2009). Cognitive gains in 7-month-old infants. *Proceedings of the National Academy of Sciences, 106*(16), 6556–6560.

Kuhl, P., Williams, K.A., Lacerda, F., Stevens, K.N., & Lindblom, B. (1992). Linguistic experience alters phonetic perception in infants by 6 months of age. *Science, 255,* 606–608.

Lambert, W.E. (1977). The effects of bilingualism on the individual: Cognitive and socio-cultural consequences. In P.A. Hornby (Ed.), *Bilingualism: Psychological, social and educational implications* (pp. 15–28). New York: Academic Press.

Macnamara, J. (1966). *Bilingualism and primary education.* Edinburgh, Scotland: Edinburgh University Press.

Maneva, B., & Genesee, F. (2002, November). Bilingual babbling: Evidence for language differentiation in dual language acquisition. In B. Skarabela, S. Fish, & A.H.-J. Do (Eds.), *Proceedings of the 26th Boston University Conference on Language Development* (pp. 383–392). Somerville, MA: Cascadilla Press.

Marchman, V.A., Martínez-Sussmann, C., & Dale, P.S. (2004). The language-specific nature of grammatical development: Evidence from bilingual language learners. *Developmental Science, 7*(2), 212–224.

National Reading Panel. (2000). *Teaching children to read: An evidence-based assessment of scientific research literature on reading and its implications for reading instruction* (NIH Publication No. 00-4769). Washington, DC: U.S. Government Printing Office.

Nicoladis, E. (2001). Finding first words in the input. In J. Cenoz & F. Genesee (Eds.), *Trends in bilingual acquisition* (pp. 131–147). Amsterdam: John Benjamins.

Oller, D.K., Eilers, R.E., Urbano, R., & Cobo-Lewis, A.B. (1997). Development of precursors to speech in infants exposed to two languages. *Journal of Child Language, 24,* 407–426.

Padilla, A.M., & Liebman, E. (1975). Language acquisition in the bilingual child. *Bilingual Review, 2*(1–2), 34–55.

Paradis, J., & Genesee, F. (1996). Syntactic acquisition in bilingual children: Autonomous or interdependent? *Studies in Second Language Acquisition, 18,* 1–25.

Patterson, J.L., & Pearson, B.Z. (2004). Bilingual lexical development: Influences, contexts, and processes. In B.A. Goldstein (Ed.), *Bilingual language development & disorders in Spanish–English speakers* (pp. 77–104). Baltimore: Paul H. Brookes Publishing Co.

Peal, E., & Lambert, W.E. (1962). The relation of bilingualism to intelligence. *Psychological Monographs, 76,* 1–23.

Pearson, B.Z., Fernández, S.C., & Oller, D.K. (1993). Lexical development in bilingual infants and toddlers: Comparison to monolingual norms. *Language Learning, 43,* 93–120.

Petitto, L.A., Katerelos, M., Levy, B.G., Gauna, K., Tetreault, K., & Ferraro, V. (2001). Bilingual signed and spoken language acquisition from birth: Implications for the mechanism underlying early bilingual language acquisition. *Journal of Child Language, 28,* 453–496.

Polka, L., Rvachew, S., & Mattock, K. (2007). In E. Hoff & M. Shatz (Eds.), *Blackwell handbook of language development* (pp. 153–172). Malden, MA: Blackwell.

Raven, J.C. (1965). *The Coloured Progressive Matrices Test.* London: Lewis.

Rosenblum, T., & Pinker, S.A. (1983). Word magic revisited: Monolingual and bilingual children's understanding of the word–object relationship. *Child Development, 54,* 773–780.

Sebastián-Gallés, N., & Bosch, L. (2005). Phonology and bilingualism. In J.F. Kroll & A.M.B. De Groot (Eds.), *Handbook of bilingualism: Psycholinguistic approaches* (pp. 68–87). Oxford, England: Oxford University Press.

Vihman, M.M., Thierry, G., Lum, J.A.G., Keren-Portnoy, T., & Martin, P. (2007). Onset of word form recognition in English, Welsh, and English–Welsh bilingual infants. *Applied Psycholinguistics, 28,* 475–493.

Werker, J.F., & Tees, R.C. (1984). Cross-language speech perception: Evidence for perceptual reorganization during the first year of life. *Infant Behavior and Development, 7,* 49–63.

Understanding Bilingual and Second Language Development

Language Development in Simultaneous Bilingual Children

This chapter discusses the language development of simultaneous bilingual children—those who acquire two languages from birth or at least before the age of 3—from infancy to the school-age years. James, Bistra, and Gabriela, profiled in Chapter 1, are all simultaneous bilingual children. The contexts in which James, Bistra, and Gabriela are growing up are the most common, but they are not the only routes to simultaneous bilingualism. Some parents expose their children to another language from birth via a full-time caregiver who speaks another language. An example of this is an English-speaking family living in Los Angeles who hires a live-in, Spanish-speaking nanny when their child is an infant (see Chapter 1). If the child's exposure to Spanish is frequent and sustained over the preschool and school-age years, she could be considered a simultaneous bilingual, even though the child's parents do not speak Spanish. Children of parents who travel or live outside their home country for business or personal reasons might also experience simultaneous bilingual acquisition through child care arrangements. Finally, it is important to keep in mind that we have set the distinction between simultaneous bilingualism and second language acquisition at 3 years of age in this book, but this distinction is not a clear-cut one. Some of the information on school-age bilingual children in this chapter might be applicable to children who begin to learn a second language shortly after age 3. Conversely, some of the information in Chapter 6 on second language learning could be applicable to children who begin to learn an additional language at age 2½.

Our primary goal in this chapter is to provide information about what is typical in the language development of simultaneous bilingual children during the preschool and elementary school years. Regardless of whether simultaneous bilingual children are destined to become bilingual adults, their parents, educators, speech-language pathologists, and other health practitioners should be aware of the impact of simultaneous dual language exposure on children's language development in the preschool and early school years. In particular, they need to set appropriate expectations for these children's oral language abilities in order to gauge whether children's language development appears to be typical or shows signs of delay/impairment. We often use monolingual children as a reference point in our descriptions, and we highlight the similarities and differences between typical bilingual children and typical monolingual children in order to permit better identification of aspects of bilingual development that truly should be a cause for concern.

The information in this chapter is organized according to the following questions:

1. Do children exposed to two languages from birth learn bilingually at first? That is, do they have one single language system or two separate language systems?

2. If bilingual children have two separate language systems, do the languages interact in development? Does this interaction cause bilingual children to show some unique patterns from monolingual children?

3. Are bilingual children slower to learn language than monolingual children, and if so, how much slower? Do bilingual children show similar rates of development in both of their languages?

4. Are multilingual children distinct from bilingual children? Is learning three or four languages early on too burdensome or confusing for children?

Although there may not be as many differences between bilingual and monolingual language development as one might expect, the previous questions involve comparisons. Therefore, before we begin to answer this list of questions, we briefly discuss alternative ways of viewing differences between monolingual children and bilingual children. Historically, bilingualism in young children was thought to put them at an intellectual disadvantage, which concerned educational policy makers (see Chapter 3). Because of this historical attitude, differences between bilingual and monolingual language development are often viewed negatively.

Bilingual children have often been considered typically developing only if they appear to be similar to monolingual children; they are considered to be not developing typically or to have disabilities if they show any differences. This kind of attitude results when monolingual children's development is taken as the norm, even though, as discussed in Chapter 1, childhood bilingualism is most likely as common worldwide as monolingualism. Given how widespread bilingualism in childhood is, we cannot help but acknowledge that the human mind is just as capable of bilingual development as monolingual development, even if there are some differences (see Chapter 3). Any differences between the two should not be taken immediately to imply that bilingualism has pernicious effects on language development as a whole. We believe that a more appropriate attitude is that there is more than one path to acquiring language, and that one of these paths is to acquire two languages at a time.

BOX 4.1

Raising Children Bilingually: Questions from Parents

Dear Dr. Genesee,

We hope you can shed some light on a question about infant bilingualism. My Russian wife and I hope to raise our soon-to-be-adopted 10-week-old infant bilingually. (The infant comes from Georgia, a former Russian republic.) My wife insists on the importance of almost exclusively speaking Russian. I was born and raised in California and have only begun to learn Russian. I would like my wife mostly to speak English to our infant when I am around. My question: Will my wife's speaking Russian almost exclusively increase the chances of our child becoming bilingual? I suspect there are both cognitive and affective factors.

Thank you for any assistance,
A father

Dear Dr. Paradis,

We live in Western Canada and our son is in a French day care, where there is very strong encouragement to speak French in the home in order to maintain a French-speaking environment at the day care. Because of this, we committed to speaking French as much as possible, even though my French is at an intermediate level. However, now that he is 2, I have begun to question whether my French language abilities have been constraining him, and more importantly, feeling like I cannot fully express myself in my mother tongue to him—which I feel will constrain our language communication and relationship development. I have now decided to speak English, though I recognize the challenges this poses in being a part of a French day care, and later school. Perhaps you could suggest some helpful resources that will continue to help me understand what is best for my son in a mixed-language family.

Sincerely,
A mother

Parents often ask us what the best way is to raise children bilingually. Although many different methods can work, the one that people use the most is the one parent–one language method. In this method, each parent speaks his or her native language exclusively with the child (see Chapter 5 for more about this method). This ensures that the child will get sufficient and rich input in both languages. This is especially important when one language is a minority language and spoken very little outside the home. It is also important for parents to feel able to fully express themselves when speaking with their children.

DO BILINGUAL CHILDREN
HAVE ONE LANGUAGE SYSTEM OR TWO?

When an infant is experiencing input from two languages, the infant is not consciously aware that he is learning two languages, and it is not until a bilingual child is much older—perhaps closer to 3 years of age—that he demonstrates explicit awareness of being a dual language learner by talking directly about it. It is therefore not surprising that researchers have asked whether children exposed to two languages acquire those languages bilingually from the outset. In other words, do they represent the language input they hear around them in their minds as a single or dual language system at first? From the beginning of the 20th century until the early 1990s, researchers tended to support the idea that bilingual children do not acquire language bilingually at first. An influential model of this, the **Unitary Language System Hypothesis** (see Figure 4.1), was put forth by Virginia Volterra and Traute Taeschner (1978). They proposed that bilingual children begin the acquisition process with a single language system that combines the words and the grammatical rules from their dual language input. At the next stage, the words differentiate into two vocabularies/lexicons, but the system of grammatical rules remains the same for both languages. In the final stage, around 3 years of age, the system of grammatical rules becomes differentiated, and the bilingual child can be said to have separate linguistic systems, as bilingual adults do. An alternative view to Volterra and Taeschner's model is one put forth by Fred Genesee (1989), the **Dual Language System Hypothesis** (see Figure 4.2), which assumes that children exposed to two languages from birth establish two separate linguistic systems from the outset of acquisition. According to this view, children with simultaneous dual language exposure never go through a noticeable period in which their linguistic representations are unified and later separate from one into two systems.

Both the Unitary Language System and the Dual Language System Hypotheses refer to the nature of the language representation in a child's mind, so it is relevant to ask whether this is a meaningful distinction for understanding the child's language behavior, especially for the practical concerns of parents, educators, and health care practitioners. It is meaningful, because these two viewpoints make very different predictions about how young bilingual children will use their languages and what developmental stages they will go through. If young bilingual children initially have a

Figure 4.1. Unitary language system in early bilingualism.

Figure 4.2. Dual language systems in early bilingualism.

unitary vocabulary and grammar, then one would expect them to frequently mix words and phrases from both languages together, regardless of language context or conversation partners. One might also expect them to use grammar rules from one language with words from another and even blend the rules from both languages together. Furthermore, it is possible that the process of differentiating two language systems could be cognitively costly for a bilingual child, causing a slowdown in their language development between the ages of 2–3 years and unique patterns of language use during this reorganization. However, current research on bilingual acquisition overwhelmingly supports the Dual Language System Hypothesis. We review this research herein with respect to several domains of language.

Speech Perception

In Chapter 3, an infant's fundamental capacity to cope with dual language input in the first year of life was discussed. This discussion included evidence that infants who will be bilingual can hear the difference between their two languages early on and go through a developmental reorganization in their perception of phonetic segments, such as consonants and vowels, at the same time as infants exposed to just one language. Not only does the timing of this developmental reorganization support the view that infants are born with the capacity to acquire more than one language early on, but also the details of this process provide evidence in favor of the Dual Language System Hypothesis. Two teams of Canadian researchers examined the speech perception abilities of infants exposed to French and English from birth. Burns, Yoshida, Hill, and Werker (2007) tested these infants on their abilities to perceive subtle acoustic differences in how [p] and [b] are pronounced in French and English. Burns and colleagues found that bilingual infants were able to perceive language-specific acoustic properties of [p] and [b] when they were between 10 and 12 months of age—the same age when monolingual infants become language-specific listeners. French and English also have subtle differences in the acoustic properties of the phonetic segment [d], and Sundara, Polka, and Molnar (2008) found that infants exposed to both French and English were able to perceive [d] in the language-specific English way at age 10–12 months, but French monolingual infants could not. The results of both studies suggest that infants exposed to two languages are establishing separate perceptual systems for each language, rather than a unified perceptual system for both, toward the end of the first year of life. However, there are further nuances and some conflicting findings in the research on bilingual speech perception in infants; see Werker, Byers-Heinlein, and Fennel (2009) for a comprehensive technical review.

Phonology

Some researchers have presented evidence to support the Unitary Language System Hypothesis with respect to the sound system of children's spoken language. For example, Celce-Murcia (1978) noted that the French–English bilingual child she studied had the same phonological substitution processes in both languages. Phonological substitution processes occur when a child uses an easier-to-pronounce phonetic segment instead of the correct segment. For example, many young children substitute a vowel for an [l] at the ends of words so that the word *ball* would be pronounced "ba-o" or "ba-u." This kind of evidence for a unitary language system is problematic, because these substitution processes are very common across children and languages. Therefore, two monolingual French- and English-speaking children the same age as Celce-Murcia's bilingual child could easily have displayed identical phonological substitutions in their speech.

Given that the early phonological system of children is so similar cross-linguistically, how can we tell whether bilingual children have one or two phonologies? Johnson and Lancaster (1998) examined the use of phonetic segments exclusive to either Norwegian or English phonology in the word productions of a Norwegian–English toddler younger than 2 years of age. Even at this early age, the production and distribution of these sounds in the boy's words showed that he was building separate sound segment inventories for his two languages. Johanne Paradis (2001) used an elicitation task to determine whether French–English bilingual children age 2½ had separate phonological systems in production. Children were asked to repeat four-syllable-long nonsense (made up) words in both languages. Children this age often omit syllables when they repeat long words, but which syllables in the words are omitted differs between French and English, because the languages differ in their rules for syllable structure. The bilingual children omitted syllables in French and English differently, showing similar patterns to their monolingual peers. This result would not have occurred if they had had a unitary phonological system for both languages.

Vocabulary

One of Volterra and Taeschner's (1978) sources of evidence for a unified vocabulary in production was the initial absence of **translation equivalents** in bilingual children's productive vocabularies. A translation equivalent is a word that has the same meaning in two languages, such as *zapatos* in Spanish and *shoes* in English. The two girls studied by Volterra and Taeschner had few pairs of translation equivalent words in their combined vocabularies. These researchers suggested that bilingual children learn lexical labels for concepts on a one-to-one basis and avoid learning words with the same meaning. For example, if a child exposed to Spanish and English acquired the word *zapatos,* she would not have *shoes* in her vocabulary right away, because this concept had already been labeled. When children start to use translation equivalents, this is considered evidence for two vocabularies, and hence for two language systems. Although the two girls studied by Volterra and Taeschner (1978) may have had few translation equivalents, they appear to be anomalous among the many other bilingual children studied. Researchers examining Spanish–English, Portuguese–English, and French–English bilingual children have all found translation equivalents from the earliest stages, even before children have vocabularies of 50 words (Nicoladis & Genesee, 1996; Nicoladis & Secco, 2000; Pearson, Fernández, & Oller, 1995; Quay, 1995). In a study examining 27 Spanish–English bilingual children in the Miami area, Barbara Pearson and her colleagues found that on average, 30% of bilingual toddlers' early vocabularies are translation equivalents (Pearson et al., 1995). Thus, there is compelling empirical evidence to suggest that bilingual children establish two vocabularies from the onset of acquisition.

It is worthwhile to ask why bilingual children would have only 30% translation equivalents in their vocabularies. Why don't bilingual children have a larger number of translation equivalents? The answer to this question becomes clear when we consider how words are learned. Children learn new words as they interact with the world around them while hearing speech. Children do not duplicate every experience in both languages. A bilingual child may acquire certain words during an activity with her Spanish-speaking grandmother and not learn the English equivalents for some time, because she does not engage in that activity with English-speaking playmates. If English is spoken by the child mainly while at child care, then she will learn many English words related to that environment, and there may be many home-related vocabulary items lacking in her English vocabulary. Even fluent bilingual adults have gaps in their vocabularies due to experiential factors. Therefore, bilingual individuals—particularly bilingual children—should not be expected to have a translation equivalent for absolutely every word. Pearson and her research group in Miami looked at how the proportion of *singlets,* or words that do not have a translation equivalent, changes over time in Spanish–English bilingual children's vocabularies. The percentage of singlets in their dual language vocabularies was 50% in first grade (age 6) and declined to 30% by fifth grade (age 11). Bilingual students attending college still had an average of 10% singlets (Pearson, 1998). In other words, these bilingual children acquired more and more translation equivalents as their language development and experiences expanded, but they never reached a point at which they had 100% translation equivalents.

Morphosyntax

Morphosyntax refers to two elements of language that combine to form grammar: morphology and syntax. Morphology refers to freestanding function words such as articles (*the/a*), auxiliary verbs (*she is going, does she like milk?*), prepositions (*to, at, in, on,* etc.), or negative markers (*she does not like milk*), and to inflections that attach to words such as nouns and verbs in the form of suffixes or prefixes, as in -*s* in *he walk-s, the cat-s,* or *Mommy-'s sock,* or -*ed* for the past tense, as in *walk-ed, help-ed.* Syntax mainly refers to the order of function and content words in a clause or sentence. Volterra and Taeschner (1978) claimed that the bilingual children they studied had a unified syntactic rule system for their two languages until they were 3 years old. Once the children appeared to have differentiated vocabularies (i.e., when translation equivalents emerged), they still seemed to use the same syntactic rules to make sentences in both languages, even when this resulted in erroneous sentences. For example, one child formulated most of her negative sentences in both Italian and German by putting a negative marker (such as *not* in English) after the verb. This word order corresponds roughly to German syntax but not to Italian syntax, in which the negative marker comes before the verb.

Since Volterra and Taeschner's study, a wealth of research has emerged that shows that bilingual children can have separate morphosyntactic systems—in some cases, even from the beginning of their first word combinations. For example, similar to German and Italian, French and English differ in terms of the placement of the negative marker. In French, the negative marker *pas* comes after the main verb, but in English the negative marker *not* comes in between the main verb and an auxiliary verb such as *do, can,* or *is.* Compare this French sentence with its English translation in which the negative markers and main verbs are underlined: *le bébé ne boit pas le lait/the baby is not drinking the milk.* If French–English bilingual children had a unitary syntactic system, they might go through a stage in which they adopt one of these rules for both languages, so they might say *le bébé ne pas boit le lait* in French, or *the baby is drinking not the milk* in English—neither of which is a grammatically well-formed sentence. In language samples of 15 French–English bilingual children ages 2–4 years, Paradis, Nicoladis, and Genesee (2000) found only sporadic use of the wrong order for the placement of the negative marker in either language. There was no evidence from any child for a stage in which a unitary rule for negative marker placement existed in their grammars.

This example of differentiated systems with respect to the syntax of negative markers holds true for other aspects of morphosyntax and for other bilingual children. The results of research projects that have followed groups of children acquiring the same language pair over time, such as the Montreal–McGill University project in Canada (e.g., Paradis & Genesee, 1996, 1997; Paradis et al., 2000) and the DUFDE project in Hamburg, Germany (e.g., Meisel, 1989, 1994), overwhelmingly support the claim that bilingual children demonstrate the same language-specific patterns and stages in their morphosyntactic development as their monolingual peers, and thus demonstrate that they have differentiated morphosyntactic systems.

Another source of evidence for the Dual Language System Hypothesis that straddles both lexical and morphosyntactic development comes from studies examining the associations between vocabulary size, vocabulary composition (e.g., proportion of nouns, verbs, function words), and utterance—that is, sentence—length in bilingual children's speech in both languages. Barbara Conboy, Virginia Marchman, and colleagues used a standardized parent report questionnaire to measure young bilingual toddlers' lexical and morphosyntactic development in each language (Conboy & Thal, 2006; Marchman, Sussman-Martínez, & Dale, 2004). Marchman and colleagues also compared their parent report findings with direct observations of language abilities in a subset of the children. Both groups of researchers found that within each language, there were close connections among vocabulary size, vocabulary composition, and utterance length, but these connections were weak across languages. These findings are consistent with the view that dual language learners are establishing separate linguistic systems, vocabulary and grammar combined, from an early age.

To summarize, looking across evidence from speech perception in infancy, early phonological production, vocabulary building, and morphosyntax, there is a consensus among researchers that bilingual children have two language systems from the onset of their development. In other words, researchers believe that the human language faculty is perfectly capable of sorting out dual language input and establishing two linguistic systems, and there does not appear to be a stage unique to bilingual development in which a child's language system undergoes differentiation. Additional evidence for separate linguistic systems, presented later in Chapter 5, comes from young bilingual children's ability to choose which language to use based on the context of the conversation and to whom they are talking—an ability difficult to explain with the Unitary Language System Hypothesis. Therefore, parents, early childhood educators, and speech-language pathologists can expect to see bilingual children developing separate language systems and to go through the same kinds of stages that they have seen in monolingual children, on the whole. This point was also made in Chapter 3 with respect to early milestones in language development. Does this mean that bilingual children are "two monolingual children in one" in their language development? Not entirely, and in the following two sections on interactions between languages and on rate of development, we discuss the ways in which bilingual children can sometimes appear different from monolingual children.

DO THE LANGUAGE SYSTEMS OF BILINGUAL CHILDREN INTERACT DURING DEVELOPMENT?

The majority of researchers agree that bilingual children have dual language systems from early on, even at the onset of language acquisition, but this does not necessarily mean that bilingual children's two languages are hermetically sealed and utterly autonomous in development. As researchers have moved beyond the Unitary versus Dual Language System debate, they have been engaged in understanding the degrees of interconnectivity and separation between bilingual children's two developing languages. Research to date shows that bilingual children show some **cross-linguistic influence** between their two developing languages in all linguistic domains that have been studied. To introduce the concept of cross-linguistic influence, let's borrow from our previous discussion about negative sentences in French and English. Suppose a French–English bilingual child produced a sentence in English such as "the baby *drink not* the milk," in which the *not* is placed after the main verb, as it would be in French. This sentence appears to have some influence from French syntax, although it does not include French words as does a code-mixed sentence (see Chapter 5). If we see these kinds of sentences used often for a certain period of time by a bilingual child, we assume that the child has a rule in his English grammar that allows for these kinds of sentences, and this rule reflects the rule in his French grammar. It is possible, then, that this English rule is the product of cross-language contact during development. As mentioned previously, we have found very few cross-linguistic structures with negation in our corpus of 15 French–English bilingual children. So these children not only lacked a unified system for negation, but did not seem to have much cross-linguistic influence in this part of the grammar, either. However, cross-linguistic influence has been found in numerous other studies of simultaneous bilingual children. Our discussion of cross-linguistic influence will be limited to those aspects we believe would be most important for parents, educators, and health care professionals to be aware of, but the research on this topic is complex and growing. See Nicoladis and Genesee (2007), Paradis (2007), and Yip and Matthews (2007) for comprehensive technical reviews.

One of the most salient types of cross-linguistic influence is the substitution of a word order rule from one language to another. Virginia Yip and Stephen Matthews have documented this in the speech of Cantonese–English bilingual children (Yip & Matthews, 2007). For example, relative clauses in Cantonese are placed before the noun they modify, but in English they are placed after it. Yip and Matthews recorded several instances of Cantonese relative clause order in Cantonese–English children's English for a period approximately between the ages of 2½ and 4 years, when the children were more proficient in Cantonese. For example, one child asked, "Where's *the Santa Claus give me the gun?*" instead of the target English structure "Where's the gun *that Santa Claus give (gave) me?*" (Yip & Matthews, 2007, p. 155). Susanne Döpke (1998, 2000) followed a group of German–English bilingual children in Australia over time, looking at word order in their sentences in both languages. She found that a certain proportion of the children's German sentences had errors that mirrored the word order of English during the preschool years. Elena Nicoladis has found cross-linguistic influence in French–English children's use of compounds; namely, combinations of individual words that form other words, such as *brosse à dents* "toothbrush" or *taille-crayon* "pencil sharpener" (Nicoladis, 2002, 2003). Notice that the order of the words in the compounds is the opposite between French and English—*brosse à dents* translates as *brush-teeth,* word for word. Nicoladis found that French–English bilingual children are much more likely than monolingual children to reverse the word order in their compounds in both languages. Foroodi-Nejad and Paradis (2009) found similar cross-linguistic influence in the compound production of Persian–English bilingual 3-year-olds, so the phenomenon is not particular to the combination of French and English.

Some forms of cross-linguistic influence do not result in outright errors in speech, but instead have less obvious effects. Paradis and Navarro (2003) looked at the use of sentential subjects over time in a Spanish–English bilingual girl ages 1½–2½ years old, and compared their observations to those of Spanish monolingual children the same age. In Spanish, a speaker can omit the grammatical subject of a sentence, if the subject is understood between the speaker and the hearer. Thus, Spanish conversations have numerous sentences with null (omitted) subjects before the verbs. By contrast, English does not permit null subjects; thus, conversations in English would always have overt subjects, and if the subject is known to both speaker and hearer, a pronoun subject is typically used. The Spanish–English bilingual girl in this study used more overt subjects in her Spanish sentences—subjects that were sometimes redundant in the conversation—than the Spanish monolingual children her age. Paradis and Navarro suggested that the child's Spanish could have been influenced by the morphosyntactic rules of English, and that she was therefore less likely to omit subjects in her Spanish. Use of an overt subject that is redundant in Spanish is not a grammatical error per se, but it could make a child's speech sound pragmatically odd.

How long does cross-linguistic influence persist in development? Some researchers, including Döpke (2000) and Yip and Matthews (2007), have documented the rise and fall of certain cross-linguistic structures in the speech of bilingual children over time in the preschool years. So, we know that some aspects of cross-linguistic influence are temporary. But research with school-age bilingual children conducted by Ludovica Serratrice, Antonella Sorace, and their colleagues indicates that some very subtle aspects of cross-linguistic influence could extend for a long time. These researchers studied Italian–English bilingual children, ages 6–10 years, along with monolingual peers. In one study, they asked children to judge whether certain plural noun phrases were grammatical. The plural noun phrases had specific meaning, such as "the dogs are in the park," and generic meaning, such as "dogs are loyal animals"—the morphosyntactic structures for such noun phrases differ between Italian and English (Serratrice, Sorace, Filiaci, & Baldo, 2009). The bilingual children showed some cross-linguistic influence in their performance on the task, even in the oldest group, because they sometimes accepted noun phrases as grammatical in one language when those noun phrases actually had the morphosyntactic structure of the other language. It is unknown whether these bilingual children would ever produce a noun phrase with the wrong morphosyntactic structure in their everyday speech, however. Research such as this suggests that interactions between dual language systems might be a permanent feature of being bilingual, and that some subtle differences between monolingual children and bilingual children in language representation extend across the lifespan.

Two main explanations have been put forward to explain when cross-linguistic influence can be expected in bilingual children's speech. The first explanation has to do with how the rules for a structure might overlap across languages. To take the example of null subjects in Spanish, notice that although Spanish allows subjects to be null or overt, English allows only overt subjects. The presence of overlap in overt subjects between the two languages and the optional use of null or overt subjects in Spanish might "invite" influence from English to Spanish, but the other way around is less likely, because English has just one option. The second explanation that has been put forward is *language dominance*, a concept discussed in detail in the next section. If children are more proficient in one language than the other, cross-linguistic influence might take place from the dominant to the nondominant language, regardless of overlap and optionality. For example, there is zero overlap in the word order in relative clauses between English and Cantonese, and no optionality either; thus, a logical explanation for cross-linguistic influence in this case is the children's dominance in Cantonese.

Whatever the reasons are for cross-linguistic structures, we would like to emphasize that they are not rampant in the language of bilingual children. On the whole, simultaneous bilingual children use grammatical structures appropriate for their stage of development in each language. But when parents or professionals dealing with bilingual children come across structures that appear to be influenced by the child's other language, it is important to bear in mind that this phenomenon is typical of bilingual development and is not a sign of confusion or extraordinary difficulty coping with dual language input.

ARE THERE DIFFERENCES IN RATE OF DEVELOPMENT BETWEEN BILINGUAL AND MONOLINGUAL CHILDREN?

Many parents, educators, and health care practitioners have the impression that bilingual children go through the stages of language development more slowly than monolingual children because they have twice as much language to acquire in the same amount of time. As discussed in Chapter 3, there is no evidence that bilingual infants and toddlers are slower than children who are monolingual to pass through early critical milestones such as babbling, first words, and first word combinations. The concern we have in this section is whether this is also true for language development past the early months and for more

BOX 4.2

Determining the Dominant Language

Preschool children: How can one tell what a young child's dominant language is? The dominant language usually has a number of characteristics when compared with the nondominant language (see the following list). These characteristics have been noted by various researchers and are based on spontaneous, naturalistic language samples from children approximately 1½–3½ years old. Researchers sometimes use a combination of direct measures of linguistic characteristics from the two languages together with parental reports of which language is more proficient, or which language their child uses more often. We recommend determining dominance using more than one measure and, if possible, across more than one linguistic domain; that is, one vocabulary and one morphosyntax measure rather than two morphosyntax measures. The dominant language would be the language for which the child has a higher score for most measures. Odd numbers of measures, such as 3 or 5, are good, because a "tie" is not possible. If a child has very close or similar scores for each measure, then that child can be considered a balanced bilingual.

Common characteristics of a dominant language:

1. Longer mean length of utterance (MLU; average length calculated across all utterances in a stretch of discourse)

2. More frequent appearance of "advanced" morphosyntactic structures

3. Larger number of different word types—or verb types in particular—used in a stretch of discourse of a fixed number of utterances

4. Fewer pauses or hesitations in a stretch of discourse of a fixed number of utterances

5. Greater volubility: more utterances in a stretch of discourse of a fixed time length

6. Fewer code-switched utterances used in a stretch of discourse conducted (mainly) in that language

See Genesee et al. (1995), Paradis and Nicoladis (2007), or Foroodi-Nejad and Paradis (2009) for technical examples of how dominance can be determined. See also Yip and Matthews (2007) for in-depth discussions of the use of MLU cross-linguistically and of different approaches to calculating dominance.

School-age children: Calculating measures such as utterance length from spontaneous language samples may be less revealing for school-age children, because their language knowledge and ability have grown so much in complexity that such methods would not easily capture differences in language proficiency. Older children's dominant language could be ascertained by comparing their scores on language tests in both languages, if the tests are comparable in terms of what they measure and how they measure it. It is important not to rely on just one measure, such as vocabulary size, but examine at least more than one linguistic domain. Comprehensive information on the child's exposure to each language at home, at school, and outside of school could also assist in determining an older child's dominant language.

fine-grained aspects of language. The research we discuss here shows that bilingual children are within the normal range as defined by monolingual children for some aspects of language, but lag behind monolingual children for other aspects, in both the preschool and school-age years. In other words, bilingual children are not globally delayed in their lexical and morphosyntactic development. The differences in rates that are apparent from research indicate that their rates of development are sensitive to factors such as amount of exposure to each language (see Box 4.2 and the following section on language dominance), the relative complexity of the morphosyntactic structure being examined, and possibly the minority/majority status of the language in the social context. Bilingual children's sensitivity to these factors can sometimes cause them to lag behind their monolingual peers in at least one of their languages. Understanding where to expect differences in rates of language development between bilingual and monolingual children is particularly important for parents, educators, and health care practitioners who initiate referrals and for specialists such as speech-language pathologists and psychologists, who conduct language-based assessments. Before turning to research comparing bilingual and monolingual rates of development and the sources of bilingual differences, we first discuss the concept of language dominance.

Language Dominance

Almost all studies of simultaneous bilingual children have found that even though they have been acquiring two languages from birth, or shortly after, the two languages do not develop in perfect synchrony. The language in which bilingual children appear to have greater proficiency is commonly referred to as their **dominant language** and the other as the **nondominant language**. (Other commonly used terms are *stronger* language and *weaker* language.) Most researchers of simultaneous bilingual children consider **dominance** to be a measure of *relative* proficiency between the two languages that the child is learning; dominance is not usually construed as meaning that a simultaneous bilingual child is incompetent in one language or has only passive knowledge of one language.

Dominance is closely linked to the amount of input the child receives in each language, which is seldom equal. For example, if we inquired about the preschool linguistic exposure of a child such as Gabriela, we might find that she hears mainly Spanish from her mother and both Spanish and English from her father on weeknights and weekends and hears English during the weekdays at a child care center. Gabriela is receiving much more input in English, and it would be expected for her to be English-dominant at this stage in her life. Barbara Pearson and her colleagues found that Spanish–English bilingual children who received less than 25% of their input in Spanish often did not become fluent Spanish speakers (Pearson, Fernández, Lewedag, & Oller, 1997). Therefore, very low input for one language could render it a passive language rather than a nondominant language. This would mean that the child would not spontaneously speak that language, but could understand, more or less, what is addressed to him in that language. Over time, even passive ability in a language can disappear entirely, unless input in that language increases.

Expectations of balanced bilingual development in preschool children may be unrealistic, and it is more likely that bilingual children will be dominant in one language. One consequence of dominance is that a bilingual child may appear to be less advanced in the development of the nondominant language than an average monolingual child of the same age (see Box 4.2 for details on determining a child's dominant language). It is also possible that a bilingual child's proficiency in the nondominant language could be so limited that the child would display competence in that language that is below the normal range of performance based on monolingual children. For this reason, it could be inappropriate to clinically assess a child in their nondominant language, and in particular, if only the nondominant language is being assessed. (For more on this point, see our discussion of mean length of utterance later in this chapter and see Chapter 9.)

Dominance has another effect on young bilingual children: their language choices. The McGill University research project included a series of studies examining the sensitivity of bilingual children to the language preferences or abilities of their conversational partners (Genesee, Boivin, & Nicoladis, 1996; Genesee, Nicoladis, & Paradis, 1995; Nicoladis & Genesee, 1996). The researchers found that even bilingual children as young as 2 years old can tailor their language choice to their adult interlocutor. However, bilingual children are often constrained by their dominance, so when they are speaking to an adult in their nondominant language, they often interject individual words and whole utterances from their dominant language in the conversation. Furthermore, Paradis and Nicoladis (2007) found that 4-year-old French–English bilingual children in a French minority/English majority context showed an interaction between dominance and language status in their conversations with unfamiliar interlocutors. Specifically, English-dominant children felt free to use English with either a French- or English-speaking interlocutor, but French-dominant children were reluctant to use French with an English-speaking interlocutor and thus were restricted in the topics they could engage in when conversing in English. Thus, these 4-year-old children showed awareness of the fact that most French speakers in their community are bilingual, but English speakers are not. More information about bilingual children's language choice is presented in Chapter 5.

Language dominance can also be seen in school-age bilingual children, as differential amounts of exposure to each language continues to have an impact on their language abilities past the early years. The sources of differential exposure to each language in older children goes beyond parental language use at home and can also include community context, language of instruction in school, language use with friends, media choices, and more.

Vocabulary

One of the earliest vocabulary-building skills is the ability to recognize familiar word forms in the speech stream. For example, an infant might be able to recognize the word "cup" as a familiar group of sounds when spoken in isolation, but the infant also needs to be able to recognize this word when she hears it in a stretch of discourse, because words do not usually appear in isolation in natural conversation. Such word recognition abilities emerge toward the end of the first year of life. Vihman and her colleagues examined word form recognition in English monolingual and Welsh–English bilingual infants ages 9–12 months using both behavioral and brain activity measures (Vihman, Thierry, Lum, Keren-Portnoy, & Martin, 2007). They found that the timing of the bilingual infants' abilities to recognize familiar word forms in both languages was the same as that for English monolingual children: around 11 months. After being able to recognize word forms, the next step is for infants to map meanings onto those forms in order to build vocabularies. Byers-Heinlein and her colleagues found that, as with monolingual children of the same age,

14-month-old bilingual children could successfully learn new words for novel objects in an experimental task (reported in Werker et al., 2009).

However, the words used in this task were phonologically very different from each other. Language learners must eventually be able to learn word-meaning pairs when the words differ in only one sound segment, for example, *bet–pet* in English, or *boire* ("to drink")–*poire* ("pear") in French. Such words are called **minimal pairs,** because a small phonological difference—that is, one sound—signals a complete difference in meaning; all languages have minimal pairs. Learning form-meaning mappings for minimal pairs requires coordination of the emerging phonological system with cognitive word learning skills. Fennell, Byers-Heinlein, & Werker (2007) tested bilingual and monolingual toddlers' ability to learn new words for novel objects when the words were minimal pairs, such as *bih* and *dih*. They found that monolingual children succeeded in mapping form and meaning at 17 months of age, but that bilingual children succeeded in doing this closer to 20 months of age. Thus, bilingual children appear to lag behind monolingual children in this ability, although the gap is not huge.

Finally, there is evidence that language dominance can play a role even at the very early stages of children's lexical development. Conboy and Mills (2006) measured the brain activity of 19- to 22-month-old bilingual toddlers while they listened to known and unknown words. The researchers gathered information on what words would be known to the children before the experiment, and also on their exposure patterns to each language to infer language dominance. The timing and distribution of brain activity to known words was different, depending on whether the word was in the children's dominant or nondominant language. In sum, at the beginning of vocabulary learning, bilingual children show similar rates of development to monolingual children, generally speaking, but they may lag behind with regard to more challenging aspects of vocabulary acquisition, and the amount of exposure they have in each language can affect how they process words.

Researchers, educators, and speech-language pathologists often measure the size of a child's vocabulary using a standardized test in order to assess whether the child's language is developing "normally" or typically—in other words, whether it falls within the range of normal performance/ability as defined by a large cohort of children the same age; that is, within the age-expected norms. (More details on normal curve distributions and these kinds of tests are given in Chapters 9 and 10.) Differences between bilingual and monolingual children have been consistently documented in research using standardized vocabulary tests, including toddlers up to school-age children. These differences sometimes show bilingual children performing below the normal range for their age in one of their languages, yet in other cases, performing lower than a monolingual comparison group, but still more or less within age-expected abilities. Furthermore, how bilingual children compare to their monolingual peers in vocabulary development depends on input exposure factors, possibly including social context.

Young Spanish–English bilingual preschoolers in the United States usually score lower on standardized vocabulary tests in each language than monolingual children (Conboy & Thal, 2006; Pearson, Fernández, & Oller, 1993). In addition, vocabulary size in each language varies directly in proportion to relative amount of exposure to each language (Marchman et al., 2004)—the more exposure to a language, the larger the vocabulary, other things being equal. A large-scale study of Spanish–English bilingual children in both English-only and Spanish–English instructional programs in Miami schools revealed that vocabulary size differences between monolingual children and bilingual children persisted until at least Grade 5 (Oller & Eilers, 2002). Exposure time to each language in school made a difference. Bilingual children in Spanish–English instructional programs had bigger vocabularies in Spanish than their peers in English-only programs. The bilingual children in English-only programs had bigger vocabularies in English than their bilingual peers in the Spanish–English program early on, but interestingly, this effect diminished between second grade and fifth grade (see Chapter 8 for more on the outcomes of bilingual education programs).

A Canadian study of vocabulary size in French–English bilingual children attending French-language schools in an English-majority city, Edmonton, showed similarities and differences with this research from Miami (Paradis, 2009). The main similarity was that the size of bilingual children's vocabularies in each language was sensitive to the amount of exposure to that language at home and in school. The main difference was that the majority of bilingual children had vocabulary sizes equivalent to monolingual age peers in French in first grade and sixth grade. In these French medium schools, English language arts instruction is introduced in third grade. This seemed to make a difference in the children's English vocabulary scores, which were slightly lower than the monolingual English average in first grade, but comparable to the monolingual English average in sixth grade. In sum, the magnitude of bilingual–monolingual differences in vocabulary size was smaller in the Canadian study than in the American study, even though an identical measure of vocabulary size was used. One reason for this difference could be that because schooling was nearly exclusively in the minority language, French, this helped the Canadian bilingual children to "balance out" the impact of English exposure in the larger community. Whatever the reason is, the importance of the contrast between these studies is that parents and professionals need not assume that bilingual children will *always* lag behind in their vocabulary development throughout the school years, but instead can expect that bilingual children *could* lag behind in vocabulary development, at least in some contexts.

What do these findings suggest for our case study children such as James and Gabriela? Remember, James is a French–English bilingual attending school in French in a bilingual city, Montreal, and Gabriela is a Spanish–English bilingual attending a bilingual school in the New York City area. First, the findings suggest that children in a social context such as James's are more likely to acquire vocabulary similarly to monolingual children for both languages earlier on than children in a social context similar to that of Gabriela. Second, they suggest that for the language not taught at school or taught less at school, discrepancies between a bilingual child's vocabulary and monolingual-based norms would be expected, because literacy and academic language in school build vocabulary. In other words, the more literacy and academic language skills are developed in a language, the more likely it is a child's vocabulary in that language will also be enhanced. Therefore, because James is attending a French-language school with continuous but limited English instruction, his parents might be advised to encourage him to read in English at home. Because Montreal has a large English-speaking community, as does Canada as a whole, it is reasonable to expect that James will acquire English successfully. Gabriela's situation is somewhat different. Because she is attending a transitional bilingual school with little or no Spanish instruction after third grade (see Chapter 8 for more details on this kind of program), her parents might also be advised to make sure that she continues to develop literacy skills in Spanish at home and participates in other linguistically rich activities in Spanish on a regular basis. Furthermore, because Spanish is not a majority language in the New York City area (although it is a widely spoken minority language), ensuring long-term proficiency in this language will take some effort on the part of both schools and parents.

Why do bilingual children tend to have smaller vocabularies than monolingual children? Because bilingual children have the same cognitive abilities and limitations with respect to memory capacity as monolingual children, one would expect that their vocabulary in each of their languages would be smaller than that of monolingual children, especially in the early years. Viewed this way, it is not surprising that bilingual children may not have accumulated the same absolute number of word–concept pairings in two languages in the same amount of time as monolingual children do for one language. Pearson and her colleagues assessed the vocabulary of bilingual Spanish–English toddlers in Miami using parent report checklists of the words the children spoke and understood in both languages. They found that when the vocabularies of both languages were combined, and translation equivalents were counted once only, their total "conceptual" vocabulary was similar in size to that of monolingual norms (Pearson, 1998; Pearson, Fernández, & Oller, 1993). This shows that bilingual children are not slower than monolingual children to assign word labels for concepts, the basic process that underlies vocabulary building, and that they are able to learn the same number of word–concept pairings as monolingual children.

To summarize, bilingual children use the same mechanisms to acquire words as monolingual children, and thus are successful word learners. When bilingual children are compared to monolingual children, the size of their vocabularies in each language can seem smaller, but this depends on amount of exposure to each language, as determined by home, school, and perhaps even the broader social context.

Morphosyntax

In Chapter 3, we discussed research showing that exposure to two languages at the same time does not delay when simultaneous bilingual children begin to use word combinations or simple sentences to express themselves. A common measure of children's early morphosyntactic development is **mean length of utterance (MLU)**, which refers to the average length of a child's utterances, calculated across numerous utterances in a sample of that child's spontaneous speech. In young children, "sentences" can consist of single words or phrases, which is why utterance is the preferred term rather than sentences. Miller and Chapman (1981) published a set of norms for MLU development in English based on the language of over a hundred monolingual children. MLU was calculated using morphemes per utterance, so a word such as *cats* would count as two morphemes: *cat-s*. Do the MLUs of bilingual children increase with age at the same rate according to these monolingual norms? A query from a speech-language pathologist in the United States on this question (see Box 4.3) prompted our analysis here. Detailed information on the MLUs of the three children studied in Paradis and Genesee (1996) are given in Box 4.4, along with the normal range of MLUs (one standard deviation above and below the mean) from Miller and Chapman's sample of children. The bilingual children we examined were growing up in the same context as the case study child, James. Some cautions are in order, as these are norms for English and we are using them to judge French as

---

BOX 4.3

Mean Length of Utterance as an Indicator of Typical Development

Dear Dr. Paradis,

Is MLU (mean length of utterance) a good indicator of a language impairment before the age of 4 for children developing two languages or hearing one language spoken by parents and another in their community/TV/non–home environment? In other words, should we expect an MLU of, say, 2.0 for a 2-year-old who is processing two languages—or 3.0 for a 3-year-old? I am having a difficult time finding research on this exact topic, but thousands of Spanish-speaking preschoolers in the United States are being identified as language impaired based on their MLU before the age of 4, which concerns me greatly, even when their receptive language is measured as well within normal limits.

Thank you for any help or direction you can give me in this endeavor.
A speech-language pathologist

The information in Box 4.4 illustrates the difference between the MLUs of a bilingual child with language delay and two bilingual children with typical development, as referenced to monolingual children. For school-age Spanish–English bilingual children in the United States, normative information on MLUs from a storytelling task can be found on the SALT web site at http://www.languageanalysislab.com.

---

well; in addition, there are some minor differences between our calculations and those used by Miller and Chapman. Nevertheless, two of the children, Gene and Oliver, had MLUs within or close to the normal range in both their languages from the ages of 2 to 3 years, although their MLUs tended to be at the lower bound of the range for monolingual children. The MLUs of the bilingual children were not exactly equivalent in both languages, which is most likely the result of unequal exposure to both languages, that is, language dominance. Similar findings on early MLU development in three Spanish–English bilingual children were reported in Padilla and Liebman (1975).

We found that the pattern for Gene and Oliver held for other children in the Montreal–McGill University study, except for William. Toward the end of the study, around the age of 3 years, William was identified by a speech–language pathologist as having expressive language delay, and he received speech therapy services before entering school. This was unknown to us or to his parents at the outset of the study. Notice that his MLUs are consistently lower than age-based monolingual expectations in both languages. Thus, William illustrates the development of MLU in a bilingual child who has language delay. The fact that his MLU values are distinct from those of Gene and Olivier shows how typically developing bilingual children are not delayed in their growth in MLU compared to monolingual children, although they tend not to be at the upper end of the monolingual range. (More research on bilingual children affected by language delay and impairment is presented in Chapter 9.) Moving on to the acquisition of more specific aspects of

BOX 4.4

Mean Length of Utterance in Bilingual Children and Monolingual Children

The MLUs from the bilingual children are from Paradis and Genesee (1996, p. 11). They are calculated as MLU in morphemes and are compared to the norms for ranges of MLUs by age from Miller and Chapman (1981, p. 158). The two children with typical development, Gene and Oliver, have MLUs that fall close to the lower bound or the middle of the normal range at all ages. The child with language delay, William, has MLU values that fall below the 1 standard deviation boundary for monolingual children.

Child	Age	English MLU	French MLU	Monolingual English −1 to +1 standard deviation range for age
Gene (typically developing)	1;11	2.04	1.92	1.47—2.37
	2;7	2.17	2.12	1.97—3.11
	3;1	2.44	2.36	2.47—3.85
Oliver (typically developing)	1;11	1.55	2.32	1.47—2.37
	2;6	2.18	2.59	1.97—3.11
	2;10	2.31	2.40	2.22—3.48
William (language delay)	2;2	1.29	1.26	1.72—2.74
	2;10	1.54	1.35	2.22—3.48
	3;3	2.19	1.60	2.71—4.23

morphosyntax during the preschool years, research shows some differences between bilingual and monolingual children can occur in rates of development. Paradis, Crago, and Genesee (2005/2006) found that French–English bilingual 3-year-olds were as accurate as French monolingual children in their use of French object pronouns—a notoriously difficult aspect of French morphosyntax to acquire, unlike in English. In contrast, Pérez-Leroux and her colleagues found that bilingual 3-year-olds lagged behind monolingual children in their use of object pronouns in French (Pérez-Leroux, Pirvulescu, & Roberge, 2009). The difference in these findings could be due to social context. The French–English bilingual children Paradis and colleagues studied were residing in the bilingual city of Montreal, whereas the children studied by Pérez-Leroux and colleagues lived in the English-majority city of Toronto. Nicoladis and colleagues found that French–English bilingual children's accuracy in using verbs in the past tense, such as *ran* (*run*) or *pick-ed,* in both languages was slightly lower than their monolingual peers at 4–6 years of age (Nicoladis, Palmer, & Marentette, 2007). However, these researchers did not look at the children's performance in their dominant language in particular. In a follow-up study, Paradis, Nicoladis, and colleagues found that bilingual children could be as accurate as monolingual children at this age in their use of the past tense in their dominant language (Paradis, Nicoladis, Crago, & Genesee, in press). Comparisons between

Spanish–English bilingual children and monolingual children in the United States have yielded parallel findings for similar aspects of morphosyntax (Gutiérrez-Clellen, Simon-Cereijido, & Wagner, 2008). In sum, it appears that for some aspects of morphosyntax, simultaneous bilingual children can keep pace with monolingual children—at least in their dominant language and/or in the majority language of their social context.

The studies of vocabulary discussed thus far that took place in Miami and Edmonton also included measures of children's morphosyntactic development in both languages (Gathercole, 2007; Oller & Eilers, 2002; Paradis, 2009, in press). The results for morphosyntactic measures largely paralleled those for vocabulary. First, bilingual children's morphosyntactic abilities in each language were influenced by how much exposure they had in that language in both studies. Second, in the Miami study, bilingual children lagged behind monolingual children in both languages, but nearly closed the gap by fifth grade (Gathercole, 2007; Oller & Eilers, 2002). In contrast, in the Edmonton study, bilingual children, as a group, performed similar to monolingual children in French. The only bilingual children who did not were those who spoke mainly English at home, and differences with monolingual children were evident only in first grade and not in sixth grade (Paradis, 2009). For English morphosyntax, bilingual children lagged behind monolingual children in first grade, but bilingual children who came from homes where English was the predominant language, or where English was spoken equally with French, performed comparably to monolingual children (Paradis, 2009, 2010).

As with vocabulary, the main distinction between the Miami and Edmonton studies was that the magnitude of bilingual–monolingual differences was smaller for the French–English bilingual children in Edmonton. The amount of the minority language taught at school could be at the root of this difference between the studies, as mentioned for vocabulary findings, but another reason could be the morphosyntactic structures examined. Because different aspects of morphosyntax were examined in each study, it is possible that the aspects of French and English that were studied were "easier" to learn than the aspects of English and Spanish studied in the children in Miami, giving the appearance of smaller differences in the Edmonton study. The complexity of a morphosyntactic structure can influence how much input and practice is necessary to learn it, which in turn could mean that bilingual children would take a lot longer to acquire complex structures than monolingual children. The impact of structure complexity was shown in a large-scale study of Welsh–English bilingual children in Welsh-medium schools (Gathercole, 2007). In Welsh, there are numerous phonological changes in noun phrases when nouns have feminine gender, but fewer when nouns have masculine gender. Virginia Gathercole and colleagues found that bilingual children's accuracy with noun phrases in Welsh varied directly with how much Welsh was spoken at home, but this variation was much more pronounced for the more complex feminine forms (Gathercole, 2007).

Studies of simultaneous bilingual learners do not usually extend past the late elementary school years. This leaves us with the question of whether bilingual children ever become indistinguishable from their monolingual peers in their morphosyntax, regardless of dominance, instructional program, and complexity of structures. In her 2008 book, Silvina Montrul reviews several studies she has conducted with adult university students who grew up speaking both English and Spanish, but attended school only in English. Many of these adults would have been simultaneous bilingual children. She consistently found that these individuals differed somewhat from Spanish monolingual individuals in their grasp of subtle aspects of grammatical expression and knowledge. It is possible that the absence of schooling in one of a bilingual person's two languages could affect long-term outcomes. It is also possible that insufficient early exposure to Spanish, due to the societal predominance of English, causes what Montrul refers to as "incomplete acquisition." However, it is important to point out that the bilingual adults studied by Montrul were not necessarily incompetent in Spanish; many were very proficient in this language, particularly in a conversational context. Turning to our case study children, Montrul's findings are more applicable to Gabriela than to James. Children such as James in any part of Canada can have both their languages supported through schooling. Children such as Gabriela might experience limited, transitional, or no Spanish language instruction in school, reinforcing our earlier point about how important it is to encourage parents of children in a situation similar to that of Gabriela to enrich their children's language experiences in Spanish, including literacy, as much as possible. What is important here is to recognize that the linguistic limitations of the adults studied by Montrul do not reflect limitations in these individuals' ability to learn both languages, but rather reflect the complexity of the learning environments in which they acquire them.

Bilingual Bootstrapping and Rate of Development

What about cross-linguistic influences that could benefit language development by facilitating acquisition? To the best of our knowledge, the term **bilingual bootstrapping** was first used by Gawlitzek-Maiwald and Tracy (1996) to describe what they observed in a German–English girl's use of code-mixing. The girl seemed to mix words from German into English in order to stretch her expressive abilities in English; English was a nondominant language for this child. Since this study, *bilingual bootstrapping* has been used with a slightly different meaning. It generally refers to the idea that a bilingual child's development in one language can be advanced by the other, dominant language, and/or that the two languages can be mutually advanced by virtue of sharing some linguistic–conceptual knowledge. This means that development might proceed more rapidly than one might expect if a bilingual child were acquiring each language in absolute isolation. For example, a bilingual child might not have to "discover" all the linguistic concepts and develop all the details of linguistic representations twice. In this way, bilingual bootstrapping could explain why bilingual children, in spite of some lags relative to monolingual children, are not substantially delayed in their overall language development. Put differently, some bilingual children might receive half the input that monolingual children do, but not be twice as far behind monolingual children; on the contrary, they can display competence that falls within monolingual norms in some cases.

Is there direct evidence for bilingual bootstrapping? The studies discussed earlier on cross-linguistic influence show that the two languages of a bilingual do not develop in isolation. However, generally speaking, this research has focused on unique patterns that arise as a consequence of interaction between a bilingual's two developing languages, and not on whether rates of development can be positively affected by connections between the languages. Fabiano-Smith and Goldstein (2010) examined accuracy in pronouncing phonetic segments in both Spanish and English in bilingual preschool children, as compared to monolingual children. They put forward the proposal that phonetic segments that are similar, or shared, between the two languages might be easier for bilingual children to master than nonshared sounds because production or practice with shared sounds would be more frequent than with nonshared sounds—children would use the shared sounds no matter which language they are speaking. They argue that such facilitation might explain why bilingual children can be more or less within the normal range for monolingual children in their rate of phonological acquisition, despite less exposure to one or both languages. It is possible that what Fabiano-Smith and Goldstein found for phonology could extend to morphosyntax as well. Concerning vocabulary, sharing at the conceptual and semantic levels for words is likely to take place in the developing bilingual lexicon (Gathercole, 2007). Thus, bilingual children might need to learn separate phonological labels for words in each language, but they might not necessarily need to learn separate conceptual and semantic features for all of them. In addition, facilitative interdependence between bilingual children's languages has been noted by several researchers and in several reviews in domains related to academic language abilities and literacy in particular (e.g., Oller & Eilers, 2002; Riches & Genesee, 2006). These studies will be discussed in some detail in Chapter 8.

It is also possible that bilingual bootstrapping reflects the sharing of cognitive processes and/or knowledge that underpins language learning, rather than the sharing of linguistic constructs themselves. As discussed in Chapter 3, research by Ellen Bialystok has shown cognitive advantages that can result from early bilingualism, particularly in what are called *executive functions*. These cognitive processes are important not just for other cognitive functions or academic skills, but also for learning language itself. It could be that bilingual development enhances cognitive skills that, in turn, further enhance bilingual development. However, not enough research has been conducted on bilingual bootstrapping to know for certain which aspects of shared linguistic or enhanced cognitive abilities might contribute to it.

Development of the Minority Language: Dominance and Language Loss

James, Bistra, and Gabriela are all simultaneous bilingual children, although a key difference between them is the minority/majority status of the two languages they are learning. Gabriela and James are learning two languages that are relatively widely used in the cities where they live. Bistra, however, is learning Bulgarian and English in the United States in a city where there are very few Bulgarian speakers other than her mother. We have already discussed James and Gabriela in the context of the research, but what about Bistra?

The importance of the minority/majority language distinction is how it can influence children's early language dominance and their ultimate success at learning both languages, because it influences children's opportunities to experience rich and frequent input in both languages. Many simultaneous bilingual children such as Bistra may be proficient in both languages when they are 3 or 4 years old but shift to become much more proficient in the majority language—typically the language of schooling—when they are older, and they may even end up not being bilingual adolescents and adults. Much of the early research on bilingual preschool children was based on children such as Bistra, who are the children of so-called linguistically mixed marriages, in which the parents have different native languages and each parent speaks his or her native language to the child. In these cases, however, one language is not frequently used in the community outside the home. This kind of situation is called **family bilingualism.** Montrul (2008, Chapter 4) reviews case studies of early bilingual children such as Bistra who are learning a minority language along with English—for instance, Hebrew or Russian—in the United States. These studies showed that rapid decline and loss of some morphosyntactic features of the minority language, especially upon entry to an English preschool program, is common. Anderson (2001) reports erosion of some morphosyntactic and lexical abilities over time in two Puerto Rican children whose families moved to the United States when they were preschoolers. Even though Spanish is less of a minority language than Hebrew or Russian, it is important to highlight two points about the children in Anderson's study: 1) they were residing in a small city in the midwestern United States where there is less concentration of Spanish speakers and no Spanish instruction in school, and 2) the parents were fluent English speakers and thus may have been using both languages comfortably at home. In contrast, our own research and that of our colleagues in Wales and in Miami are based on children such as James and Gabriela, who are growing up in both a bilingual family and a bilingual community where they may have educational opportunities that support both languages. These children are expected to develop their bilingualism past their early childhood years, although with some differences between them, as discussed earlier. In sum, it will be a challenge for Bistra's parents to ensure that she maintains fluency in Bulgarian past the preschool years and, as with the other two children, it is recommended that acquiring literacy in Bulgarian could help her to maintain the language.

EARLY MULTILINGUAL DEVELOPMENT

The information presented thus far has been based on children exposed to two languages in their early years, but there are some children who learn three, or even four, languages early on; that is, multilingual children. In Chapter 3, we put forward evidence suggesting that human infants have the capacity to learn more than one language, but what about three languages? There is very little research on children who are exposed to three languages early on, and all are case studies. Typically, the children are exposed to two minority languages at home and to a third majority language as a result of attending day care or preschool programs at an early age. What these case studies tell us is that trilingual children are not much different from the bilingual children we have just discussed in the early preschool years, but developing comparable proficiency in all three languages as they grow older can be a challenge.

Simona Montanari has examined many aspects of the language development of a Tagalog–Spanish–English trilingual girl growing up in California (Montanari, 2008, 2009). The girl began to produce word combinations in all three of her languages just after her second birthday, her emerging vocabularies included translation equivalents in all three languages, and the word order in her sentences reflected language specific patterns from the outset. In addition, she tailored her language choice according to the interlocutor by using more of the interlocutor's preferred language when speaking with him or her. Thus, trilingual exposure appeared to not cause major setbacks in basic milestones, and differentiation of three languages was evident. Similar to that of bilingual children, this child's vocabulary size and MLU in each language reflected the amount of input she was receiving in each. Montanari reported that the girl's MLU in words at age 2 years, 4 months was 1.31 for Tagalog, 1.6 for English, and 1.27 for Spanish (Montanari, 2008, p. 8). We cannot compare these to the table in Box 4.4, because those MLUs are based on

---

BOX 4.5

Multilingualism in Young Children

Dear Professor Genesee,

I live in California. My daughter is 2. Her mother is Brazilian and speaks only Portuguese with her. Our nanny is Mexican and speaks only Spanish. I speak English with her. We have been considering a French immersion school for her, as I am aware of some of the benefits of a bilingual education. My fear, however, is that asking her to learn a fourth language will tax her too much, and overwhelm her.

Sincerely,
A father

We often receive emails from parents and professionals that concern rather complex cases of multilingualism in young children. Most of the time, these queries are about whether children can learn three or four languages early in life. Our answers to these queries always include one central point: children's capacity for full bi- or multilingualism is dependent on their ability to receive rich and frequent exposure to both/all of their languages over time. The more languages, the more of a challenge this is.

---

morphemes, not words. But Paradis and Genesee (1997) calculated MLU in words for two French–English bilingual children at the same age: Yann had 1.49 for English and 1.58 for French, and Mathieu had 1.22 for English and 1.60 for French (Paradis & Genesee, 1997, p. 103). Thus, for MLUs, this trilingual girl does not appear to be lagging behind her bilingual peers. Other case studies of trilingual children have also noted language-specific word order patterns in early sentences, the children's ability to differentiate use of their languages with different interlocutors, and how their development is sensitive to the amount of input they receive in each language (Hoffman, 1985; Maneva, 2004).

Parents, educators, and speech-language pathologists often ask us if learning three or four languages would be "overload" for young children, or whether it is even realistic to expect a child to be proficient in three or four languages learned at once. The e-mail message in Box 4.5 represents a typical query from a parent about the feasibility of early multilingualism. The results of the case studies point in a positive direction for trilingual children in the early stages; they seem to indicate that children can sort out and separate input from three languages and that critical developmental milestones emerge over time. However, it should be noted that the case studies reported in scientific reports are based on children from families where trilingualism is a conscious choice that is managed by the parents. Children can also be exposed to three languages in the preschool years for other reasons. Recall one of the children profiled in Chapter 1, Faisal, whose family spent time in a refugee camp in Kenya before coming to Canada. Although we have profiled Faisal as a second language learner, a child from a similar background could have experienced

Somali–Swahili bilingualism simultaneously from birth, with English introduced after migrating to Canada around the age of 3 years. In these situations, families do not necessarily drop the "old" majority language immediately, and so a child such as Faisal might be an early trilingual child, although his trilingualism is likely to be transitional because English is likely to replace Swahili over time. The issue of minority language status is important for all trilingual children. In Montanari's case study, as soon as the child entered an English language preschool, her English advanced considerably (Montanari, 2008). It is possible that the language that has the least support, Tagalog, might recede as the child enters school. One of the biggest challenges facing families who want to raise their children as multilingual speakers is to arrange for them to have sufficient and rich exposure to all the languages over time. Without such rich and sufficient exposure, it is not likely that children will maintain and continue to develop all of their languages.

KEY POINTS AND IMPLICATIONS

Key Point 1

Children exposed to two languages from birth have two separate but interconnected linguistic systems from the outset. Developmental stages and patterns are the same *overall* for monolingual and bilingual children. For the most part, the same kinds of "errors" occur in the language of bilingual and monolingual children while they are en route to mastering the adult language system. When bilingual children occasionally produce unique errors in their language, it is most likely the result of cross-linguistic influence, which is a natural process in bilingual development.

Implications

Parents, educators, and health care practitioners should not assume that bilingual children will display unique stages or patterns in their language development because dual language input might confuse them. Bilingual children can be expected to appear as "two monolingual children in one" much—but not all—of the time, and can differentiate between their two languages. Parents, educators, and health care practitioners should not be concerned if bilingual children sometimes produce sentences in one language that follow the grammatical rules of their other language; this kind of cross-linguistic influence is typical, is mainly temporary, and is not a sign of confusion or impairment. It is simply one of the few ways in which bilingual children are not always "two monolingual children in one" (see also Chapter 5 on code-mixing).

Key Point 2

There is no scientific evidence that children's language learning ability is limited to one language. On the contrary, research indicates that infants have the capacity to acquire two languages without significant costs to the development of early milestones. Although bilingual children do not always keep pace with monolingual children in every aspect of their subsequent lexical and grammatical development, they often do so in their dominant language (see Key Point 3). The rate of language development for bilingual children is sensitive to their exposure time to each language at home, at school, and in the community. Any apparent differences in the rate of development between bilingual children and monolingual children are not a sign that dual language learning is too burdensome for young children. Rather, such differences reflect the complex linguistic environment of bilingual children and its impact on their developmental trajectories.

Implications

Parents and health care professionals should not assume that any clinically significant delays or difficulties a bilingual child is experiencing in language development are the result of dual language exposure. Dual language exposure is not a risk factor for language development per se; we discuss this in greater detail in Chapter 9. However, bilingual children might lag behind their monolingual peers for some aspects of development, and it is important to distinguish between variation in rates of development that might be due to having less exposure to a language and variation in rates of development that are truly clinically significant and signal an inherent language learning disability (more about this issue in Chapter 9). One of the most common results of variation in exposure is language dominance (see Key Point 3). What appear to be "delays" in the development of one of a child's languages could be due to less exposure to that language compared to his other language. In order to ensure full bilingualism—or even trilingualism—it is vital that children be given consistent, continuous, and rich exposure to their languages on a regular basis. Finally, it is worth keeping in mind that "the whole is greater than the sum of its parts" insofar as the combined communicative and linguistic competence of bilingual children is concerned, and viewed from this perspective, any differences they display relative to monolingual children may be unimportant when proficiency in the two languages combined is considered.

Key Point 3

Dominance or unbalanced development of the two languages is expected and typical in bilingual acquisition, particularly among preschoolers. Bilingual children may appear more advanced in one of their two languages. Dominance is closely related to which language the child hears and speaks more often in the home and in preschool/school settings. The majority/minority status of a language can contribute to the frequency of input in that language and, in turn, to language dominance.

Implications

Health care professionals should try to determine which of a bilingual child's two languages is the dominant language before assessing the child's language development. This can be achieved by asking the parents about the child's language environment in order to ascertain which language the child is exposed to and uses more often. The language of greatest exposure is typically the dominant language. This can be determined by asking parents a series of questions about language use around the child. More precise measures of language dominance for preschool children would include examining vocabulary size, sentence length and complexity, and volubility in each language. When assessing a bilingual child, the dominant language is the one to examine for the upper limits of that child's linguistic development. This can be problematic for cases where the societal or majority language is the language of the clinician, but the child's more proficient language is a minority language, because the clinician lacks competence in the appropriate language of assessment. Strategies for dealing with this mismatch are presented in Chapter 9. Testing bilingual children in their nondominant language could result in substantial underestimation of the child's linguistic abilities. Clinicians should be very aware of the pitfalls of testing bilingual children in their nondominant language and be appropriately cautious in coming to conclusions from such testing.

REFERENCES

Anderson, R. (2001). Lexical morphology and verb use in child first language loss: A preliminary case study investigation. *International Journal of Bilingualism, 5,* 377–402.

Burns, T.C., Yoshida, K.A., Hill, K., & Werker, J. (2007). The development of phonetic representation in bilingual and monolingual infants. *Applied Psycholinguistics, 28,* 455–474.

Celce-Murcia, M. (1978). The simultaneous acquisition of English and French in a two-year-old child. In E. Hatch (Ed.), *Second language acquisition: A book of readings* (pp. 38–53). Rowley, MA: Newbury House.

Conboy, B., & Mills, D. (2006). Two languages, one developing brain: Event-related potentials to words in bilingual toddlers. *Developmental Science, 9,* F1–F12.

Conboy, B., & Thal, D. (2006). Ties between the lexicon and grammar: Cross-sectional and longitudinal studies of bilingual toddlers. *Child Development, 77,* 712–735.

Döpke, S. (1998). Competing language structures: The acquisition of verb placement by bilingual German-English children. *Journal of Child Language, 25*(3), 555–584.

Döpke, S. (2000). The interplay between language-specific development and cross-linguistic influence. In S. Döpke (Ed.), *Crosslinguistic structures in simultaneous bilingualism* (pp. 79–103). Amsterdam: John Benjamins.

Fabiano-Smith, L., & Goldstein, B. (2010). Phonological acquisition in bilingual Spanish-English speaking children. *Journal of Speech, Language and Hearing Research, 53,* 160–178.

Fennell, C., Byers-Heinlein, K., & Werker, J. (2007). Using speech sounds to guide word learning: The case of bilingual infants. *Child Development, 78,* 1510–1525.

Foroodi Nejad, F., & Paradis, J. (2009). Crosslinguistic transfer in the acquisition of compound words in Persian-English bilinguals. *Bilingualism: Language and Cognition, 12,* 411–427.

Gathercole, V.M. (2007). Miami and North Wales, so far and yet so near: A constructivist account of morpho-syntactic development in bilingual children. *International Journal of Bilingual Education and Bilingualism, 10,* 224–247.

Gawlitzek-Maiwald, I., & Tracy, R. (1996). Bilingual bootstrapping. *Linguistics, 34,* 901–926.

Genesee, F. (1989). Early bilingual development: One language or two? *Journal of Child Language, 6,* 161–179.

Genesee, F., Boivin, I., & Nicoladis, E. (1996). Talking with strangers: A study of bilingual children's communicative competence. *Applied Psycholinguistics, 17,* 427–442.

Genesee, F., Nicoladis, E., & Paradis, J. (1995). Language differentiation in early bilingual development. *Journal of Child Language, 22,* 611–631.

Gutiérrez-Clellen, V., Simon-Cereijido, G., & Wagner, C. (2008). Bilingual children with language impairment: A comparison with monolinguals and second language learners. *Applied Psycholinguistics, 29,* 3–20.

Hoffmann, C. (1985). Language acquisition in two trilingual children. *Journal of Multilingual and Multicultural Development, 6,* 479–495.

Johnson, C., & Lancaster, P. (1998). The development of more than one phonology: A case study of a Norwegian-English bilingual child. *International Journal of Bilingualism, 2*(3), 265–300.

Maneva, B. (2004). "Maman, je suis polyglotte" [Mommy, I'm a polyglot]: A case study of multilingual language acquisition from 0 to 5 years. *The International Journal of Multilingualism, 1,* 109–122.

Marchman, V., Martínez-Sussman, C., & Dale, P. (2004). The language-specific nature of grammatical development: Evidence from bilingual language learners. *Developmental Science, 7,* 212–224.

Meisel, J. (1989). Early differentiation of languages in bilingual children. In K. Hyltenstam & L. Obler (Eds.), *Bilingualism across the lifespan: Aspects of acquisition, maturity and loss* (pp. 13–40). Cambridge, England: Cambridge University Press.

Meisel, J. (1994). *Bilingual first language acquisition: French and German grammatical development.* Amsterdam: John Benjamins.

Miller, J., & Chapman, R. (1981). The relation between age and mean length of utterance in morphemes. *Journal of Speech and Hearing Research, 24,* 154–161.

Montanari, S. (2008). Pragmatic differentiation in early trilingual development. *Journal of Child Language, 36,* 495–527.

Montanari, S. (2009). Multi-word combinations and the emergence of differentiated ordering patterns in early trilingual development. *Bilingualism: Language and Cognition, 12,* 503–519.

Montrul, S. (2008). *Incomplete acquisition in bilingualism: Re-examining the age factor.* Amsterdam: John Benjamins.

Nicoladis, E. (2002). What's the difference between "toilet paper" and "paper toilet"? French–English bilingual children's crosslinguistic transfer in compound nouns. *Journal of Child Language, 29,* 843–863.

Nicoladis, E. (2003). Cross-linguistic transfer in deverbal compounds of preschool bilingual children. *Bilingualism: Language and Cognition, 6,* 17–31.

Nicoladis, E., & Genesee, F. (2007). Bilingual first language acquisition. In E. Hoff & M. Shatz (Eds.), *Handbook of Language Development* (pp. 324–342). Oxford, England: Blackwell.

Nicoladis, E., & Genesee, F. (1996). A longitudinal study of pragmatic differentiation in young bilingual children. *Language Learning, 46*(3), 439–464.

Nicoladis, E., & Secco, G. (2000). Productive vocabulary and language choice. *First Language, 20*(58), 3–28.

Nicoladis, E., Palmer, A., & Marentette, P. (2007). The role of type and token frequency in using past tense morphemes correctly. *Developmental Science, 10,* 237–254.

Oller, K.D., & Eilers, R. (Eds.). (2002). *Language and literacy in bilingual children.* Clevendon, England: Multilingual Matters.

Padilla, A.M., & Liebman, E. (1975). Language acquisition in the bilingual child. *Bilingual Review, 2*(1–2), 34–55.

Paradis, J. (2010). Bilingual children's acquisition of English verb morphology: Effects of language exposure, structure complexity, and task type. *Language Learning, 60,* 651–680.

Paradis, J. (2001). Do bilingual two-year-olds have separate phonological systems? *International Journal of Bilingualism, 5,* 19–38.

Paradis, J. (2007). Early bilingual and multilingual acquisition. In P. Auer & Li Wei (Eds.), *Handbooks of Applied Linguistics: Vol 5. Multilingualism* (pp. 15–44). Berlin: Mouton/de Gruyter.

Paradis, J. (2009). *Oral language development in French and English and the role of home input factors.* Edmonton, Alberta, Canada: Report for the Conseil Scolarie Centre-Nord [North-Central School Board]

Paradis, J., & Navarro, S. (2003). Subject realization and crosslinguistic interference in the bilingual acquisition of Spanish and English. *Journal of Child Language, 30,* 371–393.

Paradis, J., & Nicoladis, E. (2007). The influence of dominance and sociolinguistic context on bilingual preschoolers' language choice. *The International Journal of Bilingualism and Bilingual Education, 10,* 1–21.

Paradis, J., Crago, M., & Genesee, F. (2005/2006). Domain-specific versus domain-general theories of the deficit in SLI: Object pronoun acquisition by French-English bilingual children. *Language Acquisition, 13,* 33–62.

Paradis, J., Nicoladis, E., Crago, M., & Genesee, F. (in press). Bilingual children's acquisition of the past tense: A usage-based approach. *Journal of Child Language.*

Paradis, J., & Genesee, F. (1996). Syntactic acquisition in bilingual children: Autonomous or interdependent? *Studies in Second Language Acquisition, 18,* 1–15.

Paradis, J., & Genesee, F. (1997). On continuity and the emergence of functional categories in bilingual first language acquisition. *Language Acquisition, 6*(2), 91–124.

Paradis, J., Nicoladis, E., & Genesee, F. (2000). Early emergence of structural constraints on code-mixing: Evidence from French-English bilingual children. *Bilingualism: Language and Cognition, 3*(3), 245–261.

Pearson, B. (1998). Assessing lexical development in bilingual babies and toddlers. *International Journal of Bilingualism, 2*(3), 347–372.

Pearson, B., Fernández, S., Lewedeg, V., & Oller, D.K. (1997). The relation of input factors to lexical learning by bilingual infants. *Applied Psycholinguistics, 18,* 41–58.

Pearson, B., Fernández, S.C., & Oller, D.K. (1993). Lexical development in bilingual infants and toddlers: Comparison to monolingual norms. *Language Learning, 43,* 93–120.

Pearson, B., Fernández, S., & Oller, D.K. (1995). Cross-language synonyms in the lexicons of bilingual infants: One language or two? *Journal of Child Language, 22,* 345–368.

Pérez-Leroux, A.T., Pirvulescu, M., & Roberge, Y. (2009). Bilingualism as a window into the language faculty: The acquisition of objects in French-speaking children in bilingual and monolingual contexts. *Bilingualism: Language and Cognition, 12,* 97–112.

Quay, S. (1995). The bilingual lexicon: Implications for studies of language choice. *Journal of Child Language, 22,* 369–387.

Riches, C., & Genesee, F. (2006). Literacy: Instructional issues. In F. Genesee, K. Lindholm-Leary, W. Saunders, & D. Christian (Eds.), *Educating English language learners: A synthesis of research evidence* (pp. 109–175). Cambridge, England: Cambridge University Press.

Serratrice, L., Sorace, A., Filiaci, F., & Baldo, M. (2009). Bilingual children's sensitivity to specificity and genericity: Evidence from metalinguistic awareness. *Bilingualism: Language and Cognition, 12,* 239–257.

Sundara, M., Polka, L., & Molnar, M. (2008). Development of coronal stop perception: Bilingual infants keep pace with their monolingual peers. *Cognition, 108,* 232–242.

Vihman, M., Thierry, G., Lum, J., Keren-Portnoy, T., & Martin, P. (2007). Onset of word form recognition in English, Welsh, and English-Welsh bilingual infants. *Applied Psycholinguistics, 28,* 475–493.

Volterra, V., & Taeschner, T. (1978). The acquisition and development of language by bilingual children. *Journal of Child Language, 5,* 311–326.

Werker, J., Byers-Heinlein, K., & Fennel, C. (2009). Bilingual beginnings to learning words. *Philosophical Transactions of the Royal Society B, 364,* 3649–3663.

Yip, V., & Matthews, S. (2007). *The bilingual child: Early development and language contact.* Cambridge, England: Cambridge University Press.

CHAPTER 5

Code-Mixing in Bilingual Development

Virtually all children who acquire two languages simultaneously code-mix. It is important to discuss code-mixing in some detail because it is widespread among bilingual children and is often the source of concern and misunderstanding. Fortunately, there is an extensive body of research on code-mixing that provides practical insights about what it means from a language development point of view. In this chapter, we first define bilingual code-mixing (BCM) and then discuss adult BCM in order to get a long-term developmental perspective on child BCM. Next, we turn to research that has sought to explain why children code-mix and whether child BCM is grammatically systematic or random. Finally, we consider the implications of mixing for the assessment of bilingual children's language abilities in particular, and how parents, educators and speech-language pathologists should view mixing in these children's development more generally.

WHAT IS CODE-MIXING?

Code-mixing is the use of elements from two languages in the same utterance or in the same stretch of conversation. When the elements occur in the same utterance, it is called **intra-utterance code-mixing**, and when they occur in two different utterances in the same conversation, it is called **inter-utterance code-mixing**. Some researchers talk about *intra-sentential* and *inter-sentential* mixing, but we choose to refer to "utterances" because children—and adults—seldom speak in complete sentences. Examples 1 and 2 in Box 5.1 are instances of intra-utterance and inter-utterance mixing in Spanish and English. To facilitate the understanding of these examples, we present what was actually said in quotation

---

BOX 5.1

Definition of Bilingual Code-Mixing and Examples

Bilingual code-mixing—use of phonological, lexical, morphosyntactic, or pragmatic patterns from two languages in the same utterance or stretch of conversation. Mixing within an utterance is called *intra-utterance mixing*. Mixing from one utterance to another is called *inter-utterance mixing*.

1. **Intra-utterance mixing (from Zentella, 1999, p. 119)**
   "*Alguien se murió en ese cuarto* that he sleeps in." ("Someone died in that room . . .")

2. **Inter-utterance mixing (from Zentella, 1999, p. 118)**
   "*Pa, ¿me vas a comprar un jugo?* It cos' 25 cents." ("Are you going to buy me juice?")

3. **Mixing words (from Poplack, 1980, p. 241)**
   "*Estamos como marido y* woman" ("We are like man and . . .")

4. **Mixing phrases (from Zentella, 1999, p. 119)**
   "I'm going with her *a la esquina*" (". . . to the corner")

5. **Mixing clauses (from Zentella, 1999, p. 118)**
   "You know how to swim but *no te tapa*." (". . . it won't be over your head")

6. **Mixing pragmatic patterns (from Genesee & Sauve, 2000)**
   "*Donne moi le cheval; le cheval;* the horse!" ("Give me the horse; the horse; . . .")
   Child loudly asks for "the horse" when repeated attempts to get a toy horse from his father using French had failed.

   Rontu (2007) gives examples of pragmatically driven bilingual code-mixing in conversations involving two young siblings and their mother; one of the children, Vera, switches to Swedish during a conversation with her older sister and mother that was otherwise in Finnish in order to shift her mother's attention away from her older sibling to herself.

---

marks, with the non–English segments in italics and the English segments in Roman. Translations of non–English segments are provided in parentheses following the quotations. Also as shown in Box 5.1, the mixed elements can include whole words, phrases, or clauses, and even pragmatic patterns. In other words, mixing can involve small units of language (e.g., sounds, inflectional morphemes, words) as well as larger chunks (e.g., phrases, whole clauses). Examples 3–6 illustrate the different elements that can be mixed.

There are individual differences in how much children code-mix. Some mix a lot, and some mix very little; children may even mix differently and at different rates with different members of their family. However, virtually all bilingual children code-mix at some time. In our work in Montreal with children who are learning French and English from their parents in the home, we generally find that children mix within utterances less than 10% of the time, although there are very large individual differences. Some of the children we have studied mix as little as 2% of the time, whereas others mixed much more fre-quently (Genesee, Nicoladis, & Paradis, 1995). It has been our experience that children mix much more from utterance to utterance than within the same utterances, although this clearly depends on the child's stage of development. Children in the one-word and early two-word stages mix primarily across utterances; as their competence grows and their utterances increase in length and complexity, they have more and more opportuni-ties to mix within a single utterance. A lot of research has been conducted to identify the factors that account for why some children mix a lot and others mix less, and we discuss this research later.

ADULT CODE-MIXING: THE END POINT FOR CHILD CODE-MIXING

Before proceeding with our discussion of child BCM, it is useful to look at it in the broader developmental perspective that is afforded by examining bilingual adults. Under-standing how, when, and why adults code-mix can help us better understand child BCM because the patterns we see in adults give us an indication of the developmentally typical trajectory or end point of child code-mixing.

Bilingual adults, as do bilingual children, mix languages both within an utterance (even switching from one grammatical system to the other to insert segments or strings of words from the other language), and from one utterance to another in the same conver-sation. Adults are much more likely to mix in informal settings during casual conversa-tions than in public settings, when formal or careful language is called for (Zentella, 1999). The preference to mix under these circumstances probably reflects the general belief that mixing is a casual, even improper, form of usage. When adults switch languages from one utterance to another, each utterance is grammatically well formed according to the rules of the host language, so inter-utterance code-mixing (or switching) is not very controversial. Mixing that occurs in a single utterance, or intra-utterance mixing, is much more controversial because it gives the appearance that the grammars are mixed—or even mixed up—and thus that the utterance is incorrect.

There has been extensive research on the grammaticality of adult intra-utterance mixing. Without exception, all researchers agree that in most cases, each language seg-ment of a mixed utterance is well formed according to the rules of its respective language; the instances that are not grammatical are probably a result of performance errors. In Examples 1–6 in Box 5.1, the non-English segments of each utterance are correct accord-ing to the grammar of that language, and the English segments are correct according to the grammar of English. Also, the shift from one language to the other in these examples of intra-utterance mixing occurs at places in the sentence that correspond to one another in each language. For example, in the utterance "I'm going with her *a la esquina* (to the corner)" from Example 4 in Box 5.1, the speaker shifts from English to Spanish after the English pronoun *her* and before the Spanish preposition *a* ("to," in English). What is important to notice here is that this shift is correct according to both English and Span-ish word order; in other words, it is perfectly correct to have a prepositional phrase after the first segment of this utterance whether you apply English rules or Spanish rules. The same pattern holds for the other examples of intra-utterance code-mixing in Box 5.1.

Researchers have discovered that the types of mixing that bilingual adults and adoles-cents use depend to some extent on their level of proficiency in their languages. Those who are proficient in both languages can switch between languages fluently and flawlessly in the middle of the utterance, avoiding violations of the rules of each language as they do so, much as we have just described. Such patterns may sound funny and even ungrammatical to people who are not used to hearing languages mixed in this way, but as we noted, careful analysis of such mixing reveals that these individuals clearly know the rules of both languages and are able to apply them flawlessly and in tandem in order to integrate segments from both languages in the same utterance. By contrast, learners who are in the process of developing proficiency in a second language often mix in ways that are different from fluent bilingual learners. Generally speaking, second language learners lack the linguistic competence that is needed to engage in the fluent, flawless mixing that is characteristic of simultaneous bilingual learners or those who are already fluent in both languages. Transfer is often evident in the mixing of second language learners; that is, the structure of the host language is imposed on the mixed segments from the other language, often resulting in violations of one or both languages.

In Example 7, below, English grammatical structure has been imposed on the utterance, and the Spanish elements are made to conform to this structure, resulting in an incorrect utterance. *Enseñar* ("to teach," in Spanish) is inserted in its infinitival form, resulting in a double infinitive; *leer* ("to read," in Spanish) is inserted without the particle *a,* which is required in Spanish for infinitival compliments. This example of mixing was probably motivated by the speaker's lack of grammatical competence in Spanish.

7. Grammatical error (from Zentella, 1999, p. 116)

"Yo have been able to enseñar Maria leer." ("I . . . teach Maria to read.")

Filling lexical gaps in their proficiency is another common reason for mixing among second language learners. Fluent bilingual people and bilingual learners often mix to fill lexical gaps as well; however, in contrast to the fluent and generally unmarked lexical mixing of proficient bilinguals, second language learners are more likely to "flag" their mixing by pausing, asking for help in finding the correct word or expression in the target language, or interjecting in their stronger language to say that they are about to mix. In Example 8, the speaker indicates that he knows that he is mixing and that it might not be correct by explicitly giving his reason for switching. Fluent bilingual people seldom need to do this. Flagging is a pragmatic strategy that second language learners can use to isolate the mixed elements because they may not know how to integrate them grammatically; in effect, the speaker is signaling to the listener that he is about to mix and that he might make a mistake in the process. Evidence of these strategies can be taken as an indication that mixing is motivated by proficiency issues.

8. Flagging

"Hier, je suis allé au . . . hardware store—how do you say hardware store in French?" ("Yesterday, I went to the. . . .")

Finally, research on adults and adolescents has revealed that BCM serves a number of important sociopragmatic and cultural functions. Bilingual adults and adolescents might code-mix in order to express their bilingual ability to other bilingual people—a kind of identity marker (see Myers-Scotton, 1993, and Poplack, 1987). They might code-mix as an indication of intimacy and ethnic solidarity with others who share their language or culture. For example, simultaneous bilingual children such as James and Gabriela from Chapter 1 probably code-mix with friends who are also fluent bilingual children because it is something they can do and it is part of who they are. It is less likely that our other simultaneous bilingual child, Bistra, from Chapter 1, would be able to engage in code-mixing with friends because—in contrast to James and Gabriela—she does not live in a bilingual community and most likely none of her friends would be Bulgarian speakers. Bilingual people might code-mix in order to narrate episodes that themselves were bilingual in nature or to talk about unique cultural aspects of their lives. They might code-mix out of respect for others in the conversation who are more proficient in one or the other language. Alternatively, they might code-mix in order to show they are different from the monolingual people around them. In short, BCM serves a number of important socio-pragmatic functions and is thus part of bilingual people's communicative competence, something that makes them different. In summary:

- BCM is a typical and virtually ubiquitous feature of language use among bilingual adults.
- It serves important linguistic, communicative, social, and cultural purposes.
- Adult BCM is grammatically, socially, and culturally constrained; it is not random.
- Proficient bilingual people and second language learners engage in mixing with different characteristics and for different reasons, although there is overlap.

WHY DO BILINGUAL CHILDREN CODE-MIX?

In sharp contrast to the view of adult BCM that research has shown us, many people, including some parents, educators, and speech-language specialists, believe that child BCM is a cause for concern because it indicates that the child is not developing language typically or is confused and cannot separate his two languages (see quote from Leopold in Box 5.2), or, in the extreme, that the child has actually formed a single language system made up of elements from both languages. According to this view, the child is actually similar to a monolingual child (with a blend of two languages) rather than a true bilingual child. In this section, we review research that examines this interpretation of child BCM and the more general questions of why and when children code-mix. The focus of this discussion will be on children who are in the process of acquiring two languages and who are between 2 and approximately 4 years of age because this age range is the most controversial with respect to BCM in children.

BOX 5.2

Code-Mixing as Evidence for a Unitary Language System?

"The free mixing of English and German vocabulary in many of her sentences was a conspicuous feature of her speech. But the very fact that she mixed lexical items proves that there was no real bilingualism as yet. Words from the two languages did not belong to two different speech systems but to one . . ." (Leopold [1949] in E. Hatch, 1978, p. 27)

Unitary Language System Hypothesis

A common explanation of child BCM is that young bilingual children mix words and other elements (e.g., inflectional morphemes, phrases, grammatical rules) from their two languages in the same utterance because their languages are not differentiated in the early stages of development. This is referred to as the Unitary Language System Hypothesis. As discussed in Chapter 4, according to this point of view, children in the process of learning two languages initially represent the languages in a single (or unitary) neurocognitive system. Differentiation takes place later in development, around 3 years of age. We have already provided evidence against the Unitary Language System Hypothesis in Chapter 4 on other grounds, but we consider this explanation for BCM in some detail here because belief in this explanation for BCM is widespread, even among some researchers. Because this interpretation views the bilingual child's code-mixing as a symptom of confusion and, in the extreme, incompetence, it has serious implications for the way educators, parents, and clinicians might respond to bilingual children who code-mix. Thus, it is important to determine whether this view is valid.

There are many problems with this argument, the chief one being that it is entirely circular—children's code-mixing is taken as evidence of lack of differentiation of their developing languages, and lack of differentiation is used to explain BCM. In order to substantiate this explanation, it is necessary to provide independent evidence that bilingual children cannot differentiate their languages. One way to test this is to document how children use language with others to see if they use their languages without regard to the language of their conversational partners. Finding evidence that they use their languages appropriately with others can rule out the confusion argument. When addressing this issue, most early research on language differentiation focused exclusively on how often bilingual children code-mixed and ignored how often they used the appropriate language with others. Looking at appropriate language use along with BCM is critical for examining whether bilingual children mix because they have a single language system or for some other reasons.

In order to examine how bilingual children use language with others, we observed English–French bilingual children from Montreal during naturalistic interactions with their parents in their homes (Genesee et al., 1995). The parents, who spoke different native languages, used primarily their native language with their children—exhibiting the so-called **one parent–one language rule** (see Box 5.3). Thus, the parents presented different language contexts. The children were observed on three separate occasions: once with their mothers alone, once with their fathers alone, and once with both parents present. By observing the children with each parent individually and when both parents were present, we were able to observe the children's ability to keep their languages separate in different language contexts. The children were between 22 and 26 months of age and were in the one- and early two-word stage of language development. We examined not only the frequency of the children's mixing (within and between utterances), but also the frequency with which they used single-language utterances that were appropriate to each parent (e.g., French utterances with the French-speaking parent, English utterances with the English-speaking parent).

Even at this young age, we found that these children were able to use their two languages in a context-sensitive manner. They used more French with their French-speaking

---

BOX 5.3

One Parent–One Language Rule

The *one parent–one language rule is a* pattern of parental language use in bilingual families in which each parent uses only, or primarily, one language (usually his or her native language) with the child. This pattern is often recommended to parents on the assumption that by keeping the languages separate, parents will make it easier for children to distinguish between the two languages and to keep them separate as they learn them. It is also recommended as a presentation style in order to discourage or eliminate code-mixing.

Although we know that this method works to raise children bilingually, in fact, there is little systematic evidence to support the claim that this is the optimal, or only, way to raise children bilingually, or evidence that it reduces code-mixing. In fact, all the French–English bilingual children we have studied were raised with this style of presentation, and they all code-mixed to some extent. It is important to keep in mind that there are other ways of raising children as simultaneous bilinguals, as mentioned in Chapters 1 and 4. Of the children profiled in Chapter 1, James and Bistra are being raised with the one parent–one language rule, but Gabriela was not, yet all of them are becoming bilingual. Finally, it is worth keeping in mind that the one parent–one language rule can be adhered to more easily when the family is alone. When visitors come, or when the family is in the community, language use will necessarily be tailored to suit the needs of the context and the interlocutors present.

---

parent than with the English-speaking parent and more English with their English-speaking parent than with their French-speaking parent. When the parents were together with the children, the children likewise used more of the father's language with the father than with the mother, and vice versa for the mother's language; see Figure 5.1 for the results of five children. The fact that these children used their two languages appropriately with each parent, whether alone or together, is incompatible with the Unitary Language System Hypothesis. According to the Unitary Language System Hypothesis, one would expect random use of each language, regardless of language context. At the same time, you will notice from Figure 5.1 that most of the children tended to use one language more than the other with both parents. In every case, this was the child's more proficient—or dominant—language, and the child was simply using that language more because he knew it better. Because the parents in these families themselves knew both languages and sometimes used both languages with their children, this strategy allowed these children to express themselves using all of their linguistic resources. Monolingual children do this when they overextend the meaning of common words, such as referring to all adult males as "daddy" until they learn more specific appropriate terms. The difference between bilingual and monolingual children is that bilingual children have two sets of resources to draw on, whereas monolingual children have only one. See Chapter 4 for more details about dominant and nondominant languages in bilingual development.

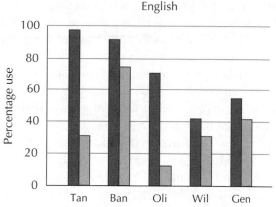

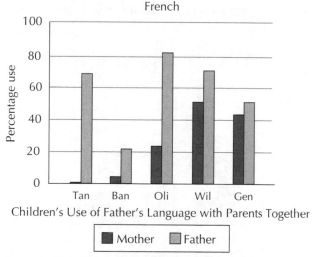

Figure 5.1. Children's use of French and English with parents together. Note that Mothers were English speaker and Fathers were French speakers.

We conducted a follow-up study to examine the limits of young bilingual children's ability to use their developing languages appropriately (Genesee, Boivin, & Nicoladis, 1996). Our initial study may have overestimated the ability of bilingual children to differentiate their languages because the children had had more than 2 years of experience with their parents, giving them ample time to learn to associate each language with each parent. If their languages are truly differentiated, then we should find evidence that the children can use their languages differentially and appropriately even with unfamiliar conversational partners. Our second study was intended to see whether young bilingual children could do this. In order to examine this question, we observed a number of additional French–English bilingual children during play sessions with monolingual strangers; the children were, on average, 26 months of age, and their mean length of utterances in French varied from 1.08 words to 1.59 words and in English from 1.33 words to 1.66 words. In other words, they were in the one-word or early two-word stage of development. Strangers were selected as conversational partners on the assumption that the children were not aware of each stranger's preferred language. Evidence that they could use the appropriate language with the strangers would attest to their ability to identify the stranger's preferred language and to make adjustments to accommodate the stranger even though they did not know her, a sign of true communicative competence. Monolingual strangers were selected in order to ascertain the children's ability to stick to one language as much as possible because, in contrast to their parents, who knew both languages, the stranger knew only one. Because the language spoken by the stranger was the less-proficient language of three of the four children we examined in this study, this was a particularly rigorous test of their abilities to accommodate the stranger. The children had to draw on all of the resources of their less-proficient language if they were to communicate with the interlocutor.

Three of the four children gave evidence of adjustments to the stranger by using more of the stranger's language with the stranger than with their parents and, in particular, the parent who spoke the same language as the stranger, usually the father; we have presented the results for two of these children in Figure 5.2. The same three children also used less of the language that was not known by the stranger with the stranger than with either parent. One of the children did not modify her language use appropriately with the stranger. In short, these results indicate that three of these children were extending

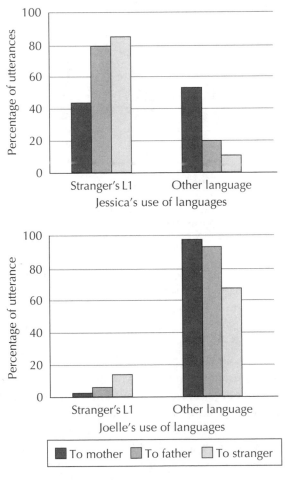

Figure 5.2. Children's use of their languages with a stranger and with parents.

their use of the strangers' language as much as possible and minimizing their use of the language the stranger did not know as much as possible. Thus, despite the fact that these three children had had no prior experience with this adult and they were compelled to use their nondominant language with her, they not only used the appropriate language, but also used it more frequently with the monolingual stranger than with the parent who also spoke that language. Again, these findings do not support the confusion hypothesis. The fact that the children in our study used a great deal of the language not known by the stranger simply reflects their dominance in that language, a pattern that was observed even when children talk with their parents. It is also noteworthy that the children in the stranger study did not all perform alike. One of the children did not appear to accommodate the stranger at all. This should not be surprising given the large individual differences that have been documented in a variety of other aspects of language acquisition. There is no reason to believe that the development of communicative competence (bilingual or monolingual) is not subject to the same individual variation among children that is demonstrated in other aspects of language acquisition.

In summary, and contrary to many commonsense interpretations, child BCM does not reflect linguistic confusion or lack of differentiation in the child's developing languages. As noted in Chapter 4, researchers now agree that the Unitary Language System Hypothesis is not valid and, to the contrary, that bilingual children raised in communities where the two languages are used can and do differentiate their languages from the earliest stages of verbal production—perhaps even earlier. Many case studies of bilingual children growing up in Europe indicate that these children, as do the children in our research in Montreal, generally use the appropriate language with their conversational partners (De Houwer, 1990; Lanza, 1992; Meisel, 1990). Moreover, in a study of BCM in Spanish–English bilingual children in the United States, Vera Gutiérrez-Clellen and her colleagues found that children with specific language impairment did not display more BCM or more atypical mixing than bilingual children without specific language impairment (Gutiérrez-Clellen, Simon-Cereijido, & Leone, 2009). Thus, even children with a language learning disorder are not susceptible to the kind of linguistic confusion suggested by the Unitary Language System Hypothesis.

Gap-Filling Hypothesis

As shown previously, bilingual children do not code-mix because they are confused or cannot differentiate between their languages. In this and the following sections, we consider alternative explanations for code-mixing. BCM has multiple explanations, and more than one can apply to the same situation or conversation. In other words, no single explanation accounts for all BCM. Understanding why bilingual children code-mix provides some nonobvious insights into their linguistic and communicative competence.

One alternative explanation for child BCM is that it serves to fill gaps in the developing child's linguistic competence. The simplest illustration of this is the case of lexical (word) mixing. According to the **Lexical Gap Hypothesis**, bilingual children mix words from language X when using language Y because they do not know the appropriate word in language Y. Mixing syntactic patterns might also occur in order to fill syntactic gaps in the child's knowledge of the target language. There is considerable evidence in favor of this explanation. First, this explanation would account for the general observation, noted previously, that young bilingual children mix more when they use their less-proficient or nondominant language. By definition, their lexical and syntactic competence in their nondominant language is less developed than in their other language, and thus they might be compelled to draw on the resources of their dominant language in order to express themselves fully when using their less-developed language. Second, there is direct evidence that bilingual children are much more likely to mix words for which they do not know the translation equivalent in the target language than for words for which they do, regardless of whether they are using their dominant or nondominant language.

We asked two sets of parents who were raising their children bilingually to keep detailed diary records of their sons' language use during a 3-week period (Genesee, Paradis, & Wolf, 1995). We asked them to focus especially on new words that the children used. Because the boys were 1 year, 8 months and 2 years of age, this task was feasible: the children were not producing many words. We did this so that we could identify how often the children code-mixed and whether they code-mixed words more often when they did not know the appropriate word in the language of their conversational partner. We then looked at the parents' diary entries carefully to see what kinds of words the boys code-mixed. We found that both boys were more likely to code-mix words for which they did not know the translation equivalent in the appropriate language. This was especially true of one boy; 100% of the words he code-mixed with his father were words the boy did not know in his father's language. For the other boy, as well, the majority of words that he code-mixed were words for which he did not know the translation equivalent; to be specific, he did not have translation equivalents for 65% of the words he code-mixed. Similar results have been reported in case studies of other children (Nicoladis & Secco, 2000).

In some cases of lexical mixing, it might not be a matter of the child not knowing the appropriate word, but rather that an appropriate word might not exist in the target language. For example, the French word *dodo* is a word that is used primarily with children and means "nap" or "sleep" (from French *dormir,* "to sleep"). There is no exact equivalent in English because all such terms in English are equally appropriate with adults and children. It is not uncommon in bilingual families in which French and English are spoken for parents to use *dodo* at all times, even when speaking English. There are many examples of bilingual adults who mix words because an exact equivalent does not exist in the target language; for example, *scolarité,* "years of schooling"; *bourse,* "fellowship, scholarship, or grant"; *formation,* "training"; and *stage,* "internship" are all French words that are commonly used by English speakers in Montreal because they have a particular meaning in Quebec. In fact, borrowing is a well-documented phenomenon by which languages acquire new vocabulary. English is a particularly good example. For example, many English words associated with food and eating are derived from French: *beef, mutton, ragout, veal,* and so on. We are witnessing a dramatic reversal in this pattern of borrowing. Words and expressions related to computers and electronic technology are being coined in English and then borrowed by many other languages (e.g., *fax, spam, the web, the Internet, mouse*).

Mixing to fill gaps in children's lexical or syntactic knowledge in one or the other of their languages reflects bilingual children's flexibility in using all their linguistic resources in order to satisfy their communication needs; in other words, it reflects their communicative competence. Because many bilingual children grow up with other children and adults who are also bilingual, this strategy can be effective and appropriate. When bilingual children use this strategy inappropriately with monolinguals, it is usually not because they are not learning the language or that they have a language impairment that requires remediation. It is probably that they do not know the specific word in the target language. Some bilingual children may persist in code-mixing with monolingual people because they have failed to grasp that their interlocutor is monolingual; monolingual people may be rare in their day-to-day lives. A unique aspect of growing up bilingual is that children may encounter monolingual adults who are less linguistically competent than they are. As we saw in the stranger study, bilingual children must learn to accommodate the linguistic incompetence of monolingual adults. Given sufficient time, bilingual children make this adjustment.

Pragmatic Explanations

Yet another explanation of BCM concerns the pragmatics of communication. Bilingual children may code-mix for pragmatic effect—to emphasize what they are saying, to quote what someone else said, to protest, to narrate, and so forth. For example, when speaking English, Spanish–English bilingual children may interject expressions in Spanish in order to emphasize the importance of what they are saying, in much the same way that monolingual children might repeat themselves, altering their wording slightly in order to emphasize an important detail (e.g., "I was terrified, scared to death!"). See Example 6 in Box 5.1 for an illustration of pragmatically motivated code-mixing from a French–English bilingual boy in Montreal.

For some bilingual children, one of their languages may have more affective or emotional load than the other, and they may use that language to express emotion when they speak. Mixing in order to quote what someone else said or when narrating events can be a way of rendering one's discourse more authentic if the event or material being quoted took place in the other language. For example, bilingual teenagers may use English and Spanish to describe a music video they saw in Spanish on television. They may use English and Spanish to describe what they did at school during the Spanish part of the day or during recess if they were playing with their Spanish-speaking friends. Bilingual children may use the language of schooling to talk about school when at home, even if the language of the home is different. Mixing speech or speaking styles is common in everyday discourse; it makes discourse colorful, authentic, and varied. Bilingual children have the advantage of being able to use two languages to enrich their discourse.

Social Norms

A third explanation of child BCM is related to social norms. We discuss social norms that are community based and family based and how they might influence child BCM. These different normative influences do not operate in isolation of one another. Children exposed to two languages are exposed to the normative patterns of BCM in their communities, and they learn these patterns at the same time as they learn the sounds, words, and grammatical patterns of the languages. Acquiring appropriate community-based patterns of code-mixing is an important part of bilingual children's language socialization (see Chapter 2).

Communities have different social norms with respect to appropriate kinds of mixing, when and where mixing occurs, and how often mixing is appropriate (e.g., see research by Poplack, 1987, and Myers-Scotton, 1993). In some communities, there is a great deal of tolerance and acceptance of mixing. Children raised in such communities learn to code-mix more than children in communities where mixing is frowned on or not tolerated. The specific forms of code-mixing children learn are also shaped by social norms in their community. For example, in an early seminal study on code-mixing, Shana Poplack (1980) examined code-mixing patterns in a Spanish-speaking Puerto Rican community in New York City. She found that members of this community engaged in an especially fluent form of mixing in which the same utterance could include several switches from Spanish to English and back again (see Example 9 in Box 5.4). BCM can be an important marker of social identity, and, in the Puerto Rican community that Poplack studied, rapid, fluent mixing served to identify the speaker as both Spanish and English speaking and, thus, as both Puerto Rican and American (see also Zentella, 1999). Establishing their dual identity and allegiance was important for members of this community.

In contrast, the norms regarding BCM are quite different among French–English bilingual people in the Ottawa region of Canada (Poplack, 1987). Generally speaking, bilingual people in this community—especially if they identify as French Canadian—use a different form of mixing. Their mixing tends to be less frequent and less fluent; it is often flagged to indicate that the discourse is bilingual (see Example 10) and is often restricted to private conversations or settings. The flagged mixing exhibited by this group was not due to lack of proficiency—as we saw in the case of second language learners—but rather to identity issues. More specifically, it is likely that this pattern of mixing reflects the desire among members of this community to identify with the French-speaking community in Canada and to set themselves apart from English Canadians. To use French and English as Puerto Ricans in New York City use Spanish and English would blur their identity. The form of mixing that Poplack noted in the Ottawa community, with its particular focus on keeping the languages separate, is also probably linked to their concerns about preserving French in the face of the dominating influence of English in North America. This was not a concern in the Puerto Rican community in New York City

---

BOX 5.4

Multiple Code-Switches in Discourse

Example 9: "But I used to eat the *bofe* (brain), the brain. And then they stopped selling it because, *tenían, este, le encontraron que tenía* (they had, uh, they found out that it had) worms. I used to make some *bofe! Después yo hacía uno d'esos* (then I would make one of those) concotions: the garlic *con cebolla, y hacía un moho, y yo dejaba que se curare eso* (with onion, and I'd make a sauce, and I'd let that sit) for a couple of hours. Then you be drinking and eating that [expletive]. Wooh! It's like eating anchovies when they drinking. Delicious!" (Poplack, 1980, p. 238)

because members of that community could and often did return to Puerto Rico, where Spanish is the dominant language and is flourishing.

10. Flagging (from Poplack, 1987, p. 61)

"Mais je te gage par exemple . . . excuse my English, *mais les odds sont là."* ("But I bet you that . . . but the odds are there.")

Children growing up bilingual in each of these areas learn distinct patterns of bilingual usage in order to fit into and to be fully functional members of the community. Children who have spent their whole childhood in their own communities may not be accustomed to patterns of language use in other communities and thus may need time to learn new patterns so that they can fit into the new community. Some bilingual children may even have difficulty keeping their languages separate because they have grown up with other bilingual people; it may take them some time to accommodate the monolingualism of others. Most children can learn new patterns easily, if they need to and if given appropriate time and encouragement. The challenges these children face when learning new patterns of language usage are not related to language learning problems or impairment but rather to social adaptation.

It is reasonable to ask at what age young bilingual children's code-mixing begins to reflect their understanding of the social community outside the home. When we compare across the three profiled bilingual children—James, Gabriela, and Bistra—we could hypothesize that Bistra might be less willing to code-mix Bulgarian into English when interacting with an adult, even to fill lexical gaps because she encounters so few Bulgarian-speaking adults. In contrast, James and Gabriela are growing up in bilingual communities where numerous adults speak both languages. This hypothesis was tested by Suyal (2002). She compared code-mixing in two French–English bilingual siblings ages 2 and 4 years, and two Nepali–English bilingual siblings, also 2 and 4 years old, living in Edmonton, Canada. In Edmonton, there is a small but vibrant French-speaking community where virtually all adults speak English as well, and the two siblings and their parents were active participants this community. But there is no Nepali-speaking community in Edmonton because there are so few speakers of this language. Suyal observed the children in interaction with their parents and with an unfamiliar adult and found that the French–English children were more likely to code-mix with the unfamiliar adult than the Nepali-speaking children. Furthermore, there seemed to be a shift with age because the 2-year-olds were less able to restrict themselves to the language of their interlocutor than their 4-year-old siblings. This shift could have been caused by two factors. The older children may have been more aware of the broader social context, and they knew more of both languages, and thus did not need to fill lexical gaps. In a related study, Paradis and Nicoladis (2007) observed interactions between eight French–English bilingual 4-year-olds and adult interlocutors, also in Edmonton. They found that children's dominance influenced their code-mixing in the ways we have discussed already, but also that this seemed to interact with their knowledge of the broader social context, where French is the minority language. English-dominant children felt free to code-mix English into French discourse when interacting with a French-speaking adult, but the French-dominant children rarely code-mixed French into English discourse when interacting with an English-speaking adult, even when this meant restricting their topics of conversation.

Social norms in individual families can also influence child BCM. The pattern and frequency of code-mixing can vary from one family to another in the same community because some families and even individual parents within the same family are more tolerant of mixing than others. Elizabeth Lanza (1997), for example, described bilingual parents in Norway who were raising their child, Siri, bilingually. Although both parents were bilingual, Lanza observed that Siri code-mixed much less with her native English-speaking mother than with her native Norwegian-speaking father. Upon closer examination, Lanza noticed that Siri's mother discouraged Siri from code-mixing by avoiding mixing herself, by pretending that she did not understand Siri when she said something in Norwegian, or by indicating in her reply to Siri that she wanted Siri to express herself in English. By using these patterns of discourse with Siri, Siri's mother was sending the message that she preferred English and wanted Siri to use English as much as possible. One might imagine that Siri's mother sought to encourage Siri to use only English because this was one of the few opportunities Siri got to use English; elsewhere, everything took place in Norwegian. In contrast, her father indicated that using both English and Norwegian was acceptable. He did this by code-mixing himself and by indicating that he understood Siri even when she used his nonnative language, English. Consequently, Siri's language choice was not an issue with her father as it was with her mother.

Another example of the influence of family norms on child BCM comes from Suzanne Döpke, in a study of German–English bilingual families in Australia. Döpke (1992) observed that some of the bilingual families she was studying were more successful than others in promoting the use of the minority language (German) in a community that was otherwise dominated by English. Döpke attributed this success, in part, to the use of child-centered discourse styles by the parent who spoke the minority language:

> *The results of the present study indicate a relationship between the parents' awareness of their roles as language teachers and the children's active acquisition of the minority language, in that those children whose minority language parent provided more structurally tailored input than did their majority language parent acquired an active command of the minority language. (Döpke, 1992, p. 191)*

Lanza's and Döpke's findings illustrate that children differ in their style and frequency of BCM as well as in their preference to code-mix or stick to one language as a result of the different discourse styles of their parents.

Some bilingual children may overextend the mixing patterns they have learned in their family and neighborhood community to new settings in which they are not appropriate or effective. Most children can and will learn new patterns, given sufficient time and encouragement. Persistence in using inappropriate patterns of mixing even after some experience in a new setting might suggest that other factors are at play:

1. Code-mixing fills gaps in the child's proficiency in the target language.
2. Code-mixing is pragmatically strategic.

3. Code-mixing might be the norm in the child's family or community.

4. Code-mixing asserts the child's identity as a bilingual person or a member of a different cultural group.

Because these explanations are likely to account for the majority of patterns that one is likely to encounter, they should be examined and ruled out before issues linked to language learning difficulties are entertained seriously.

In summary, bilingual children, as do all children, learn the social norms that pervade their lives. Their acquisition and adherence to these norms are essential to their fitting in with their family, community, and cultural group. Community- and family-specific norms shape the code-mixing behavior of bilingual children. Looking at the social context in which bilingual children have learned their two languages can give a better understanding of why individual children are using their languages in certain ways. Parents, clinicians, and other professionals who are concerned about a child's code-mixing should first seek to understand what BCM means to the child in the context of her family, the neighborhood community in which the child lives, and the cultural group(s) of which she is a member. Looking to these sources of influence is especially important in the case of professionals who are not members of the child's community or cultural group and who are not themselves bilingual, because the norms that are influencing the child are likely to be unfamiliar. Special effort is called for in such cases to ensure that the professional has a broader picture of the child's mixing.

IS CHILD BILINGUAL CODE-MIXING GRAMMATICALLY DEVIANT?

When two languages are used in the same utterance, grammatical incompatibilities can arise between them due to differences in word order or inflectional morphology; these, in turn, can result in patterns of language use that are awkward or illicit. Indeed, a commonly held perception of code-mixing is that it is a "bastardized" (ungrammatical) form of language. This is one of the reasons why parents and others are often concerned about child BCM and even avoid code-mixing with children. The stigma about the grammatical status of intra-utterance code-mixing is evident in adult BCM as well. When questioned, many bilingual adults will say that they think code-mixing is not a proper form of language. As we noted previously in this chapter, however, it is clear from extensive research that adult BCM is constrained by the grammars of both languages and, contrary to some lay opinions, the most proficient bilingual adults engage in the most sophisticated forms of mixing.

But what about child BCM? Is children's code-mixing grammatically constrained or deviant? An extensive body of research has examined the grammatical properties of intra-utterance code-mixing by children acquiring a variety of language pairs, including English and French (Genesee & Sauve, 2000; Paradis, Nicoladis, & Genesee, 2000), French and German (Köppe, 2009; Meisel, 1994), English and Inuktitut (Allen, Genesee, Fish, & Crago, 2002), English and Norwegian (Lanza, 1997), and English and Estonian (Vihman, 1998), among others. All of these studies indicate that the vast majority of bilingual children's code-mixing is systematic and, specifically, conforms to the grammatical constraints of the two participating languages. This is true for bilingual children as soon as they begin to use multiword utterances, when grammatical constraints become important in their language use. Children who are in the one-word stage cannot engage in intra-utterance mixing because by definition it entails the use of more than one word or morpheme. The finding that bilingual children code-mix grammatically as soon as they begin to organize their language according to grammatical principles is very important because it means that they learn how to code-mix grammatically at the same time as they learn their two languages. It is not something extra they have to learn; it comes automatically with being a bilingual learner. At the same time, they do learn the frequency or patterns of mixing that characterize their own families and communities.

A few examples follow to illustrate exactly what it means to say that children's code-mixing is grammatical. A common form of code-mixing by young bilingual children entails the mixing of single content words (e.g., nouns, verbs, adjectives) from one language into an utterance or sentence that is organized according to the grammar of the other language. This form of mixing is common in young children because they produce short, syntactically simple sentences that usually lack conjoined elements. When children mix single words, they usually treat the mixed word as if it were part of the host language and thereby produce grammatically correct constructions. Examples 11–14 illustrate this kind of mixing and are all taken from children younger than 4 years of age. Examples 11–13 were produced by French–English bilingual children in Montreal, and Example 14 is from a bilingual child learning English and Inuktitut in northern Quebec. In every case, the English word has been inserted in the correct place, assuming that the word is being treated as a member of the host language; the host language is considered to be the dominant language of the child's interlocutor, which was English, French, French, and Inuktitut for Examples 11–14, respectively. Example 13 is particularly interesting because in this case the child used the English subject pronoun (I) with a French verb (*aime,* "like"). There are other examples of this sort from his corpus. Subject pronouns in French are prohibited from appearing with certain verb forms, but in English they are not. This child obeyed this restriction when he mixed subject pronouns; he put English pronouns with a number of French verbs, but he only put French pronouns with English verb forms that followed the restricted category in French. In this way, he respected the distributional restrictions of English and French when he mixed pronouns.

11. *Mixing single content words into English (from Paradis, Nicoladis, & Genesee, 2000, p. 255)*

"big *bobo*" ("bruise" or "cut")

12. *Mixing single content words into French (from Paradis et al., 2000, p. 257)*

"*je veux aller manger* tomato" ("I want to go eat . . .")

13. *Mixing single content words into French (from Paradis et al., 2000, p. 257)*

"*I aime pas ça, moi*" (". . . do not like that, me")

14. *Mixing single content words into Inuktitut (from Allen et al., 2002)*

"monkey-*uqquungimmat*" ("it's probably not a . . .")

Example 14 is also interesting because it shows a young Inuktitut–English child inserting an English noun (monkey) in an otherwise Inuktitut utterance; it is a case in which the word order in English and Inuktitut are different, yet the child inserted the English word in the correct position for Inuktitut. It is also interesting because the English noun "monkey" is transformed into a verb by the Inuktitut morpheme *u* ("to be"); in effect, the noun *monkey* becomes "to be a monkey." Known as *noun incorporation,* this is a common construction in Inuktitut. This child demonstrated that he knew how to use this construction even with an English noun. In short, evidence from code-mixing in simultaneous bilingual people, even young children, indicates that their mixing is constrained and reflects their grammatical competence in both languages.

As children get older, they mix larger fragments of language and use code-mixing for more sophisticated pragmatic functions. Examples 15–17 illustrate mixing of word combinations.

15. Child who is 3 years, 5 months old (from Paradis et al., 2000, p. 258)

"*Elle coupe* her hair" ("she cuts . . .")

16. Child who is 12 years old (from Zentella, 1999, p. 100)

"*ello(h) te invitan a bailar,* so I GO, you know" ("they invite you to go dancing . . .")

17. Child who is older than 8 years (from Zentella, 1999, p. 95)

"*Ella tiene*—shut up! Lemme tell you." ("She has . . .")

Example 15 is from an English–French bilingual child, and Examples 16 and 17 are from English–Spanish bilingual children. All of these instances are grammatical, insofar as the word order of the participating languages is respected; in other words, the switch from one language to the other occurs at a point in the utterance where there is grammatical equivalence in the two languages (e.g., in Example 15 between the verb and object; in Examples 16 and 17, the switches occur when the speaker makes an interjection). Example 17 is particularly interesting because it illustrates the use of switching to emphasize a point—in this case, the speaker's annoyance with the listener and his insistence that the listener pay attention. Thus, not only do the forms of code-mixing become more sophisticated with age, but also they serve pragmatic functions.

Even trilingual children code-mix in grammatically organized ways.

18. Trilingual code-mixing (from Hoffmann & Stavans, 2007, p. 65):

". . . ki the moscos dvorim . . ." (Hebrew "because" + English "the" + Spanish "the flies" + Hebrew "bees": "because the flies . . . bees . . . ")

KEY POINTS AND IMPLICATIONS

What does BCM tell us about the language development of bilingual children, and what are the implications of child BCM for parents, educators, and clinicians?

Key Point 1

BCM is a typical and ubiquitous pattern of language use among bilingual children and adults. Multiple sources of evidence indicate that in most cases, child BCM is not a cause for concern. Chief among these sources is the fact that most child BCM is grammatical and, as found by Gutiérrez–Clellen and her colleagues, children with specific language impairment do not display more BCM or more atypical mixing that bilingual children without specific language impairment (Gutiérrez–Clellan et al., 2009). Thus, BCM is best viewed as a reflection of the child's developing linguistic competence. Indeed, in order to code-mix grammatically, bilingual children must be acquiring both grammars, and they must have access to both grammars online in order to integrate the languages in a single utterance.

Implications

BCM should not be taken as evidence for language delay or impairment in bilingual children in most cases and without careful further examination. Parents and educators should not reprimand children for code-mixing. Nor should they be singled out in any way that would stigmatize them because they are bilingual and code-mix. Language development specialists, educators, and other professionals should not recommend that children use only one language or that parents desist in using both languages on the assumption that this will rectify any language learning problems.

Key Point 2

BCM is a communicative resource. Bilingual children are being resourceful in calling on both languages when they code-mix. They may be especially prone to draw on their dual language resources during stages of development when full proficiency in each language has not been achieved, but BCM is a resource even for fully proficient bilingual people who want to talk about ideas, events, or things that are part of their unique lives as bilingual individuals or that are best expressed in one or the other language.

Implications

Most bilingual children will adapt to the communicative demands of monolingual social situations, given appropriate time and supportive encouragement. Efforts to get a child to express himself or herself monolingually should not be punitive, but instead should always be positive; for example, provide the child with monolingual paraphrases or words that he wants to say, while praising the child for making whatever efforts he makes. If individual bilingual children persist in code-mixing in settings or with individuals where it is inappropriate or ineffective, even after considerable time for adjustment is given, then the communicative demands of the situation should be examined for evidence of gaps in the child's communicative competence. If there are identifiable gaps in certain domains of the child's language proficiency, then language enrichment in the relevant areas should be provided, followed by careful monitoring of growth in the areas of concern. In most cases, it is recommended that the child continue in the situation or setting where concerns have arisen. Referring children to specialists or special classes is not likely to be effective in resolving the identified communication problems if the child is isolated from the positive incentives that are provided by contact with peers and mainstream language models. Moreover, referrals that are unwarranted stigmatize children for being bilingual.

Key Point 3

BCM is shaped by social norms in the families and communities in which bilingual children live. All children are socialized to the patterns of language use and social behaviors that are characteristic of their families and communities. Family and community norms guide their behavior in most settings they encounter, familiar and unfamiliar.

Implications

Bilingual children who exhibit language or social behaviors that differ from mainstream monolingual/monocultural children should not automatically be singled out for special attention or referred for further examination because of suspicions of underlying language learning disorders. Most bilingual children will acquire the social norms appropriate to a new situation if they are given sufficient time and positive encouragement (see Key Point 2). Professionals should familiarize themselves with the patterns of language and social behavior that characterize life in the child's family and community in order to better understand the child's language behavior. This may require interviews with caregivers or others in the community who are well informed about community norms; a home visit may even be called for. Where significant differences are found to exist between the home or community and the new situation, then steps must be taken in the new setting to help the child adjust.

Key Point 4

BCM may reflect the child's cultural identity. Language is an important marker of one's identity; this is why individuals and groups are willing to go to great lengths to defend their right to use their own language. For young language learners and school-age children, language is a fundamental part of who they are because it has been an inextricable part of the social world they have grown up in. To denigrate a child's language or refuse her the possibility of using her language(s) for self-expression is to diminish the child as an individual. Many adults have personal resources for dealing with the complexities of being a member of a minority group or of having a dual identity. Most children lack these resources; this is particularly true for children from minority group backgrounds. Therefore, it is particularly important that adults be understanding and supportive of bilingual children who are adapting to monolingual situations.

Implications

It is incumbent on professionals, clinicians, and other adults caring for bilingual/bicultural children to nurture the children's unique identities, protect them from the challenges of being different, and provide them with strategies for coping with these challenges. Educators, clinicians, and other professionals should provide positive recognition and support to bilingual children who express affinity to or identity with another culture, especially a minority culture. At the same time, if bilingual children are not fully socialized to the majority cultural group, they should be given assistance in acquiring the social skills and cultural understandings they need to make friends and function effectively in majority group settings. Steps should be taken to ensure that bilingual children from minority cultures do not become isolated from other children; for example, providing the child with a "buddy" who is bilingual and well integrated is one way of helping the child to socialize to a new group while minimizing the risks of isolation.

REFERENCES

Allen, S., Genesee, F., Fish, S., & Crago, M. (2002). Patterns of code-mixing in English–Inuktitut bilinguals. In M. Andronis, C. Ball, H. Elston, & S. Neuvel (Eds.), *Proceedings of the 37th Annual Meeting of the Chicago Linguisitic Society* (Vol. 2, pp. 171–188). Chicago: Chicago Linguistics Society.

De Houwer, A. (1990). *The acquisition of two languages from birth: A case study.* Cambridge, England: Cambridge University Press.

Döpke, S. (1992). *One parent one language: An interactional approach.* Amsterdam: John Benjamins.

Genesee, F., Boivin, I., & Nicoladis, E. (1996). Talking with strangers: A study of bilingual children's communicative competence. *Applied Psycholinguistics, 17,* 427–442.

Genesee, F., Nicoladis, E., & Paradis, J. (1995). Language differentiation in early bilingual development. *Journal of Child Language, 22,* 611–631.

Genesee, F., Paradis, J., & Wolf, L. (1995). *The nature of the bilingual child's lexicon.* Unpublished research report, Psychology Department, McGill University, Montreal, Quebec, Canada.

Genesee, F., & Sauve, D. (2000, March 12). *Grammatical constraints on child bilingual code-mixing.* Paper presented at the Annual Conference of the American Association for Applied Linguistics, Vancouver, British Columbia, Canada.

Gutiérrez-Clellen, V.F., Simon-Cereijido, G., & Leone, A.E. (2009). Code-switching in bilingual children with specific language impairment. *International Journal of Bilingualism, 13,* 91–109.

Hatch, E.M. (1978). *Second language acquisition: A book of readings.* Rowley, MA: Newbury House.

Hoffmann, C., & Stavans, A. (2007). The evolution of trilingual code-switching from infancy to school age: The shaping of trilingual competence through dynamic language dominance. *International Journal of Bilingualism, 11,* 55–72.

Köppe, R. (2009). Is codeswitching acquired? In Jeff MacSwan (Ed.), *Grammatical theory and bilingual codeswitching.* Cambridge, MA: The MIT Press.

Lanza, E. (1992). Can bilingual two-year-olds code–switch? *Journal of Child Language, 19,* 633–658.

Lanza, E. (1997). *Language mixing in infant bilingualism: A sociolinguistic perspective.* Oxford, England: Clarendon Press.

Leopold, W. (1949). *Speech development in a bilingual child: A linguist's record. Grammar and general problems.* Vol. 3. Evanston, IL: Northwestern University Press.

Meisel, J.M. (1990). *Two first languages: Early grammatical development in bilingual children.* Dordrecht, Germany: Foris Publications.

Meisel, J.M. (1994). Code-switching in young bilingual children: The acquisition of grammatical constraints. *Studies in Second Language Acquisition, 16,* 413–441.

Myers-Scotton, C. (1993). *Social motivation for codeswitching: Evidence from Africa.* Oxford, England: Oxford University Press.

Nicoladis, E., & Secco, G. (2000). The role of a child's productive vocabulary in the language choice of a bilingual family. *First Language, 58,* 3–28.

Paradis, J., & Nicoladis, E. (2007). The influence of dominance and sociolinguistic context on bilingual preschoolers' language choice. *The International Journal of Bilingualism and Bilingual Education, 10,* 1–21.

Paradis, J., Nicoladis, E., & Genesee, F. (2000). Early emergence of structural constraints on code-mixing: Evidence from French–English bilingual children. In F. Genesee (Ed.), *Bilingualism: Language and cognition* (pp. 245–261). Cambridge, England: Cambridge University Press.

Poplack, S. (1980). "Sometimes I start a sentence in English y termino en Español": Toward a typology of code-switching. *Linguistics, 18,* 581–618.

Poplack, S. (1987). Contrasting patterns of code-switching in two communities. In E. Wande, J. Anward, B. Nordberg, L. Steensland, & M. Thelander (Eds.), *Aspects of multilingualism: Proceedings from Fourth Nordic Symposium on Bilingualism, 1984* (pp. 51–77). Uppsala, Sweden: Ubsaliensis S. Academiae.

Rontu, H. (2007). Codeswitching in triadic conversational situations in early bilingualism. *International Journal of Bilingualism, 11,* 337–358.

Suyal, C. (2002). *Bilingual first language acquisition: Code-mixing in children who speak a minority language.* Unpublished master's thesis, Department of Linguistics, University of Alberta, Edmonton, Alberta, Canada.

Vihman, M. (1998). A developmental perspective on codeswitching: Conversations between a pair of bilingual siblings. *International Journal of Bilingualism, 2,* 45–84.

Zentella, A.C. (1997). *Growing up bilingual.* Malden, MA: Blackwell Publishers.

CHAPTER 6

Second Language
Development in Children

I n Chapter 1, we presented profiles of nine different dual language children, six of whom—Samantha, Trevor, Bonnie, Luis, Faisal, and Pauloosie—were described as second language (L2) learners, as opposed to simultaneous bilinguals, because they began to learn another language after their first language had been established. As with the simultaneous bilingual children—James, Bistra, and Gabriela—one key difference between the language learning situations for Samantha and Trevor versus the other L2 learners is the distinction between majority and minority languages. Samantha and Trevor are majority language speakers of English who are acquiring their second languages through schooling, and in the case of Samantha, her L2, Spanish, is a minority language in the community. Bonnie, Luis, Faisal, and Pauloosie all have minority languages as their first languages (L1): Mandarin, Spanish, Somali, and Inuktitut, respectively. They all began learning the majority language as their L2 through both schooling as well as through contact with the majority ethnolinguistic community. Although Inuktitut-speaking people are the majority in Pauloosie's community in Northern Quebec, English and French speakers are the majority in this province and across Canada.

This minority/majority language situation of a child often has an effect on the ultimate proficiency a child acquires in her L2 and on the maintenance of her L1. One can consider young L2 learners such as Samantha to be privileged because they typically experience additive bilingualism, a concept discussed in Chapter 3. Majority language children who learn a minority second language become bilingual by choice and, generally speaking, do not have to cope with sociocultural integration and adaptation at the same time as they are learning a new language and beginning school. The language learning situations and outcomes for majority language children similar to Samantha are discussed mainly in Chapter 8; however, some of the information in this chapter, about stages of L2 learning in particular, apply to both majority and minority L2 learners. Nevertheless, most of the research and issues we focus on in this chapter pertain to the situation of minority language children such as Bonnie, Luis, Faisal, and Pauloosie. In North America, the United Kingdom, and Australia, minority L1 children who are in a majority English social context and who attend school in English are commonly referred to as **English language learners (ELLs)**, *English learners* (ELs), or *English as a second language* (ESL)/*English as an additional language* (EAL) learners. In this chapter, we often discuss research that was conducted with ELL children from Canada and the United States; however, because these findings could apply to other minority L1 children leaning another majority L2 elsewhere, and to reduce the use of abbreviations, we refer to them as "English L2" children.

Children and youth can come into contact with an L2 at any age, but our focus in this chapter is limited to L2 learners during the preschool and early elementary school years. We focus on this age range because this is when children's development is most commonly assessed for purposes of identifying language and learning disabilities. In addition, this is the age when concern over how to provide the most appropriate educational programming for L2 learners is greatest. It is important to keep in mind that many L1 minority children who become L2 learners during this time in their lives were born in the host society. Not all of these children are immigrant or refugee children such as Bonnie and Faisal. For instance, Luis was born in the United States, and many Spanish L1 children in the United States who begin to learn English at school entry come from families who have lived in the United States for more than one generation. Also, Pauloosie was born in a region of North America where his people, the Inuk, have lived for at least a thousand years. Despite this, his language is now a minority language and has been replaced by English and French as the majority societal languages.

To reiterate a point made in Chapter 1: Bonnie is a relatively fortunate immigrant child. Her parents have good jobs in their host country and high levels of education, and, moreover, they could function in the majority language when they arrived in their new country. Many immigrant L2 children in both North America and Europe are not as fortunate, in that their families may have to cope with financial hardships and sometimes with the stress of forced relocation, as is the case for Faisal's family. Often, parents of children learning the majority language as an L2 do not speak the language of the host country very well and, as a result, they cannot communicate easily with educators and health practitioners, as is the case for both Luis's parents, even though they have lived for some time in the United States. It is important to remember that these kinds of challenges can influence the extent to which parents can be involved in their child's schooling and can monitor and support their child's L2 learning. In Chapters 1 and 4, we discussed how the division between simultaneous and sequential bilinguals (L2 learners) is not always clear-cut. We have set the boundary at roughly 3 years of age because this seems to be the boundary used most commonly by researchers, and because children at his age would have acquired enough of the first language to possibly display transfer effects and differences in developmental stages between their L1 and their L2. However, as mentioned in Chapter 4, it is possible that early sequential bilinguals—such as children between 3 and 4 years of age—could display patterns in their dual language development that are more consistent with simultaneous bilinguals and, conversely, some "late" simultaneous bilinguals—such as children who were not exposed to two languages from birth—could display patterns more consistent with those discussed in this chapter. Therefore, the distinction between simultaneous and sequential bilinguals should be thought of as a rough guideline only.

The purpose of this chapter is to discuss the oral language development of L2 learners. The literacy skills and academic progress of L2 children are discussed in Chapters 8 and 10. This chapter is organized to address the following general questions:

1.   What are the stages children go through in learning to speak their L2?
2.   How long does it take L2 learners to approach native-speaker proficiency?
3.   What factors influence L2 learners' rates of language development?
4.   What happens to the L1 of minority language children in a majority L2 context?

Throughout the chapter, we provide examples of English L2 children's language that come from research conducted by Johanne Paradis with children from migrant families in Edmonton, Canada (for more information, see http://www.ualberta.ca/~jparadis/). These children are 4–8 years old and come from a variety of L1 backgrounds, the largest groups being Spanish, Arabic, South Asian (Punjabi/Hindi/Urdu), and Chinese (Mandarin and Cantonese). The children vary in their length of exposure to English from 4 months to 3½ years. A variety of measures of these children's oral language proficiency have been collected, including both naturalistic methods and standardized tests. We use the term *Edmonton ELL Corpus* when we refer to the data from this research. (This is the only place in this chapter where "ELL" is used.)

STAGES OF SECOND LANGUAGE DEVELOPMENT IN CHILDREN

Children's First Exposure to the Second Language

Patton Tabors (2008) describes a study of English L2 children in a university nursery school in Massachusetts, where she observed the children several mornings a week for two years. She used her extensive observations together with research from L2 children in other early education settings to put forward the following stages in early L2 development: 1) home language use, 2) nonverbal period, 3) formulaic language use, and 4) productive language use. Before we discuss what generally happens at each stage, we emphasize that there are large individual differences among L2 children, so that some children appear to skip Stage 2 and others remain in Stage 2 for months. Understanding the typical characteristics of these stages is useful for establishing general expectations, but they do not necessarily apply to every child.

Stage 1, or the period of home language use, refers to children using their L1 in the English environment, even though no one else speaks it. This period can be very brief—sometimes just a few days—because children try their home language in their new environment but rapidly realize that other children and adults do not speak that language. Occasionally, L2 children persist in using their home language some of the time in an English-language classroom for longer, even 2–4 months, but this is not typical (Saville-Troike, 1987). The **nonverbal period**, Stage 2, follows the home language period, and during this time children are accumulating receptive knowledge of the L2 but produce very few or no words in the L2. Tabors found that during this period, the L2 children in her study developed a system of communication that relied heavily on gesture to get meaning across; therefore, not talking during this period does not imply a complete lack of communication and interaction. The nonverbal period can last a few weeks to a few months, and in general, younger children stay longer in this stage than older ones. During this nonverbal period, social interaction with peers is a crucial factor in enabling L2 children to get exposure to more of the L2, and to be motivated to begin speaking.

At Stage 3, when children first begin to produce some of the L2, they do not use full and original sentences right away. Instead, their utterances are often short or imitative, with little original content (**formulaic language**). The first English produced by the children Tabors observed consisted of one-word utterances to label objects or to count and identify colors; thus, the children were not using full sentences. The first sentence-like utterances were often memorized phrases that may not have consisted of separate words for the child, for example, *I don't know, Excuse me, So what?* and *What's happening?* Wong Fillmore (1979) characterized English L2 children's approach to learning at this stage as including two key strategies: 1) give the impression—with a few well-chosen words— that you can speak the language; and 2) acquire some expressions you understand, and start talking. By using these strategies, the L2 children can engage and function in social interaction and therefore increase their exposure to the L2.

Gradually, L2 children start to construct sentences that are productive. A productive sentence is one that does not consist entirely of a memorized word sequence; the child uses some of her own repertoire of nouns, verbs, or adjectives and constructs an utterance that is wholly or partially original. Some beginner sentences in L2 English appear to have a semiformulaic frame and slot construction, for example, "*I do* + <u>noun</u>" or "*I want* + <u>noun</u>," in which the child does not use another pronoun or form of the verb but just varies the thing (noun) that the child does or wants (e.g., *I do <u>a ice cream</u>, I do <u>letter B</u>*).

Wong Fillmore noted how one child, Nora, started with a formula that she would use frequently across contexts, "*How do you do dese?*" Then, she expanded on it to say things such as "*How do you do dese <u>in English</u>?*" and "*How do you do dese <u>little tortillas</u>?*" Next, she began to substitute words in the formula: "*How do you <u>make the flower</u>?*" and "*How do you <u>gonna</u> do dese <u>in English</u>?*" (1979, p. 214). Eventually, L2 children move beyond the frame and slot stage into a real productive period for language, Tabors's Stage 4, where they can vary what words they use to fill in all of the slots in a sentence. Then, they are well on their way toward developing some fluency in their L2. English L2 children usually reach Stage 4 during their first year in a preschool or school program in English, but there is always variation among individuals—some children may appear to be at Stage 4 after one semester, and others may be starting Stage 4 only at the end of the school year.

When children have reached this fourth stage and can use their L2 productively, this does not mean that they sound as if they were native speakers of the language. Even small children can have a foreign accent when they are learning their L2. They may mispronounce words and make errors in vocabulary choice and grammar. Often L2 children's first sentences sound abbreviated, or "**telegraphic**" in form, such that many of the **grammatical morphemes** are missing. Grammatical morphemes are verbal and nominal inflections, such as plural *-s* or past tense *-ed,* and freestanding function words such as articles (*the, a*) or auxiliary verbs. An English L2 child at the early stages of learning might say "he no like play car" instead of "he doesn't like to play cars." It is important to keep in mind that both formulaic and telegraphic language use are a normal part of the language learning process—even children acquiring their L1 go through this process—and that these kinds of language use patterns are therefore not a sign of any language or learning difficulty.

Characteristics of L2 Children's Interlanguage

The period in second language development between when the learner starts to use the language productively until the learner achieves competence similar to a native speaker is referred to as **interlanguage.** Interlanguage is a systematic and rule-governed linguistic system, but it does not have the same characteristics as the target system, the L2. Traditionally, interlanguage has been thought to consist of **developmental errors** and **transfer errors**—both error types make interlanguage appear distinct from the target. Our objective in this section is to familiarize readers with the characteristics of interlanguage—for English in particular. We use the more general term "patterns" more often than the term "errors," because there are some developmental and transfer-based patterns that are not, strictly speaking, errors in the target language. Furthermore, by creatively constructing sentences in the language they are learning, whether L1 or L2, children are practicing and thus advancing their expressive and receptive linguistic abilities in that language. Therefore, describing their language use as mainly errorful depicts their language learning in a negative light and misses the important fact that they are progressing toward native-like competence.

Developmental Patterns in English L2   Many developmental patterns in L2 interlanguage are common across learners regardless of their L1, suggesting that transfer from the L1 is not the only source for interlanguage patterns. In fact, most researchers agree that the majority of interlanguage patterns are developmental, rather than transfer based. Developmental patterns in child L2 English also have many parallels with the patterns in the monolingual acquisition of English by younger children. One example from phonology—the sound system of language—is how learners acquire consonant clusters. Consonant clusters are simply groups of consonants in a row, unbroken by vowels, such as at the beginning of words such as *play* or *truck*. Young children acquiring English as their L1 usually go through a stage where they delete one of the consonants in a cluster, and so

---

BOX 6.1

Interlanguage

"The term interlanguage was coined in 1972 by Selinker to refer to the language produced by learners, both as a system which can be described at any one point in time as resulting from systematic rules, and as the series of interlocking systems that characterize learner progression. In other words, the notion of interlanguage puts the emphasis on two fundamental notions: the language produced by the learner is a system in its own right, obeying its own rules, and it is a dynamic system, evolving over time." (Mitchell & Myles, 1998, p. 31)

BOX 6.2

Use of *Do* as a General All-Purpose (GAP) Verb

These examples are from Golberg, Paradis, and Crago (2008, p. 13). The children who used them come from a variety of L1 backgrounds, and had between 9 and 34 months of exposure to English. There are more examples from children with less exposure to English because as children learn more English, their vocabularies grow and they do not depend as much on GAP words.

GAP *do* utterance	More appropriate/specific verb for context
he *do* ribbit, ribbit	say
I *do* the bigger one	want
he *do* a baseball	throw
how to *do* ring-around-the-rosie?	play, sing
I can *do* any night	play
spiderman *do* like this	sprays [his web]
my dad can *do* a person	draw, make
we *do* our name	write
I *do* some grass over here too	cut
then we *did* recess	have
I *did* some loud	blow
[a nurse] *do* needles	give
I *do* like this [protects face with hands]	put my hands in front of my face

---

pronounce the word *play* as *pay/pei/*. Similarly, consonant clusters can pose problems for L2 learners—even those whose L1s have consonant clusters in the phonology. L2 learners deal with these difficult-to-pronounce consonant clusters in two ways: 1) by deleting one of the consonants similar to L1 children, or 2) by inserting a vowel between the consonants. Both of these strategies make the clusters easier to pronounce (Gilhool, Burrows, Goldstein, & Paradis, 2009; Sorenson Duncan, Tessier, & Paradis, 2009).

Regarding lexical learning, young L2 children are often in situations where they need to stretch their limited vocabulary to communicate, such as in a classroom setting. Consequently, a lexical developmental pattern shown by L2 children is the use of what are called *general all-purpose* (GAP) words, when more specific words would be appropriate and characteristic of a native speaker. Verbs such as *do* in English are often candidates to become GAP verbs because *do* has a broad and flexible meaning. Golberg, Paradis, and Crago (2008) found many instances of *do* as a GAP verb in the speech of children from the Edmonton ELL corpus, shown in Box 6.2. The GAP word phenomenon shows that L2 children have conceptual/cognitive abilities beyond their linguistic abilities in the L2, and that they are resourceful in their attempts to express their thoughts in the L2. The GAP word phenomenon has also been documented in majority English L1 children who are learning French as an L2 in immersion schooling (Harley, 1992).

One of the most studied aspects of English L2 interlanguage is the developmental sequence for grammatical morphemes. In their seminal research in this field, Dulay and Burt (1973, 1974) found that 85% of the errors in spoken English by Spanish–L1 children were developmental in origin (i.e., not traceable to Spanish), and were errors with grammatical morphemes. They also noted that the sequence in which children acquired them was parallel with what has been found for monolingual children acquiring English as an L1. For instance, both L1 and L2 children become more accurate with certain morphemes before others. Generally speaking, the verbal inflections of past tense *-ed*, as in *walk-ed*, and third-person singular *-s*, as in *walk-s*, are used accurately much later than plural *-s* in *cat-s* or progressive *-ing* as in *walk-ing*. More recent research reinforces these findings from the 1970s about the sequence of acquisition (Haznedar, 2001; Jia & Fuse, 2007; Paradis, 2005, 2008; Paradis, Rice, Crago, & Marquis, 2008), but with one exception, the "precocious" acquisition of the verb *be* in L2 children. Monolingual L1 children acquire *be* as an auxiliary verb, *she is walking,* or *the bears are sleeping,* about the same time as they acquire verbal inflections such as *-ed* and *-s,* but L2 children acquire *be* forms in advance of inflections. This research on sequences in English grammatical morphology shows that children may master the use of one grammatical morpheme, but still produce developmental errors for another. In the Edmonton ELL corpus, for example, after about 10 months of exposure to English, the children were accurate in their use of plural *-s* about 71% of the time in spontaneous speech but were accurate in their use of the past tense *-ed* only about 22% of the time in the same spontaneous speech (Paradis, 2005). Being aware of sequences in acquisition is relevant to educators and clinicians when evaluating children's progress in the L2. English L2 children should not be expected to acquire the whole set of grammatical morphemes at the same time.

Children's errors with grammatical morphemes in the L2 can be categorized as **errors of omission** and **errors of commission.** Errors of omission refer to the deletion of the morpheme, which gives rise to the telegraphic nature of interlanguage. Errors of commission refer to the substitution of one morpheme for another, or producing a creative phonological form of the target morpheme. These terms are used to categorize errors in any L2 interlanguage, not just English L2 interlanguage. To illustrate these kinds of errors, the following examples are given from the Edmonton ELL corpus. In Example 1, the child (CHI) is telling the experimenter (EXP) a story about something that happened in the past and uses bare verb forms instead of the correct (irregular) past tense forms of the verbs. In Example 2, the child omits the third-person singular *-s*, plural *-s*, and the irregular past form of *give*. This same child also omits possessive *-s*, as shown in Example 3. Note that ages of the children in the examples are given as *years;months* (e.g., 1 year, 4 months is written as 1;4).

1. **Randall (exposure to English: 5 months; age: 7;9)**
    CHI: And then the boat *go* like that. [went] [Child tips the toy boat up.]
    EXP: The boat sank, huh?
    CHI: Yeah.
    EXP: And what happened to the people?
    CHI: They *get* some. [got]

2. **Oleg (exposure to English: 13 months; age: 6;7)**
    CHI: He like-Ø carrot-Ø [like-s, carrot-s]
    CHI: And one time I *give* to him carrot-Ø. [gave, carrot-s]

3. **Oleg (exposure to English: 13 months; age: 6;7)**
    EXP: T-Rex!
    EXP: Is that your favorite dinosaur?
    CHI: Yes.
    EXP: Umhum.
    CHI: Not it's my friend-∅ favorite dinosaur. [*friend-'s*]

In contrast, commission errors occur when a grammatical morpheme is used incorrectly. In Example 4, the child uses the correct irregular past tense form *had* for *have,* but also adds a superfluous *-ed,* so he double-marks the past. In Example 5, the child adds a third person singular *-s* to the verb form *got,* which does not take this agreement morpheme. Double-marking, faulty agreement, and overregularization of the past—where the *-ed* is added to a verb form that typically has an irregular past-tense form (e.g., *comed* instead of *came*)—are typical kinds of commission errors. Although these kinds of commission errors are often salient when English L2 children make them, they are far less frequent overall than errors of omission (Paradis, 2005; Paradis et al., 2008).

4. **Felipe (exposure to English: 10 months; age: 5;8)**
    EXP: Were there robbers in Columbia?
    CH1:   Yeah.
    EXP: Mmhm?
    CH1:   That's why we *haded* to move. [had-∅]

5. **Felipe (exposure to English: 10 months; age: 5;8)**
    EXP: What's different about this house?
    CH1:   Um, it's bigger.
    CH1:   And it *gots* basement. [(It's)got-∅]

When L2 children are in the process of acquiring grammatical morphemes, they often use a morpheme correctly once, and then make an error with it, even within the same conversation. Refer to Example 6, in which the child uses the past tense for the first two verbs in his story but then slips into using the bare verb forms for the rest. This kind of alternation between correct and incorrect usage is a typical part of the language learning process. In fact, even regression from a consistently correctly used form is possible. In a case study of a Turkish L1/English L2 boy, Haznedar (2001) noted that the boy used some irregular past-tense forms correctly and then switched to overregularization later on in his interlanguage development. Two examples of this are given in Example 7, and the dates show that the correct forms emerged earlier than the incorrect ones. Wong Fillmore (1979) suggested that this appearance of regression might happen because the correct structure represented more formulaic or memorized usage. When children really begin to become productive speakers of the L2, creative errors such as overregularization emerge.

Educators and clinicians need to be aware of this back-and-forth correct use of grammatical morphology in order to set appropriate expectations. Even if an L2 child uses a morpheme once or twice correctly, this does not necessarily mean that the child will use the morpheme correctly from then on. Children vacillate between correct and incorrect forms, and between supplying a form and not supplying it, before their use of the correct form is high and stable (steady at 90% or greater accuracy in obligatory context). This occurs not only for grammatical morphemes, but for other aspects of morphosyntax as well. Thus, it is important to recognize that inconsistent use of correct forms is not necessarily a sign of a problem; it is often typical of both L1 and L2 learners.

6. **Oleg (exposure to English: 13 months; age: 6;7)**
   CHI: I *went* one time, *was* in the line at first, and then he *come push* outta the line and *come stand* beside me first.

7. **Erdem (Turkish L1, English L2; from Haznedar, 2001, p. 19)**
   CHI: My Daddy *brought* a toy. (February 14, 1995)
   CHI: She *bringed* me some new clothes. (May 19, 1995)
   CHI: Because it was not working, that's why I *broke* it. (February 22, 1995)
   CHI: Daddy opens the window and the window *breaked*. (May 19, 1995)

How many errors with grammatical morphology do English L2 learners make in their interlanguage throughout a conversation? Are they frequent, occasional, or rare? At the early stages, it is possible that L2 children will produce almost none of these morphemes correctly, so error rates can be very high, greater than 80%. Naturally, error rates decline as children are exposed to more English, but this decline does not happen very quickly, as we discuss in the section "How Long Does It Take for L2 Children to Approach Native-Speaker Proficiency?"

L1 Transfer in L2 Development Interlanguage patterns come, in part, from the L1 of L2 learners, which is why L2 learners who have the same L1 often have similar foreign accents. Both adults and children rely on their existing linguistic knowledge from their L1 when acquiring their L2 and this L1 influence on the L2 is often referred to as transfer from the L1. In the past, transfer was thought to be very detrimental to L2 learning, and there was a strong pedagogical orientation toward eliminating the effects of transfer. However, the L1 is now viewed as a valuable reservoir of linguistic resources for L2 learning. The phonology, vocabulary and grammar of the L1 can provide essential scaffolding for building knowledge of the L2, and this reliance on the L1 is most prominent at the beginning of the productive language period in the L2, when learners' resources in the L2 are limited. When the L1 is different from the L2 with respect to, for example, word order in sentences or rules for pronunciation, this reliance on the L1 may result in transfer errors in children's interlanguage. In contrast, if the L1 and L2 share patterns, then L2 acquisition is facilitated. We often see evidence of transfer only when it results in errors; this is probably why it is often seen as problematic. When transfer results in the right pattern, it is invisible, and—as a result—we do not see its facilitative effects.

The phonological system is often a major source of transfer from the L1. For example, in Spanish, consonant clusters at the beginning of words, such as /st/ or /sp/, typically have a vowel in front of them. Spanish speakers often transfer this pronunciation rule to English and pronounce the word *stop* /stap/ as "*estop*" /ɛstap/. Even very small children can transfer phonological features from their L1 to their L2. In a case study of his son, Alvino Fantini (1985) noted that when Mario first began speaking English, around the age of 2½, some of his first English words were pronounced using features of Spanish phonology. For example, English has tense and lax vowel pairs for the vowels /i/ (b*ea*t) /ɪ/ (b*i*t) and /u/ (b*oo*t) /ʊ/ (b*oo*k), whereas Spanish has only the tense vowels /i/ and /u/. Mario used tense vowels only in his first English words, so he said "*bili*" for /bɪli/ (i.e., Billy) and "*luk luk*" for /lʊklʊk/ (i.e., look look).

Morphosyntax can be a common place for transfer to occur when the L1 and the L2 have different rules for word order. Unsworth (2005) studied word order in the L2 Dutch of English L1 children. Dutch has several differences in the word order of sentences from English. In particular, the placement of the object of the verb can move in Dutch to either side of an adverb or negator, and the placement of the object signals a meaning difference, such as whether a specific or nonspecific object is being referred to. By contrast, in English, the object of the verb is placed after the verb, without an intervening negator or adverb, as in *he often watches TV/*he watches often TV*, or *he doesn't watch TV often/*he watches not often TV* (the asterisk denotes an ungrammatical sentence). Effectively, English has more "rigid" word order rules than Dutch, and Unsworth found that the children sometimes used their English L1 word order rules in their Dutch L2. Zdorenko and Paradis (2009) examined how English L2 children acquired the structure of questions in English. The morphosyntax of questions in English involves an inversion of an auxiliary verb and the subject; for example *The kitty is resting* versus *Is the kitty resting?* Numerous other languages, including Chinese languages, do not have this kind of morphosyntax for questions. Zdorenko and Paradis found that children whose L1 was a language with auxiliary verbs and the use of inversion for questions, such as in Spanish, produced questions with inversion and correct auxiliaries in English more often than children whose L1 did not have inversion or auxiliary verbs. Thus, L1 transfer was a benefit to the Spanish-speaking children in their acquisition of this aspect of English. Note that transfer of word order patterns—whether facilitative or not—is similar to the transfer of word order discussed in Chapter 4 as part of cross-linguistic influence. One difference, however, is that in the context of L2 acquisition, the directionality of transfer is typically from L1 to L2, but in simultaneous bilingual acquisition, more bidirectionality is possible.

L1 influences can lead not only to outright transfer errors, but can also be manifest in the L2 in more subtle ways. For instance, a distinction between Spanish and French versus English is the construction of possessives. In English, one can say "the dog's house" or "the house of the dog". In Spanish and French, only the second construction exists (e.g., *la casa del perro*, *la maison du chien*). Spanish- and French-speaking learners of English have often been noted to prefer saying "the house of the dog" instead of "the dog's house" in English, even though most native speakers of English would agree that the latter is more natural. This preference on the part of the L2 learners is a subtle transfer effect from their L1 because the effect does not produce a grammatical error. Instead, it leads the L2 learner to choose a less frequent construction that might sound odd, but that is not, strictly speaking, a grammatical error. Another and even more subtle kind of L1 transfer—or influence—is avoidance of certain structures in the L2. In contrast to English, in French, the object pronoun comes before the verb, rather than after it; for example *je le vois* ("I see him/it"). In our research, we have observed that English L1 learners of French as an L2 sometimes avoid using direct object pronouns, presumably because of the contrast in word order between the two languages. So, instead of saying "je le vois," they might use the demonstrative pronoun in French, which comes after the verb, and say "je vois ça" ("I see that"), or they might use a lexical object instead of a pronoun, even though it might sound redundant in the conversation. As in the preference transfer example, avoidance does not lead L2 learners to produce, strictly speaking, grammatical errors. Thus, three kinds of L1 influence patterns can be observed in the morphosyntax of child L2 learners: 1) direct transfer of L1 structure into the L2, 2) preference for a structure in the L2 that parallels the L1, and 3) avoidance of an L2 structure that contrasts with the L1 structure for the same concept.

Finally, the presence of L1 transfer errors in L2 interlanguage can be salient, but, as mentioned in the previous section, most researchers find that developmental patterns are a more prominent characteristic of L2 interlanguage. What this means is that the overall stages in the L2 development of any language are largely similar across learners, regardless of L1 background. Another distinction between developmental patterns and transfer is that L1 transfer is more observable at early stages of L2 acquisition (Unsworth, 2005; Zdorenko & Paradis, 2008, 2009), and developmental patterns are a defining characteristic of interlanguage in children up until they approach native-speaker competence in their L2.

To illustrate the interplay of developmental and transfer-based patterns, let us consider what could be expected in the interlanguage of the minority L2 children we profiled in Chapter 1. First, even though Bonnie has Mandarin Chinese as her first language, Luis has Spanish, and Faisal has Somali, it is likely that they will all simplify the pronunciation of consonant clusters early on, use some GAP verbs, and acquire English grammatical morphemes in a similar sequence. However, because Spanish is a language with auxiliaries and inversion in question formation, as in English, and Mandarin Chinese is not, it is possible that Luis will make fewer errors with the morphosyntax of English questions than Bonnie because he can transfer grammatical rules from his L1.

Interdependence Between the First and Second Language In Chapter 4, we discussed the concept of *bilingual bootstrapping*, in which the development of two languages is interdependent on some level such that bilinguals might not need to acquire every part of each language twice. For example, some aspects of linguistic–conceptual knowledge and language learning skills can be shared between the two languages. It is logical to assume that such interdependence takes place in sequential as well as in simultaneous bilinguals, especially because, by definition, L2 learners have prior linguistic knowledge to draw upon. One of the first researchers to discuss the possibility of interdependence was Jim Cummins from the Ontario Institute for Studies in Education at the University of Toronto. In Chapter 3, we discussed Cummins's threshold hypothesis, whereby high proficiency in both the L1 and the L2 could result in cognitive enhancements for bilingual children. Related to the threshold hypothesis are Cummins's hypotheses of **interdependence** and **common underlying proficiency** (Cummins, 1979, 1991, 2000). He proposed that many language skills in the L1 could be shared or transferred to the L2 because they draw on similar common underlying proficiencies, such as abstract linguistic concepts, language learning skills, and perceptual cognitive skills. In this way, interdependence can be viewed as broad-based facilitative transfer. Some researchers have found evidence for interdependence between the L1 and L2 of young children. Castilla, Pérez-Leroux, and Restrepo (2009) examined morphosyntactic and lexical/semantic knowledge in Spanish L1/English L2 4½-year-old children in an English preschool program. The children were tested in Spanish at the outset of the program, before they had had much exposure to English, and then in English at the end of the school year. These researchers found that children who had richer, stronger oral language abilities in their L1 also had richer, stronger oral language abilities in their L2 at the end of the year. Very similar findings emerged in a study of Turkish L1/Dutch L2 children in the Netherlands

(Verhoeven, 2007). However, we should point out that, in general, researchers have found more consistent evidence for interdependence in L2 children's academic language and literacy abilities than they have in their oral language abilities (Cummins, 2000; López & Greenfield, 2004; Oller & Eilers, 2002; Riches & Genesee, 2006).

HOW LONG DOES IT TAKE FOR L2 CHILDREN TO APPROACH NATIVE-SPEAKER PROFICIENCY?

A frequently asked question about the interlanguage period is, "How long does it last?" In other words, when do L2 children begin to sound as if they were native speakers? This question is important because L2 children who may appear to learn the L2 very slowly can cause concern for parents and professionals alike. Adult L2 learners might always have a foreign accent, but L1 minority children are expected to eventually become similar to native speakers of the majority L2. A popular belief is that young children can learn a language practically overnight. Some people think that when young children are exposed to a new language they "soak it up like a sponge." There is considerable research evidence showing this popular belief to be false, and it is important for professionals working with L2 children to be aware of how long it can really take to acquire native-like competence in a second language, and whether L2 children actually ever become identical to native-speakers in all respects of linguistic competence. At the early stages of L2 acquisition, children can function in an English conversation without using much English. To illustrate this point, let's examine a conversation that took place between Johanne Paradis and a 7-year-old boy. This child spoke Spanish as his L1 and had been exposed to English in elementary school in Canada for 4 months.

8. **Samuel (exposure to English: 4 months; age: 7;3)**
    EXP: So, what grade are you in at school?
    CH1: Two.
    EXP: Wow, Grade 2 already. What's your teacher's name?
    CH1: Mrs. Munro.
    EXP: What's the name of your school?
    CH1: Lendrum.
    EXP: I've heard of that school. I think one of our other grad students sent their kids there. Do you like school here in Canada?
    CH1: Yeah. Oh yeah.
    EXP: What's your favorite subject? What do you like best at school?
    CH1: Um, math.
    EXP: That's great. Not everybody likes math, but it's important. Do you take English second language classes?
    CH1: Yeah . . . some days.
    EXP: What do you think about all the snow? Does it snow like this in Chile?
    CH1: I like it, the snow.
    EXP: Do you go tobogganing with your friends?
    CH1: Yeah, I like it.
    EXP: The cold doesn't bother you?
    CH1: [shrug] No.

BOX 6.3

How Long Does It Take? Questions from Clinicians

One of the questions we are frequently asked by professionals is when L2 children attain similar linguistic abilities as monolingual children. The reason for the question usually has to do with the decision to use standard assessment instruments with L2 children, and/or how to interpret the results of such assessment tools when given to L2 children. The discussion in this section shows that there is no simple answer to this question, but generally speaking, clinicians should be very cautious in administering tests normed for monolinguals with L2 children. We discuss this topic further in Chapter 9.

Hello Dr. Paradis,

I'm wondering if I can pick your brain a little about the rate at which a child acquires ESL. There is a 9-year-old child who has been referred to our clinic for a neurodevelopmental assessment who arrived here from the Philippines about one year ago. He was reported to not know his alphabet and to have trouble remembering things already reviewed. His teacher wrote that she thought this boy's learning problems were not just due to a lack of English. Is that a reasonable expectation? It seems awfully fast to expect a child to be up to speed in a second language in one year. And I'm not sure if the teacher appreciates the difference between spoken, conversational language ability and written academic language ability.

Thanks,
A psychologist

Dear Dr. Genesee,

I'm currently employed at a child development center where we see children ages birth to 6 who require more than one therapist (occupational, physical, and/or speech and language). A third of families in our area speak a language other than English at home. As an SLP, I must assess these children, often using a translator, and determine whether they are "within normal limits." This is a very difficult task, especially given that we do not have language norms for those other languages. For example, if I assess a child, age 3, who has grown up speaking Punjabi and has not yet begun attending preschool, we would expect them to have minimal skills in English. What about the same child at age 4 who has been going to a preschool for one year? I've come across several children who, after attending preschool for 1 year, appear to be doing fine in their home language yet have not managed to pick up much English. Should this be a concern?

Thank you for your help,
A speech-language pathologist

At the end of this exchange, several people remarked on how good this child's English was. But, can this child's English language skills really be judged from this exchange? The child's part of the conversation consisted mainly of one-word answers to questions on familiar topics: school and the weather. His comprehension may appear to be impeccable, but he could have used many kinds of nonlinguistic information to comprehend what was being asked (e.g., real-world knowledge about schools, experience with this line of questioning about school). More important, the expectations of the adult interlocutor and listeners were low. Many people do not expect children to initiate and elaborate much in conversation with an unfamiliar adult. Therefore, in terms of basic conversational skills and social expectations of a 7-year-old, this boy performed extremely well in an English language exchange, but actually, he might know very, very little English.

The point we want to make is that in casual conversations, L2 children can often appear more linguistically advanced than they really are because their linguistic abilities are not being stretched in these situations. To put it differently, the ability to communicate and participate in an informal social interaction does not necessarily reflect an L2 learner's full or real competence. So how long does it really take? Hakuta, Goto Butler, and Witt (2000) examined language test information from over 1,800 English L2 children in the San Francisco area and concluded that these children took between 3 and 5 years of full-time English schooling to have oral English abilities similar to those of native speakers. Saunders and O'Brien (2006) reviewed numerous studies of L2 children's English abilities and also found that it was not until the senior elementary school grades that they were able to perform as well as native speakers. Saunders and O'Brien (2006) also found that the children's rate of English development changed over time. Specifically, the children made rapid gains to moderate proficiency levels up until third grade, but the pace of their development slowed in the later elementary school years, and thus it took them two or more years to close—or nearly close—the gap with their native-speaker peers. This makes sense when one considers that it is usually easy to show progress when one begins learning something new; it is mastering the small details in the later stages that often takes time when acquiring any skill. This finding about changes in pace is particularly important for educators and parents to keep in mind when called upon to make decisions about appropriate educational programming for L2 children. It would be wise to not assume that the pace of early L2 development will be sustained throughout the elementary school years—L2 children might need special language support for longer than their initial gains would lead one to believe.

In order to look more closely at the question of how long it takes for L2 children to achieve native-like proficiency, we now consider the timeframe of development for separate domains of language.

Phonological Development

Snow and Hoefnagel-Höhle (1977) studied the pronunciation of Dutch words by 47 English speakers (from 3 to 60 years old) learning Dutch as an L2 in the Netherlands. They found that after one year, the children had surpassed the adult learners in their pronunciation abilities in the L2. However, even after 18 months of exposure, none of the children had achieved perfect pronunciation of Dutch. A recent study based on the Edmonton

ELL corpus examined children's correct pronunciation of English consonants after roughly 1 year of exposure to English in school. The children's accuracy in producing consonants in English was, generally speaking, very good—greater than 90% for many types of consonants and vowels. The children had less than 80% accuracy in their pronunciation of fricative consonants in particular (/s/, /z/, /f/, /v/, /ʃ/ "sh," or /ð,θ/ "th"), and so this group of consonants was taking longer for them to acquire (Gilhool et al., 2009). Therefore, although it is widely accepted that young children can eventually achieve native-like pronunciation of their L2, it could take more than two years to reach this level. It is also worth keeping in mind that some L2 children are exposed to varieties of the target language that differ from the mainstream variety in pronunciation, and thus the endpoint of their phonological development would more closely model the variety they are exposed to in their community. For example, see Goldstein (in McLeod, 2007) for a discussion of Spanish-influenced English in the United States.

Morphosyntactic Development

Learning to use grammatical morphemes appropriately has a definable end point for speakers of a language—usually considered to be 90% or greater correct use in contexts requiring that morpheme; for example, the plural reference of a count noun requires adding -*s*, *two kitten-s are playing with the string.* Native-like mastery of grammatical patterns is not 100% correct use because even monolinguals might make a small mistake when speaking quickly, or changing thoughts in mid-sentence, and so on. It takes years for children to achieve this end point in their L2. Jia (2003), Jia and Fuse (2007), and Paradis (2008) examined English L2 children's production of grammatical morphemes over time. These studies found that after 2–3 years of exposure, L2 learners were using the early-acquired morphemes, such as plural -*s* and progressive -*ing*, quite accurately, but that it took longer, between 3 and 5 years, for them to become accurate with the late-acquired grammatical morphemes, such as verbal inflections -*s* and -*ed*. Zdorenko and Paradis (2008) examined English L2 children's acquisition of definite and indefinite articles in particular, such as *the* and *a/an*. Numerous languages do not have definite/indefinite articles in their morphosyntax, and the rules for when to use the definite article, the indefinite article, or no article, are complicated in English and depend on subtle nuances in semantics and pragmatics. Therefore, it is not surprising that many adult L2 learners take a long time to learn these rules, and even very fluent L2 adults can make mistakes with articles from time to time. The L2 children we studied learned very early on to place an article before a noun in English, and so they were relatively quick to figure out where the English language requires an article. However, even after 2–3 years of exposure, the children were still making mistakes regarding which article to use; most notably, they tended to use the definite article, *the*, in place of the indefinite article. Interestingly, this error is also common in monolingual children acquiring English as their L1. Taken together, these studies of grammatical morphology support the findings from Hakuta et al. (2000) that it can take between 3 and 5 years for L2 children to attain oral English proficiency similar to native speakers. They also support the observation made in the section "Stages of Second Language Development in Children" that sequences in morphosyntactic acquisition are largely parallel between child L2 learners and younger monolingual learners of the same language.

Vocabulary Development

How long it takes for children to accumulate vocabulary in their L2 on par with their native speaker peers has been studied extensively, possibly because breadth and depth of vocabulary is an important factor in reading comprehension (see Chapter 10), and therefore vocabulary is regarded as crucial to L2 children's academic achievement. The available evidence suggests that it can take a long time for L2 children to achieve a vocabulary size and composition comparable with their native-speaker peers, and sometimes they never do. Oller and Eilers (2002) compared Spanish L1/English L2 children's receptive vocabulary size with that of same-age monolingual English peers in Grades 2 and 5. Both groups of children were in the same school system from kindergarten. They found that the L2 children came close to closing the gap with the monolinguals by Grade 5—after 6 years of schooling in English, but that some differences between them persisted. Golberg et al. (2008) followed 19 children from the Edmonton ELL corpus for 2 years using the same receptive vocabulary test as Oller and his colleagues. We found, in contrast to the result from Oller and Eilers, that L2 children in Edmonton nearly closed the gap with native speakers after just 3, instead of 6, years of schooling in English. One possible reason for the discrepancy between these two studies is that the children studied by Golberg and colleagues had diverse L1 backgrounds and were residing in communities where English was the lingua franca inside and outside of school. This might have contributed to their faster acquisition of English vocabulary in comparison with the L2 children in Miami who shared the same L1. However, more research is necessary to know how robust differences are among English L2 children across social contexts. Regarding vocabulary, the study by Oller and Eilers (2002) also included a test of productive vocabulary in which children had to name pictures. L2 children tended to score somewhat lower on productive than receptive vocabulary in English, although the same overall trends were found for both receptive and productive vocabulary in that children came close to native-speaker levels in fifth grade. The important implication of these American and Canadian studies is that L2 children did not close the gap completely by the end of either study, so L2 children should not be expected to acquire vocabulary knowledge on par with native speakers within the early elementary school years.

What are the consequences of children not quite closing the gap in vocabulary? Roessingh and Elgie (2009) discuss how initial vocabulary gains in English L2 children— up until third grade—are not necessarily sustained into the senior elementary school years. They found that L2 children's breadth and depth of vocabulary in elicited narratives (e.g., use low-frequency words and synonyms) was limited compared with native speakers, and it is suspected that this can cause limitations in reading comprehension in Grades 4–6, and possibly beyond, when children transition from learning to read to reading to learn. These authors recommend more enriched and intensive vocabulary instruction in the early grades for English L2 children.

In sum, L2 children may demonstrate some differences in comparison with monolinguals in their vocabulary knowledge and use beyond the stage where their pronunciation and their basic morphosyntactic abilities in English seem to be near those of native speakers. Why might this happen? Two factors in L2 vocabulary learning are important to keep in mind. First, L2 children are trying to hit a "moving target" when they are acquiring L2 vocabulary because their native-speaker peers are also accumulating vocabulary rapidly during the elementary school years, and vocabulary learning can continue across the lifespan (Cummins, 2000). This contrasts with phonological and morphosyntactic learning in the sense that once the sound and grammatical system of a language has been acquired, there are no new rules to be learned; they are finite systems. Second, as discussed in Chapter 4, bilingual children, both simultaneous and sequential, possess two lexical systems (not one), and the distributed nature of concept–word associations can influence vocabulary size in both languages (see Chapter 4; Oller & Eilers, 2002; and Oller, Pearson, & Cobo-Lewis, 2007). Both of these factors might explain some of the long-term outcomes for vocabulary learning that have been documented in L2/bilingual children and youth.

The research on vocabulary development raises the broader question of whether it is appropriate to expect bilinguals to become identical to monolinguals in all aspects of language, or whether some differences in the configuration of linguistic competence should be expected between them—in this case, for vocabulary knowledge. There are two points to keep in mind when considering the possibility of bilingual–monolingual differences. First, in our view, it is important to understand that any kind of difference between bilinguals and monolinguals should not be automatically considered as negative, but instead should be considered in the context of the many advantageous linguistic and cognitive consequences of bilingualism. Second, it is also not clear whether any bilingual–monolingual differences in long-term vocabulary knowledge are inevitable, or whether they are the product of the complex social and educational circumstances in which minority L1 children develop their two languages, as these are often subtractive bilingual contexts (see Chapters 3 and 8).

Profile Effects in Approaching Native-Speaker Norms

One final point to be made about L2 children's developmental trajectories is that they do not approach native-speaker proficiency in all linguistic domains at the same pace. Instead, they display what have been called *profile effects*. Oller et al. (2007) found that Spanish L1/English L2 children could have basic word-decoding skills equivalent to those of monolingual age peers, while their vocabularies in English lagged behind these same peers. Paradis and Schneider (2008) compared the storytelling or narrative abilities of children from the Edmonton ELL corpus with those of monolingual children residing in the same city. They examined the macrostructure and microstructure of the stories children told when looking at picture sequences. The macrostructure of a story means how children refer to the characters, setting, events, and outcomes to make a coherent story. The microstructure refers to the diversity of vocabulary and grammatical complexity used in children's sentences. The L2 children had a unique profile of narrative abilities because they often had very high scores for macrostructure—within the range of the monolinguals—and at the same time, very low scores for microstructure; monolingual peers tended to be either high or low for both. What could be the reason for profile effects? The concepts of interdependence and common underlying proficiency might explain them. For example, the skills required to decode written words are largely perceptual–cognitive in nature and can be shared across two languages. Also, the macrostructure of narratives has a large conceptual component not tied to any specific language, and thus could be shared across languages. In contrast, many aspects of vocabulary and grammar are specific to the L2.

To illustrate the extent of profile effects in L2 development, some data from the Edmonton ELL corpus are presented in Figure 6.1. These data are from 25 children whose English was tested every 6 months for 2 years. The tests measured receptive vocabulary size, verbal morphology, and narrative macrostructure. The bars in the figure show what percentage of the children achieved a score within the normal age-expected range for native speakers on that test. The striking aspect of Figure 6.1 is that the bars do not get bigger in synchrony, but instead are uneven at every time period. The overall pattern is that these L2 children approached native-speaker performance for narrative macrostructure ahead of vocabulary, with verbal morphology being the slowest to develop. The pattern shown by these 25 children is the same when more than 200 children from a cross-sectional sample of the Edmonton ELL corpus are examined.

The presence of profile effects is particularly relevant to speech-language pathologists, psychologists, and special educators who often administer language and literacy assessments with L2 children. It is important for these professionals to understand how to interpret the sometimes uneven performance of L2 children on an assessment battery, and to be aware of where their relative strengths and weakness in the L2 may lie. In short, profile effects mean that the answer to the question "How long does it take?" is not straightforward because different domains of language take longer than others. If our explanation is on the right track, then one could expect children to make more rapid progress in domains of language and literacy whose fundamental components can be transferred or shared with the L1.

WHAT FACTORS CAN ACCOUNT FOR INDIVIDUAL DIFFERENCES IN CHILDREN'S RATES OF SECOND LANGUAGE ACQUISITION?

One striking facet of children's rates of L2 acquisition is the degree of variation among individuals. Substantial individual variation is noted by virtually all researchers of child L2 learners, and there is clearly evidence of such variation in the Edmonton ELL corpus. In the longitudinal data from 25 children shown in Figure 6.1, at the first round, when the children had been exposed to English for about 1 school year, their scores on the test of grammar were highly variable; the mean score was 27% correct, with a range from 0% to 94%. We found similar variation for scores on the receptive vocabulary test; the mean standard score was 77, with a range of 49–114. Thus, some individual L2 children had English grammatical and vocabulary skills within the native-speaker range after just one year, while others were trailing far behind. In this section, we discuss some factors that might cause these large individual differences in children's rates of learning their L2. Factors influencing individual differences in academic language skills and academic outcomes are discussed in Chapter 8. For more technical and comprehensive reviews of individual differences in child L2 learners, see Paradis (2007) and Saunders and O'Brien (2006).

Factors that explain individual differences in language learning can be categorized as child internal and child external. Child-internal factors are those that the child brings with them to the L2 learning situation: motivation, personality, language learning aptitude, cognitive maturity (age), and the structure of their L1. Child-external factors are those that exist in the environment outside the child; for example, how much L1 and L2 the child hears and uses at home, the quality of language interactions between the child and

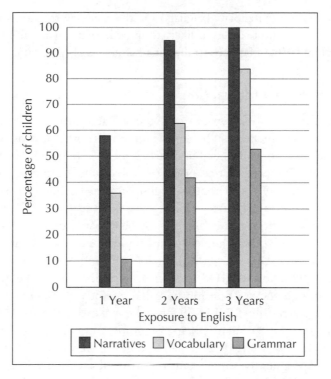

Figure 6.1. Percentage of English L2 children meeting native-speaker expectations of performance on tests of narrative ability, vocabulary, and grammar.

parents at home, the richness of the L2 the child is exposed to outside of school, and the nature of language use in the classroom. It is important for parents, other caregivers, educators, and health care practitioners to be aware not only of the factors that influence how quickly children will acquire a L2, but also of which factors can be changed to promote more effective L2 learning. Aside from motivation, there is little about child-internal factors that can be influenced by parents or professionals. In contrast, modifications to some aspects of child-external factors are possible.

Motivation

Attitudes, emotional factors, and beliefs about the language being learned and the cultural group who speak it combine to determine an individual's motivation for learning the L2. High motivation is consistently associated with L2 success in adult learners, particularly those in a foreign language classroom (Dörnyei & Skehan, 2003). Motivation may also be an important predictor of L2 attainment for adult immigrants who—for various complex ethnic, religious, and cultural reasons—vary in their desire to integrate with the host society. However, absence of motivation is not a common characteristic of L1 minority children. Wong Fillmore (1979) noted that some of the Spanish L1 children she examined were initially reluctant to learn English, but this did not persist, and moreover was most likely due to the fact that they had other Spanish-speaking children to play with and a vibrant Spanish-speaking community where they lived in California. It is difficult to imagine a child whose L1 is not spoken by any other child in his class having low motivation for an extended period of time to learn the majority language. On the contrary, the desire of minority children to assimilate to the host society is likely to impede their L1 maintenance, as discussed in the section titled, "What Happens to the First Language of Minority Children?"

Personality and Social Interaction

Investigations of the role of personality factors in L2 acquisition tend to suffer from the "which came first, the chicken or the egg?" problem. In other words, are children with outgoing personalities more advanced in their L2 because they seek out English-speaking playmates and thus get more practice, or are they able to be outgoing and seek out these playmates because they are competent in English and have achieved this competence for other reasons? It is always important to keep this issue in mind when considering the impact of personality factors. Personality factors have not been found to be consistently good predictors of L2 success in adults, but a couple of studies indicate they could matter in child L2 learning (Dörnyei & Skehan, 2003; Strong, 1983; Wong Fillmore, 1983). Wong Fillmore (1983) followed 48 Spanish L1 children in Berkeley, California, for 2 years, and examined the relationship between personality traits of the children and their success at learning the L2. Personality characteristics she looked at defined the "social style" of the children, such as being outgoing and talkative versus shy and introverted. Children who were highly social and outgoing were successful English learners, and these children frequently sought out opportunities to speak English through peer interaction. Strong (1983) similarly found that personality variables associated with amount of social contact with native speakers were significantly correlated with greater proficiency in English grammar, vocabulary, and pronunciation by L2 children in kindergarten. However, Wong Fillmore also found that children who were shy and not very sociable, but very attentive in class and highly academically skilled, also managed to learn the L2 very well. Perhaps these children's strong cognitive and analytic skills compensated for their reduced social interactions.

Language Aptitude

Among studies conducted with adult L2 learners, the variable that most consistently correlates with language learning success is **language aptitude** (Dörnyei & Skehan, 2003; Sawyer & Ranta, 2002). Language aptitude is related to, but distinct from, general intelligence or intelligence quotient (IQ). Language aptitude includes a combination of working memory and analytic abilities, and individuals vary in their language aptitude much as they vary in their IQ. Also as with IQ, language aptitude is considered to be an intrinsic, rather than an acquired, ability. For example, individuals with the ability to rapidly and accurately decode unfamiliar speech into phonetic (sound) units and analyze unfamiliar written language into parts of speech (e.g., nouns, verbs, adjectives) have high language aptitude. Because language aptitude is more explanatory of individual differences in adult learners than many other factors and because it is an intrinsic characteristic, it is most likely a relevant factor in explaining why some children acquire their L2 faster than others. However, the language aptitude tests used for adults cannot easily be administered to young children because of the complexity in format and literacy requirements, and thus the impact of language aptitude on L2 acquisition has not been widely studied in young

---

BOX 6.4

Language Aptitude

"Foreign language learning aptitude has been defined by John Carroll, the most prominent scholar in this area as 'some characteristic of an individual which controls, at a given point of time, the rate of progress that he will make subsequently in learning a foreign language' (1974). Studies investigating L2 success in relation to language aptitude have generally yielded correlation coefficients in the .4 to .6 range (Carroll, 1981, p. 93). These are considered moderate to strong correlations, and although they imply that considerable learner variation remains to be explained by additional factors, they also demonstrate that language aptitude has consistently been the single best predictor of subsequent language learning achievement." (Sawyer & Ranta, 2002, p. 320)

---

children. Researchers who have looked at older children and adolescents have results that parallel the findings for adult L2 learners (Harley & Hart, 1997; Ranta, 2002).

In order to examine the impact of language aptitude on the acquisition rates of young children, language aptitude must be assessed using tests of the basic components of language aptitude that are appropriate for young children. Short term or working memory abilities are often measured in young children using digit span or nonword repetition tasks. For example, children listen to a sequence of digits or an unfamiliar word and must repeat it back as accurately and quickly as possible. This kind of task measures phonological short term memory in particular. Strong **phonological memory** is associated with strong language learning, and with vocabulary building in particular, in monolingual children, and deficits in phonological memory are often found in children with specific language impairment (Gathercole, 2006; see also Chapter 9).

Looking at 155 children ages 5–7 years from the Edmonton ELL corpus, we found that both nonverbal IQ and phonological memory were strong predictors of children's vocabulary size and accuracy with verbal morphology in English (Paradis, 2010; see also Genesee & Hamayan, 1980). In fact, in the Edmonton L2 children, these child-internal factors predicted more about children's English outcomes than some of the child-external, input-based factors we discuss shortly. These findings indicate that language aptitude could be as important in predicting individual differences in child L2 as it is in adult L2.

Age of Acquisition

It is clear even to nonspecialists that age of acquisition has an effect on L2 learning because individuals who learn an L2 as adults usually have a foreign accent and make grammatical errors when they speak. However, age effects on L2 learning have been observed even when L2 learning begins in the childhood years. Indeed, differences in long-term phonological and morphosyntactic outcomes for L2 learners with variations in age of arrival within childhood have been well documented (see Hyltenstam & Abrahamsson, 2003, for a comprehensive review). In brief, this body of research indicates that children who begin to learn an L2 starting between the ages of 6 and 8 years or older might not be identical to native speakers in all respects of their L2 competence when they become adults, although the differences with native speakers can be quite subtle. What we are more concerned with in this section is whether there are short-term age effects, or individual differences in children's developmental rates due to variations in age of L2 onset. Beginning to learn English as an L2 in the middle, rather than early, elementary school years has been found to be advantageous for the acquisition of academic English skills (Collier, 1987, 1989; Roessingh, Kover, & Watt, 2005). Presumably older is better than younger in this case because older children's more developed cognitive skills give them an advantage in learning strategies over younger children. In addition, older learners' previous experience with schooling and literacy can transfer to English as part of the interdependence between the languages (see also Chapter 3 and 8). Regarding oral language abilities, Golberg et al.'s (2008) longitudinal study of vocabulary development, described earlier, included children who were 4–7 years old at the outset of the study. We found that the children who began to learn English when older than 5 years of age had consistently larger vocabularies in English over the 2-year period than the children who began to learn English when younger than 5 years of age. Jia and Fuse (2007) also examined the effects of age in their study of grammatical morpheme development; children/adolescents ranged in age from 5 to 16 years old when they arrived in the United States. Jia and Fuse found that older children/adolescents acquired grammatical morphemes in English faster than the younger children at first. However, at the end of the study, the children who started learning English younger achieved closer to 90% correct use of these morphemes than the adolescents. A similar pattern is noted in Chapter 7 for IA children. Therefore, when it comes to age of acquisition within the childhood years, younger seems to be better in the long term, but older seems to be better in the short term. In the latter case, "younger" means younger than middle childhood. There is no evidence to date that differential long-term outcomes emerge when children learn English as a second language at different ages younger than 6–8 years, although there is a general lack of research on this age group.

Findings concerning age of acquisition have implications for professionals who are asked for advice by parents of L1 minority children about when to introduce the L2. Immigrant and refugee parents often want their children to learn English before school entry, so that they can get a head start. As the evidence reviewed here demonstrates, earlier is not necessarily better. Moreover, research discussed in Chapter 8 on bilingual schooling indicates that sometimes educational support of the minority language during the early school years results in higher levels of English language achievement among L2 learners than English-only schooling. Indeed, some would argue that maintenance of the minority L1 could be put in jeopardy if English is introduced too early. We elaborate on this point in the next major section, "What Happens to the First Language of Minority Children?"

Structure of the First Language

A final child-internal source of individual differences is the distance between the L2 and L1 in terms of phonological or grammatical structure. In other words, when a child's L1 is very different from the L2, this can affect the child's rate of L2 development.

We have already discussed the concept of L1 transfer in the earlier section, "Stages of Second Language Development in Children," with respect to the unique patterns that can emerge in the L2 that are traceable to the L1. In this section, we are concerned with how L1 transfer—or the lack of it—can influence the rate of L2 development. For example, Mandarin Chinese does not have definite and indefinite articles (*the, a*), but Spanish does. Would it be harder for a Mandarin L1 child to learn English articles than a Spanish L1 child? If Spanish L1 children could transfer the grammatical concept of definiteness, the knowledge that there are words in the language that denote this concept, and even some rules about how to use articles in sentences—all of this might give them an advantage in acquiring English articles. Zdorenko and Paradis (2008, in press) found that children whose L1 was Spanish indeed had an advantage in the acquisition of English articles over their peers whose L1 was Mandarin. In terms of phonology, there are some indications that overlap between the L1 and L2 can facilitate development. Goldstein (2004) and Fabiano-Smith and Goldstein (2010) found that early sequential bilingual children's pronunciation of phonetic segments (sounds) in English that are "shared" with Spanish—that is, pronounced in a similar way—was superior to their pronunciation of nonshared phonetic segments. For speech-language pathologists, an understanding of how L1 transfer can affect a child's error patterns, and rate of phonological and morphosyntactic development in English could be important for making decisions about the presence of phonological or language disorders. *The International Guide to Speech Acquisition* (McLeod, 2007) contains descriptions of the phonological systems and phonological acquisition patterns of 24 languages and can be a useful resource for clinicians to predict substitution patterns and acquisition difficulty for L2 learners. To date, no such guide exists for morphosyntactic structures across languages.

Quantity and Quality of L2 Exposure

Child-external factors that affect L2 development are related to their experiences with the L2. For example, length of time learning the L2, and amount of practice they get with the L2 at school, at home, and in the community are all factors that contribute to the quantity of L2 input children receive. Furthermore, the quality of the L2 exposure can also be considered—that is, the variety and depth of interactions in the L2 and contact with native speakers, media, and L2 reading material that exposes children to rich vocabulary and complex grammar. Gisela Jia and colleagues measured "richness" of the English L2 environment outside the classroom for Mandarin L1 children based on information about hours of English TV watched, number of English books read, number of English native-speaker friends, and the percentage of time they spoke English at home (Jia & Aaronson, 2003; Jia & Fuse, 2007). They found that faster acquisition of English was associated with richness of the L2 environment and that this might be a more important factor than age of arrival for immigrant children.

However, it is important to point out that these findings do not necessarily mean that frequent or exclusive use of the L2 among family members in the home should be encouraged. On the contrary, frequent use of the L1 at home should be encouraged for a variety of reasons that we elaborate on in the next section. There is no evidence that frequent use of the L2 in the home is essential to children's successful acquisition of the L2 and, importantly, the quality of the L2 input at home should be considered. If parents who are not proficient in the L2 are using this language most of the time with their children, the benefits of this "extra" L2 exposure may be curtailed once children are past the early stages of acquisition because the parents' limited L2 skills means that they are not able to provide their children with rich L2 input. In the Edmonton ELL corpus, this appears to be the case; the benefit of exposure to English at home was tied to how fluent parents were in English (Paradis, 2010). We also found that English use at home among families had a separate impact on children's English than factors such as contact with native-speakers, activities in English outside of school, and media contact in English. The latter factors often had a greater positive impact on children's English abilities, particularly after the first year of schooling in English. The issue of native-speaker contact could be a point of difference between the profiled children Luis and Faisal. Luis is growing up in a community in California where the vast majority of his peers are other Spanish-speaking L2 children; Faisal is growing up in a community where there are many L2 children, but these children have diverse L1 backgrounds, and there are some English monolinguals as well. This difference could mean that Faisal gets more practice with English and native-speaker contact in the community than Luis.

A factor that has been widely associated with quantity and quality of the input is *socioeconomic status* (SES) of the family, usually measured by mother's level of education. Maternal education level is a strong predictor of children's outcomes in their L1, and there are two reasons for this effect: 1) higher educated mothers speak more to their children, and 2) higher-educated mothers have an interactive style that encourages complex language use by their children (Hoff, 2006). Oller and Eilers (2002) showed that higher-SES Spanish–English bilingual children had better proficiency in English than their lower-SES peers. Golberg et al. (2008) also found that in the cohort of L2 children we followed for 2 years, the children of mothers with postsecondary education had consistently bigger vocabularies than the children of mothers with secondary education only. Interestingly, in this study, the higher education mothers were more likely to speak the L1, and not the L2, at home with their children, yet their children were doing better in English than their peers. This finding seems rather paradoxical, but it might be the case that the quality of language interactions at home, no matter what language they are in, is more important and beneficial to children's acquisition of both languages. Recall that of our profiled children, only Bonnie had university-educated parents, and the parents of Luis and Faisal had low levels of education. This SES difference could be a source of difference in how quickly Bonnie learns English compared with the other two children.

A final input factor to consider is language use at school. In the French immersion context in Canada, for example, where English-speaking children learn French as an L2 through the medium of schooling, Genesee and Hamayan (1980) found that children who used French more frequently in class, at recess, and in the halls, had higher French proficiency at the end of kindergarten. The Wong Fillmore (1983) study with Spanish L1 children, discussed previously, also included an examination of how the classroom situation interacted with personality factors to influence L2 outcomes. She found that teacher-centered classroom settings helped shy and attentive learners to advance because they were exposed to a great deal of English through teacher talk and did not have to initiate social contact with their peers in order to get input. Children who were more outgoing and peer-oriented in their interactions, however, got more out of a classroom structured around group activities in which they could interact with other children. However, the advantages of an outgoing social style would backfire in a classroom with lots of group activities if many of the children spoke the same L1 and there were few English native speakers. Some highly social minority children observed by Wong Fillmore spent an entire year in an English classroom and learned very little English because they spoke mainly Spanish with their peers during group activities. One important implication of this study is that there is no single combination of learner and classroom characteristics that result in rapid success in the L2; even children who are shy can be, relatively speaking, quick to advance in their L2, and not every classroom setting suits every learner's style.

WHAT HAPPENS TO THE FIRST LANGUAGE OF MINORITY CHILDREN?

Immigrant and refugee parents often feel divided between their desire to have their children grow up speaking their native language and their desire to have their children learn the majority language as quickly as possible, on the assumption that this will help them succeed in the host society. The truth is that parents need not feel divided on this issue because the goals of L1 maintenance and L2 acquisition are mutually supportive of each other, rather than being at odds with each other. On the face of it, it may seem contradictory to suggest that maintaining the L1 is important. We have just discussed how long it can take L2 children to catch up to native-speaker peers in English, and we identified the potential importance of social interaction in the L2 as a factor in development. However, dual language learning is not a zero-sum game. As we pointed out in Chapter 3, the limited capacity hypothesis is not tenable. It is not the case that there is only so much space for language in the brains of young children; therefore, the L1 must be dropped to make room for the L2. Nor is it true that simply increasing "time-on-task" will ensure better progress in the L2 (see Chapter 8). Although it is commonly believed that children need to maximize exposure to the L2 and reduce exposure to other languages in order to make maximal gains in their L2, this—as does the "soak it up like a sponge" theory— enjoys little empirical support.

Minority children learning a majority L2, such as migrant children in North America, Western Europe, and Australia, are often in subtractive bilingual environments because they often lose competence in their L1 as proficiency in the L2 grows. As a result, their ultimate bilingual proficiency might be low, and they may therefore not experience the cognitive advantages conferred by high levels of dual language competence that comes from being in an additive bilingual environment, as discussed in Chapter 3. Moreover, they may not reap the academic benefits conferred by interdependent development of academic language skills in the L1 and L2. The clearest example of positive interdependent development is L2 reading. Minority language children who have acquired emergent literacy skills or initial literacy skills in their L1 prior to coming to school make faster progress in L2 literacy than children who lack such skills. The link between L1 and L2 literacy is even more evident when considering the case of language minority students who have already acquired reading skills in the L1. For these children, acquisition of literacy skills in an L2 is straightforward. Further elaboration on the advantages of maintaining the L1 for enhanced performance in L2 school settings is covered in Chapters 8 and 10.

BOX 6.5

Consequences of L1 Loss in Minority Children

"What is lost when children and parents cannot communicate easily with one another? What is lost is no less than the means by which parents socialize their children: When parents are unable to talk to their children, they cannot easily convey to them their values, beliefs, understandings, or wisdom about how to cope with their experiences. They cannot teach them about the meaning of work, or about personal responsibility or what it means to be a moral or ethical person in a world with too many choices and too few guideposts to follow. . . . Talk is a crucial link between parents and children: It is how parents impart their cultures to their children and enable them to become the kind of men and women they want them to be. When parents lose the means for socializing and influencing their children, rifts develop and families lose the intimacy that comes from shared beliefs and understandings." (Wong Fillmore, 1991, p. 343)

A subtractive bilingual environment can create ambivalence toward the home language and culture on the part of young language learners and their caregivers. The home language comes to be seen as an impediment to acquisition of the majority language and a marker of minority group inferiority, with the result that the home language is abandoned. A corollary effect is that parents no longer provide rich linguistic input to their children as they strive to interact with them in a language that they themselves have usually not mastered. In effect, the bilingualism of the child is devalued, and the rich linguistic input that is critical to full acquisition is compromised. Thus, there are significant psychological and sociocultural reasons for promoting the maintenance of the L1 in children whose L1 is a minority language, in addition to the cognitive/academic reasons noted previously. Lily Wong Fillmore passionately expressed why loss of the L1 can be detrimental to such children and their families in her 1991 article titled "When Learning a Second Language Means Losing the First," shown in Box 6.5. In spite of the importance of L1 maintenance for the minority child's personal well-being and academic success, many of these children gradually lose their L1 abilities over time. This process of language loss is referred to as **L1 attrition.** Some attrition can occur even in children whose L1 is supported in their surrounding community, such as Spanish in some regions of the United States. It is important for professionals working with children to expect that the L1 abilities of many minority language children will not remain stable and will not be the same as those of monolingual speakers of that language from the home country. Gradual shift from the L1 to the majority language is inevitable for most migrant families in the United States, Canada, Western Europe, and Australia.

Characteristics of Language Shift and Language Attrition

Sequential bilingual children begin the process of learning an L2 with the L1 as their dominant, or most proficient, language. However, for minority L1/majority L2 children, the dominant language typically shifts to the L2 over time, in particular when the L2 is the language of schooling (see Chapter 4 for a discussion of dominant language in bilingual children). This transitional phase between descending L1 abilities and ascending L2 abilities has been examined by Kathryn Kohnert and her colleagues in Spanish L1/ English L2 children and adolescents in California (Kohnert & Bates, 2002; Kohnert, Bates, & Hernandez, 1999). These researchers examined the speed and accuracy with which these participants recognized and named words in both Spanish and English at different ages, from 5 to 16 years of age. The participants' word-processing skills were stronger in Spanish initially until they had approximately 10 years of experience with English, at which point their dominance shifted from Spanish to English. In terms of comprehension, this shift occurred earlier, after about 7 years of exposure to English. These children and adolescents lived in a community where their L1 was widely spoken, and this may have contributed to the timeframe of the shift in the dominant language. It is possible that minority L1 children living in communities where their L1 is not widely spoken might experience earlier shifts to the L2 as the dominant language. We return to the issue of L1 community size when discussing causes of L1 attrition.

Although dominant language shift to the L2 does not necessarily go hand in hand with L1 attrition, or complete L1 loss, in some cases it does lead to these outcomes. L1 attrition in minority children is evident in multiple aspects of their linguistic knowledge and use. Anderson (2004) discusses the many features of Spanish that undergo attrition in bilingual children in the United States; here are some examples (Anderson, 2004, p. 202):

1. Children might have limited vocabularies, so they frequently use demonstrative pronouns, such as *éste* ("this one") instead of the name for an object, or they code-mix the word from English into their Spanish sentence.

2. Children might make errors in their verb morphology, such as *ellos come* ("they eat[singular]") instead of *ellos comen* ("they eat[plural]"), or make errors with the gender in noun phrases, such as *el casa rojo* ("the[masc] house[feminine] red[masc]").

3. Children might also use English word order in phrases in Spanish, such as *el grande vaso* ("the large glass") instead of the appropriate *el vaso grande* ("the glass large").

Silvina Montrul has extensively studied adult Spanish heritage language speakers in the United States and has found numerous and often subtle differences in their morphosyntactic competence when compared with monolingual Spanish speakers, even though many of these heritage speakers were comfortable and fluent speakers of Spanish (Montrul, 2008). Montrul points out that some of the differences between heritage speakers and monolinguals are more likely to reflect incomplete acquisition, as opposed to attrition, because heritage language speakers may not have had the opportunity to fully acquire all the morphosyntactic complexities of their L1 in the first place, rather than losing it after it was acquired. For example, full acquisition of the syntax and semantics of the Spanish subjunctive mood might rarely be in place by the time children are 3 years old, but this might be the time when they begin consistent and sustained exposure to the majority language. Furthermore, lack of schooling in Spanish might mean they are never exposed to the subtler aspects of the subjunctive mood in Spanish. For a comprehensive technical review of L1 attrition/incomplete acquisition in heritage language children and adults, see Montrul (2008). Although L1 attrition, or incomplete acquisition, is commonplace, we want to emphasize that the extent of its effects vary immensely across individuals and, moreover, that pronounced L1 attrition is not inevitable for all L2 minority children. Some dual language learners do grow up to be proficient in both the minority and the majority language. Nevertheless, the characteristics of L1 attrition are important for parents and professionals to be aware of so that minority children are not mistaken for having language learning difficulties or disorders because of restricted and errorful use of their L1.

Many researchers and practitioners working with young L2 children have noticed that some of these children can go through a transitional period when their L1 ability has declined considerably and rapidly, but their L2 ability is nowhere near complete or native-like. This transitional period has often been labeled **semilingualism.** Children in this transitional period are also referred to as "non-nons," or nonspeakers of either English or the home language. These terms are very controversial because they imply that the child is in a kind of linguistic vacuum from which there may be no escape, and that his or her situation might be analogous to impaired language development. We believe these terms should be avoided for many reasons. First, there is much doubt about how linguistically deficient children are in this transitional period. Children always have some level of proficiency in their L1 and L2 during this period, and recall that their L2 interlanguage is a language; it is systematic; it has a grammar; and it is a functional system for communication. Second, in our experience, the label of "semilingual" is often inappropriately applied to minority children whose L2 models in the home might cause concern because adults are using an incompletely mastered L2, and not their L1, with the children. In other words, the language models experienced by these children could be characterized as impoverished in some sense. However, this is a separate issue from semilingualism because monolingual children can also be exposed to impoverished linguistic models. It is important to keep in mind that these minority children will be exposed in school and through media sources to richer and academic varieties of the L2. A final flaw with the concept of semilingualism is that it is often linked to testing issues. Many minority language children are labeled semilinguals (or non-nons) because they have scored poorly on a test of language ability that was designed for monolingual native speakers of the test language who are familiar with test taking routines and the majority/mainstream culture and variety of that language. The test results in such circumstances are unreliable and invalid for a variety of cultural and linguistic reasons, as elaborated upon in Chapter 9. In sum, rapid transition from the L1 to the L2 such that L1 attrition is accelerated is observable in some children. But, there is no evidence that this phenomenon causes "semilingualism" and that these children have some kind of environmentally caused language impairment.

First Language Attrition: Causes and Prevention

Many immigrant families we have dealt with complain that their children refuse to speak the L1; they can understand it, but they answer back in the L2. This refusal can often turn into language loss over time, or may be the result of the process of loss already in progress. There are many, often interrelated, causes for L1 attrition or complete loss. Some of the causes of loss or attrition are within the control of families and the professional community to change. In this section, we discuss the causes of attrition and also suggest strategies to help minority children maintain their L1 past early childhood.

Small Minority L1 Community   In Chapter 1, we pointed out that the concept of a minority language is on a continuum. For example, although Spanish and Kurdish in the United States are both, technically speaking, minority languages, they are on opposite ends of this continuum. L1 minority children who are growing up in communities where their L1 is spoken outside the home by many other families and in many contexts, such as in stores, at religious services, and at cultural events, stand a greater chance of maintaining and developing their L1 because they can use it more frequently and in a variety of situations. Families who speak a minority language with what has been called low *ethnolinguistic vitality* (Hardwood, Giles, & Bourhis, 1994), should find as many opportunities as they can for their children to experience the L1 to promote maintenance and development of that language; this could include seeking out media such as books and DVDs in the language, identifying social or play groups with children who speak the language, and even travel to regions where the language is spoken widely. We have often heard from families who have traveled with their children to the home country for a holiday that the visit acted as a "tonic": It renewed the child's interest in the home language and culture, and their children began using the language much more once they returned. Our profiled L2 migrant children fall along this continuum of minority language status. Luis is growing up in a mainly ethnically Mexican, Spanish-speaking community in California, and it is likely that he will have many opportunities to use his L1 in day-to-day life outside his home. Likewise, Bonnie and her family are members of the very large and vibrant Chinese cultural community in Vancouver, and they also visit Taiwan on a regular basis. In contrast, the Somali community in Edmonton that Faisal and his family belong to is much smaller, and it is spread out in various neighborhoods. There are few, if any, written or other media available in this language. Also, for political and economic reasons, Faisal and his family cannot travel home to Somalia. Therefore, based on community factors, Faisal is probably more at risk for L1 attrition than the other two children.

Learning the L2 at a Young Age   In the earlier section on individual difference factors, we discussed the impact of age of acquisition on the short and long term outcomes of L2 learning. We now discuss how age of L2 acquisition should be a consideration when supporting the maintenance of a minority L1. Wong Fillmore (1991) and Montrul (2008) argue that early introduction of English, particularly in the preschool years, can precipitate L1 attrition and loss in minority children in the United States. They document cases where children effectively "give up" speaking their L1 once they have contact with the majority language. If this happens at a young age, the L1 is not acquired completely and, as a result, is even more prone to loss or attrition. This is not always the case, however. In fact, some American researchers found that preschool exposure to English did not have negative effects on L1 maintenance (Winsler, Díaz, Espinosa, & Rodriguez, 1999). The extent to which early introduction of the majority language jeopardizes L1 maintenance most likely depends on how subtractive the bilingual environment is, and on the other factors discussed in this section. Because delaying exposure to the majority L2 does not have a negative impact on L2 development, and because it might protect and support development of the L1 for some children, we often recommend not introducing minority language children to the majority L2 too early in their development.

Lack of Educational Opportunities in the L1   Education is a cornerstone of language learning in many societies because the vocabulary and grammar associated with academic and literacy activities are learned primarily in school. Education is similarly important for maintaining and further developing minority languages because it provides sustained and enriched input in languages that might otherwise not get such support outside school. The importance of education for dual language learning among minority language children is evidenced by the documented success of bilingual programs in the United States. In these programs, speakers of a minority language are initially schooled, at least in part, through their minority home language. Research, reviewed in Chapter 8, shows that minority language students in these programs acquire greater levels of competence in both oral and written forms of the home language than students in English-only programs. At the same time, they often achieve higher levels of proficiency in oral and written English than minority language students in English-only programs. In support of these studies on dual language learning during the elementary grades, Wong Fillmore (1991) reports results of a large-scale parent survey that found that minority children who participated in preschool programs exclusively in their L1 were more likely to maintain the L1 into the early elementary school years than children in English-only preschool programs. Thus, there is evidence that both preschool and school experiences in minority languages can support development and maintenance of those languages.

Not all children from minority ethnolinguistic communities will have access to regular schooling in the home language. Some minority communities establish weekend schools so that their children can learn and practice the home language and gain some literacy skills as well. One of the profiled children, Bonnie, attends such a weekend school. Minority language families should be encouraged to pursue educational opportunities for their children in the home language if they want their children to maintain their competence in the home language. There is no evidence that these experiences threaten their L2 development. On the contrary, the process of interdependence suggests that the two languages would build on each other, especially in domains related to literacy and academic language.

Desire for Assimilation and Integration   When minority language children arrive in English-only schools, they are confronted head on with the majority culture and language. Their home language and culture may not be represented at all, or very little, and they quickly come to realize that being accepted into the social fabric of the school and developing a sense of belonging depends on learning the majority language and assimilating to the majority culture (Wong Fillmore, 1991). This drive for assimilation can come at the price of feelings of inferiority for being a minority. In our view, minority children and their parents need to be encouraged to believe that dual cultural identity, like dual language knowledge, is a realistic and healthy possibility for minority children. But in order to do this, educational institutions need to demonstrate their openness to diversity and true intercultural exchange with newcomer and longstanding minority groups. Such openness may start with greater representation of diverse cultures and languages in the classroom décor, and then develop more deeply through curriculum changes based on parent and community engagement. Educators and the educational system have a pivotal role to play in helping minority children to balance their dual cultural identities and maintain their dual language competence.

Language Shift in the Home As the pressure from all these factors increasingly pushes minority language children to use the majority language, this could in turn influence language use among all family members in the home. Such a child-driven shift is taking place among all the siblings in Faisal's home. Also, parents themselves often try to speak as much of the majority language at home, in the belief that this will help their children learn the majority language faster. But the evidence indicates that if parents want their children to continue to speak the L1 as they grow older, they need to resist doing this; moreover, using the minority language at home will not necessarily detract from their children's development of the majority language. Hakuta and D'Andrea (1992) conducted a large-scale study of adolescents of Mexican descent in California. They gathered information through interviews about the adolescents' family backgrounds, their language use in various settings, and their attitudes about Spanish. The key finding from this study was that proficiency in Spanish was much more related to parental use of the language in the home than to the teenagers' attitudes about Spanish. Proficiency in Spanish was lowest among participants whose parents spoke English in the home. Also important, English language proficiency was high and relatively stable among the teenagers who had resided in the United States for about 8 years, regardless of how well they spoke Spanish. This study indicated that if parents want their children to maintain their abilities in their L1, they must use that language in the home as much as possible, and this practice does not take away from minority language children's chances at success in acquiring English.

KEY POINTS AND IMPLICATIONS

Key Point 1

Children acquire phonological and grammatical proficiency and build vocabularies in their L2 slowly; they do not "soak language up like a sponge." They may even go through a nonverbal period when they first come into contact with the new language. When they start speaking their L2, their first utterances are usually short and formulaic. L2 children may become good communicators with their peers and with adults within a few months of exposure to the L2, but this does not mean that their grammatical competence, the size and diversity of their vocabulary, and their pronunciation is in the range of their native-speaker peers. It usually takes L2 children 3–5 years to become similar to their native-speaker peers in oral language proficiency. Finally, some domains of the L2 develop faster than others. For example, L2 children might be very close to native speakers in their abilities to construct and sequence events to form a story, but at the same time distant from native speakers in terms of their accuracy with grammar in the same story.

Implications

If an L2 child seems reluctant to speak at all or responds to questions with one-word answers in a classroom or assessment context, it is important to determine how long he has had *consistent* exposure to the L2 before considering whether he might have language delay or disorder. By consistent exposure to the L2, we mean schooling or full-time preschool in the L2. If the child has had less than a year of exposure, it is possible that he is in the early stages of L2 acquisition, when this kind of behavior is typical. It may also be the case that the child's seemingly uncommunicative behavior is culturally determined; for example, in the child's culture, being talkative with adults is not encouraged. Another factor may be that the child has recently experienced some emotional trauma due to recent relocation, time spent in a refugee camp, or forced separation from one or both parents. These kinds of experiences can be sources of uncommunicative behavior in young L2 children.

Be careful using and interpreting results of standardized assessment instruments with L2 children. Even if the test does not probe oral language directly, these children's more limited oral language skills could influence the results of the test. Research has yet to tell us when exactly such tests would be appropriate for L2 children, but they are most likely not appropriate for L2 children within the first 3 years of exposure (see Chapter 9 for more discussion on this issue).

Given that English L2 children approach native-speaker abilities for some domains of language before others, when interpreting the results of formal or informal assessments of their performance, a general rule of thumb would be that the more a test or subtest is based on specific accumulated knowledge of the target language, the less likely children who are just beginning to acquire that language will perform as if they were native speakers. In contrast, for tests and subtests tapping into more cognitive–linguistic and perceptual–linguistic interface skills, such as narrative structure or word decoding, L2 children might perform closer to—but not necessarily the same as—native speakers.

Key Point 2

There is a great deal of individual variation among children with regard to how quickly they learn an L2. Length of exposure to the second language—for instance, grade in school—does not always clearly determine how advanced a child will be. Some children can carry on a conversation easily after one year of schooling in English, but others may be just beginning to speak the language productively after the same amount of time. Factors that might determine how quickly a child learns the L2 include personality/social style, language aptitude, age of acquisition, structure of the L1, and quantity and quality of L2 input and exposure.

Implications

The range of individual variation is another reason for exercising caution when interpreting results from standardized assessments for L2 children. Gathering information on a child's background, such as parental education and occupation, language use in the home and community, premigration experiences of the family and so on, could provide some insights that will help to set expectations for a child's developmental pace in English.

There are sources of individual differences that parents and professionals have the ability to influence, and sources that they do not. For example, most internal factors cannot be changed by professionals, yet external factors, such as language exposure factors, can be influenced in a positive direction. For example, educators could increase the richness of a child's L2 environment in the classroom and at home through materials that are appropriate for the child's needs and interests while at the same time challenging them to develop their vocabularies and grammatical skills further.

Key Point 3

The interlanguage of L2 children is characterized by phonological, lexical, and grammatical features that make it different from how the target language is used by native speakers. Some of these differences might appear as errors in the L2 caused by transfer of the sound system and grammatical rules from the L1. But most of the time, these differences, and errors, are developmental in nature; they are the same for all learners of that language, and in many cases, they parallel the developmental stages that young monolingual children go through when they learn that language as an L1. In learning English as a second language, one salient domain for errors is grammatical morphology. L2 children can take more than 3 years to accurately produce grammatical morphemes on a consistent basis. During this time, they may become more accurate with one morpheme before another, and they may alternate between accurate and inaccurate uses of the same morpheme. One of the reasons we highlight this aspect of L2 English is because errors with grammatical morphology are also characteristic of children with language disorders. We elaborate on this in Chapter 9.

Implications

Learning about the phonological and grammatical structure of a child's L1 could help teachers and speech-language pathologists identify features of the L2 that could benefit from practice and therapy. However, most of the errors that L2 children make are not traceable to the L1; thus, targets for practice or therapy built around common developmental errors could be particularly useful when working with L2 children from a variety of L1 backgrounds.

If an L2 child seems to vacillate between using correct and incorrect sounds and grammatical structures, one should realize that this behavior is a typical part of L2 acquisition and that it should not be considered to be a sign of language learning difficulties. Such back-and-forth behavior is expected in L2 learner language, even when a particular sound or grammatical structure is the focus of a lesson.

It is important for professionals to devise intervention strategies that fit with or complement the developmental stages of L2 learning. It is unlikely that children can be made to skip stages or double their learning pace in the L2 through intervention or instruction, however focused and intensive. Rather, classroom teachers and language specialists should assist an L2 child to move forward by providing intervention at the appropriate level—with some element of challenge—and introduce more advanced material in increments, taking note of the child's pace of learning.

Key Point 4

Shifts in dominance from the L1 to the L2 and L1 attrition and loss are all commonplace in the experience of minority language children. However, maintaining proficiency in the L1 is beneficial for both psychosocial and cognitive/educational reasons, in particular for L2 children in subtractive bilingual environments. Maintenance of the L1 is more difficult in circumstances such as when the L1 community is small, there are limited educational opportunities in the L1, children's desire to assimilate is very strong, or the entire family is shifting away from using the L1 at home.

Implications

The L1 abilities of children who have no schooling in the L1 and who grow up in an L2 majority language environment may be limited. This does not mean that they cannot speak the L1, only that they have a different range of abilities in the language, and that their abilities have been influenced by contact with the L2, by lack of educational experience in that language, and also, by features of L1 attrition. This is a natural outcome and should not be cause for concern about the child's language learning capacity. If parents are worried about how their child speaks the L1, that he sounds "funny" or does not speak it well, this may not be a sign of impairment, but instead a sign of L1 attrition.

Dual language children should be given full support, affective and linguistic, to learn both languages fully wherever possible. Continuous, consistent, and rich exposure to both languages is important for full dual language development and for children to reap the benefits of bilingualism in the long term. The child's dual language skills should be viewed positively and reinforced as much as possible. Those who work with or care for dual language children (e.g., teachers, child care workers) should be taught to view the child's dual language skills as a positive personal and social asset without detrimental consequences. It is important that they, in turn, support the child's language learning and nurture the child's self-esteem as a dual language learner. Advice to parents should be centered on the importance of using the L1 at home, and parents need to be informed as much as professionals about how continuing to learn and use the L1 does not take way from success in learning the L2.

Advising parents to use the L1 mainly or exclusively at home ought to be combined with discussion about how the L1 is currently used by household members with each other, the times of day and activities when and where they have contact with their children, and how they usually speak to, or read to, their children. Understanding these details and exploring language use possibilities with parents could make the advice about L1 use more effective and easier to implement. In our experience, many parents use the L1 mainly to direct children's behavior, rather than to converse with them. This can come about for cultural reasons (as discussed in Chapter 2), because parents might be too busy, or because parents themselves do not see the home language as having much value for their child, even if it is the only language parents speak well. Whatever the reason, if a child's only experience with the L1 is a few directive utterances a day, it is difficult to imagine how she will develop proficiency in that language. Parents might need to expand the frequency, topics, and occasions of L1 use so that children have a full and rich experience in that language. In situations in which cultural or other factors make it difficult for parents to converse often with their young children, it might be possible that rich L1 experiences can be obtained through sibling conversations and community-based activities. The main point here is that dialogue with parents is essential in order to make advice about how to use the home language meaningful.

REFERENCES

Anderson, R. (2004). First language loss in Spanish-speaking children: Patterns of loss and implications for clinical practice. In B. Goldstein (Ed.), *Bilingual language development and disorders in Spanish–English speakers* (pp. 187–212). Baltimore: Paul H. Brookes Publishing Co.

Castilla, A.P., Pérez-Leroux, A.T., & Restrepo, M.A. (2009). Individual differences and the developmental interdependence hypothesis. *International Journal of Bilingual Education and Bilingualism, 12*(1), 1–16.

Collier, V. (1987). Age and rate of acquisition of second language for academic purposes. *TESOL Quarterly, 21,* 617–641.

Collier, V. (1989). How long? A synthesis of research on academic achievement in a second language. *TESOL Quarterly, 23,* 509–531.

Cummins, J. (1979). Linguistic interdependence and the educational development of bilingual children. *Review of Educational Research, 49,* 221–251.

Cummins, J. (1991). Interdependence of first and second language proficiency in bilingual children. In E. Bialystok (Ed.), *Language processing in bilingual children* (pp. 70–89). New York: Cambridge University Press.

Cummins, J. (2000). *Language, power and pedagogy: Bilingual children in the crossfire.* Clevedon, England: Multilingual Matters.

Dörnyei, Z., & Skehan, P. (2003). Individual differences in second language learning. In C. Doughty & M. Long (Eds.), *The handbook of second language acquisition* (pp. 589–630). Oxford, England: Blackwell.

Dulay, H., & Burt, M. (1973). Should we teach children syntax? *Language Learning, 24,* 245–258.

Dulay, H., & Burt, M. (1974). Natural sequences in child second language acquisition. *Language Learning, 24,* 37–53.

Fabiano-Smith, L., & Goldstein, B. (2010). Phonological acquisition in bilingual Spanish–English speaking children. *Journal of Speech, Language, and Hearing Research, 53,* 160–178.

Fantini, A. (1985). *Language acquisition of a bilingual child: A sociolinguistic perspective.* San Diego: College-Hill Press.

Gathercole, S. (2006). Non-word repetition and word learning: The nature of the relationship. *Applied Psycholinguistics, 27,* 513–543.

Genesee, F., & Hamayan, E. (1980). Individual differences in second language learning. *Applied Psycholinguistics, 1,* 95–110.

Gilhool, A., Burrows, L., Goldstein, B., & Paradis, J. (2009). English phonological skills of English language learners. Poster presented at the annual meeting of the American Speech and Hearing Association, New Orleans.

Golberg, H., Paradis, J., & Crago, M. (2008). Lexical acquisition over time in minority L1 children learning English as a L2. *Applied Psycholinguistics, 29,* 1–25.

Goldstein, B. (2004). Phonological development and disorders. In B. Goldstein (Ed.), *Bilingual language development and disorders in Spanish–English speakers* (pp. 259–286). Baltimore: Paul H. Brookes Publishing Co.

Hakuta, K., & D'Andrea, D. (1992). Some properties of bilingual maintenance and loss in Mexican background high-school students. *Applied Linguistics, 13*(1), 72– 99.

Hakuta, K., Goto Butler, Y., & Witt, D. (2000). *How long does it take English learners to attain proficiency?* Policy report for the University of California Linguistic Minority Research Institute. Retrieved March 31, 2004, from http://www.stanford.edu/~hakuta/

Hardwood, J., Giles, H., & Bourhis, R. (1994). The genesis of vitality theory: historical patterns and discoursal dimensions. *International Journal of the Sociology of Language, 108,* 167–206.

Harley, B. (1992). Patterns of second language development in French immersion. *French Language Studies, 2,* 159–183.

Harley, B., & Hart, D. (1997). Language aptitude and second language proficiency in classroom learners of different starting ages. *Studies in Second Language Acquisition, 19,* 379–400.

Haznedar, B. (2001). The acquisition of the IP system in child L2 English. *Studies in Second Language Acquisition, 23,* 1–39.

Hoff, E. (2006). How social contexts support and shape language development. *Developmental Review* (doi:10.1016/j.dr.2005.11.002)

Hyltenstam, K., & Abrahamsson, N. (2003). Maturational constraints in SLA. In C. Doughty & M. Long (Eds.), *The handbook of second language acquisition* (pp. 540–558). Oxford, England: Blackwell.

Jia, G. (2003). The acquisition of the English plural morpheme by native Mandarin Chinese–speaking children. *Journal of Speech, Language, and Hearing Research, 46,* 1297–1311.

Jia, G., & Aaronson, D. (2003). A longitudinal study of Chinese children and adolescents learning English in the United States. *Applied Psycholinguistics, 24,* 131–161.

Jia, G., & Fuse, A. (2007). Acquisition of English grammatical morphology by native Mandarin-speaking children and adolescents: Age-related differences. *Journal of Speech, Language, and Hearing Research, 50,* 1280–1299.

Kohnert, K., & Bates, E. (2002). Balancing bilinguals, II: Lexical comprehension and cognitive processing in children learning Spanish and English. *Journal of Speech, Language, and Hearing Research, 45,* 347–359.

Kohnert, K., Bates, E., & Hernandez, A. (1999). Balancing bilinguals: Lexical-semantic production and cognitive processing in children learning Spanish and English. *Journal of Speech, Language, and Hearing Research, 42,* 1400–1413.

López, L., & Greenfield, D. (2004). The cross-language transfer of phonological skills of Hispanic head Start children. *Bilingual Research Journal, 28,* 1–18.

McLeod, S. (2007). *The international guide to speech acquisition.* Clifton Park, NY: Thomson Delmar Learning.

Mitchell, R., & Myles, F. (1998). *Second language learning theories.* London: Arnold.

Montrul, S. (2008). *Incomplete acquisition in bilingualism: Re-examining the age factor.* Amsterdam: John Benjamins.

Oller, K.D., & Eilers, R. (Eds.). (2002). *Language and literacy in bilingual children.* Clevendon, England: Multilingual Matters.

Oller, D.K., Pearson, B.Z., & Cobo-Lewis, A. (2007). Profile effects in early bilingual language literacy. *Applied Psycholinguistics, 28,* 191–230.

Paradis, J. (2005). Grammatical morphology in children learning English as a second language: Implications of similarities with specific language impairment. *Language, Speech and Hearing Services in the Schools, 36,* 172–187.

Paradis, J. (2007). Second language acquisition in childhood. In E. Hoff & M. Shatz (Eds.), *Handbook of language development* (pp. 387–405). Oxford, England: Blackwell.

Paradis, J. (2008). Tense as a clinical marker in English L2 acquisition with language delay/impairment. In E. Gavruseva & B. Haznedar (Eds.), *Current Trends in Child Second Language Acquisition: A Generative Perspective* (pp. 337–356). Amsterdam: John Benjamins.

Paradis, J. (2010). Sources of individual differences in English L2 children. Paper presented at the Annual German Linguistics Society Meeting (*DGfS*), Humboldt University, Berlin.

Paradis, J., Rice, M., Crago, M., & Marquis, J. (2008). The acquisition of tense in English: Distinguishing child L2 from L1 and SLI. *Applied Psycholinguistics, 29,* 1–34.

Paradis, J., & Schneider, P. (2008). Distinguishing bilingual children from monolinguals with SLI: Profile effects on the Edmonton narrative Norms Instrument. Poster presented at the *Symposium on Research in Child language Disorders.* University of Wisconsin, Madison.

Ranta, L. (2002). The role of learners' language analytic ability in the communicative classroom. In P. Robinson (Ed.), *Individual differences and instructed language learning* (pp. 159–181). Amsterdam: John Benjamins.

Riches, C., & Genesee, F. (2006). Literacy: Crosslinguistic and crossmodal issues. In F. Genesse, K. Lindholm-Leary, W. Saunders, & D. Christian (Eds.), *Educating English language learners: A synthesis of empirical evidence* (pp. 64–108). New York: Cambridge University Press.

Roessingh, H., & Elgie, S. (2009). Early language and literacy development among young English language learners: Preliminary insights from a longitudinal study. *TESL Canada Journal, 26,* 24–45.

Roessingh, H., Kover, P., & Watt, D. (2005). Developing cognitive academic language proficiency: the journey. *TESL Canada Journal, 23,* 1–27.

Saunders, W., & O'Brien, G. (2006). Oral Language. In F. Genesse, K. Lindholm-Leary, W. Saunders, & D. Christian (Eds.), *Educating English language learners: A synthesis of empirical evidence* (pp. 24–97). New York: Cambridge University Press.

Saville-Troike, M. (1987). Bilingual discourse: The negotiation of meaning without a common code. *Linguistics, 25,* 81–106.

Sawyer, M., & Ranta, L. (2002). Aptitude, individual differences, and instructional design. In P. Robinson (Ed.), *Cognition and second language instruction* (pp. 319–353). New York: Cambridge University Press.

Snow, C., & Hoefnagel-Höhle, M. (1977). Age differences in the pronunciation of foreign sounds. *Language and Speech, 20*(4), 357–365.

Sorenson Duncan, T., Tessier, A.M., & Paradis, J. (2009, June). Preferences for vowel epenthesis and child ESL cluster reduction. Poster presented at the Child Phonology Conference, University of Texas at Austin.

Strong, M. (1983). Social styles and the second language acquisition of Spanish-speaking kindergartners. *TESOL Quarterly, 17,* 241–258.

Tabors, P.O. (2008). *One child, two languages: A guide for preschool educators of children learning English as a second language* (2nd ed.). Baltimore: Paul H. Brookes Publishing Co.

Unsworth, S. (2005). *Child L2, adult L2, child L1: Differences and similarities. A study on the acquisition of direct object scrambling in Dutch.* Doctoral dissertation. Utrecht Institute of Linguistics, Utrecht, The Netherlands.

Verhoeven, L. (2007). Early bilingualism, language transfer, and phonological awareness. *Applied Psycholinguistics, 28,* 425–440.

Winsler, A., Díaz, R., Espinosa, L., & Rodríguez, J. (1999). When learning a second language does not mean losing the first: Bilingual language development in low-income, Spanish-speaking children attending bilingual preschool. *Child Development, 70,* 349–362.

Wong Fillmore, L. (1979). Individual differences in second language acquisition. In C. Fillmore, D. Kempler, & W.S.-Y. Wang (Eds.), *Individual differences in language ability and language behavior* (pp. 203–227). San Diego: Academic Press.

Wong Fillmore, L. (1983). The language learner as an individual: Implications of research on individual differences for the ESL teacher. In M. Clarke & J. Handscombe (Eds.), *On TESOL '82: Pacific perspectives on language learning and teaching* (pp. 157–173). Washington, DC: Teachers of English to Speakers of Other Languages.

Wong Fillmore, L. (1991). When learning a second language means losing the first. *Early Childhood Research Quarterly, 6,* 323–346.

Zdorenko, T., & Paradis, J. (2008). The acquisition of articles in child L2 English: Fluctuation, transfer, or both? *Second Language Research, 24,* 227–250.

Zdorenko, T., & Paradis, J. (2009). *The development of auxiliaries BE and DO in child L2 English.* Paper presented at International Symposium on Bilingualism 7, University of Utrecht, The Netherlands.

Zdorenko, T., & Paradis, J. (in press). Initial stages in child L2 English: Evidence for modular L1 influence in an interface phenomenon. *First Language.*

CHAPTER 7

Language Development in Internationally Adopted Children

In this chapter, we discuss the language development of internationally adopted children, or IA children. As we noted in Chapter 1, these are children who have been adopted by families that speak a language different from that spoken by the children prior to adoption; for example, children who were born and raised in China for 1 year but are adopted by English-speaking families in Canada or the United States. These children might be more appropriately called *cross-language adopted children* because not all internationally adopted children are necessarily raised speaking a new language, but we use the term that is most often used in the scientific literature. The number of international adoptees is substantial in some areas of the world. For example, more than 200,000 children were adopted in the United States from other countries over the last decade (U.S. Department of State, 2008, in Scott, 2009). These are unique second language learners because they discontinue learning their first, or birth, language once they are adopted and are exposed to the language of their adoptive families. They are of particular interest in this book because they are often thought to be at risk for problems with language development, a point we return to shortly.

One might well ask why the language development of these children is being considered in a book on dual language learning. It is an interesting question. We consider these children a special case of dual language learning, although most of them do not become bilingual. They are unique language learners because, in most cases, they discontinue acquisition of the birth language upon adoption. In fact, it has been claimed that IA children forget or lose any competence they have in their birth language shortly after adoption (De Geer, 1992; Nicoladis & Grabois, 2002) and there is some evidence that they retain no traces of the birth language over time, although the evidence on this point is limited and inconsistent (Hyltenstam, Bylund, Abrahamsson, & Park, 2009; Pallier et al., 2003). Thus, the language

146

development of these children is difficult to classify. Unlike simultaneous bilinguals who acquire two languages from birth, IA children acquire two languages successively, although acquisition of the birth language is discontinued. However, they cannot easily be considered second language learners in the usual sense of this term because the adoptive language is, arguably, acquired more like a first language—it is the only language they learn during the infant/toddler period in most cases. Their language learning has sometimes been referred to as "second first language acquisition" (De Geer, 1992; Glennen, 2002).

Scientifically speaking, it is difficult to know whether IA children's acquisition of the adoptive language is like that of first language learners, second language learners, or simultaneous bilinguals because there is currently incomplete information on the effect of discontinued learning of the birth language on acquisition of the adopted language. There are some aspects of language acquisition by IA children that look like first language acquisition (e.g., Glennen, Rosinsky-Grunhut, & Tracy, 2005; Snedeker, Geren, & Shafto, 2007), yet there are also indications that they do not acquire or use some aspects of the adopted language in the same way as native speakers (Gauthier, Genesee, & Kasparian, 2009); we discuss these studies in more detail later. How best to conceptualize IA children's language development—like that of first, second, or simultaneous bilingual language learners—is not only an interesting theoretical challenge but also an important practical one because it can help parents, educators, and clinicians formulate expectations about what can be expected of these children, which in turn can be useful for identifying problem areas and strategies for intervention.

We also consider IA children in depth in this book because these children are considered to be at risk for language development. There are a number of reasons for this. First, abrupt termination of acquisition of the birth language might put IA children at risk for acquisition of the adopted language. Whether, precisely how, and to what extent cessation of the birth language might affect acquisition of another language is not well understood at this time. There is growing evidence that the first months and year of life are significant for language learning, of either a first or another language, because of changes that occur in the brain during the first months of life as a result of exposure to language (Kuhl, Williams, Lacerda, Stevens, & Lindblom, 1992). Thus, the abrupt shift in language exposure that IA children experience upon adoption might undermine, or at least change, the normal neurocognitive systems that support language acquisition and might as a result put at risk, or alter, the patterns and outcomes of acquisition that IA children exhibit in the adopted language.

A more important and direct source of risk for the language development of IA children comes from the fact that many IA children are raised in orphanages prior to adoption, although some children in countries like China are sometimes raised in foster homes. Orphanages are complex, high-risk environments for young children (Zeanah, Smyke, & Dumitrescu, 2002). Children raised in orphanages are often deprived of consistent and durable interpersonal relationships, due to frequent changes in caregivers and low caregiver–child ratios (Gunnar, Bruce, & Grotevant, 2000), and they often experience a lack of general stimulation and impoverished language experiences (Johnson & Dole, 1999). According to Johnson and Dole, it is nearly impossible for children to not be negatively affected by their stay in an institution, although some of these effects may be short-lived after adoption. Fortunately, as we will discuss shortly, many of these fears are not realized. Suffice it to say here that the institutional care that many IA children experience before adoption is not optimal for language learning and raises concerns about their acquisition of their new language, as well as about their general adaptation to their new homes. The IA child profiled in Chapter 1, Kristina, spent time in an orphanage, and her physical and language development after adoption as described in Chapter 1 suggest the possibility of lingering effects of suboptimal experiences early in her life.

Finally, IA children might be at risk for acquisition of their adopted language because although many begin to learn the language within 2 or 3 years of life, they still experience a lag in exposure to the language in comparison with typical first language learners. This is a concern that implicates the critical period hypothesis. It is argued by many that competence in a second language is likely to be native-like in the long run only if it is acquired before a certain critical age, often thought to occur around puberty, or 12–15 years of age. In contrast, less than native-like competence is to be expected if acquisition of a second language begins after the critical period. This is a widely held view of second language learning. However, there are many controversies around the question of whether there is a critical period, or age, for language learning. Chief among these is how early in development such age effects might emerge. There is some evidence that acquisition of a second language even during the preschool years is not likely to result in truly native-like competence, if competence is examined in a detailed and rigorous way (Abrahamsson & Hyltenstam, 2009). In other words, the age at which it is necessary to begin learning a new language for native-like competence to result may be much earlier in development than previously thought. If this is true, then even IA children who are adopted between 1 and 2 years of age and begin to learn the adopted language within the first 2–3 years of life might not acquire complete native-like competence. This does not mean that their language development would be impaired, but it could mean that they might differ from native language learners in some respects. As we noted earlier, it is important to understand whether the differences in language competence that some children exhibit reflect impairment or simply differences in their language learning experiences.

As in the case of other dual language learners discussed in this book, it is important to have a solid scientific understanding of IA children's language development in order to establish appropriate expectations as to what is typical for such learners, to identify whether individual children are making appropriate progress, and to ascertain who needs additional support and what kind of support they need. In short, understanding these children's language development and the factors that influence it are critical for providing them with learning environments and supports that foster their language competence as much as possible. The remainder of the chapter is organized to address the following two general questions:

1. What do we know about IA children's language development during the preschool years?

2. Do adopted children experience language or academic difficulties in school?

WHAT DO WE KNOW ABOUT THE LANGUAGE DEVELOPMENT OF IA CHILDREN DURING THE PRESCHOOL YEARS?

In this section, we focus attention on the language outcomes of IA children during the preschool years. We know of no studies on IA children who were adopted at an age greater than 5 years. We discuss the language abilities of IA children who were older than 5 years of age at the time of testing, but these children were adopted prior to 5 years of age. Thus, when discussing school-age adoptees in the next section, we are considering the performance of preschool adopted children when they go to school. It is important to treat the findings for IA children who are younger than 5 years of age and those who are older than 5 years of age at the time of testing separately because the contexts for language learning are very different during the preschool and school years. Research on preschool IA children provides insights about their critical early language learning, immediately after adoption, and in the short to medium term after adoption. The focus is on acquiring the language. This is a period when IA children are adjusting to major changes in their personal, social, cultural, linguistic, and physical environments. Research on IA children when they are in school provides insights about how well the new language skills they acquired during the preschool years prepare them for the demands of schooling and, in particular, for using the language for higher-order cognitive purposes and in written as well as in oral forms. These are not issues that preschool adoptees face.

By far, the majority of published studies have examined children adopted into monolingual English-speaking families, usually in the United States (but see publications by Gauthier & Genesee, in press, for French; Hyltenstamm et al., 2009, and Hene, 1988, for Swedish; and Van IJzendoorn, Juffer, & Poelhuis, 2005, for Norwegian). Many studies on preschool age IA children have used data based on survey and parent report measures, such as The MacArthur Communicative Development Inventories (MCDI; Fenson et al., 1993) and the Language Development Survey (LDS; Rescorla, 1989). Parent reports and surveys are sometimes the best way to collect evidence about the language development of infants and toddlers, as more formal methods such as collecting and analyzing spontaneous language samples are difficult and are not useful when children are in the preverbal stage. Parent report instruments also permit researchers to collect information on language learners before they are verbalizing extensively from people who know their language well–their parents. They have the added advantage of allowing researchers to collect data on children who are geographically distributed and thus otherwise difficult to access. Typically, these instruments provide indicators of children's expressive and receptive vocabulary and their ability to comprehend and produce short phrases; they may also include ways of assessing children's mean length of utterance, or MLU (that is, the average number of words or morphemes children use in each utterance—see Chapter 4 for details about MLU), and indicators of nonverbal communication, such as the use of gestures. Children's performance on such instruments can be interpreted with reference to norms that the test developer provides; these are scores that indicate the levels of performance that are typical for native speakers and those that are characteristic of children who score above and those who score below typical levels of performance broken down by age. Often the norms take the form of percentile scores or age-equivalent scores.

We have organized the following discussion around four topics: 1) language outcomes in general; 2) factors that can influence language outcomes; 3) prevalence of risk for language difficulties in IA children; and 4) methodological considerations. These are followed by a brief summary.

Language Outcomes in General

Most preschool adoptees display remarkable progress in acquiring their new language. This is evident in both their progress immediately after adoption and their subsequent progress prior to starting school. For example, Sharon Glennen, who has been a very active researcher in this field of study, found that most of the IA children from Eastern Europe in her study could understand words and simple phrases and that many were producing some words only 2.5 months after adoption (Glennen, 2005, 2009). Snedeker and Geren (2005) report that after only 3 months exposure to their adopted language, adoptees from China had vocabularies like those of 24-month-old nonadopted children, as surveyed by the MCDI. Although most IA children display remarkable progress early after adoption, Glennen cautions that the results of very early assessments—those done within 2–3 months of adoption—are likely to fall in the low range because IA children have had insufficient exposure to their new language for much learning to take place. Thus, there is a lag before most IA children give evidence of learning their new language, much as there is for native speakers, but it is much shorter than that experienced by native speakers who typically produce their first words around 12 months of age; that is, after 12 months of exposure (Meacham, 2006).

Researchers who have studied adoptees' language acquisition in detail by examining their acquisition of specific types of words, such as nouns, verbs, and specific grammatical morphemes, such as regular plural *-s, cat-s,* and the regular past tense *-ed, walk-ed,* report that they demonstrate the same patterns of acquisition as nonadopted children (Glennen, Rosinsky-Grunhut, & Tracy, 2005; Snedeker & Geren, 2005). In the case of grammatical morphemes, however, Glennen and her colleagues note that the IA children from Russia in their study had not fully mastered the four morphemes they examined by 36–40 months of age; they examined the use of the progressive *-ing,* regular plural *-s,* regular past tense *-ed,* and possessive *-s.* The IA children were also not as accurate in their use of these morphemes as nonadopted children (see Chapter 6 for details on how L2 children acquire these grammatical morphemes). These results are important because they indicate that, despite early impoverished linguistic environments, loss of the birth language, and delayed exposure to the adopted language, IA children do not appear to lose their basic capacity to learn a new language. Indeed, generally speaking, IA children score within the normal range, and sometimes even above normal, on a variety of standardized measures of language before entering school at 5 years of age (Krakow & Roberts, 2003; Roberts et al., 2005; Tan & Yang, 2005; see Roberts & Scott, 2009, for a review; and Gauthier & Genesee, in press, for IA children learning French).

The impressive gains that most adopted children display in acquiring their new language after adoption can be attributed, in large part, to the supportive environments they experience in their new homes (Capron & Duyme, 1989). Adoptive families provide multiple protective influences that can offset the effects of impoverishment and adversity that adopted children might have experienced before adoption, and they can stimulate adopted children's development after adoption (Gauthier, Genesee, Dubois, & Kasparian, 2009; McGuinness, McGuinness, & Dyer, 2000). Adoptive parents are typically older and highly educated, are usually of relatively high socioeconomic status, and are often screened for and/or trained in parental duties. Recall that Kristina's parents both had postgraduate university degrees, and they made the decision to adopt when they were older than the average age for parents to have a first child because they tried for some time to have a child of their own but found out that they could not. Even domestic adoptees who do not undergo a change in language experience advantages from adoption. This is illustrated in an early study by Duyme (1988), who found that domestic adoptees who were adopted into families in a relatively high social class performed significantly better in school than children adopted into families of relatively lower social class. Socioeconomic status has been found to be a significant correlate of language development in nonadopted children (Hoff, 2006) and is another factor that probably contributes to the generally positive language outcomes that IA children display after adoption.

Factors that Can Influence Language Outcomes

Notwithstanding these findings, there is wide variation in language outcomes among IA children. Understanding the reasons for this variation can help parents, educators, and clinicians better understand the progress of individual IA children and, thereby, help them better determine if individual children are progressing as expected or are experiencing significant lags.

Age at Adoption   Age has repeatedly been found to be linked to language and other outcomes in IA children. More specifically, younger adoptees tend to display better language outcomes and, in particular, are more likely to achieve parity with nonadopted peers during the preschool years than older adoptees, and to do so sooner (Gauthier & Genesee, in press; Glennen & Masters, 2002; Krakow, Tao, & Roberts, 2005). In contrast, older adoptees tend to make faster initial progress in acquiring their new language, but they are slower and less likely to achieve parity with age norms prior to starting school (Glennen, 2009; Krakow et al., 2005; Meacham, 2006; Pollack, 2005). Pollack's results are instructive here. She found that IA children adopted after 24 months of age acquired 400 words in 6 months; children adopted between 13 and 24 months of age acquired only 200 words after one year; and children adopted between 7 and 12 months acquired only 50 words after one year. However, viewed in terms of chronological age, the younger adoptees were more likely to score within the typical range for their age group than the older adoptees, presumably because the older adoptees had more to learn and thus required more time to reach parity with their nonadopted peers of the same age. In a related vein, Glennen (2009) found that children adopted at 3–4 years of age made greater gains in vocabulary, assessed at 3, 9, and 14 months after adoption, than children adopted at 2 years of age who were assessed at the same intervals after adoption. Age of adoption has also been found to be related to school-related outcomes, as we will see in the next section. More details on the relationship between age of adoption and language development are given in Box 7.1.

IA children adopted before 24 months of age usually achieve parity with age norms, other things being equal (Gauthier & Genesee, in press; Glennen & Masters, 2002; Tan & Yang, 2005). However, IA children who experience severe deprivation in orphanages before adoption can experience language delays and/or long-term problems even when adoption occurs at a very young age. For example, Croft and colleagues found that IA children from Romania who were institutionalized for only 6 months before adoption displayed lags in language (and cognitive) development into the school years (Croft et al., 2007). In contrast, they found no discernible effects of institutionalization on the language (or cognitive) development of IA children from Romania if institutionalization did not extend beyond 6 months of age. As Croft and colleagues note, the children in their

---

BOX 7.1

Focus on Age at Adoption and Language Development

Glennen and Masters (2002) and Pollack (2005) examined the language outcomes of children longitudinally as a function of how old they were at adoption. To be specific, Pollack looked at subgroups of children from China who had been adopted between 7 and 12 months of age, 13 and 18 months of age, or older than 24 months of age. Each child's language development was surveyed, using the MCDI, every 3 months, starting when the children had been in their new homes, on average, for 6.2 months, until they were 3 years of age or had acquired 600 words. A similar design was used by Glennen and Masters to examine the language outcomes of children from Eastern Europe. The children were divided into subgroups based on the following ages of adoption: 0–12 months, 13–18 months, 19–24 months, and 25–30 months. Testing was then carried out every 3–6 months until the children were 36 months of age. The results from these two studies corroborate one another and provide useful elaborations on the general patterns of results discussed in this chapter so far:

- Younger adoptees tend to make slower initial progress in lexical development than older adoptees.

- Older adoptees tend to produce more words at initial assessment after adoption and at each subsequent testing than younger adoptees.

- Both younger and older adoptees display a vocabulary growth spurt, as do non-adopted children, with older adoptees experiencing it several months earlier after adoption than younger adoptees.

- Similar patterns are found for measures of MLU.

- Children who are younger at adoption are more likely than children who are older at adoption to achieve parity with age norms and/or to achieve higher levels of competence, at least within the age ranges they examined.

- Glennen and Masters found that the frequency of speech and language services required by children was positively correlated with their age at adoption.

---

study had experienced extreme deprivation; therefore, their results indicate that although most children are resilient in the face of institutionalization prior to adoption, institutional care that entails extreme deprivation can have lasting effects on adopted children (see also Meacham, 2006; Morison, Ames, & Chisholm, 1995). These findings are also instructive in highlighting the importance of examining the length and quality of institutional care experienced by IA children before adoption when trying to evaluate individual IA children's progress in acquiring the adopted language after adoption.

It is useful to consider why age at adoption is so important. First of all, IA children who are relatively young at the time of adoption arguably retain more developmental plasticity than older children, which permits them to adjust and thrive in their new homes, and more specifically, to overcome any adverse effects associated with their preadoption environments. Moreover, they will have experienced less deprivation than IA children who are older at the time of adoption. In contrast, children who are older at the time of adoption will have had extended experiences of a variety of types prior to adoption that could compromise their language as well as their general development. For example, older adoptees may have lived in dysfunctional or stressed families for longer periods of time; they may have lived for extended periods of time in institutions or foster families that provided minimal or impoverished social, cognitive, or linguistic stimulation, and/or inadequate health care and nutrition; and in the case of language development, their exposure to their new language will have been delayed longer. Individual children will have experienced varied amounts and forms of deprivation that could compound the impact of having lived in an orphanage.

Country of Origin   Another factor that distinguishes adopted children from one another and can influence their language outcomes is their country of origin. IA children from China and Eastern Europe, and especially Russia, have received the most research attention, although there is research on children from African countries, other countries in Eastern Europe, such as Romania, and children from other areas around the world, such as Korea and Colombia. We can illustrate how country of origin can make a difference in all aspects of development by examining adoptions from China. In 1981, China passed legislation making it illegal, with some exceptions, for families to have more than one child (Johnson, Banghan, & Liyao, 1998). Despite the law, many families give up first-born children who are not boys and second- and later-born children for adoption. Most adoptees from China are abandoned soon after birth and are subsequently raised in orphanages or foster families (Johnson et al., 1998). As a result, IA children from China often differ from IA children from other countries. Specifically, families from all social strata in China give children up for adoption, although wealthy families are less likely to do so because they are able to pay the fines associated with violations of the law. As well, children given up for adoption in China are generally less likely than adoptees in other countries to suffer from the effects of the following: parental alcoholism, drug abuse, and/or poor mental health; poverty; general neglect and abuse; and general familial dysfunctionality—all factors that can challenge families in other countries who give children up for adoption. Indeed, it is often because of these challenges that domestic and international families give their children up for adoption. As noted earlier, the more adoptees suffer such adversities and the longer they experience them, the poorer their physical and mental health is likely to be and the greater the risks they experience after adoption.

The point here is not to single out certain countries as exemplary donors, because individual children from any country can have experienced relatively favorable or unfavorable care prior to adoption. Rather, the point is that it is critical to examine the preadoption care that every adoptee receives and the circumstances surrounding a child's adoption, as much as possible, in order to better understand and plan for the child's postadoption development. As Croft and her colleagues point out, adoption per se is not a risk factor; it is the preadoptive care and health of individual children that puts adopted children at risk (Croft et al., 2007). Adopted children are remarkably resilient, and their long-term development can best be fostered after adoption by parents, educators, and speech and language specialists who are fully cognizant of each child's particular background.

Prevalence of Risk for Language Difficulties

We have reviewed research evidence indicating that, on average, IA children tend to score in the average range on a variety of standardized language tests and report measures. At the same time, there is yet other evidence that there is a subgroup of IA children who exhibit significant language delays or difficulties that is larger than what one finds in the general population of nonadopted children (Roberts, Pollock, & Krakow, 2005; Tan, Dedrick & Marfo, 2007). The prevalence of difficulty appears to be larger the older the children at adoption. For example, in their longitudinal study of children from Eastern Europe, Glennen and Masters (2002) found that 47% of the IA children who had been adopted before 12 months of age had had speech-language pathology assessments; 58% of the children who had been adopted between 13 and 18 months of age had had speech-language pathology assessments; and 73% of those who had been adopted between 19 and 24 months of age underwent clinical assessment. There was also an increase in the number of children who were recommended for treatment as age of adoption increased. These rates of referral for assessment and treatment are higher than one would expect based on similar statistics for nonadopted children. For example, a developmental language disorder like specific language impairment (SLI), which is not environmentally caused, affects about 7% of the general population (Leonard, 1998; Tomblin et al., 1997; see also Chapter 1). Referral for assessment and/or speech and language services could be an indication of language learning difficulty, or it could reflect adoptive parents' elevated level of concern about their children's progress in acquiring their new language. Recall that the parent of our profiled child, Kristina, took the initiative on their own to have her overall development assessed shortly after adoption. Thus, these elevated rates of referral, assessment, and treatment must be interpreted with caution as evidence for increased prevalence of developmental or acquired disorders in adopted children. However, even when objective direct testing of IA children's language outcomes are carried out, there is evidence of an unexpectedly high prevalence of low performance. For example, Glennen (2007) used the Communication and Symbolic Behavior Scales Developmental Profile™ (CSBS DP™; Wetherby & Prizant, 2002) and the MCDI to assess the language outcomes of 27 IA children who were between 11 and 23 months of age at the time of adoption; the children were from Eastern Europe. She found that 22% of the children were considered to be developing language slower than their peers at the time of the last assessment, when the children were, on average, 31 months of age.

Further evidence that a greater than expected percentage of IA children have important language learning problems comes from a study by Roberts, Pollock, and Krakow (2005). They examined the language development of the 10 lowest performing IA children from a larger cohort of 55 IA children. All the children were tested twice, at a 2-year interval. They were 5 years and 10 months old at the time of the second assessment and had had a total of 4½ years exposure to English, on average. The authors hypothesized that the 2 additional years between the first and second assessment would allow the low-performing children to catch up to the other IA children, who were scoring in the typical range. However, the low performers continued to score significantly lower than the comparison group, suggesting that time alone would not resolve their delays and that the low performers had an underlying language learning problem. Eighteen percent (i.e., 10 out of 55 children) is a higher rate of language impairment than is typically reported for SLI in nonadopted children (noted earlier). Therefore, the language learning problems in these children who were adopted likely included not only SLI as a source, but could have also included nonspecific language impairment (language impairment with mild cognitive deficits) and/or language impairment that is more properly characterized as acquired, rather than developmental or genetic, in origin.

Methodological Considerations

Interpreting the results of published research on IA children can be difficult for methodological reasons that we want to discuss briefly in this section. Generalizing findings based on group data in order to better understand the progress of individual IA children can be particularly problematic, owing to these methodological issues. Conducting research on IA children is difficult because IA children are widely different from one another and sampling is often based on convenience, not scientific principles of selection; that is, the researcher includes as many children as possible in the study in order to obtain a reasonable sample size. As a result, the children often vary with respect to a variety of important factors. For example, different studies may include adoptees from different countries, and the same study may include children from different countries, making it difficult to compare results from study to study because of differences between samples in the preadoption environments characteristic of different countries, as discussed previously. Similarly, individual studies may include a broad age range of children, both with respect to age at adoption and at testing, or different studies may have tested children of different ages or with different age ranges. As a result, one must be cautious in generalizing group results from specific studies to individual children.

Studies also often differ with respect to the methods of assessment they use. Many studies have used parent report methods, such as the MCDI or other parent report methods, as we indicated earlier. This has made it possible to collect data on a large number of children and to solicit participation from families in different regions of the country. However, these methods of data collection can be subject to biases or inaccuracies if parents do not understand precisely how to complete the report. Moreover, overestimations of difficulty and even impairment can creep into the assessments if parents are overly concerned about the development of their child; conversely, underestimations can result if parents are reluctant to identify potential problems that their children might be having. However, numerous studies have shown parent report measures like the MCDI to be reliable instruments, in general, by comparing the results of parent reports with direct measurement of children's abilities (see Paradis, Emmerzael, & Sorenson Duncan, in press, for a review). Other studies of adopted children have used direct assessments based on standardized tests to obtain objective indices of development; this is a useful way to reduce any biases that might be present in parent reports. Many studies interpret adoptees' performance on such tests with reference to test norms. However, test norms seldom take into account factors that favor language development, such as parental socioeconomic level, and that are disproportionately represented in adoptive in comparison with nonadoptive families at large. Some studies interpret their results relative to comparison groups who may or may not be matched to the adoptees on critical variables, such as gender, age, or socioeconomic status. When such controls are used, results can differ from what is reported when controls are not implemented (Cohen, Lojkasek, Zadeh, Pugliese, & Kiefer, 2008; Gauthier & Genesee, in press).

There may also be important cohort effects. That is, the outcomes of IA children from the same country might differ depending on when they were adopted. If countries modify their criteria for allowing children to be adopted by foreigners, then children with better or worse preadoptive environments may be included in specific studies, depending on when they were carried out. In our own research, for example, we found that one cohort of IA children from China whom we had been studying longitudinally exhibited problems with object pronouns in French, yet a later cohort of children of the same age did not. Although we are not certain how to explain this difference, cohort effects are one possibility. At present, there are no systematic data to know whether and to what extent cohort effects are occurring, however.

The results of many studies of IA children can also be difficult to interpret definitively because little information is provided about the children's preadoptive living environments. This is a virtually intractable problem because of the difficulty obtaining such information from donor countries. This can make it difficult to fully understand the progress of individual children. It is critical that parents, educators, and clinical professionals be aware of and consider these methodological issues when reading and interpreting research reports on adopted children, especially if they are using data from published reports as a reference point for assessing the development of an individual child.

In summary, IA children display remarkable resilience in their language development after adoption. The majority make very quick initial progress and catch up to age-norms during the preschool years. Children who are younger at the time of adoption are more likely to reach parity with age norms than children who are older at the time of adoption, but the latter are more likely to make faster initial progress. Factors that appear to affect language outcomes include: age at adoption, length of exposure to and nature of preadoption environment, and possibly cohort and country, although there are few direct comparisons between children from different countries or cohorts.

DO IA CHILDREN EXPERIENCE LANGUAGE OR ACADEMIC DIFFICULTIES IN SCHOOL?

There is a small, but growing, body of research on the language abilities, academic achievement, and behavioural adjustment of IA children during the school years (see Scott, 2009, for a review). Much of this research has compared IA children directly with nonadopted children in the host country (or the country of origin, in some cases; see Van IJzendoorn et al., 2005, for a review of this work). These studies have examined a variety of outcomes, in addition to language, including academic achievement, frequency of diagnoses of learning disabilities and behavioral problems, and the prevalence of speech/language and special education problems and services. In question here is whether the language competencies that IA children acquire during the preschool years are adequate for the demands of schooling when they are required to use language to learn complex, abstract subject matter and skills, for problem solving, and for literacy. Researchers in the educational field refer to such language skills as language for academic purposes or "academic language" (see Chapter 8 for an expanded discussion of this concept). Also in question is whether the linguistic environment of schooling will provide enrichment that will enhance the language competence of the minority of IA children who do not score within the range that is typical for their age group during the

---

BOX 7.2

Internationally Adopted Children in the School Years at a Glance

- IA children generally perform as well as, or better in some cases than, non-adopted comparison children on measures of cognitive ability, such as IQ (see Van IJzendoorn et al., 2005, for a review).

- IA children often perform academically as well as expected for their age group (Dalen & Rygvold, 2006) and even better in some cases (Lapointe et al., 2006).

- Many IA children compare favorably with their nonadopted peers on measures of everyday language (Dalen & Rygvold, 2006) and reading (Delcenserie & Genesee, 2010; see Scott, 2009, for a review).

- IA children are generally well adjusted and well integrated into their new families (see Juffer & Van IJzendoorn, 2005, for a review).

- IA children perform better than siblings or nonadopted peers who were left behind in the country of birth on measures of cognitive development and academic achievement, and they display fewer mental health problems (Van IJzendoorn et al., 2005) and are referred less often to mental health professionals than domestic adoptees (Juffer & Van IJzendoorn, 2005).

---

preschool years, permitting them to catch up to their nonadopted peers. Alternatively, the linguistic demands of school might challenge their language abilities further, resulting in continued or possibly even greater lags in their language abilities relative to nonadopted peers.

The resilience that IA children demonstrate during the preschool years continues to show itself during the school years. A summary of the general trends for developmental outcomes of IA children the school years is presented in Box 7.2.

Despite multiple signs of successful adaptation and development during the school years for most IA children (see Box 7.2), there is also evidence that there may be a significantly larger percentage of IA children who experience language and/or academic difficulties than is found in the general school-age population. For example, in a study of 6- to 9-year-old adoptees from Eastern Europe, Glennen and Bright (2005) found that, according to parent and teacher responses to a survey, 17.4% of these children were receiving accommodations in the classroom or were in special education programs, 27.3% had received speech-language pathology services in the previous year, 11.4% were currently diagnosed with a speech-language delay or disorder, and 11.4% had a learning disability. All the children had been adopted before 30 months of age. In another survey of IA children from Eastern Europe, Tirella, Chan, and Miller (2006) report similarly high indices of difficulty. More specifically, 36% of the 8- to 12-year-old adopted children in this study were reported to have learning disabilities and 38% had attentional problems. Moreover, 61% of the children were receiving special education services as part of an individualized education plan; this was a significantly higher participation rate than that of the general population, namely 9% in 2006–2007 (U.S. Department of Education, 2009). In a study of school-age adoptees from China, Scott, Roberts, and Krakow (2008) found that—despite the fact that, as a group, these children scored in the average range on a variety of oral and written language tests—more than half were receiving supplementary academic or special education services. These findings are instructive in highlighting how important it is to consider multiple indices of language ability or school performance when assessing the language and academic outcomes of IA children.

There is some evidence, admittedly indirect, that these relatively high prevalence rates of difficulty are differentially related to country of origin. Dalen (2001), for example, found that IA children from Korea who participated in his study were judged significantly more positively on a scale of academic performance than IA children from Colombia in the same study. In contrast to the relatively high rates of referral for clinical assessment and participation in individualized support programs for IA children from Eastern Europe in some studies, results for IA children from China appear to be relatively more favourable. For example, Dalen and Rygvold (2006) found no significant differences in teachers' ratings of the academic performance or language abilities (both everyday and academic) of a group of 77 IA children from China and native Norwegian-speaking students in Norway. However, they found considerably more individual variation among the adopted than among the nonadopted children. Lapointe, Gagnon-Oosterwal, Cossette, Pomerleau, and Malcuit (2006) found that the majority of adopted children from China in their study performed at an above-average level academically. Our profiled child, Kristina, was born in an Eastern European country, Russia, and made somewhat slow progress at first in producing English words. Although it is important not to uncritically generalize from group studies to an individual child, Kristina's country of origin, her physical characteristics at adoption (suggesting a suboptimal preadoption experience), as well as her relative slowness in developing English skills, all point to her being a child whose progress is worth monitoring carefully throughout the school years.

Although the incidence of referrals and special services for IA children reported in these studies is quite high, it is important to remember the methodological issues discussed in the previous section. To repeat, many studies include IA children with a wide range of ages at adoption and at assessment and there is therefore wide variation in the length and nature of the environments they experienced preadoptively. Depending on the composition of the children who make up the sample in a particular study, the results for IA children as a group could be skewed by a subgroup who have experienced prolonged and/or adverse preadoptive care. Similarly, the use of rating scales and report measures to assess academic achievement and to monitor rates of referrals for special education services, for example, is subject to bias. On the one hand, ratings could skew results toward the low end if respondents are concerned that IA children be given as much additional support as possible; on the other hand, ratings can be biased favorably if those doing the rating, such as teachers, have a positive stereotype of the learners being rated. Thus, it is important to interpret the magnitude of these results and differences with caution.

One way in which researchers analyze data from a number of studies that takes into account differences related to subject selection, assessment procedures, statistical methods, and so on, is called *meta-analysis*. Meta-analysis is a systematic statistical process for synthesizing and describing results from a large number of similar studies in order to assess the reliability and magnitude of the effects associated with some factor, such as adoption. In effect, a meta-analysis treats each study as a subject in a large multiple-study experiment. Van IJzendoorn and colleagues (2005) carried out such a meta-analysis on 62 studies involving 17,767 adopted children from diverse countries (except China); both domestically and internationally adopted children were included. The focus of this study was on the cognitive, academic, and linguistic outcomes of adopted children in comparison with those of nonadopted children. They found that adopted children, both domestic and international, had significantly higher IQs and better academic outcomes than children from similar backgrounds who remained in institutions or in their birth families. IA children did not differ from their nonadopted peers in their adoptive environments on IQ. However, the language skills and school performance of IA children were significantly poorer than those of their nonadopted peers in the adoptive environment, and they exhibited more learning problems. This pattern of results was evident for both domestic and international adoptees. Contrary to some common-sense expectations, Van IJzendoorn and colleagues found that gender was not a significant factor, so male and female adoptees displayed the same general patterns of development.

These results indicate that adoption has a positive impact on the cognitive development of adopted children. This is evident in the results of IA children on measures of cognitive and academic ability in comparison with that of peers and siblings who were left behind. However, Van IJzendoorn and colleagues' analyses also indicate that adoptees, both domestic and international, are often not able to catch up completely to nonadopted peers in their new environments with respect to language and academic outcomes. Although these differences were statistically significant, the effect sizes were small. Statistical significance is an estimate of the reliability of a finding; that is, how consistently it is found from study to study. Effect size is an indicator of the magnitude of the differences calculated across all studies in the analysis, taking into account methodological variation among the studies. A statistically significant difference that yields a small effect size is a reliable but small difference. This is important because it reinforces our previous comments that results from individual studies, although empirically reliable, do not necessarily provide empirically accurate estimates of the magnitude of differences between IA and other children. When appropriate statistical procedures are used to systematically examine the size of the differences between IA and nonadopted children in different studies, it turns out, as Van IJzendoorn and colleagues show, that the differences are rather small. At the same time, even a small effect size indicates that IA children deserve attention as they begin and progress through school.

In summary, IA children continue to exhibit developmental resilience during the school years. More specifically, most IA children perform as well as, or better in some cases than, nonadopted children on measures of general intelligence or cognitive ability, general language ability, and behavioral adjustment. At the same time, they may not perform as well as nonadopted peers on measures of academic achievement or academic language, and there is a larger than expected prevalence of children who appear to experience academic and language-related difficulties. Although reports of difficulty are fairly common in a number of studies, a meta-analysis indicates that the magnitude of the differences between IA and nonadopted children is small, albeit statistically significant. Because of large and important methodological differences among individual studies, the results of specific studies must be generalized with caution. Most importantly, the performance of individual IA children should be interpreted with respect to the results of specific studies only with extreme caution since group or average results reported in specific studies mask extensive variation among the children who make up study samples.

KEY POINTS AND IMPLICATIONS

Key Point 1

IA children exhibit remarkable developmental resilience during the preschool and school years. Most IA children make early and impressive progress acquiring their new language during the preschool years, and many achieve parity with age-appropriate expectations before starting school. In school, most IA children perform as well as, or better than, children of the same age on tests of general cognitive ability and they outperform siblings who remained in their birth families or children who were left in institutions. Studies of IA children's behavioral adjustment indicate that they are generally very well adjusted and are well integrated into their new families and communities.

Implications

Adoption is not a risk factor for poor language, academic, or socioemotional development. In fact, most adoptive families provide adopted children with enriched and highly supportive environments that permit them to adapt well to their new lives and, in many cases, to recover from any adverse experiences that they may have had prior to adoption.

Key Point 2

Despite evidence of generally positive and age-appropriate outcomes for most IA children in most domains, there is wide individual variation among IA children in their developmental outcomes, including language. Moreover, there appears to be a relatively high prevalence of language and academic difficulty among IA children in comparison with what is typically found among nonadopted children in general. At present, there is insufficient research to indicate if there are particular areas of linguistic or academic difficulty that IA children experience since most research to date has relied on assessments that are broad in scope. The apparent difficulties in language development exhibited by some preschool IA children do not get resolved in many cases with more exposure to the target language and with the enrichment that comes with schooling (Delcenserie & Genesee, 2010). Studies on IA children also vary considerably with respect to a number of important methodological issues, and methodological factors may be contributing to the individual variation in adoptees' developmental outcomes.

Implications

The language and academic progress of IA children should be monitored carefully for signs of difficulty, with a view to providing additional support if and where necessary, especially during the school years. Great caution should be exercised when using results from specific published studies as benchmarks for assessing the progress of individual children. This is particularly true for studies that do not differentiate among IA children with respect to age of adoption, country of origin, and age at testing.

Key Point 3

Although research on factors that influence the language and academic achievement of IA children is still growing, it is evident that a number of factors are related to IA children's short- and long-term development after adoption; these include age at adoption, length and quality of institutionalized care prior to adoption, and general health and mental well-being at adoption. Children who are relatively old at the time of adoption; those who have had extended institutionalized care, and especially adverse or impoverished care, preadoption; and adoptees whose health and mental health have been compromised prior to adoption are at greater risk of delayed and even below-normal development in the long term than children with more favorable preadoption experiences.

Implications

Parents and health care professionals should collect as much information about the pre-adoption care and rearing environments of adopted children as possible so that they are able to provide postadoption environments and professional attention that will optimize IA children's overall development after adoption.

Key Point 4

The language development of IA children exhibits significant continuity from shortly after adoption to several years after adoption and into the school years. IA children's knowledge of their birth language, time taken to produce first words in the adopted language, and early indices of acquisition of the adopted language (Gauthier & Genesee, in press) all correlate significantly with later language abilities, even into the school years. At the same time, IA children's language abilities in the adopted language are likely to fall at the low end in comparison with test norms and/or the performance of same-age peers if they are assessed shortly after adoption.

Implications

Signs of knowledge of the birth language at adoption, signs of acquisition of the adopted language relatively soon after adoption, and signs of relatively fast progress in acquiring the adopted language augur well for later development. In contrast, children who do not exhibit these signs warrant ongoing attention in order to gauge their need for additional language support. Clinically speaking, attempts to assess IA children's language skills within the first months of adoption should be undertaken with the understanding that they are in the very beginning stages of acquisition and, therefore, will score in the low range in comparison with age-matched norms or peers. More discussion on assessment and diagnosis of IA children is presented in Chapter 9.

REFERENCES

Abrahamsson, N., & Hyltenstam, K. (2009). Age of acquisition and native-likeness in a second language: Listener perception vs. linguistic scrutiny. *Language Learning, 59*(2), 249–306.
Capron, C., & Duyme, M. (1989, August 17). Assessment of effects of socio-economic status on IQ in a full cross-fostering study. *Nature, 340,* 552–554.
Cohen, N.J., Lojkasek, M., Zadeh, Z.Y., Pugliese, M., & Kiefer, H. (2008). Children adopted from China: A prospective study of their growth and development. *The Journal of Child Psychology and Psychiatry, 49,* 458–468.
Croft, C., Beckett, C., Rutter, M., Castle, J., Colvert, E., Groothues, C., et al. (2007). Early adolescent outcomes of institutionally-deprived and non-deprived adoptees: Language as a protective factor and a vulnerable outcome. *Journal of Child Psychology and Psychiatry, 48,* 31–44.

Dalen, M. (2001). School performances among internationally adopted children in Norway. *Adoption Quarterly, 5,* 39–58.

Dalen, M., & Rygvold, A.-L. (2006). Educational achievement in adopted children from China. *Adoption Quarterly, 9,* 45–58.

De Geer, B. (1992). *Internationally adopted children in communication: A developmental study.* (Working Papers, No. 39). Lund, Sweden: Department of Linguistics.

Delcenserie, A., & Genesee, F. (2010). *Language abilities of internationally adopted children from China during the early school years.* Unpublished manuscript, Psychology Department, McGill University, Montreal, Quebec, Canada.

Duyme, M. (1988). School success and social class: An adoption study. *Developmental Psychology, 24,* 203–209.

Fenson, L., Dale, P., Reznick, J., Thal, D., Bates, E., Hartung, J., et al. (1993). *The MacArthur Communicative Development Inventories: User's guide and technical manual.* San Diego: Singular.

Gauthier, K., Genesee, F., & Kasparian, K. (2009). *Acquisition of complement clitics and tense morphology in internationally adopted children acquiring French.* Unpublished manuscript, Department of Psychology, McGill University, Montreal, Quebec, Canada.

Gauthier, K., & Genesee, F. (in press). Language development in internationally adopted children: A special case of early second language learning. *Child Development.*

Gauthier, K., Genesee, F., Dubois, M.E., & Kasparian, K. (2009). *Communication patterns between internationally adopted children and their mothers: Implications for language development.* Unpublished manuscript, Department of Psychology, McGill University, Montreal, Quebec, Canada.

Glennen, S.L. (2002). Language development and delay in internationally adopted infants and toddlers. *Journal of Speech-Language Pathology, 11,* 333–339.

Glennen, S.L. (2005). New arrivals: Speech and language assessment for internationally adopted infants and toddlers within the first months home. *Seminars in Speech and Language, 26*(1), 10–21.

Glennen, S.L. (2007). Predicting language outcomes for internationally adopted children. *Journal of Speech, Language, and Hearing Research, 50,* 529–548.

Glennen, S.L. (2009, January/March). Speech and language guidelines for children adopted from abroad at older ages. *Topics in Language Disorders, 29*(1), 50–64.

Glennen, S.L., & Bright, B.J. (2005). Five years later: Language in school-age internationally adopted children. *Seminars in Speech and Language, 26*(1), 86–101.

Glennen, S., & Masters, G. (2002). Typical and atypical language development in infants and toddlers adopted from Eastern Europe. *American Journal of Speech-Language Pathology, 11,* 417–433.

Glennen, S., Rosinsky-Grunhut, A., & Tracy, R. (2005). Linguistic interference between L1 and L2 in internationally adopted children. *Seminars in Speech and Language, 26*(1), 64–75.

Gunnar, M.R., Bruce, J., & Grotevant, H.D. (2000). International adoption of internationally reared children: Research and policy. *Development and Psychopathology, 12,* 677–693.

Hene, B. (1988). Language development of inter-country adoptees. Presentation of a Swedish research project. *SPRINS Report No 39.* Department of Linguistics, University of Göteborg, Sweden.

Hoff, E. (2006). How social contexts support and shape language development. *Developmental Review, 26,* 55–88.

Hyltenstam, K., Bylund, E., Abrahamsson, N., & Park, H.S. (2009). Dominant-language replacement: The case of international adoptees. *Bilingualism: Language and Cognition, 12,* 121–140.

Johnson, D., & Dole, K. (1999). International adoptions: Implications for early intervention. *Infants and Young Children, 11,* 34–45.

Johnson, K., Banghan, H., & Liyao, W. (1998). Infant abandonment and adoption in China. *Population and Development Review, 24,* 469–510.

Juffer, F., & Van IJzendoorn, M.H. (2005). Behavior problems and mental health referrals of international adoptees, *Journal of the American Medical Association, 293*(20), 2501–2515.

Krakow, R.A., & Roberts, J.A. (2003). Acquisition of English vocabulary by young Chinese adoptees. *Journal of Multilingual Communication Disorders, 1,* 169–176.

Krakow, R.A., Tao, S., & Roberts, J. (2005, February). Adoption age effects on English language acquisition: Infants and toddlers from China. *Seminars in Speech and Language, 26*(1), 33–43.

Kuhl, P.K., Williams, K.A., Lacerda, F., Stevens, K.N., & Lindblom, B. (1992). Linguistic experience alters phonetic perception in infants by 6 months of age. *Science, 255,* 606–608.

Lapointe, M.-N., Gagnon-Oosterwal, N., Cossette, L., Pomerleau, A., & Malcuit, G. (2006, May). *Développement cognitif d'enfants adoptés en Russie, en Chine, et dans d'autres pays d'Asie depuis leur arrivée dans leur famille québécoise jusqu'en début de scolarisation.* Poster session presented at the 74th Congrès de l'Association canadienne-française pour l'avancement des sciences (ACFAS), Montreal, Quebec, Canada.

Leonard, L.B. (1998). *Children with specific language impairment.* Cambridge MA: The MIT Press.

McGuinness, T., McGuinness, J., & Dyer, J. (2000). Risk and protective factors in children adopted from the former Soviet Union. *Journal of Pediatric Health Care, 14*(3), 109–116.

Meacham, A.N. (2006). Language learning and the internationally adopted child. *Early Childhood Education Journal, 34,* 73–79.

Morison, S.J., Ames, E.W., & Chisholm, K. (1995). The development of children adopted from Romanian orphanages. *Merrill-Palmer Quarterly, 41*(4), 411–430.

Nicoladis, E., & Grabois, H. (2002). Learning English and losing Chinese: A case study of child adopted from China. *The International Journal of Bilingualism, 6,* 441–454.

Pallier, C., Dehaene, S., Poline, J.-B., LeBihan, D., Argenti, A.-M., Dupoux, E. et al. (2003). Brain imaging of language plasticity in adopted adults: Can a second language replace the first? *Cerebral Cortex, 13,* 155–161.

Paradis, J., Emmerzael, K., & Sorenson Duncan, T. (in press). Assessment of English language learners: Using parent report on first language development. *Journal of Communication Disorders.*

Pollock, K.E. (2005). Early language growth in children adopted from China: Preliminary normative data. *Seminars in Speech and Language, 26*(1), 22–32.

Rescorla, L. (1989). The Language Development Survey: A screening tool for delayed language in toddlers. *Journal of Speech and Hearing Disorders, 54,* 587–599.

Roberts, J.A., Pollock, K.E., & Krakow, R.A. (2005). Continued catch-up and language delay in children adopted from China. *Seminars in Speech and Language, 26*(1), 76–85.

Roberts, J.A., Pollock, K.E., Krakow, R.A., Price, J., Fulmer, K.C., & Wang, P.P. (2005). Language development in preschool-age children adopted from China. *Journal of Speech, Language and Hearing Research, 48,* 93–107.

Roberts, J.A., & Scott, K.A. (2009, January/March). Interpreting assessment data of internationally adopted children: Clinical application of research evidence. *Topics in Language Disorders, 29*(1), 82–99.

Scott, K.A. (2009, January/March). Language outcomes of school-aged internationally adopted children: A systematic review of the literature. *Topics in Language Disorders, 29*(1), 65–81.

Scott, K.A., Roberts, J.A., & Krakow, R. (2008). Oral and written language development of children adoption from China. *American Journal of Speech-Language Pathology, 17,* 150–160.

Snedeker, J., & Geren, J. (2005). International adoption as a natural experiment in language acquisition. *Proceedings of 27th Annual Conference of the Cognitive Science Society (July 21–23)* (pp. 2038–2043). Mahwah, NJ: Lawrence Erlbaum Associates.

Snedeker, J., Geren, J., & Shafto, C. (2007). Starting over: International adoption as a natural experiment in language development. *Association for Psychological Science, 18,* 78–87.

Tan, T.X., Dedrick, R.F., & Marfo, K. (2007). Factor structure and clinical implications of child behaviour checklist/1.5–5 ratings in a sample of girls adopted from China. *Journal of Pediatric Psychology, 32,* 807–818.

Tan, T.X., & Yang, Y. (2005). Language development of Chinese adoptees 18–35 months old. *Early Childhood Research Quarterly, 20,* 57–68.

Tirella, L.G., Chan, W., & Miller, L.C. (2006, Summer). Educational outcomes of children adopted from Eastern Europe, now ages 8–12. *Journal of Research in Childhood Education, 20*(4), 245–254.

Tomblin, J.B., Records, N.L., Buckwalter, P., Zhang, X., Smith, E., & O'Brien, M. (1997). The prevalence of specific language impairment in kindergarten children. *Journal of Speech, Language, and Hearing Research, 40,* 1245–1260.

U.S. Department of Education. (2009). National Center for Education Statistics. *Indicator 9 (2009) children and youth with disabilities.* Available at http://nces.ed.gov/programs/coe/2009/section1/indicator09.asp

Van IJzendoorn, M.H., Juffer, F., & Klein Poelhuis, C.W. (2005). Adoption and cognitive development: A meta-analytic comparison of adopted and nonadopted children's IQ and school performances. *Psychological Bulletin, 131,* 301–316.

Weatherby, A.M., & Prizant, B.M. (2002). *Communication and Symbolic Behavior Scales Developmental Profile*^{TM} *(CSBS DP*^{TM}*).* Baltimore: Paul H. Brookes Publishing Co.

Zeanah, C., Smyke, A.T., & Dumitrescu, A. (2002). Attachment disturbances in young children, II: Indiscriminate behavior and institutional care. *Journal of the American Academy of Child and Adolescent Psychiatry, 41,* 983–989.

CHAPTER 8

Schooling in a Second Language

This chapter discusses children who are educated in part or entirely through the medium of a second language (L2). These children are linguistically diverse. For example, many immigrant children begin to learn English when they start school in Canada, the United States, Australia, and other countries where English is the majority language. In many regions of the world, there are school children who grow up speaking a language other than the majority language of the community in which they have been born and raised—for example, the child profiled in Chapter 1, Luis, who is growing up speaking primarily Spanish in California, but whose schooling is in English. Another profiled child, Pauloosie, is living in a region where the primary ethnolinguistic community is an indigenous group, the Inuit, and where Inuktitut is the dominant language. However, English and French are the majority languages of the province and country, and thus he is learning French as an L2 through his schooling. For children like Luis and Pauloosie, even though they were born in a country where their language is technically a minority language, their first significant experiences with the majority group language and culture are often when they begin school. Other children profiled in Chapter 1, like Faisal and Bonnie, were born in non–English-speaking countries, but migrated to English-speaking regions of Canada with their families, and thus are being educated in their L2. The children of expatriate parents—that is, those who work in foreign countries—often attend schools where the national language is used, like Trevor, and thus they are also being educated in their L2. We have categorized Trevor as a majority L1/majority L2 learner because of the temporary nature of his residence in Germany, and because of the international importance of English.

Children from minority language backgrounds are not the only ones who are educated in their L2. An increasing number of children speak the majority group language, such as English in Canada and the United States, but in their communities attend schools where a substantial proportion of their school subjects are taught through the medium of a second or foreign language; Samantha from Tucson, Arizona, is an example of such a child. These programs are often referred to as *immersion programs*, after the St. Lambert French immersion program that was established in Quebec in 1965 (Lambert & Tucker, 1972), but are sometimes also referred to as *dual language programs*.

We refer to children who come to school speaking a language other than the one spoken by the majority of the larger community in which they live as **minority language students**. We refer to children who speak the dominant language of the society in which they live, but who may or may not attend school in another language, as **majority language students**. As noted in Chapter 3, children who speak a minority language are likely to experience subtractive bilingual learning environments unless special care is taken to support continued development of their native language, whereas children who speak a majority group language usually experience additive bilingual learning environments. This chapter focuses on children from each language background—minority and majority—and their language and academic development in school. We first consider minority language students and then turn to research on majority language students in immersion programs. We exclude from our discussion majority language students whose only exposure to a second or foreign language in school is limited to conventional foreign or L2 instruction. These children are excluded because their L2 learning experience is very limited and does not raise serious concerns among parents, educators, or clinicians. We discuss the literacy outcomes, primarily reading, of minority and majority language students in L2 school programs, but we do not discuss the processes involved in learning to read in an L2, nor do we discuss what research has to say about students who face difficulty learning to read in an L2. These issues are discussed in Chapter 10, along with a discussion of issues related to identifying and providing intervention for L2 readers who experience reading difficulties.

MINORITY LANGUAGE STUDENTS

As already noted, in many regions of the world, children learn a language at home that differs from that which is used for instructional and social communication in school. When they begin school, they must learn the majority group language in order to fit in socially and to succeed academically. Although we highlighted the situation in industrialized countries in our introduction, such children can be found in countries in virtually all corners of the world, regardless of their economic and political status. Migration resulting from voluntary movement of people for social or economic reasons or from involuntary movement due to war, political oppression, or economic plight is common and, as a result, there are large numbers of minority language students being schooled in their second language. These diverse patterns of migration also mean that children can begin schooling in another language at any age, ranging from typical school entry (around 5 years of age) all the way to the secondary school level.

Most such children are educated exclusively through the language dominant in the society, with little attention paid to their native language. In some regions of the world, most notably the United States, some minority language children have the possibility of being educated partially through the native language along with the majority language of the dominant society. These are often referred to as *bilingual programs* or **bilingual education**. There are alternative forms of bilingual education, which we describe shortly.

In this chapter, we examine a number of issues concerning the language and academic development of minority language students who participate in bilingual programs, as well as those in programs in which only the L2 is used. We treat each form of education (i.e., L2 only and bilingual) on par with one another because there are minority language students in each type of program. At the same time, and for developmental and educational reasons, we support bilingual forms of education for all children where resources are available and parental support is strong. It is important that parents, educators, clinicians, and other professionals be familiar with evidence concerning these students' development in school so that they can make appropriate decisions about their education and, in the case of children who might be experiencing difficulties, about additional supportive services.

Some people have argued against bilingual education for minority language students on the grounds that education in part or in total through their native language delays or even retards their acquisition of the majority language (e.g., Porter, 1990; Rossell & Baker, 1996). In fact, there is no evidence for these claims. Systematic reviews of evaluations of bilingual programs for minority language students in the United States have found that minority language students tend to perform as well as, and often better than, similar students in programs in which only English is used for instructional purposes (e.g., August & Shanahan, 2006; Goldenberg, 2008; Lindholm-Leary & Borsato, 2006). We review evidence about the effectiveness of bilingual education for minority language students in more detail later in this chapter. To argue for educational programs that result in loss of any child's native language is wasteful, squandering a language resource that these children bring to school. It is also disrespectful of these children's cultural skills and backgrounds, in some cases to their educational detriment. The purpose of the following discussion is not to engage in this debate, but rather to consider the educational outcomes, especially with respect to language and reading development, and the implications of each form of education for minority language students who are at risk or experience language or learning impairments.

Minority Language Students in Second Language–Only School Programs

Educating minority language students through the medium of the majority language is by far the most common form of education for minority language students, even in the United States, where some forms of bilingual education are offered (Goldenberg, 2008; see Genesee, 1999, for a summary of bilingual forms of education for minority language students). Programs in which only the L2 is used are sometimes referred to as **submersion** or **sink-or-swim programs** on the grounds that they do not take into account the students' special language learning needs and their particular cultural backgrounds. We use the more neutral term *L2-only programs*, also known as **second language–only programs**.

In this chapter, we consider the development of both oral and written language skills. We do not provide evidence for the effectiveness of L2-only programs for minority language students because there is wide variation in how effective L2-only education is;

some minority language students do well in L2-only programs, but many do not (e.g., see Genesee & Lindholm-Leary, in press; and Goldenberg, 2008, for data on the achievement of English language learners in the United States). It is difficult to ascertain with precision how successful minority language students in L2-only programs are because we are aware of no statistics that disaggregate minority language students who know the majority language from those who do not. We do know, however, that in many—if not most—industrialized countries, immigrant and other ethnic minority students are generally overrepresented in the underachieving categories and in special education classes. This would imply that, notwithstanding some successes, minority language students face a higher than average risk of failure or difficulty in L2-only programs. Students in L2-only programs face multiple challenges: They must acquire a new language; they must integrate socially and culturally into a new peer group; and they must learn new academic skills and knowledge.

There are a number of factors to consider when examining the performance of minority language students in L2-only programs in order to ascertain the causes of their difficulty and, in particular, whether the difficulty is linked specifically to language and whether it is of clinical significance. The factors we discuss are related to the nature of language proficiency, culture, prior language and literacy experiences, and family background.

The Nature of Language Proficiency for Academic Success

An important concept in understanding student performance in school is *academic language*, first proposed by Jim Cummins (1984) in his distinction between "basic interpersonal communicative skills" and "cognitive academic language proficiency." It is widely believed that successful performance in school requires proficiency in language for academic purposes. A number of definitions of academic language have been proposed (e.g., Bailey & Butler, 2007; Scarcella, 2003; Short & Fitzsimmons, 2007). A succinct definition that we like is that of Chamot and O'Malley (1987), who define academic language simply as "the language that is used by teachers and students for the purposes of acquiring new knowledge and skills . . . imparting new information, describing abstract ideas, and developing students' conceptual understanding" (p. 40). To expand on Chamot and O'Malley's definition, academic language refers to the specialized vocabulary, grammar, discourse/textual, and functional skills associated with academic instruction and mastery of academic material and tasks. Box 8.1 includes an example[1] of academic language use between a teacher (T) and a student (S) during a lesson on using graphs to represent change in the manufacturing industry in California.

Note in this example that there is technical vocabulary (e.g., *manufactured, line graph, trace, related rise*), sentences that include complex clausal constructions (e.g., "*What might happen if there were not products to manufacture*"), and the use of explicit reference to what is being talked about (e.g., ". . . *the graph would then indicate a decline. The line would go down . . .*"). Note also that students must have specific background knowledge without which the language used in this interchange would be even more challenging. In addition, academic language can be oral or written, even though this example is oral.

---

[1]We would like to thank Jana Echevarria, California State University, Long Beach, California, for providing us with this example.

BOX 8.1

Example of Academic Language

T: *Many things are manufactured in California, from airplanes to computer chips. Suppose you wanted to find out how many people worked in manufacturing jobs in California for the last 25 years. A line graph could help you. Look at the line graph on page 51 and trace the line to see changes over time. Why would the line be expected to move up over time?*

S: *More jobs.*

T: *That's right. Because manufacturing had increased over time, the line indicates the related rise in the number of jobs. What happened around 1990?*

S: *It stays the same.*

T: *Yes, the job market stabilized so there was only a slight increase—hardly discernable—in the line. What might happen if there were not products to manufacture?*

S: *People lose their jobs.*

S: *Some would move away.*

T: *That's right, and the graph would then indicate a decline. The line would go down in that case.*

The specific academic language that is characteristic of one school subject, such as science, can differ from that associated with another subject, such as mathematics, with respect to the specific grammatical forms and discourse patterns that are typically used when talking or writing about these subjects. For example, whereas science might call for grammatical skills that allow students to formulate hypotheses using subjective verb forms and to express relationships in probabilistic terms (e.g., *if the boats were heavier, then they would probably sink*), or to express causal relationships (e.g., *humidity is a function of both temperature and proximity to large bodies of water*), mathematics might call on these grammatical forms and discourse functions much less often. There is undoubtedly some overlap in the academic language associated with different academic domains; therefore, it is usually a matter of what grammatical forms or discourse patterns are relatively frequent in each academic domain.

Definitions of academic language often contrast with language used in everyday social situations. Cummins (1984), for example, characterized academic language as decontextualized and cognitively demanding, and social language as contextualized and cognitively undemanding. Although it is useful to contrast social and academic uses of language, it is important to guard against thinking that they are entirely distinct from one another and, moreover, that there is something inherent in social language that makes it less sophisticated or less cognitively demanding than language used in academic contexts. For example, inflectional morphology on verbs, such as the past tense, appear in English regardless of whether it is for social or academic purposes; as discussed in Chapter 6, L2 learners can take a long time to acquire such morphology (see also Paradis,

2007). It is differences in the overall prevalence of different kinds of linguistic constructions, vocabulary, and discourse patterns in and outside school that distinguish academic and social communication.

It is thought, and there is some evidence to support the claim, that day-to-day conversational skills can be acquired more quickly than academic language skills. This makes sense when one considers that L2 learners usually have greater exposure to social uses of language—from peers and adults inside and outside school, whereas their exposure to academic language is usually limited to school and their teachers. But it is important to not equate conversational language with oral language in general—academic language is both oral and written, as mentioned earlier. Nevertheless, it is still the case that children gain competence in academic language use primarily, and often only, through schooling. As students progress from the lower to higher grades, they are required to use language in more and more abstract and complex ways as the subject matter of teaching and learning becomes more abstract and complex. Acquisition of native-like academic language skills in the L2 is additionally challenging because minority language students face a moving target. As their academic language skills develop, so too do those of majority language students. Because majority language students have a head start in the language, minority language students must, in fact, acquire academic language skills at a faster rate than majority language students if they are to catch up to their native-speaking peers. It has been estimated, based on research on student performance in school settings, that minority language students can take 5–7 years to achieve proficiency in English for academic purposes that is on par with that of native speakers (Cummins, 2000; Lindholm-Leary & Borsato, 2006; Thomas & Collier, 2002). An important caveat is called for here. The fact that minority language students may require some time to master language for academic purposes does not mean that they cannot or should not be taught age-appropriate, challenging academic content. Linguistic modifications are called for to make such content comprehensible (see, e.g., Echevarria, Vogt, & Short, 2000). Moreover, the best way to teach academic language skills is to teach them in meaningful academic contexts.

The distinction between language for academic and social communication is useful in understanding the school performance of minority language students. When minority language students begin schooling in an L2, they often have some conversational skills in the language of schooling because these skills can be acquired from their peers, older siblings, television, and on the street. In contrast, they are much less likely to have acquired English for academic purposes, especially if they begin schooling in the L2 beyond the primary grades. As a result, these students often experience a significant gap in their ability to communicate effectively in English in social contexts in contrast to academic contexts.

Educators, special educational professionals, and speech and language specialists need to be sensitive to the possibility that minority language students may be unresponsive or even inept in the classroom—not because they have a learning disability or language impairment, but simply because they have not yet acquired sufficient proficiency in the L2 for academic purposes to interact actively and appropriately. Teachers and other professionals working with minority language students who fail to understand this distinction might be prone to interpret the child's behavior in class or during testing situations as signs of a learning disability, on the grounds that the child appears to know the language in social situations and, therefore, his behavior in class must be due to more general learning or behavioral problems. Many standardized tests of oral language development designed for children in the middle and upper elementary grades focus heavily on academic language. As a result, typically developing minority language students who have incomplete mastery of English academic language could perform like students who have language and learning disabilities on such tests. Indeed, minority language students are often overrepresented in special education classes, arguably because their incomplete acquisition of the language of instruction has been misinterpreted as a learning problem (Genesee & Lindholm-Leary, in press).

The challenge of acquiring academic language is not only about students being able to follow lectures in class or about their engagement in classroom discussions; it is also about learning to read in the language of instruction. A growing body of research, to be discussed in Chapter 10, indicates that acquisition of efficient and effective skills for comprehending written text is related to students' mastery of complex syntactic and semantic aspects of language. This makes sense when you think that academic texts that students read in the higher grades contain complex and sophisticated language; difficulty processing that language can interfere with students' understanding of what they are reading. In short, when trying to understand why minority language students may be having difficulty learning to read written text, especially in the higher grades, it is important to consider that it may be because they also have to acquire the oral language skills that support reading comprehension; they probably are not reading impaired.

Cultural Factors   Cultural factors should also be considered when trying to understand individual minority language children's patterns of L2 use, especially if learning difficulties or language impairment are suspected. As we discussed in Chapter 2, different cultures have different sets of expectations concerning appropriate patterns of language use and social interaction on the part of children and adolescents (see Roseberry-McKibbin, 2002, for descriptions of some of the differences that distinguish various cultures). In our discussion, we refer primarily to English as the majority or societal language and **Anglo-Western culture** as the dominant culture, because we are most familiar with this language and culture and because we assume our readers are familiar with English and share some knowledge of the cultures that underlie English-speaking communities.

In Chapter 2, we noted that most English-dominant and European cultures treat children as legitimate and important conversational partners and expect them to actively engage in, initiate, and maintain conversation with adults. Such cultures also expect school children to show off what they have learned in school by responding actively and verbally to teachers' probes and encouragements. Eye contact between students and teachers is considered appropriate and is taken as a sign that the student is attending to the teacher and is engaged in learning. Boys and girls are generally held to the same general expectations and work and learn together. Not all cultures share these norms and expectations. In some cultures, students are not regarded as appropriate conversational partners for adults, and as a result, children are expected to be seen and not heard and to show deference to adults during verbal encounters by averting their gaze. In such cultures, students are not expected, or appreciated, when they initiate verbal exchanges or actively assert themselves verbally. Students in such cultures often learn primarily by watching others, and they demonstrate what they have learned in groups or discreetly on their own. Students from certain cultures may be uncomfortable in mixed-gender groups in school. It is important to emphasize here that these are characterizations of cultural differences and members of different cultures; not all individuals who belong to the same cultural group share these norms and expectations, so we must be careful not to overgeneralize.

Children who speak a minority language bring the socialization patterns that they have learned at home to school. As a result of differences in the cultures of the home and school, some children avoid initiating talk with their teachers or other adults; they are uncomfortable or even unwilling to give an individual response to a direct question or request from their teachers; they avoid eye contact or physical proximity with adult inter-locutors; and they may be uncomfortable and even resist working in groups with students of the other sex. Such cultural norms can influence learners' social interactions with others long after they have acquired competence in the language of schooling because these norms constitute part of their personal identity. Children who speak a minority language from cultures with language socialization patterns that differ from Anglo-Western cultures could give the impression that they have language delays or impairments or that they have learning disabilities because they do not respond actively, the way teachers from the Anglo-Western cultures expect.

An example of this comes from research in Inuit schools. When a speech-language pathologist asked for a list of children who the southern Canadian non-Inuit teachers thought had speech-language problems, she was presented with a list of the names of one third of the children in the school. Next to each name was written *Does not talk in class.* Because the number of children listed far exceeded the typical incidence rate for speech-language problems in the childhood population, the speech-language patholo-gist asked for help from a local Inuk special education teacher. This experienced Inuk educator looked at the list and said with a discouraged tone, "These Qallunaat (non-Inuit) teachers never seem to learn that well-raised Inuit children should not talk in class. They should be learning by looking and listening" (Crago, 1988, p. 212). In instances in which there is no cultural expert to interpret such information for Anglo-Western educators and clinicians, this kind of misunderstanding could place minority children at a severe educational disadvantage.

Cultural effects can influence children's language use in yet other ways—through the sheer nature of the experiences children have when growing up. For example, children from cultural minority groups may not have had the same experiences with doctors, dentists, or other professionals as children from the mainstream culture. Their experiences with food, music, toys, and religious customs are often different as well. As a result, they may find it difficult to engage in classroom discussions or activities that involve experi-ences that are foreign or novel to them. This may, in turn, dampen their language use because they are simply unfamiliar with the subject of the activity. When planning les-sons, teachers should be sensitive to the fact that not all their students share the same life experiences outside school. Including themes and activities in lesson plans based on the cultural backgrounds of minority students might encourage their participation.

Teachers, educational specialists, and clinicians working with minority language stu-dents from different cultural backgrounds must consider the role of cultural factors in their language use and development when seeking to identify children suspected of hav-ing specific language impairment, reading difficulties, or learning disabilities of a more general nature. In particular, they must take care to avoid misattributing culturally condi-tioned patterns of language use to underlying impairments of a linguistic or general learning nature. It can be a real challenge for teachers and educational specialists who are monolingual and monocultural, and even for those with diverse cultural experiences, to know all of the cultures of the minority language children they are dealing with when students come from diverse cultural backgrounds. When educators and speech-language professionals encounter a child from a culture with which they are unfamiliar, they should seek input from members of that culture or from other professionals who have had more experience with the culture in question. At the same time, professionals must work to help minority language students expand their cultural repertoires to include the norms of the majority group. After all, their successful integration into the broader community will depend on their becoming bicultural as well as bilingual.

Family Background Factors   The performance of L2 learners in school, including their language use, can also be influenced by a host of factors that are linked to family background. Here we talk about the importance of the socioeconomic status of families; in the next section, we talk about their use of language in the home. Research has shown that performance in school, as indicated by grades and other formal indicators of progress, is correlated with socioeconomic status (SES). For example, in a review of research on the literacy development of English language learners in the United States, Genesee and Riches (2006) found that SES was correlated with performance on a variety of literacy measures, so students from low-SES backgrounds scored significantly lower than students from higher SES backgrounds (see Chapter 6 for discussion of SES and oral language development). SES, however, is not a causal factor in and of itself, but is associated with a variety of other factors that can mediate the effects of low SES, such as preschool literacy experiences, amount and kind of language used in the home, and health and nutrition. Research indicates that many family-related variables are especially important for literacy development in school, a point we return to in the next section. Students from relatively advantaged SES backgrounds enjoy the benefits of these influences more than students from less advantaged homes. We know that minority language students are overrepresented in low-SES categories, and thus minority language students may experience less rapid progress or even retarded progress in language and literacy development in school because of the influence of such SES-related factors. Research indicates further that the effects of low SES on school performance are particularly likely for minority language children who live in communities and attend schools that are populated by large numbers of families and children from low-SES backgrounds (Goldenberg, 2003).

These kinds of factors should be considered when assessing the source of individual minority language students' difficulty with language, reading, and learning in school. The effects of these factors on school performance should not be mistaken as evidence for impairment or disability. It is also important not to overgeneralize these general patterns to individual children and assume that all students who speak a minority language lack the benefits of these influences even if they come from low-SES families. The general patterns that have emerged from research on students from low-SES backgrounds are just general patterns and do not necessarily pertain to every minority language student.

Prior Literacy and Language Experiences   It is important when trying to understand the school performance of individual minority language students to also look at the language and literacy practices of the families and communities in which individual children live. There is growing consensus in the research community that language and especially literacy-related experiences in the home and community before starting school can play an important role in laying the foundations for the acquisition of academic language and literacy skills in school (Neuman & Dickinson, 2003). In particular, learning to read and write in school is easier for young school children who have had prior experiences with reading and writing at home. Many of the preschool experiences that facilitate children's literacy development in school do not involve direct experiences with actual reading and writing, but rather indirect experiences, such as being read to, having their own books and engaging in pretend reading, engaging in rhyming games or other activities that expose them to the alphabetic principle, and even conversations with parents or other caregivers that stretch their vocabulary skills and expand their use of language to explain themselves or to relate events in a coherent, logical manner. It makes sense that certain kinds of early oral language skills facilitate later literacy development, as reading and writing are written forms of oral language.

As well, and of particular importance for dual language learning, there is a growing body of evidence that many of the foundational skills that underlie learning to read and write are transferable from one language to another, especially in the early stages of learning to read and write (August & Shanahan, 2006; Erdos, Genesee, Savage, & Haigh, in press; Genesee, Lindholm-Leary, Saunders, & Christian, 2006). To be more specific, it has been shown that knowledge of the names and sounds of the alphabet and certain kinds of phonological awareness skills are critical for word decoding, which in turn is important for later reading comprehension. Children who acquire these skills and these kinds of knowledge before coming to school learn to read and write more easily in school than children who do not. In addition, children who have acquired these skills at home in the native language can apply those skills to learning to read and write in a second language. Transfer of these skills is greater when the two languages are typologically similar and share similarities with respect to grapheme-to-sound patterns and grammar (like English and Spanish or French) and less so when they are different (like English and Chinese), but there is transfer even when languages differ a great deal. Indeed, there is lots of evidence of positive correlations between students' scores on tests of phonological awareness and knowledge of the alphabetic principle in their home language before or at school entry and their later word decoding and reading comprehension skills in a second language in school (August & Shanahan, 2006; Erdos et al., in press; Genesee et al., 2006) and between bilingual students' reading scores in one language with their reading scores in the other language.

In sum, when examining the performance of minority language students in L2-only or bilingual programs, especially their acquisition of early reading and writing skills, it is important to consider what kinds of early literacy-related language experiences they have had in the home and in the home language. Difficulties in acquiring initial literacy skills in school, no matter what the program, could reflect long-term risk for reading and writing development, or it could simply reflect the extent to which a child has or has not had the benefits of preschool language experiences that support formal literacy instruction (see Cloud, Genesee, & Hamayan, 2009).

Let us consider how these factors might affect the school achievement of our profiled L2 children from minority backgrounds: Pauloosia, Faisal, Luis, and Bonnie.

Considering the information on language socialization of Inuit families discussed in Chapter 2, it is possible that Paulooise did not experience the kinds of literacy-enhancing language patterns discussed in this chapter at home before starting school. As well, he may be unfamiliar and uncomfortable with the patterns of individual language use expected in an Anglo-Western classroom. Pauloosie's transition from home to school was facilitated by having instruction from kindergarten to second grade in the Inuktitut language using culturally specific teaching methods. However, in third grade, he is making the transition to a different language and classroom culture. Regarding SES and home language use, Faisal might also be at a disadvantage. His parents are newcomers who work long hours at low-paying jobs. This can have an impact on every facet of his life, from the quality and availability of food to the amount of parent–child interactions in the home. It is also important to mention how traumatic premigration experiences could affect the mental health of family members and, in turn, parent–child interactions. Whatever the language socialization patterns typical of Somali culture may be, pre- and postmigration experiences might disrupt those patterns within Faisal's family. Although born in the United States, Luis, like Faisal, also comes from a low-SES family, with a culture that is distinct from the mainstream. In contrast, there appears to be few factors in Bonnie's case that might negatively impact her school outcomes. She comes from a high-SES family, and her parents engaged in literacy-based activities with her even before she started school.

Minority Language Students in Bilingual Programs

We focus our discussion of minority language students who are educated in bilingual programs on programs in the United States because bilingual programs for minority language students have been well documented there. There has been a strong civil rights influence on the development of educational alternatives for students from such backgrounds in the United States. Providing students who speak a minority language with access to education through their native language has been a major outcome of this initiative. In bilingual programs, the students' native language, along with the majority language (English, in the case of the United States), is used for instructional purposes.

There are alternative models of bilingual education. The main ones are **transitional bilingual, developmental bilingual,** and **two-way bilingual/immersion** (see Genesee, 1999, for detailed descriptions of these programs). In developmental bilingual and two-way bilingual programs, academic and literacy instruction are provided through both the students' native language and English, starting in kindergarten. The portion of the school day that is taught through English and the native language differs in different program models, the most common patterns being 90% first language (L1) and 10% English, or 50% L1 and 50% English. These are referred to as the *90/10* and *50/50* models, respectively. Use of both languages for instruction is continued throughout the elementary grades and, ideally, during secondary school as well.

Developmental bilingual programs differ from two-way immersion programs in that all of the students in the former are minority language students, whereas half of the students in two-way programs are members of the majority language group. Two-way programs aim to promote bilingualism among both minority and majority language students, and they seek to do this by using each group's language for academic instruction to teach a portion of the curriculum. Developmental and two-way bilingual models are considered additive forms of bilingual education because they both aim to maintain students' native languages at the same time as they promote competence in the other language. These two forms of bilingual education see minority language students' native languages as important personal assets and resources and as an essential foundation on which to build their competence in the L2 and in academic domains. Two-way programs see bilingualism as an asset for all students, including majority language students.

Transitional programs are the most limited form of bilingual education, but have been the most prevalent in the United States. All students in transitional bilingual programs are from minority language backgrounds. The typical transitional program provides initial instruction in literacy and some academic subjects, like mathematics, through the students' native language, along with instruction in English oral language development; nonacademic subjects, such as music and physical education, are often taught through English. The most common minority language used in transitional bilingual programs is Spanish, followed by Vietnamese, Hmong, Cantonese, and Korean (Kindler, 2000). As students acquire proficiency in English, there is a shift toward greater use of English to teach academic subjects and a commensurate decrease in the use of the students' native language. The shift is often completed by third grade, at which point the native language ceases to be used at all. Transitional bilingual programs are considered subtractive forms of bilingual education insofar as the students' native language is used only until they can make a transition to L2-only instruction. Consequently, the goal of this program is not bilingual proficiency but proficiency in English only. Socioculturally, transitional programs can convey to students the impression that their native language is not useful or viable in the long run, but is a crutch to be used until they learn sufficient English to be schooled exclusively through English. In fact, participation in such programs often results in loss of the native language, especially with respect to reading and writing, as English assumes a stronger role in their daily lives. The simultaneous bilingual child profiled in Chapter 1, Gabriela, is in a transitional program, even though she already spoke English when she started school. Her parents may have chosen this program because they wanted some Spanish instruction at school, even if limited. Minority language students are often viewed by school administrators, and even teachers, as a homogenous group, when in fact they vary in terms of their proficiency in the majority language.

A number of important questions arise concerning the language development of minority language students in bilingual programs that are relevant to our concerns in this book. We address the following: 1) Does schooling in bilingual programs enhance or retard students' acquisition of the majority language? and 2) What is the relationship between amount of exposure to the minority language in school and acquisition of that language? An ancillary question is: Which program models are most effective in building bilingual proficiency? The answers to these questions are important because they provide valuable information that can be used to distinguish atypical from typical patterns of school achievement and language development.

Does Schooling in Bilingual Programs Enhance or Retard Students' Acquisition of the Majority Language?

We address this question with respect to both minority language and majority language student outcomes; we begin with the former. Diametrically opposite arguments have been made for and against bilingual education for minority language students, particularly concerning their effectiveness in promoting the acquisition of the majority language. On the one hand, critics of bilingual education in the United States (e.g., Baker & de Kanter, 1981; Porter, 1990; Rossell & Baker, 1996) have argued that use of minority language students' native language for significant portions of their schooling detracts from their acquisition of English because it reduces their exposure to English. This is what is referred to as the ***time-on-task argument***. On the other hand, others have argued that the language capacity of children is not limited to the acquisition of one language (e.g., Lindholm-Leary & Borsato, 2006) and, moreover, that development of the native language in the case of minority language students is a useful scaffold for developing competency, especially literacy, in the L2 (Cummins, 2000; Riches & Genesee, 2006). According to these latter points of view, additive forms of bilingual education should either enhance or have no detrimental effect on the development of the L2 of minority language students. What does the research evidence say about these possibilities?

Two patterns of results have emerged from evaluations of bilingual education. In some cases, there is evidence of an advantage to minority language students in developmental and two-way bilingual programs over students in **English-only programs** or transitional bilingual programs (see, for example, Lindholm, 2001; Lindholm-Leary & Borsato, 2006; Ramirez, Yuen, & Ramey, 1991; Thomas & Collier, 2002). In particular, minority language students in developmental bilingual alternatives—especially those that continue to use the native language for instruction throughout the elementary school years—demonstrate higher levels of proficiency in English in comparison with students in nonbilingual or transitional bilingual programs. In other cases, there has been no evident advantage or disadvantage for minority language students in developmental and two-way bilingual programs. In these cases, minority language students have been shown to perform at the same level as minority language students in English-only programs or on par with district- or state-level standardized achievement test results (see Lindholm-Leary & Borsato, 2006, for a review of these studies).

A related question concerning bilingual education often arises: What is the relationship between amount of instruction in or exposure to the majority language in school and level of proficiency attained in that language? It is widely believed that there is a correlation between students' exposure to language in school and their acquired competence in that language. Clearly, in the extreme, such a relationship is bound to occur. Students with very little exposure and those with a great deal of exposure are likely to differ, obviously, to the advantage of the latter. However, research does not support this expectation within the language allocations of current models of bilingual education. To be more specific, minority language students with more exposure to English in school (such as those in 50/50 bilingual programs) show an initial advantage in English over students with less exposure to English (those in 90/10 programs), but this advantage is marginal and short lived. By the end of third grade, minority language students in 50/50 two-way bilingual programs no longer show this advantage, despite their considerably greater exposure to English in the beginning, in comparison with 90/10 students.

This pattern is also evident when comparisons are made between minority language students in English-only programs and those in developmental bilingual and two-way immersion programs. The former often show an initial advantage in English, but there is usually no difference or a difference in favor of bilingual program participants by the later elementary or middle school grades (Lindholm-Leary & Borsato, 2006; Oller & Eilers,

2002). These findings mirror a pattern that has been reported for majority language students in L2 immersion programs, to be discussed in the next section. One of the profiled children, Luis, is in an English-only program, and it is possible that his parents believe that an English-only program is the best choice because they want him to get as much English as he can; that is, the time-on-task argument. However, research evidence indicates otherwise; Luis might acquire English just as well in the long run and, in addition, have the benefit of acquiring more oral language and literacy skills in Spanish, if he were in a bilingual program.

These results for bilingual programs can be explained, at least in part, by students' exposure to the majority language outside school. The extended exposure that students have to English in an English-dominant community offsets differences in exposure between groups of students in different programs in school. Reduced exposure to English in bilingual programs is also offset by transfer of L1 skills to English. Transfer is most evident in the development of literacy; the more developed minority language students' skills in L1 literacy, the faster they acquire literacy skills in English, their L2. In effect, the reduced exposure that minority language students have to English in bilingual programs is offset by the reduced time they need to acquire literacy in school due to transfer. Enhancement of L1 literacy skills is more likely in developmental and two-way bilingual programs than in transitional and English-only programs and the longer students stay in bilingual programs. Indeed, in their review of bilingual education in the United States, Lindholm-Leary and Borsato (2006) found that minority language students in developmental and two-way programs and in extended bilingual programs were more likely to close the achievement gap with majority language students than minority language students in L2-only (i.e., English only) programs. Moreover, contrary to the time-on-task hypothesis, there is evidence that minority language students with greater exposure to the home language in school outperform minority language students in English-only programs (Lindholm-Leary & Borsato, 2006). Myers (2009) found that English language learners (ELLs) classified as having a learning disability who were participating in a two-way Spanish-English program performed as well as similarly labeled ELL students with learning disabilities in English-only programs on a variety of standardized language and non-language tests administered in English. In short, despite their learning disabilities, the ELLs in the bilingual program were performing as well as similar students in monolingual English programs on a number of important tests of academic and language achievement.

These results do not indicate that minority language students in additive bilingual programs always achieve the same level of competence in English literacy as native speakers of English. In fact, they frequently do not, but often these residual differences can be traced to other factors, such as the quality of the program itself. For example, Lindholm-Leary and Borsato (2006) found that minority language students who had consistent exposure to coherent bilingual programs demonstrated higher levels of language and academic achievement than students whose program of instruction varied from year to year. As well, minority language students, as a whole, generally have lower SES backgrounds than majority language students, as a whole, and we know that students from low SES backgrounds, whether they are minority language or majority language, generally do worse on tests of literacy and academic achievement than students from advantaged SES backgrounds.

What about the English language development of majority language (i.e., English speaking) students in bilingual programs—students like Samantha? There are two forms of bilingual education for majority language English-speaking students: 1) two-way immersion in the United States, as described earlier; and 2) immersion programs in Canada and the United States, as well as in other counties, which we describe in the next part of this chapter. Immersion programs include only majority language students who are taught through a second language for at least 50% of the day, usually for 2 or more years; variations in these programs are described in more detail later. What is important for our purposes here is that evaluations of the language, including literacy, and academic achievement of majority language students in both types of bilingual education have shown these students demonstrate the same levels of achievement in English, including reading and writing, as similar majority language students in English-only programs.

In short, participation in a bilingual program does not compromise acquisition of the majority language by either minority or majority language students (e.g., Genesee, 2004; Holobow, Genesee, & Lambert, 1991; Lindholm-Leary & Borsato, 2006).

What Is the Relationship Between Amount of Exposure to the Minority Language in School and Acquisition of that Language?

Contrary to the pattern we just noted for the majority language, amount of exposure to the minority language in school does make a difference to proficiency. Minority language students who have more exposure to the minority language in school acquire greater proficiency in that language than students with less exposure (Lindholm-Leary & Borsato, 2006). This stands to reason, given the relative lack of exposure to the minority language in the broader community, especially when it comes to forms of the language linked to literacy. These findings are important because they indicate that extending exposure to the minority language in school provides minority language students with greater opportunities to develop high levels of bilingual proficiency; extending exposure to the minority language does not detract from their development of the majority language, but enhances their native language skills. These findings are also significant because Lindholm and Aclan (1991) found that higher levels of bilingual proficiency among minority language students are associated with higher levels of academic language proficiency. In short, and contrary to some people's expectations, the evidence indicates that additive bilingual education that includes significant portions of instruction through the native language of minority language students contributes to their bilingual proficiency and their academic development. It also follows that minority language students with higher levels of bilingual proficiency are likely to experience the cognitive benefits reported by Bialystok (2001) and Cummins (2000; see also Chapter 3).

MAJORITY LANGUAGE STUDENTS

Although we probably associate schooling in an L2 with immigrants, indigenous language groups, and others who grow up speaking a minority language, there is a growing number of children who acquire a majority language as their L1 but are nevertheless educated through the medium of a second, or even third, language—children like Samantha

BOX 8.2

Questions from Parents About Immersion Programs

One of the biggest distinctions between L2 education programs for majority versus minority language students is that, for majority language students, parents have a choice in the language of their children's education and, therefore, have a choice as to whether to raise their children to be bilingual. For minority language students, education choices might be limited to majority language–only programs, and bilingualism for their children is usually not a choice. Because immersion education is a choice for majority language children, parents often ask us questions about these programs. The following email messages are typical examples of the kinds of questions parents ask. The information in this chapter provides answers to these questions.

Hello Dr. Paradis,

Our neighborhood school is a French immersion one, and I am having a tough time making the decision to send my daughter there for the next school year. She will be ready to begin kindergarten and many parents in my neighborhood think I am foolish to have reservations about it. Do bilingual kids lag behind in both languages? My concern is that she would not excel in either language but might end up being mediocre at both. Is there any published research to back up what I'm feeling?

Sincerely,
A mother

Professor Genesee:

I am writing to you with a question on total French Immersion programs in the US and the introduction of English language instruction at the fourth-grade level. My children are enrolled in a program where there is no English instruction provided until the second part of fourth grade when the students have 45 minutes twice each week of English. In the fifth grade, they have 45 minutes per day of English. The rationale for the instruction of English is that it will ease the transition to middle school (where there is only partial immersion). My question is this—are you aware of any research (or have you done any yourself) that speaks to the importance of providing that English language instruction? The research I have read does play out in our school—the immersion students wind up doing quite well in their native tongue but not right away. Plus they are frankly nervous about the transition to middle school where the majority of their work is in English.

Thank you in advance
A mother

or Trevor. A common form of L2 education for students who speak a majority language is *immersion*. Immersion programs were first developed in the French majority province of Quebec, Canada, in order to provide English-speaking Quebec students with opportunities to learn French along with English (see Genesee, 2004, and Lyster & Genesee, in press, for reviews). We focus our discussion in this chapter on immersion forms of bilingual education for majority language students because of the extensive body of descriptive and empirical literature on them.

Students in immersion programs receive all or a significant portion (usually a minimum of 50%) of their academic instruction, including language arts and literacy instruction, through the L2. The rationale behind immersion is that students can learn a language effectively if it is used for significant periods of time and for substantive communication in school, much as children learn their native language in the home (see Genesee, 2004, for a detailed description; see Lyster, 2007, for an alternative view). The risk that immersion in a second language will jeopardize students' native language development is minimal in the case of majority language students, it is argued, because they have extensive exposure to the native language outside school. Since their inception in 1965, immersion forms of education have been implemented in other regions of Canada, the United States, and worldwide (see Christian & Genesee, 2001, and Johnson & Swain, 1997, for case studies of immersion around the world). Immersion students also receive instruction through their native language; thus, these programs are additive forms of bilingual education. In addition to the general goal of bilingualism, immersion programs serve a variety of linguistic and cultural objectives that differ from country to country (from Christian & Genesee, 2001):

- To promote national policies of bilingualism (e.g., French immersion for English-speaking students in Canada)

- To promote national languages in countries with students who do not speak the dominant language of the community (e.g., Estonian immersion for Russian-speaking students in Estonia)

- To promote proficiency in important regional and/or world languages (e.g., English immersion in Japan)

- To promote proficiency in heritage languages (e.g., Hungarian immersion in Slovakia)

- To promote indigenous languages that are at risk (e.g., Mohawk immersion in Canada; Hawaiian immersion in Hawaii)

There is a variety of alternative forms of immersion. They differ with respect to the grade/age level when the L2 is used for intensive academic instruction and the amount of instruction provided through the second and native languages. One can distinguish **early immersion** (beginning in kindergarten or first grade) from delayed or **middle immersion** (beginning in fourth or fifth grade) and **late immersion** (beginning in seventh grade or the initial grades of secondary school). Programs that provide a delayed or late start provide core L2 instruction to students in those grades that precede the beginning of immersion (e.g., from kindergarten to Grade 6 in the case of a Grade 7 late immersion program). This means that students do not begin academic instruction through the L2 without having had some prior instruction in the target language. Schematic representations of early, delayed, and late immersion

Early immersion

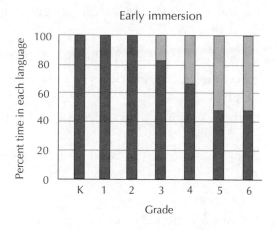

Delayed immersion

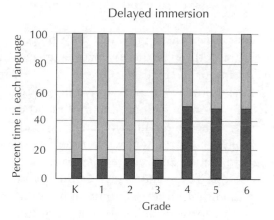

Late immersion

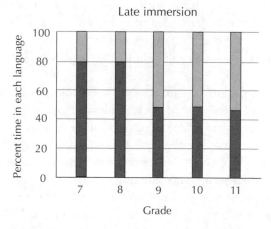

Figure 8.1. Models of second-language immersion programs.

program models are presented in Figure 8.1. Programs also differ with respect to the extent of instruction through the L2. In **partial immersion** programs, 50% of instruction in a given year is presented in the L2 and 50% in the native language of the students. In **total immersion** programs, all instruction for 1 or more years is presented through the L2.

Notwithstanding their different programmatic characteristics and goals, these programs share a number of core objectives:

1. Development of full, native-like proficiency in the students' native language
2. Development of advanced functional proficiency in all domains of the L2: reading, writing, speaking, and listening
3. Grade-appropriate levels of academic achievement in core school subjects, such as mathematics, science, and history
4. Understanding and appreciation of the culture of the target language group, along with understanding and appreciation of the culture of the student's own group

In effect, these programs aim for the same native language and academic goals as monolingual school programs, while also aiming for bilingual competence and cultural tolerance.

It is important to differentiate these programs from programs in which minority language students are educated through the majority language. In the United States, English-only programs for minority language students are often referred to as *English immersion* by some educators, but they are more aptly referred to as *submersion,* as noted earlier, because there is little accommodation made to these students' particular linguistic and cultural needs most of the time. Minority language students may be pulled out for English as a second language instruction, while receiving most of their other academic instruction along with native English-speaking students. Students in these kinds of submersion programs are often expected to give up their native language and culture for the sake of acquiring English. In direct contrast, immersion programs for majority language students are additive forms of bilingual education that aim to promote full bilingual proficiency. Most important, immersion teachers modify their instructional strategies to serve the special language learning needs of student who speak the majority language throughout the day, as they teach math, science, and so forth, and in all grade levels (see Cloud, Genesee, & Hamayan, 2000, and Met, 1998, for descriptions of these accommodations).

Majority language students in immersion-type programs are of relevance to our concerns in this book because some of these students experience learning or language difficulties and may be referred to learning specialists or clinicians for diagnosis and additional support. It is important that parents, educators, and clinicians understand what research has to say about typical outcomes of immersion education as well as outcomes for students with language and learning challenges so that they can decide on the suitability of immersion-type programs for students from majority language backgrounds who are at risk for language and reading impairment. There is often the belief that majority language students with language or learning difficulties are not good candidates for these programs, on the assumption that learning through a second language will put them at great risk of academic and language learning difficulty than they would face in a native language program. In the following sections, we review what we know about the language, literacy, and academic development of both typically developing students and students with learning challenges who belong to a majority language group and are in immersion programs.

How Effective Is Immersion Education for Majority Language Students?

Systematic and comprehensive evaluations of immersion programs for majority language students have been conducted in Canada, Japan, Spain, the United States, and elsewhere (for in-depth reviews, see Christian & Genesee, 2001; Genesee, 2004; and Johnson & Swain, 1997). Thus, we are fortunate in being able to draw on a wealth of scientific information about the development of majority language students who are schooled bilingually. A detailed review of these research findings is beyond the scope of this book (see Genesee, 2004, for a detailed synopsis of this research), but we provide a general overview of the most common findings that have been reported in evaluations of immersion. Specifically, we focus on students' native and second language outcomes, including reading and writing, and their academic achievement. We also review evidence concerning the effectiveness of immersion for students from economically disadvantaged and cultural minority backgrounds and for students with language delay or impairment, because these kinds of students are often thought to be at greater risk in immersion than in programs that use only the native language.

Students in General There has been extensive research on the language development and academic achievement of majority language students in immersion programs. By far the most extensive body of research on these aspects of development has been conducted in Canada on French immersion programs for English-speaking students (Lambert & Tucker, 1972; see also Genesee, 1987, and Swain & Lapkin, 1982). The general findings from the Canadian research have been replicated, for the most part, in other regions of the world in which similar programs with majority language students have been implemented (see Christian & Genesee, 2001, and Johnson & Swain, 1997, for other examples). Our summary draws heavily on the Canadian research.

Oral and Literacy Development in the Native Language Research has shown consistently that students in immersion programs who speak a majority language usually develop the same levels of proficiency in all aspects of their native language, including reading and writing, as comparable students in programs in which the native language is used exclusively for instruction. Remember that students in immersion programs are exposed to the native language on a daily basis outside school—at home, in the community, in the media, and so forth. There can be a lag in the development of native language literacy skills (reading, writing, and spelling) among immersion students in the initial years of total immersion programs when all academic instruction is presented in the L2. Parity with comparison students who have been instructed entirely through the native language is usually achieved after 1 year of receiving language arts instruction in the native language; for example, at the end of third grade in the case of students whose first exposure to instruction in the native language begins in third grade. This rapid catch-up is probably due, in part at least, to transfer between the native language and L2. The native language development of majority language students who begin immersion education beyond the primary grades of school (in delayed or late immersion) usually shows no such lags. Students in the latter programs exhibit age-appropriate native language skills at all grade levels.

To make these findings more concrete, consider the profiled child Samantha—a native English-speaking child who was born and is being raised in Tucson, Arizona. Her parents use English in the home, and all of her language experiences in the community at large are in English, except for occasional trips to Mexican restaurants or local grocery stores where Mexican food is sold. Because Samantha's parents wanted her to know another language, they decided to enroll her in the local Spanish immersion program— Buena Vista Elementary, an early total immersion program in which English is not taught until third grade. Samantha was taught to read and write in Spanish from kindergarten to second grade (before receiving formal literacy instruction in English in third grade), and all of her school subjects (math, social studies, and science) were taught to her in Spanish until the end of second grade. English was taught for 1 hour per day starting in third grade, and the amount of English increased gradually so that by sixth grade, half the day was taught in Spanish and half in English.

The Arizona State Department of Education requires that Buena Vista test Samantha and her classmates at the end of third grade and sixth grade using standardized tests (administered in English), including language, reading, spelling, mathematics, and science subtests. Because Buena Vista parents were concerned about their children's progress in English, the school decided to extend its testing program and assess the students' English language skills at the end of every grade, beginning in kindergarten. In addition to the language and academic domains that were covered by the standardized tests required by the state, the school also examined the immersion students' speaking, listening, and writing skills in English, using locally devised assessment instruments. These are skill domains that are not usually covered by standardized tests. The school administered these latter tests to classes in a neighboring English language school that had the same demographic characteristics as Buena Vista so that they had a point of comparison for judging the progress of the immersion students at Buena Vista. In order to be extra cautious, they also decided to test the immersion students' mathematics skills, using a standardized test administered in Spanish in first and second grades; the school authorities felt that the standardized test of mathematics in English could underestimate what they had learned in Spanish.

As other early immersion schools across the United States and in Canada have discovered, the evaluation at Buena Vista indicated that Samantha and her classmates tended to score below grade level in kindergarten, first grade, and second grade on the standardized subtests in English-language reading and spelling. This was not surprising, because all their language arts instruction had been in Spanish until then; however, their speaking and listening comprehension skills in English did not differ from those of the comparison students in the all-English program in the district. They also noted that although the students' math scores were below grade level on the English standardized test, they were at grade level, or above, on the standardized math test in Spanish. Most important, and much to their relief, they found that that there was no gap between the English reading and writing scores of the Buena Vista and all-English students by third grade, after 1 year of English language arts instruction. The Buena Vista students continued to do as well as the comparison students in all their English language skills throughout the elementary grades.

Let's return to our review of the research. Researchers have found that despite the time-on-task hypothesis, majority language immersion students who receive more native language instruction do not achieve higher levels of proficiency in the native language in the long run than immersion students who receive less exposure to the native language. To be specific, students in early *total* immersion programs score at the same level on standardized tests in the native language at the end of elementary school as students who have been in early partial or **delayed immersion,** despite the fact that early total immersion students have less exposure to the native language during the elementary grades than students in other forms of immersion. Therefore, there is no direct correspondence between the amount of native language instruction and native language development in the case of majority language students. We also noted this pattern for the majority language in the case of minority language students in bilingual programs. It is likely that these findings with respect to English are due to the compensating effects of cross-linguistic transfer and extensive exposure to the majority language outside school.

Second Language Development

Researchers have also consistently found that majority language students in immersion programs acquire significantly more advanced levels of functional proficiency in the L2 than students who receive conventional L2 instruction; that is, instruction that focuses primarily on language learning and is restricted to separate, short periods of instruction. This is evidenced by their performance on tests of reading, writing, speaking, and listening comprehension. Although it is difficult to make direct statistical comparisons, many researchers have reported impressionistically that immersion students' comprehension skills (in reading and listening) are more advanced than their production skills (in speaking and writing). Immersion students' functional competence in the L2 is evident from their academic performance. More specifically, because majority language students score as well on tests of mathematics, science, and social studies administered in French as comparison English-speaking students on tests administered in English, they must have acquired considerable functional proficiency in the L2 to assimilate new academic skills and knowledge.

At the same time, researchers have noted that immersion students seldom attain native-like competence in the target language even after 11 or 12 years of immersion (Genesee, 1991; Lyster, 2007). By native-like competence, we mean performance in the L2 that is as good as that of native speakers. Immersion students often fail to master important aspects of the target language grammar, such as pronouns, verb tenses, and prepositions (Adiv, 1980; Harley & Swain, 1984); they often exhibit nonidiomatic usage (Genesee, 1991); and they tend to use simplified grammatical forms and show intrusions from their native language. Some of these aspects parallel those discussed in Chapter 6 for the developing L2 abilities of minority L1/majority L2 learners. A major challenge among educators is how to extend the language proficiency of immersion students so that these gaps are addressed (e.g., Swain, 1996); Roy Lyster's counterbalanced approach is a research-based approach that seeks to respond to these concerns (Lyster, 2007).

Academic Achievement

Returning to achievement in academic domains, such as mathematics, science, and social studies, evaluations of majority language students in immersion programs indicate that they generally attain the same levels of achievement as comparable students in native language programs. This is true whether the comparison students are native speakers of the same language as the immersion students or native speakers of the L2 who are tested in the L2. Parity with native language comparison students is often exhibited even when immersion students receive all academic instruction through the L2, provided that the assessment is conducted in the L2 and modifications are made to take into account that full competence in that language has not been acquired.

Immersion students can appear to have deficiencies in academic domains if they are tested in the noninstructional language. For example, students in early total immersion programs who receive math instruction in French (their L2) but are tested in English (their native language) may appear to have deficiencies in problem solving. This can be explained by their incomplete mastery of English reading skills because once they receive reading instruction in their native language, these disparities disappear. Moreover, they usually do not exhibit these deficiencies if tested in the language of instruction. Immersion students may exhibit what appear to be gaps in their learning of academic material if they are questioned about it in the language that was not used to teach it. If students are taught science in French, their L2, but are questioned about their knowledge of science in their native language, they may lack some of the terminology or phrasing needed to fully express what they know. The hesitations that result from these word-finding problems should be interpreted for what they are—word-finding problems—and nothing more. Bilinguals often exhibit dominance or differential proficiency in their languages when it comes to specific domains of knowledge. This is typical and easily remedied, if necessary.

Notwithstanding these qualifications, academic parity with comparison groups is usually exhibited by students in immersion programs at both the elementary and secondary levels and has been demonstrated using a variety of assessment instruments, including standardized norm-referenced tests, official government tests, and locally devised tests. In sum, there is no evidence that instruction in academic subjects through the L2 impedes the acquisition of new academic skills and knowledge on the part of majority language students in comparison with students receiving the same academic instruction through their native language.

Outcomes in Different Community, Linguistic, and Cultural Contexts   The general patterns of student achievement that we have just described have been found in diverse contexts. For example, majority language students in immersion programs fare more or less the same regardless of whether the L2 is used in their communities—communities as diverse as Montreal, Toronto, Cincinnati, Los Angeles, Estonia, Japan, Spain, and others. Undoubtedly, immersion students who have contact with native speakers of the target language outside school have the opportunity to extend their L2 learning outside school. It is also noteworthy that these general patterns occur even when typologically different pairs of languages are involved. Researchers have found the same basic results for Japanese and English (Bostwick, 2001); Hawaiian and English (Slaughter, 1997); Hebrew, French, and English (a trilingual example; Genesee, 1998); Mohawk and English (Jacobs & Cross, 2001); and Estonian and Russian (Asser, Kolk, & Küppar, 2001).

The research we have reviewed to this point has focused on students who not only speak the majority group language but are also members of the majority ethnic group in their community; for example, mainstream Anglo-American or Anglo-Canadian students in the United States and Canada, respectively. There have also been evaluations of immersion programs that serve students from minority ethnic groups, such as students from Hawaiian, African American, and Franco-American backgrounds in the United States (see, respectively, Slaughter, 1997; Holobow et al., 1991; and Caldas & Boudreaux, 1999) and students of Mohawk background in Canada (Jacobs & Cross, 2001). Students from some of these groups tend to underachieve in school in comparison with mainstream students, although not always (Garnett, 2006; Goldenberg, 2003), and thus may not be considered suitable candidates for education through a second language. The students in some of these programs are doubly interesting because they are not only members of a minority ethnic group, but may also speak a nonstandard variety of the majority language. Many African Americans speak African American English and many children of Hawaiian descent speak Hawaiian Creole English (or "pidgin English"). It could be said that, in fact, these students are learning Standard English in school as a third language, in addition to a heritage language.

Research in all of these contexts indicates that these students, even those who speak a nonstandard variety of English, attain the same levels of proficiency in the standard variety of their native language development and in academic achievement as comparable students in native language programs; in addition, they develop advanced levels of functional proficiency in the L2. It must be reiterated that all of the students in these programs spoke a variety of English outside school and that these findings thus cannot be generalized to children from a minority ethnic group who speak a minority language at home.

Taken together, these findings are reassuring from an educational point of view because they indicate that this form of bilingual education for majority language students can be effective in communities with different levels of representation of the L2, using languages that differ considerably typologically, and for students from minority as well as majority ethnic group backgrounds.

Individual Difference Factors

In this section, we review research that has assessed the performance of immersion students who differ from one another in ways that often influence their academic and language development in school (Genesee, 2007). We review this research in some detail because students with these characteristics, such as low levels of academic and native language ability or relatively low socioeconomic backgrounds, are often at risk for poor language and academic outcomes in school and, in fact, often do poorly in school in comparison with students who do not share these characteristics.

Academic Ability With respect to academic (or intellectual) ability, Genesee (1987) systematically examined the performance of both elementary and secondary-level English-speaking students in French immersion programs in Canada in relation to their intellectual ability. Students were classified as average (IQ between 85 and 115), below average (IQ below 85), or above average (IQ above 115) based on their scores on a standardized IQ test; none of the students in the below-average subgroup were considered cognitively impaired from a clinical point of view. Their school performance was assessed with respect to L1 (English) and L2 (French) outcomes and academic achievement. With respect to L1 outcomes and academic achievement, the below-average students in immersion scored at the same level as the below-average students in L1 programs on both L1 and academic achievement measures. In other words, the below-average students in immersion were not disadvantaged in their L1 development or academic achievement as a result of participation in immersion. As one might expect, the below-average students in both programs scored significantly lower than their average and above-average peers in their respective programs on the same measures. With respect to L2 acquisition, the below-average students in immersion scored significantly higher on all L2 measures than the below-average students in the L1 program who were receiving conventional L2 instruction. In other words, the below-average students were benefiting from immersion in the form of enhanced L2 proficiency.

Comparisons between elementary and secondary students revealed interesting and differential effects of academic ability on L2 achievement. Specifically, below-average students in both early and late immersion programs scored lower on measures of French language development related to literacy (reading and writing) than average and above-average students in the same immersion programs; similarly, the average students in both program types scored lower than the above-average students. A different pattern of results was found, however, for measures of speaking and listening. Whereas late immersion students exhibited the same stratification on measures of speaking and listening as they had demonstrated on measures of L2 literacy, there were no differences among the ability subgroups in the early immersion program on measures of L2 speaking and listening. In other words, academic ability influenced the development of proficiency in all aspects of L2 acquisition among secondary school students, but had much less effect on the speaking and listening comprehension skills of immersion students in the elementary school program. Although we have no definitive explanation for these results, it could be that acquisition of an L2 when it is integrated with academic instruction is more cognitively demanding at the secondary than the elementary school level and, as a result, calls on the kinds of cognitive skills that are differentially available to older students. In contrast, acquisition of L2 skills that are integrated with academic instruction at the elementary level calls on the natural language learning ability that all students possess during their early formative years. In any case, these findings suggest that early immersion is more egalitarian than late immersion because it is relatively more effective for students with different levels of general academic ability. Overall, these results indicate that low academic or intellectual ability is no more of a handicap for majority language students in bilingual education than it is in L1 programs and that to the contrary, low-performing students can experience a net benefit from immersion in the form of bilingual proficiency.

In a related vein, Maggie Bruck (1985a, 1985b) examined the role of academic ability in decisions to switch some students out of early immersion. At issue was whether academic ability, or something else, was the primary cause of students' difficulty in immersion. Bruck compared the academic, familial, and socioaffective characteristics of early immersion students who switched to an L1 program with those of students who remained in an immersion program. She found, as expected, that the students who switched scored lower on a number of achievement measures than most students who remained in immersion, but the academic difficulties of the students who switched were no worse than those of a subgroup of students who remained in immersion despite low academic performance. What distinguished the students who switched from those who remained in the program despite their academic difficulties was that the former expressed significantly more negative attitudes toward schooling (and immersion in particular) and exhibited more behavioral problems than the latter. Bruck conjectured that some immersion students with academic difficulties exhibited behavioral problems that in turn led parents to switch their children out of immersion in the hope that they would adjust more satisfactorily in an L1 program.

In a follow-up investigation, Bruck noted that the students who switched continued to have academic difficulties and to exhibit attitudinal and behavioral problems. Bruck's results suggest that the ability to cope with poor academic difficulties may be a more serious problem for some immersion students than poor academic performance per se. Her results also support the argument that academic ability alone does not distinguish students who can benefit from immersion education and those who cannot. In other words, other things being equal, students with low levels of academic ability should be eligible for immersion education.

Socioeconomic Status   Students from families with low SES often achieve at lower levels in school than students from higher SES families for reasons that are not fully understood. Because of this risk factor, researchers in the United States and Canada have examined the performance of students from low SES backgrounds in immersion programs (Genesee, 1987; Holobow et al., 1991). Canadian researchers have found that socioeconomically disadvantaged students in early immersion programs usually attain the same levels of native language competence as students from comparably low-SES families in native language programs. SES has been measured in these studies according to the educational level and occupational status of parents and the characteristics of the communities in which they live. At the same time, and as one would predict from their low SES, such low-SES students usually score significantly lower on native language literacy tests than their middle-class peers in the same programs; this is also true for students from low SES backgrounds in native language programs. The same pattern has been found for achievement in mathematics and science. For example, even though immersion students from low SES backgrounds receive all their math instruction through their L2, they score as well as students from low SES backgrounds who have received math instruction through the their native language, but not as well as students from families with higher SES.

With respect to their L2 development, it has been found that immersion students from low SES families perform significantly better than comparable students in conventional L2 programs where the L2 is taught as a subject, on all measures of L2 proficiency. Of particular note, they also sometimes perform as well as middle-class immersion students on tests of listening comprehension and speaking, although significantly lower on tests of reading, as noted earlier. Recall from our previous discussion that Cummins and others have argued that social, interpersonal communication skills develop differently from, and more quickly than, academic language skills. We know that newborns are innately prepared to acquire interpersonal communication skills during the preschool years without instruction. It could be that young school-age learners retain some innate capacity for acquiring interpersonal communication skills without instruction or with relatively little formal instruction. This could explain the differential success of students from low SES backgrounds when it comes to the acquisition of listening and speaking skills in comparison with reading and writing skills in the L2.

Working in the United States, Caldas and Boudreaux (1999) similarly reported that socioeconomic disadvantage does not put immersion students at a greater disadvantage than similar students in L1-only programs; in this case, the students were English-speaking students attending French immersion programs in Louisiana. Because these researchers did not have access to information concerning the SES of individual students, they compared entire groups of students in immersion classes with high concentrations of students living in poverty (determined by the number of students who participated in a free/reduced-price lunch program) with groups of students in classes with similarly high concentrations of impoverished students in which the native language was used for instruction. They found that the immersion students (both white and African American) tended to score higher than nonimmersion students in the same school district on standardized state-mandated tests of English and mathematics achievement administered in Grades 3, 5, and 7.

Taken together, these studies indicate that students from low SES backgrounds can maintain typical levels of native language and academic development in L2 immersion programs and, at the same time, acquire bilingual proficiency.

First Language Ability   The issue we address here is whether students with what would be considered clinically low levels of L1 ability should be excluded from dual language programs because they will be at a greater risk than if they were in an L1 program. Despite the significance of this issue, there is remarkably little systematic investigation of it, one exception being work by Bruck in Montreal. In order to examine this question, Bruck (1978, 1982) identified subgroups of third-grade immersion and nonimmersion students who were "language-disabled," to use her terminology, or "normal" (i.e., typically developing children) in their L1 development. Bruck's "language-disabled" subgroup would likely be considered to have a *lanugage impairment* in more current terminology, according to the inclusion criteria used in the study. Classification was based on teachers' judgments, an oral interview, and a battery of diagnostic tests. When Bruck tested the students on literacy and academic achievement measures, she found that the immersion students with language disabilities scored at the same level as students with similar disabilities in the L1 program, and both groups scored lower than their typically developing peers in the same programs, as would be expected from the status of the students with disabilities. At the same time, the immersion students with disabilities had developed significantly higher levels of L2 proficiency than both subgroups of nonimmersion students (with and without disabilities) who were receiving conventional L2 instruction.

In sum, students with low levels of L1 ability—that could be considered to conform to clinical criteria of impairment—have been found to demonstrate the same levels of L1 ability and academic achievement in immersion programs as students with similar language disabilities in L1 programs. At the same time, participation in the immersion program benefited the students with language disabilities with significantly superior L2 proficiency in comparison with students receiving conventional L2 instruction. In Chapter 9, we discuss the issue of whether children identified as having language delay or language impairment should be enrolled in immersion programs. In Chapter 10, we consider how to identify and support students who are learning to read in an L2 but are at risk for reading difficulties and possibly reading impairment.

KEY POINTS AND IMPLICATIONS

Many minority and majority language children begin to acquire their L2 when they begin school. For minority language students, it is a matter of being schooled in the majority group language and thus acquiring an L2 that is essential for their social integration and economic prosperity in the wider community. For majority language children, it is a matter of choosing to add competence in a second or foreign language to their linguistic repertoire. The L2 may or may not be useful in their immediate community, but it will certainly broaden their horizons. The prospects of greater opportunity that come from knowing another language prompt majority language parents to select bilingual forms of education for their children. Here are the key points from this chapter and their implications.

Key Point 1

Minority language students who are educated through the majority language face the triple challenges of acquiring an L2 for academic purposes, integrating socially into a new community of peers, and acquiring new academic skills and knowledge. Their success in the face of these challenges depends on their ability to acquire the language skills, including literacy, that are required in school and to bridge the cultural differences between their homes and the school.

Implications

Educators, clinicians, and other professionals should rule out the following factors before concluding that an individual minority language child's language or learning difficulties are cause for clinical concern: 1) lack of acquisition of language skills required for academic tasks; 2) lack of familiarity with the cultural norms that govern school behavior; 3) lack of prior experience in the home with literacy and literacy-related behaviors; 4) hardship associated with disadvantaged SES, such as inadequate nutrition; 5) dysfunctional or disruptive family circumstances; 6) medical problems; and 7) inappropriate or ineffective prior schooling or total lack of prior schooling in the case of students who begin schooling in an L2 beyond the normal starting grade.

Key Point 2

Minority language children generally develop the same or higher levels of proficiency in the majority language if they attend additive bilingual programs that provide substantial instruction in academic and language domains through the native language. At the same time, they maintain and extend their proficiency in the native language. In other words, they become bilingual and biliterate in the native and majority languages. Use of the native language can provide an important developmental scaffold for the acquisition of the majority language, especially with respect to academic language proficiency and literacy. L2-only or transitional bilingual programs often do not achieve these benefits because they fail to promote high levels of competence in the native language and, as a result, there are no positive transfer effects from the native to the majority language. The achievement of minority language students in mainstream classrooms can also be limited by the lack of properly trained teachers; that is, teachers who know how to address their specific language learning and cultural needs.

Implications

- It should not be assumed that participation in a bilingual program impedes acquisition of the majority language.
- Parents, educators, and clinicians should take a developmental perspective and expect

that early lags in acquisition of the majority language due to use of the minority language in school can, and often are, offset by later gains. In other words, minority language students may be behind other students during those grades when the native language is the predominant medium of communication, but they usually catch up rapidly once the use of the majority language is extended. The same is true for majority language students in immersion.

- A focus on the majority language is not necessarily the most effective developmental route to promoting minority language children's acquisition of that language, and, moreover, such a strategy compromises development of the native language and thus bilingual development.

Key Point 3

There are significant and positive correlations between the acquisition of literacy skills in one language and acquisition of literacy skills in another language. For example, minority language Spanish-speaking students in the United States who have already acquired foundational literacy skills in Spanish (i.e., phonological awareness and letter-sound knowledge) and/or preliteracy skills in Spanish learn to read more easily in English in school than minority language students who have not acquired foundational or preliteracy skills in the native language. As well, the predictors of success in learning to read, especially word decoding, are the same in a first and a second language, and acquisition of these skills, or failure to acquire them, in either language is a significant predictor of success in acquiring reading skills in the other language. There are also clearly other factors to consider when it comes to acquiring competence in reading and writing in a second language in comparison with the first language, but the fundamentals are much the same; we discuss these in greater detail in Chapter 10.

Implications

- Parents of children who speak a minority language should be encouraged to use language at home in ways that support literacy development in order to facilitate their children's acquisition of literacy skills in school. This might be more difficult for some families to achieve than others because of cultural differences in language use patterns in the home, and other barriers.

- Contrary to the traditional view that minority language students are better off if the minority language is set aside in favor of using the majority language at home, early literacy and literacy-related experiences in the minority language prior to and during schooling can facilitate children's acquisition of the majority language while also supporting their maintenance of the minority language. We discuss the importance of maintaining the minority language in Chapter 6.

- Children who experience difficulty acquiring literacy skills in a second language, especially during the early years, may either be at risk for reading difficulties or may have not had early experiences with foundational literacy skills and may need support acquiring those skills in school. Minority language students who begin schooling in an L2 beyond the normal starting grade may struggle learning to read and write in the L2 because they have had no or inadequate prior literacy instruction.

- Limiting children to one language is unlikely to resolve difficulties that some dual language learners face learning oral and written language. We talk more about identifying and supporting students who are at risk or experience language-learning difficulty in Chapter 9, and those who are at risk or have difficulty acquiring reading skills in Chapter 10.

Key Point 4

Most majority language students who participate in immersion programs acquire typical levels of native language development and high levels of achievement in academic domains. This has been found for a variety of students, including those with limited academic or native language abilities, students from disadvantaged socioeconomic families, as well as those from diverse minority ethnic groups; students who speak a native language that is typologically similar or dissimilar to the L2; and those in communities with or without a significant presence of the target language. Students from disadvantaged or at-risk groups often perform at lower levels than students with more advantaged backgrounds, but this is equally true for students in monolingual programs.

Implications

- It should not be assumed that the difficulties (language, literacy, or academic) experienced by some majority language students in bilingual programs are due to dual language instruction. Learning through another language is not a linguistic, cognitive, or social hardship for most majority language students.
- Educators, learning specialists and clinicians should rule out socioeconomic, cultural, and family-related factors as possible explanations of individual student's difficulties before seriously considering underlying language or learning impairments.

Key Point 5

There is relatively little systematic evidence on the language and literacy development of either minority or majority language students with language or more general learning disabilities in bilingual programs. Research on majority language students is somewhat more extensive than that on minority language students, and there is some evidence on students who would be considered to have a learning or language disability according to school-based criteria for identifying students with special needs (e.g., Myers, 2009; Bruck, 1982). Criteria for determining learning disabilities vary across districts, and therefore vary across studies. Thus, at present, we cannot say with certainty how all students who experience learning disabilities—particularly moderate to severe disabilities—would do in dual language programs. Nevertheless, the available evidence indicates that students who are challenged in school because of learning disabilities, usually of a nonclinical nature but conforming sometimes to criteria for identifying students with special education needs, are not disadvantaged more in a bilingual/immersion programs than similar students in monolingual programs, and they can acquire impressive bilingual competencies (Genesee, 2007; Genesee & Lindholm-Leary, in press; Myers, 2009). In other words, students with learning disabilities in immersion/bilingual programs have been shown to perform as well as similar affected students in monolingual programs on a variety of standardized achievement tests. The L2 development of minority L1 children with language delay and language impairment is discussed in Chapter 9.

Implications

- There is no a priori reason to exclude majority or minority language students who have learning disabilities or are at risk for learning impairments and difficulties from bilingual education on the assumption that their academic and language development will be enhanced in a monolingual program.

- It should not be assumed that majority and minority language students in bilingual programs who are experiencing academic or language learning difficulties have language or learning impairment for reasons related to their bilingualism or their bilingual schooling. Thus, these students should be given every opportunity to continue in the program, provided that parental support is strong and that appropriate support services can be provided by the school or school district. We consider in more detail how to identify and support students who are experiencing difficulties acquiring reading skills in a second language or are at risk for such difficulties in Chapter 10.

- The decision to enroll a child with learning challenges or who is likely to face learning challenges in a bilingual program, in lieu of a monolingual program, should consider a number of factors: parental support for bilingualism; the importance of bilingualism in the student's immediate and future life; and the extent to which the family, the community, and the school can provide learning support for the child. Children with learning difficulties need focused, extended, and continuous support from educational professionals as well as from the family and community if they are to achieve their full learning potential.

REFERENCES

Adiv, E. (1980). *An analysis of second language performance in two types of immersion programs.* Unpublished doctoral dissertation, McGill University, Montreal, Quebec, Canada.

Asser, H., Kolk, P., & Küppar, M. (2001). *Estonian-language immersion programme: Report on student achievement and parental attitudes for the academic year 2000–2001.* Tallinn, Estonia: Estonian Immersion Centre.

August, D., & Shanahan, T. (2006). *Developing literacy in second language learners. Report of the National Literacy Panel on minority-language children and youth.* Mahwah, NJ: Lawrence Erlbaum Associates.

Bailey, A., & Butler, F. (2007). A conceptual framework of academic English language for broad application to education. In A. Bailey (Ed.), *The language demands of school: Putting academic English to the test.* New Haven, CT: Yale University Press.

Baker, K.A., & de Kanter, A.A. (1981). *Effectiveness of bilingual education: A review of the literature.* Washington, D.C.: U.S. Department of Education, Office of Planning, Budget and Evaluation.

Bialystok, E. (2001). *Bilingualism in development: Language, literacy, and cognition.* New York: Cambridge University Press.

Bostwick, M. (2001). English immersion in a Japanese school. In D. Christian & F. Genesee (Eds.), *Bilingual education* (pp. 125–138). Alexandria, VA: Teachers of English to Speakers of Other Languages.

Bruck, M. (1978). The suitability of early French immersion programs for the language disabled child. *Canadian Journal of Education, 3,* 51–72.

Bruck, M. (1982). Language disabled children: Performance in an additive bilingual education program. *Applied Psycholinguistics, 3,* 45–60.

Bruck, M. (1985a). Consequences of transfer out of early French immersion programs. *Applied Psycholinguistics, 6,* 101–120.

Bruck, M. (1985b). Predictors of transfer out of early French immersion programs. *Applied Psycholinguistics, 6,* 39–61.

Caldas, S.J., & Boudreaux, N. (1999). Poverty, race, and foreign language immersion: Predictors of math and English language arts performance. *Learning Language, 5*(1), 4–15.

Chamot, A.U., & O'Malley, J.M. (1987). The cognitive academic language learning approach: A bridge to the mainstream. *TESOL Quarterly, 21,* 227–249.

Christian, D., & Genesee, F. (Eds.). (2001). *Bilingual education.* Alexandria, VA: Teachers of English to Speakers of Other Languages.

Cloud, N., Genesee, F., & Hamayan, E. (2000). *Dual language instruction: A handbook for enriched education.* Portsmouth, NH: Heinle & Heinle.

Cloud, N., Genesee, F., & Hamayan, E. (2009). *Literacy Instruction for English Language Learners.* Portsmouth, NH: Heinemann.

Crago, M.B. (1988). *Cultural context in communicative interaction of young Inuit children.* Unpublished doctoral dissertation, McGill University, Montreal, Quebec, Canada.

Cummins, J. (1984). *Bilingualism and special education: Issues in assessment and pedagogy.* Clevedon, England: Multilingual Matters.

Cummins, J. (2000). *Language, power and pedagogy: Bilingual children in the crossfire.* Clevedon, England: Multilingual Matters.

Echevarria, J., Vogt, M.E., & Short, D.J. (2000). *Making content comprehensible for English language learners.* Boston: Allyn & Bacon.

Erdos, C., Genesee, F., Savage, R., & Haigh, C. (in press). Individual differences in second language reading outcomes. *International Journal of Bilingualism.*

Garnett, B., (2006, October). *An introductory look at the academic trajectories of ESL students.* Paper presented at the Immigration, Integration, and Language Conference, University of Calgary.

Genesee, F. (1987). *Learning through two languages: Studies of immersion and bilingual education.* Rowley, MA: Newbury House.

Genesee, F. (1991). Second language learning in school settings: Lessons from immersion. In A. Reynolds (Ed.), *Bilingualism, multiculturalism, and second language learning: The McGill conference in honor of Wallace E. Lambert* (pp. 183–202). Mahwah, NJ: Lawrence Erlbaum Associates.

Genesee, F. (1998). A case study of multilingual education in Canada. In J. Cenoz & F. Genesee (Eds.), *Beyond bilingualism: Multilingualism and multilingual education* (pp. 243–258). Clevedon, England: Multilingual Matters.

Genesee, F. (Ed.). (1999). *Program alternatives for linguistically diverse students.* Educational Practice Report No. 1. Washington, D.C.: Center for Applied Linguistics.

Genesee, F. (2004). What do we know about bilingual education for minority language students. In T.K. Bhatia & W. Ritchie (Eds.), *Handbook of bilingualism and multiculturalism* (pp. 547–576). Malden, MA: Blackwell.

Genesee, F. (2007). French immersion and at-risk students: A review of research findings. *Canadian Modern Language Review, 63,* 655–688.

Genesee, F., & Lindholm-Leary, K. (in press). The education of English language learners. In K.R. Harris, S. Graham, & F. Pajares (Eds.), *APA educational psychology handbook: Application of educational psychology to learning and teaching* (Vol. 3). Washington, DC: American Psychological Association.

Genesee, F., Lindholm-Leary, K., Saunders, W., & Christian, D. (2006). *Educating English language learners: A synthesis of research evidence.* New York: Cambridge University Press.

Genesee, F., & Riches, C. (2006). Literacy development: Instructional issues. In F. Genesee, K. Lindholm-Leary, W. Saunders, & D. Christian (Eds.), *Educating English language learners: A synthesis of research evidence* (pp. 109–175). New York: Cambridge University Press.

Goldenberg, C. (2003). Making schools work for low-income families in the 21st century. In S.B. Neuman & D.K. Dickinson (Eds.), *Handbook of early literacy research* (pp. 211–231). New York: Guilford Press.

Goldenberg, C. (2008, Summer). Teaching English language learners: What the research does—and does not—say. *American Educator, 32*(2), 2–44.

Harley, B., & Swain, M. (1984). An analysis of verb form and function in the speech of French immersion pupils. *Working Papers in Bilingualism, 14,* 31–46.

Holobow, N.E., Genesee, F., & Lambert, W.E. (1991). The effectiveness of a foreign language immersion program for children from different ethnic and social class backgrounds: Report 2. *Applied Psycholinguistics, 12,* 179–198.

Jacobs, K., & Cross, A. (2001). The seventh generation of Kahnawàke: Phoenix or dinosaur. In D. Christian & F. Genesee (Eds.), *Case studies in bilingual education* (pp. 109–121). Alexandria, VA: Teachers of English to Speakers of Other Languages.

Johnson, R.K., & Swain, M. (1997). *Immersion education: International perspectives.* New York: Cambridge University Press.

Kindler, A.L. (2000). *Survey of the states' limited English proficient students and available educational programs and services: 2000–2001 summary report.* Washington, DC: National Clearinghouse for English Language Acquisition & Language Instruction Educational Programs.

Lambert, W.E., & Tucker, G.R. (1972). *The bilingual education of children: The St. Lambert experiment.* Rowley, MA: Newbury House.

Lindholm, K. (2001). *Dual language education.* Clevedon, England: Multilingual Matters.

Lindholm, K.J., & Aclan, Z. (1991). Bilingual proficiency as a bridge to academic achievement: Results from bilingual/immersion programs. *Journal of Education, 173*(2), 99–113.

Lindholm-Leary, K., & Borsato, G. (2006). Academic achievement. In F. Genesee, K. Lindholm-Leary, W. Saunders, & D. Christian (Eds.), *Educating English language learners: A synthesis of research evidence* (pp. 176–222). New York: Cambridge University Press.

Lyster, R. (2007). *Learning and teaching languages through content: A counterbalanced approach.* Amsterdam: John Benjamins.

Lyster, R., & Genesee, F. (in press). Immersion education. In C. Chapelle (Ed.), *The encyclopedia of applied linguistics.* Oxford, England: Wiley-Blackwell.

Met, M. (1998). Curriculum decision-making in content-based language teaching. In J. Cenoz & F. Genesee (Eds.), *Beyond bilingualism: Multilingualism and multilingual education* (pp. 35–63). Clevedon, UK: Multilingual Matters.

Myers, M. (2009). *Achievement of children identified with special needs in two-way Spanish immersion programs.* Doctoral dissertation, Graduate School of Education and Human Development, George Washington University, Washington, D.C.

Neuman, S.B., & Dickinson, D.K. (2003). *Handbook of early literacy research.* New York: Guilford Press.

Oller, K.D., & Eilers, R. (Eds.). (2002). *Language and literacy in bilingual children.* Clevedon, England: Multilingual Matters.

Paradis, J. (2007). Second language acquisition in childhood. In E. Hoff & M. Shatz (Eds.), *Handbook of language development* (pp. 387–405). Oxford, England: Blackwell.

Porter, R.P. (1990). *Forked tongue.* New York: Basic Books.

Ramirez, J.D., Yuen, S.D., & Ramey, D.R. (1991). *Longitudinal study of structured English immersion strategy, early-exit and late-exit transitional bilingual education programs for language-minority children (Final report to the U.S. Department of Education).* San Mateo, CA: Aguirre International.

Riches, C., & Genesee, F. (2006). Cross-linguistic and cross-modal aspects of literacy development. In F. Genesee, K. Lindholm-Leary, W. Saunders, & D. Christian (Eds.), *Educating English language learners: A synthesis of research evidence* (pp. 64–108). New York: Cambridge University Press.

Roseberry-McKibbin, C. (2002). *Multicultural students with special language needs.* Oceanside, CA: Academic Communication Associates.

Rossell, C.H., & Baker, K. (1996). The educational effectiveness of bilingual education. *Research in the Teaching of English, 30,* 7–74.

Scarcella, R.C. (2003). *Accelerating academic English: A focus on the English learner.* Oakland, CA: Regents of the University of California.

Short, D., & Fitzsimmons, S. (2007). *Double the work: Challenges and solutions to acquiring language and academic literacy for adolescent English language learners.* A report to Carnegie Corporation of New York. Washington, DC: Alliance for Excellent Education.

Slaughter, H. (1997). Indigenous language immersion in Hawai'i: A case study of Kula Kaiapuni Hawai'i. In R.K. Johnson, & M. Swain (Eds.), *Immersion education: International perspectives* (pp. 105–129). New York: Cambridge University Press.

Swain, M. (1996). Integrating language and content in immersion classrooms: research perspectives. *The Canadian Modern Language Review, 52,* 529–548.

Swain, M., & Lapkin, S. (1982). *Evaluating bilingual education: A Canadian case study.* Clevedon, England: Multilingual Matters.

Thomas, W., & Collier, B. (2002). *A national study of school effectiveness for language minority students' long-term academic achievement.* Santa Cruz, CA: Center for Research on Education, Diversity and Excellence.

SECTION III

Dual Language and Disorders

Language Impairment in Dual Language Children

In Section II of this book, we presented a review and synthesis of research on numerous aspects of language development and schooling in typically developing dual language children, both simultaneous bilinguals and second language (L2) learners, both minority and majority language speakers, and internationally adopted (IA) children. Throughout those chapters and in the key points and implications sections at the end of each, we drew attention to the outcomes of this research most relevant for the practice of educators and clinicians, and also for parents, who make important decisions on behalf of their children about educational choices and referrals to specialists. In Section III, we now turn to discussing the characteristics of dual language children who do not have typical language and/or reading development, and to discussing more directly, and in more detail, the issues and considerations involved in the assessment, identification, and intervention for language and reading impairment with dual language children. This chapter deals with oral language and Chapter 10 deals with reading.

This chapter is divided into two main sections. The topic of the first section is the nature of language impairment in dual language children; in other words, what characteristics of language impairment are similar or dissimilar in children who speak two languages versus children who speak just one language. This section begins with a description of language delay and impairment in all children (building on Chapter 1), and then moves on to descriptions of dual language learners affected with language delay or impairment. This section ends with a discussion of whether dual language learning is appropriate for children with language impairment. The second section of this chapter focuses on clinical practice and policy regarding dual language children. We present the many issues that can complicate effective assessment and identification with dual language children, but also present some strategies for working around some of these complications. We end this second section with a discussion of issues and strategies for intervention with dual language children.

Notice that we have used the inclusive term *dual language children* here, but in previous chapters, we tended to discuss simultaneous bilinguals and L2 learners separately. Throughout this chapter, we will be presenting research that was based on both subgroups of dual language children. At times, differentiating between these subgroups is important for the discussion. When it is important to specify whether the children we are referring to are simultaneous bilinguals or L2 learners, we do so. If it is not important, the inclusive term *dual language children* or simply *bilingual children* is used.

When we describe atypical language development in dual language children, we report mainly on bilingual children with specific language impairment (SLI); however, children affected with other neurodevelopmental disorders that have consequences for language development, like Down syndrome or autism spectrum disorder, can be bilingual as well. Where research exits on such children, we include it. Furthermore, issues concerning assessment, identification, and intervention with dual language children are not limited to children who are suspected of having SLI; on the contrary, the information we present could be relevant to professionals who are assessing dual language children for potential language learning difficulties regardless of the suspected or known source of those difficulties. However, we do not touch on issues regarding dual language children and articulatory, phonological, or fluency (stuttering) disorders. Readers can consult Goldstein (2004; new edition forthcoming) for more information on these topics.

LANGUAGE DELAY AND LANGUAGE IMPAIRMENT IN DUAL LANGUAGE CHILDREN

Defining Language Delay and Impairment

Delays in the timing of language development milestones in infants and children are a bellwether for a range of potential developmental problems. Infants can display delay in beginning to speak due to sensory deficits such as hearing impairment, due to syndromes that include neurodevelopmental deficits not restricted to language such as Down syndrome, fragile X syndrome, or autism spectrum disorder, or due to *specific* language impairment, so called because the primary source of the impairment is in language development itself (see Schwartz, 2009, or Rice, Warren, & Betz, 2005, for overviews). Rice (2007) argues that a further distinction should be made between "specific" language delay and specific language impairment, among disorders that primarily affect language. Children with "specific" language delay are slower to begin speaking and producing word combinations, and they do not show evidence of other clinically significant conditions, but their language development can normalize with time. Thus, many of these children eventually close the gap, usually before or shortly after school entry, with children who do not show early delays. In contrast, children with SLI start out with language delays, but their difficulties and protracted development of language extend into the school-age years and possibly never completely resolve over time, although they can come close to their unaffected peers for some language abilities by the end of elementary school. Children with SLI show some profound deficits in certain domains of language knowledge and processing that go beyond what their general delays in language development would indicate, and for these domains of language, they are unlikely to achieve the same abilities as unaffected children. In other words, not all children with "specific" language delay end up diagnosed with SLI, but children diagnosed with SLI typically experienced early language delay. As will be shown shortly, data from bilingual children support this distinction between (specific) language delay and SLI. In sum, delay and difficulties in the domain of language development can be a signal for a variety of developmental disorders. Understanding how dual language children can be expected to perform on language assessments is important for the accurate diagnosis of developmental disorders affecting language in this population.

In Chapter 1, we provided a sketch of the causes and basic characteristics of SLI in monolingual children. The main points from that review are summarized in Box 9.1.

Identification of SLI   We make reference here and elsewhere in this chapter to concepts that are important for the measurement of children's performance using standardized tests, such as **normal curve, normal range, percentile,** or **standard deviation.**

BOX 9.1

Summary of Characteristics of Specific Language Impairment

- SLI is a relatively common developmental disorder that affects approximately 7% of the general population.

- SLI consists of persistent language learning difficulties in the absence of other clinically significant conditions, although some mild cognitive deficits have often been found in children with SLI.

- Children with SLI, around 4–7 years old, have both general and specific delays in their language development. They show general delays, often of about 2 years, in terms of vocabulary size, sentence length, and narrative abilities. They show specific—that is, more profound—delays with some aspects of morphosyntax; for example, acquisition of late-acquired grammatical morphemes in English, like past tense *-ed*, can be more than 2 years delayed, and may never be fully acquired.

- Children with SLI also show profound delays/deficits in certain language processing skills that are critical for language learning, such as phonological memory (see Chapter 6).

- Children with SLI are at greater risk than unaffected children for reading impairment and attention-deficit/hyperactivity disorder (ADHD); however, the reasons for these connections with other disorders are not yet completely understood.

- The root causes of SLI include an inherited genetic component. The root deficits caused by SLI could be in the ability to establish linguistic mental representations, in more fundamental perceptual–cognitive processing mechanisms that underlie language learning and other cognitive functions, or in both; this is currently a matter of debate among researchers.

Because some readers may not be familiar with these concepts, we have included a brief explanation in an appendix to this chapter, "The normal curve and related concepts."

SLI is typically diagnosed based on a combination of exclusionary and inclusionary criteria. Exclusionary criteria include no presence of hearing impairment, no autism spectrum disorder, no severe intellectual disability as found in disorders like Down syndrome, no oromotor limitations, and no frank neurological trauma (Leonard, 1998). Inclusionary criteria usually include lower-than-age–expected performance on a language test battery and a nonverbal IQ standard score above 85 (i.e., within the normal range, 85–115; Leonard, 1998). In some cases, children who meet all the criteria except that their IQ scores are between 75 and 80 are considered to have "*nonspecific* language impairment" or simply "language impairment" because although their IQs are lower than the average, they are not in the range associated with intellectual disabilities (Rice, Tomblin, Hoffman, Richman, & Marquis, 2004; see also Swisher, Plante, & Lowell, 1994). How is "lower-than-age–expected performance" determined? This is based on normal curve distribution measurements (see this chapter's appendix). Most commonly, researchers consider children to be SLI if their performance on most or all language tests within a battery is 1.25 or more standard deviations below the mean (Leonard, 1998). For clinical identification, score levels that qualify for services can vary and sometimes be closer to 2 standard deviations below the mean, depending on the school or health district. The main point is that there is no universally agreed-upon definition of "lower-than-age–expected performance" for the diagnosis of SLI, apart from scores being generally lower than the normal range, and clinicians follow the criteria used in their district.

What is important about the identification of SLI for both researchers and clinicians is that other possible explanations of poor test performance—or language learning difficulties, more broadly—need to be ruled out by considering exclusionary factors before a firm diagnosis of SLI can be made. For example, in the case of dual language children, the list of exclusionary factors could include language exposure factors (we elaborate more on this in the section "Strategies for Assessment and Identification with Dual Language Children"). Because SLI, by definition, is a disorder that primarily affects language, accurate identification of SLI in dual language children tends to be more complex than for other disorders that are diagnosed, in part, on the basis of nonlinguistic inclusionary criteria. Throughout this chapter, we use the broader term *language impairment* more often than SLI because sometimes we are referring to research that included children with nonverbal IQs lower than 85 or because we are referring to children who have neurodevelopmental syndromes that have language impairment as a consequence as well as children with SLI. However, where appropriate, we use the term SLI.

What Are the Characteristics of Dual Language Children with Language Delay/ Impairment?

Despite the significant Spanish–English-speaking populations in the United States and the large French–English bilingual populations in Canada, and despite widespread immigration in these countries as well as in Australia and Western Europe, until recently, surprisingly little research attention has been paid to examining bilingual acquisition in children with language impairment. One unfortunate outcome of this lack of research is that parents, educators, and health practitioners have had limited information to guide them in making decisions about these children. The recent upsurge in research on bilingual children with language impairment means that more information is now available than when we wrote the first edition of this book. In this section, we review the existing research on dual language children with language delay/impairment, both simultaneous bilinguals and L2 learners. Our review is organized such that the linguistic characteristics of these children are compared with both their unaffected dual language peers and their monolingual peers who also have language impairment.

In Chapter 3, we discussed the limited capacity hypothesis, which is essentially the belief that the human language faculty is set to acquire one language and that acquiring two languages thus exceeds its capacity. If the limited capacity hypothesis were true, then bilingual children would show pronounced delays and difficulty in their language learning, but as we have shown in the previous chapters (especially Chapters 3 and 4), this does not happen. A summary of the main points from previous chapters is given in Box 9.2. These points show that for the key elements of early acquisition, bilingualism does not cause language delay in children. However, it is still relevant to ask whether the limited capacity hypothesis might apply to dual language children with language delays or impairment because these children are acquiring two languages with language learning disabilities. The research reviewed in this section shows that, contrary to what is often believed by parents, educators and clinicians, there is little evidence that dual language learning puts children with language delay/impairment at a disadvantage; therefore, this research also argues against the limited capacity hypothesis.

Simultaneous Bilingual Children   What happens to the language development of simultaneous bilingual children who are later diagnosed with SLI? We conducted research to address this question with a group of 7-year-old French–English bilingual children residing in Montreal. All of these children were simultaneous bilinguals from majority language backgrounds, all had been exposed to both languages in the home from birth, and all resided in communities where both languages were widely spoken and valued; in other words, they lived in an additive bilingual environment. These children were growing up very much like the profiled child James. All of the children were assessed as having SLI after they turned 4 years old, and they received intervention services. They were all below age expectations in their linguistic abilities in both languages; they had nonverbal IQ scores in the normal range; and they had no frank neurological trauma or other neurodevelopmental disorders. We examined many aspects of these children's morphosyntax in both French and English and compared them with monolinguals with SLI in each language (Paradis, 2007; Paradis, Crago, & Genesee, 2005/2006; Paradis, Crago, Genesee, & Rice, 2003). We found that the bilingual children were less accurate with verb morphology in both languages, which is expected in French- and English-speaking children with SLI, but importantly, they did not exhibit lower levels of ability with these morphemes than their monolingual age peers with SLI. The bilingual children had shorter MLUs than unaffected monolinguals their own age, but had similar MLUs as monolinguals with SLI their own age. Furthermore, the bilingual children with SLI also showed no difficulties in accurately producing early acquired grammatical morphemes, also expected as part of the SLI profile in both languages.

Therefore, these bilingual children with SLI, like monolingual children with SLI, had specific delays with late-acquired grammatical morphemes in French and English and

---

BOX 9.2

Summary of Typical Early Bilingual Development: The Issue of Delay

- Bilingual children are not delayed in the onset of the early linguistic milestones of first word and first word combinations.

- Bilingual children's early vocabularies tend to be smaller than those of monolinguals in each language, but when combined, they are as big or bigger than the vocabularies of monolinguals, and thus bilingual children are not slower to accumulate concept–word pairings, in spite of their dual language environment.

- The average length of bilingual children's early sentences (mean length of utterance [MLU]) in both languages is within the normal range, although they are often at the lower bound of that range. The one bilingual child with language delay that we studied had shorter MLUs than both his bilingual and monolingual peers from age 2 to 3 years.

- Bilingual children show productive command of the various components of morphosyntax following a similar time line as monolingual children, but they can lag behind in perfecting some details. For example, they start to use grammatical morphemes in spontaneous speech at the same age as monolingual children do, but may take longer to reach 90% or greater accuracy in producing all grammatical morphemes in both languages.

- In their dominant language, bilingual children often display vocabulary sizes and morphosyntactic abilities on par with monolingual children; in their nondominant language, they can sometimes display lower language abilities than monolingual children.

- Bilingual children's dominant language is typically the language to which they receive more exposure, and exposure to both languages is seldom equal. Bilingual children who receive 50% or more of their input in a particular language can display similar levels of development as monolingual children in that language.

---

general delays for other aspects of their language development. We found that most of these children were not strongly dominant in either language, but of those who were dominant in one language, some exhibited more pronounced morphosyntactic deficits in their nondominant language as compared with their dominant language. This pattern parallels what has been found for bilingual children with typical language development: children's language development is often more advanced in their dominant language (see Box 9.2 and Chapter 4). We also found that these bilingual children with SLI used their two languages appropriately according to their interlocutors' preferences, and they did not display indiscriminate code-mixing that might signal some pragmatic impairment (see Chapter 5). To summarize, these French–English bilingual children with SLI showed equivalent levels of morphosyntactic proficiency and equivalent morphosyntactic profiles, in both their languages, as did children also affected with SLI who were learning just one language. In addition, they exhibited the same general patterns of bilingual development as their unaffected bilingual peers.

These positive outcomes for bilingual children with SLI are not limited to children in a highly additive bilingual environment. Vera Gutiérrez-Clellen and her colleagues have studied the morphosyntactic development of Spanish–English bilingual children with SLI residing in southern California and have found parallel results (Gutiérrez-Clellen, Simon-Cereijido, & Wagner, 2008). Specifically, they found that on a storytelling task, bilingual children with SLI made errors with similar verbal morphology in English as English monolingual children with SLI, and to a similar degree. They also examined children's abilities to use overt subjects in sentences in English. In Spanish, but not in English, the subject of a sentence can be dropped if it is known to both interlocutors in a conversation. These researchers hypothesized that perhaps this difference between Spanish and English might confuse the bilingual children with SLI and cause them to drop subjects in English in the same contexts that they could be dropped in Spanish. However, they found that the bilingual children did not erroneously transfer this grammatical rule from Spanish to English. The study by Gutiérrez-Clellen and her colleagues was based on children who were 2 years younger than the French–English children in our research; therefore, their study indicated that it is possible for bilingual children with SLI to have similar proficiency to monolingual children with SLI as young as 5 years old.

Regarding language choice and code-mixing, Gutiérrez-Clellen, Simon-Cereijido, and Erickson Leone (2009) examined how Spanish–English bilingual 5-year-olds used their two languages when telling stories and having spontaneous conversations in each of them; the study included bilingual children with typical language development and those with SLI. The researchers found numerous parallels between the affected and unaffected bilingual children suggesting that SLI does not interfere with this component of bilingual language development (see Chapter 5). First, all children code-mixed more often in their nondominant language, code-mixed more often in conversation than in the more formal narrative task, and also code-mixed more in Spanish regardless of dominance. This last result possibly reflects an awareness of the minority–majority sociolinguistic status of the two languages. Second, both typically developing bilingual children and bilingual children with SLI had low levels of code-mixing overall, but the types of code-mixed structures used were similar for both groups, and importantly, both groups of children showed compliance with grammatical rules for code-mixing. In short, bilingual children with SLI displayed both pragmatic and grammatical skill in their code-mixing that was appropriate for their age.

With respect to children with other developmental disorders, research on French–English bilingual children with Down syndrome was discussed in Chapter 3. The results of this research showed that even in the face of severe intellectual disabilities, these children were able to achieve levels of linguistic proficiency in two languages within the expectations of their mental age and with the typical linguistic profile of their neurodevelopmental disorder (Kay-Raining Bird, Cleave, Trudeau, Thordardottir, Sutton, & Thorpe, 2005). Thus, whether children's language impairment is "specific" to language or the result of profound cognitive deficits, they are still capable of learning two languages.

Second Language Learners   Simultaneous bilingual development could be considered optimal for successful bilingual outcomes, because of the extensive exposure to both languages from an early age, especially if children are in an additive bilingual environment. In contrast, L2 learners, by definition, do not learn their two languages at the same time and have less exposure to one of them. More important, first language (L1) minority children learning an L2 are often in subtractive bilingual environments. It is reasonable to ask whether minority L1/majority L2 children with SLI might show some unique patterns in their L2 development when compared with monolingual children with SLI learning that language, and whether they might display greater difficulties in becoming bilingual than L2 learners with typical development.

As mentioned earlier, monolingual children with language delay and impairment are slow to learn language at first, and those with impairment have long-lasting general and specific language delays. Do children with language delay and impairment show the same kinds of developmental patterns when they learn a second language? Paradis (2008, 2010a, 2010b) examined the developmental trajectories in the L2 English of two Cantonese Chinese–speaking boys with language delay/impairment, KVNL and WLLS, as compared with their L2 peers with typical language development. KVNL, who had language delay in Cantonese, began to learn English at age 3½. For 2 years, KVNL consistently lagged behind typically developing Chinese-speaking children (Mandarin and Cantonese) with the same amount of exposure to English in his use of late-acquired grammatical morphemes (verbal morphology), but he eventually caught up to them in his third year of learning English. Thus, the language delay profile he showed in his L1 was duplicated in his L2 development and, importantly, the delay in his L2 resolved as it did in his L1 development.

WLLS, whose profile in both his languages met the criteria for SLI, began learning English at age 4. Like KVNL, WLLS lagged behind typically developing Chinese-speaking children, but unlike KVNL, he did not catch up to them by the end of the study. Jacobson and Schwartz (2005) also found that Spanish L1/English L2 children with SLI lagged behind their typically developing L2 age peers on late-acquired morphemes such as past tense -ed, even after 4 years of exposure. However, after 3 years of exposure to English, WLLS's accuracy in using these morphemes reached the level of monolingual English speakers with SLI who were the same age, which is the expected outcome for a child with SLI. Furthermore, WLLS's use of grammatical morphemes that are not particularly difficult for children with SLI to learn was very close in accuracy to that of his typically developing L2 peers; for example, his use of plural -s. Thus, WLLS exhibited the general and specific delay profile in his English common to monolingual children with SLI. Taken together, KVNL's development and WLLS's development show that the development of English in children with language delay or impairment unfolds in a similar way, whether English is a child's L1 or L2.

The case studies of KVNL and WLLS are supported by research with Turkish L1/German L2 children (Rothweiler, Chilla, & Clahsen, 2009). Rothweiler and colleagues studied a group of early sequential bilingual children with SLI who began to learn the majority language, German, around 3 years of age; they also studied a group of monolingual German children with SLI. When the children were between 4 and 8 years old, both groups showed deficits in their ability to use subject–verb agreement morphemes, but both groups were quite accurate in their use of some complex syntactic constructions. Importantly, the L2 learners with SLI had similar levels of accuracy as their monolingual peers with SLI on all measures in German. Thus, like Paradis's Cantonese–English children, these Turkish–German bilingual children with SLI displayed similar developmental profiles and similar levels of proficiency to their monolingual peers with SLI, after a certain amount of exposure to their second language.

Do minority L2 children with language delay and impairment show greater difficulties in becoming bilingual? In other words, do they show greater delays compared with typically developing L2 learners than monolingual children with SLI show compared with their typically developing peers? Paradis and Sorenson Duncan (2009) compared English L2 children with typical development with English L2 children with SLI on two measures of English found to be sources of specific delays in children with SLI: English verb morphology and English nonword repetition (a measure of phonological short-term memory). The children were 6 years old, came from various L1 backgrounds, and had approximately 2 years of exposure to English in Edmonton, Canada. As expected, the L2 children with SLI performed worse than the unaffected children on both measures, but importantly, the differentials between the scores of the children with SLI and the children with typical development was of the same magnitude as found in comparisons of monolingual children with and without SLI; in other words, the L2 children with SLI were not *extraordinarily* delayed in their English L2 development when compared with their typically developing L2 peers (see also Paradis, 2010a, 2010b).

Also related to the question of whether L2 children with SLI have greater difficulties becoming bilingual is whether they have greater difficulties continuing to develop their minority L1. In a study using parent reports of L2 children's development of the minority L1, Paradis, Emmerzael, and Sorenson Duncan (2010) found that L2 children with SLI did not seem to be more vulnerable to L1 loss than their typically developing peers. The parents of children both with and without SLI did not rate their children's L1 abilities highly overall. The parents of children with SLI consistently rated their children as having poorer L1 abilities than the parents of their unaffected peers. However, questions about L1 loss revealed that the parents of children with SLI were not more likely to answer that their children were undergoing L1 loss than the parents of children with typical development. These parent report results are consistent with direct observations of minority children's L1 abilities. Gutiérrez-Clellen, Restrepo, and Simon-Cereijido (2006) examined a range of morphosytactic measures in Spanish from Spanish L1/English L2 children with SLI, ages 4–7 years; these children were dominant in Spanish, indicating that they were in the beginner-to-intermediate stages of learning English. They found that these English L2 children with SLI performed similarly in Spanish to monolingual Spanish speakers with SLI. Therefore, the introduction of the majority language was not interfering with their Spanish language abilities, at least at that stage in their development.

In contrast to the findings on English L2 and German L2 children, Dutch researchers have found more mixed bilingual outcomes for Turkish L1/Dutch L2 children with SLI. Steenge (2006) and Orgassa and Weerman (2008) found that some gaps in Dutch morphosyntax between L2 learners with SLI and monolingual children with SLI persisted even after the L2 children had had four years or more exposure to Dutch. It is possible that the difficulties learning the majority language that are experienced by these children in the Netherlands are related to environmental factors, such as social isolation of immigrant communities, and less related to intrinsic barriers posed by SLI for the long term ability to learn two languages (see Paradis, 2010a, 2010b). Further research is needed to know for certain, but it is important to point out that the successes that have been documented do not necessarily apply to all bilingual children with SLI in all social contexts.

Should Children with Language Delay/Impairment Learn Two Languages?

In our experience, there is a widespread belief among parents and professionals that bilingualism poses too much of a burden on a child with language learning difficulties, whether the result of SLI or of other disorders. Parents of children with developmental language disorders are often counseled by educators and clinicians to use only one language with their children, and effectively arrest their children's bilingual development, or they are counseled to not consider second language/bilingual education programs for their children, or to withdraw them from such programs if they have already started. This kind of decision can have irrevocable and profound costs for a child, such as loss of educational opportunities, loss of ability to communicate fully with other family members, shift in ethnic identity, and limitations on access to an ethnic community—losses and limitations their siblings might not have. Moreover, for some families, the choice of using one language is simply unavailable; the household operates in two languages, and no one can change that; or, in the case of migrant families, everyone needs to learn the majority language, but at the same time, the parents cannot "give up" speaking their native language. Furthermore, families of a child with SLI may already be sending older siblings to a L2 immersion program. Clearly, the decision to eliminate a language from a child's environment cannot be made lightly and should not be made in ignorance. Whether to continue or initiate bilingual learning for a child with a developmental language disorder is one of the most frequently asked questions we receive in emails and phone calls from professionals and parents; some examples are given in Box 9.3. For this reason, we have included a section focused solely on this question. In the previous section, we summarized research on the characteristics of bilingual language development in children with SLI. What this research shows is that dual language learning is certainly within the capacity of children with SLI, and that therefore there is no reason to stop bilingual development on the grounds that these children's language learning difficulties might worsen if they have two languages to deal with instead of one. Furthermore, research also shows that children with SLI are able to learn a second language. Children with SLI do not appear to develop their two languages differently, or to a lower level of proficiency, than monolingual children with SLI. Moreover, these positive bilingual outcomes do not depend on whether children receive language therapy in one or two languages. The French–English bilingual children with SLI in the research we have conducted were receiving therapy in one language, usually French. The Canadian English L2 children discussed in the previous section were receiving intervention and/or attending language enrichment kindergarten programs in English only. In addition, we discussed research in Chapter 8 demonstrating that children with cognitive and linguistic disabilities can do just as well academically in second-language immersion programs as their counterparts in English-only programs. Therefore, there is no evidence for thinking that dual language learning is a risk factor for children with language delay or impairment and, in turn, there is no basis in evidence for counseling parents to switch to one language at home or to not place their children in immersion education.

In Chapter 6, we discussed the reasons why maintaining and developing the L1 is beneficial for minority language children. These reasons apply no less to L2 children with developmental language disorders. One of the main reasons given for maintaining proficiency in the L1 was so that parents and children could communicate easily with each

BOX 9.3

One of the most frequently asked questions sent to us by professionals and parents is whether dual language learning is appropriate for children with developmental speech and language disorders. Some examples of these messages are presented here. The information in this chapter shows that there is no evidence that learning two languages is a risk factor for these children, and that, for some children, continuing to learn both languages would have benefits for them.

Dear Dr. Paradis,

I work with many children with autism whose parents' first language is not English. Parents often ask if they should be speaking in English or in their first language to the child. This is a child who often is between 3 and 6 years old with little to no language. I struggle with what to say, because I know that the research says that a strong first language base helps, but these kids have no language, so I'm teaching English, because it's all I can teach. And if the parents are teaching a different language, I think it's too much for them, and they are not getting the repetition that kids with ASD so badly need. I was just wondering if there is any research out there.

A speech-language pathologist

Dear Prof. Paradis,

I have a 4-year-old child who has recently been diagnosed with SLI. My child's main language is Italian, although my wife speaks to him in English. We plan to move to Canada in July and we are obviously concerned with the change in language, as the doctor who made the diagnosis told us that it is not advisable to change languages. Is changing the main language an absolute contraindication or it is possible to do it without significant impairment in the medium-term prognosis? Is there a specific intervention by a speech and language pathologist that is addressed specifically at bilingual children with SLI? Is there anything that we can do as parents to develop our child's bilingualism even with SLI?

A father

Bonjour Mme. Paradis,

My daughter (2.5 years old) has been recently assessed as having a speech impediment. As such, we have started English speech therapy and have noted some gradual improvements in her ability (and willingness) to say a number of words. Prior to the phonology assessment, we had enrolled my daughter in a French preschool. Since the assessment was performed, our speech therapist and the administrators of the preschool she is associated with have been attempting to persuade us that she should be receiving speech therapy exclusively in English and have strongly recommended we remove her from the French preschool and enroll her in the English preschool. From my perspective, their arguments show a

> *unilingual bias, as they have not presented strong empirical evidence that would indicate that a bilingual approach to my daughter's early speech development would lead to a further delay. Considering your experience in this field of study, I was hoping you would have the time to provide your own insights in this matter.*
>
> *A father*
>
> *Dear Professor Genesee,*
>
> *My Spanish-language preschool is thriving and I am very excited to expand our program. Based on my experience, it seems to me like next year we will move towards a bilingual mode instead of a total immersion—most of the students are monolingual living in monolingual households and it makes more sense to use their native language as well as their second language. There is a family that is interested in signing up for the fall and their only concern is that their son—a 3-year-old boy adopted from Guatemala—has been diagnosed with some kind of speech delay and they are afraid that introducing a second language would do more harm than benefit his condition. My question to you is (without knowing the specifics): Is that the case with language delayed children? To what extent?*
>
> *A preschool director*

other, and we will focus on this reason here, because for children with developmental disorders, this is a crucial consideration. It is likely that for children with Down syndrome, fragile X syndrome, or autism spectrum disorders, their parents are their primary caregivers and, thus, a primary source of social interaction, for an extended period. At the same time, these children are likely to experience a great deal of contact with education and healthcare professionals who will most likely be speakers of the majority language only. If parents try to switch to using only their L2 with these children, it is difficult to see how they could provide their children with the rich linguistic input they need or feel satisfied with their ability to communicate comfortably with their children—both of these factors are vital to their children's well-being. In short, it does not seem to us that "monolingualism" is an appropriate option for these children.

Kremer-Sadlik (2005) studied language use among families of high-functioning children with autism who spoke a minority language at home in a context where English was the majority language. The study consisted of parent interviews and recordings of conversations among family members. After diagnosis, parents were all counseled to speak only English with their children, on the grounds that it would be too difficult for their children to learn two languages and that consistency between the language at home and the language of therapy was considered to be beneficial. Parents noted some or all of the following outcomes for their child with autism as a result of ceasing to interact with that child in the minority first language:

- The child did not speak the first language anymore.
- The child was left out of family conversations among parents and siblings that took place in the first language.

- The family participated less in cultural and religious activities in the first language.
- The child expressed rejection of his ethnic identity.

Parents also reported that they did not always do the social and language modeling exercises recommended by the clinician, primarily because they were not sufficiently comfortable and proficient in English. Furthermore, Kremer-Sadlik documented clear communication barriers in conversations between parents and their children with autism: barriers that they did not have with their unaffected children who continued to speak the first language. An excerpt from a family dinnertime conversation in Box 9.4 illustrates this. Finally, Kremer-Sadlik found that one family disregarded the advice of the healthcare practitioners and continued to use the first language with their child after diagnosis, with the result that their child maintained his bilingualism and with no apparent detriment to his development. This study serves as a powerful reminder of how removing a language from a child's environment can have far-reaching consequences for an entire family.

Our general advice to parents and professionals is to support, in any way they can, the dual language learning of children with developmental language disorders. This support should be forthcoming whether children are already bilingual due to home or community experience, or are in the process of becoming bilingual through schooling. However, such general advice always needs to be qualified and shaped to each individual child's situation. Bilingualism is a choice for some families and a necessity for others. For example, let us consider the contrasting situations of the profiled children, Luis and Samantha, both Spanish–English bilingual children. Luis is a Spanish L1/English L2 child growing up in California in a predominately ethnically Mexican, Spanish-speaking community. Luis's parents are much more proficient in Spanish than in English. For Luis to maintain a close relationship with his parents and to function socially in his community, he needs to speak Spanish. If a child like Luis were diagnosed with SLI or another developmental disorder, it would not be realistic for his family to raise him only speaking English, and as we have noted previously, there is no compelling reason to make such a recommendation anyway.

Luis's situation contrasts with the situation of Samantha. Samantha is an English L1 child growing up in Arizona whose parents have decided to send her to Spanish immersion school. Samantha would not face communication barriers within her own family or community if she spoke only English. If a child like Samantha were diagnosed with a developmental disorder affecting language, should her parents be advised to keep her in immersion schooling? Our recommendation in this case would be based on factors such as Samantha's parents' ability and willingness to put the extra effort needed to assist her in becoming bilingual, even though she has language learning difficulties; Samantha's enthusiasm for attending school in Spanish; and the ability of the school she attends to provide her with the speech-language services and special education support she might require. But, crucially, we would like to emphasize that if parents of a child like Samantha are advised to place her in English-only schooling, this advice should not be based on the notion that a child with language impairment is not capable of learning two languages; the evidence does not support such a notion.

BOX 9.4

Family Conversation at Dinnertime

John is a high-functioning child with autism; Jay is his older brother. John no longer speaks Mandarin Chinese, because his parents stopped interacting with him in that language after his diagnosis. The following excerpt is from Kremer Sadlik, 2005, p. 1230:

The family, the two parents, John and his older brother, are watching an avalanche on the news while eating dinner. John proposes that the avalanche was purposefully caused by a bomb. Both parents reject John's proposal. Thus, John asks for an alternative explanation. Father tries to provide a reason for the avalanche, but stops when he cannot find the word "gravity" in English. He asks in Chinese for Jay's help. Father continues to explain, but his idea is not made clear as the language is choppy. Eventually, Jay interrupts the father and goes on to explain in Chinese that John was correct. During this exchange in Chinese, John watches TV, unaware of his brother's defense. The parents then turn to John to acknowledge in English that he was correct.

John: [looking at father] How did they, um, make it go down?

Father: You know, it's heavy so, that—*Jay, chung li chiao se ma?*
             (Jay, How do you say gravity in English?)

Jay: Gravity.

Father: Gravity! OK? They pour down. Something look like this. You s-[makes gestures] you stand off this one and. . . .

Jay: That's not how they do it.

John: [Turns his look away from father and looks at the TV]

Jay: That's not how they do it.

Mother: He said.

Father: Hu?

Jay: *Ta sou de duei.*
             (He said it right.)

Father: *Sha me duei.*
             (What's right?)

Jay: *Ta sou de duei. Ta mien na bien tai dou dong shih le. Ta men bou tsi tse za, zen gou chi de shih hou, suai le, dou shih.*
             (He said it right. They have too much stuff there. If they don't blow it up, when people go across there, stuff might . . .)

Mother: Oh, so—so they <u>did</u> bomb it, huh?

Jay: Uh-huh.

Mother: OK.

Father: [looking at John] So you got it, huh?

ASSESSMENT AND INTERVENTION WITH DUAL LANGUAGE CHILDREN

Overidentification of language and learning disabilities is a well-known hazard in the assessment of children in multilingual, multicultural settings (Cummins, 2000; Donovan & Cross, 2002; Gutiérrez-Clellen et al., 2006). Overidentification occurs when a dual language child is inappropriately diagnosed with a language or a learning disability and receives unnecessary services and/or is inappropriately placed in special education classes. Overidentification can have negative consequences for children with respect to their self-esteem, their attitudes about schooling, and even their future educational opportunities. Equally important, and possibly on the rise, is the problem of underidentification (Crutchley, Conti-Ramsden, & Botting, 1997; Donovan & Cross, 2002; Roseberry-McKibbin, 1995). Underidentification occurs when a dual language child has a language or learning disability, but it goes unnoticed or undiagnosed, because it is assumed that her poor performance in school or in the majority language and in language-related academic activities are the result of learning two languages. Underidentification can also have negative consequences for a child, because academic performance can suffer as a result of the absence of needed intervention for language skills. This section is focused on uncovering the reasons for misidentification of dual language children and presenting some strategies that might help in reducing the barriers to accurate and timely identification of language impairment in dual language children. In addition, we discuss particular approaches to intervention with dual language children. For practical information on assessment and intervention with culturally and linguistically diverse children aimed at speech-language pathologists and special educators in particular, see Roseberry-McKibbin (2008). For information about the referral and language evaluation process aimed at general educators in particular, see Tabors (2008).

Issues in Assessment and Identification of Dual Language Children

This discussion is primarily oriented toward raising awareness about the problems associated with the use of language tests that are norm-referenced with monolingual children for the assessment of dual language children. However, some of the points raised are equally relevant to consider when using informal measures of bilingual children's language development. Although it is widely acknowledged that use of monolingual norm-referenced testing material with dual language children can lead to biased assessment—that is, can underestimate dual language children's linguistic competence and language learning capacities—it is nevertheless a common practice (Caesar & Kohler, 2007; Gutiérrez-Clellen et al., 2006; Roseberry-McKibbin, 2008). The primary reason for this is the absence of both testing materials appropriate for dual language children and professionals qualified to administer them. For practical reasons, the development of dual language testing materials and professional training programs would likely only be undertaken for large populations of dual language children, such as Spanish–English bilingual children in the United States or French–English bilingual children in Canada. Therefore, it is important for clinicians working with diverse linguistic and cultural communities to understand the issues that arise when monolingual standardized tests are used with dual language children.

We have divided this section according to several factors that constitute barriers to the accurate assessment and identification of children with language learning difficulties among bilingual populations.

Overlap Between L2 and SLI   We have conducted numerous studies, in both French and English, that revealed many common characteristics in the incompletely learned language of L2 children and monolingual children with SLI. In French, L2 learners and monolingual children with SLI the same age make errors with auxiliary verbs and with direct object pronouns, but have fewer difficulties with the use of articles or prepositions. Thus, the morphosyntactic profile of French L2 children is parallel to children with SLI at the beginning and intermediate stages of L2 learning (Paradis, 2004; Paradis & Crago, 2000, 2004). Similarly, we have found that typically developing children who are learning English as an L2 have an "SLI" profile in English during the early stages of learning, for example, low accuracy with verb morphology and high accuracy with nominal morphology like plural -*s* (Paradis, 2005; Paradis, Rice, Crago, & Marquis, 2008). We found only two distinguishing features between English L2 learners and monolingual children with SLI: 1) English L2 learners acquired BE morphemes, as in *the bears <u>are</u> resting, the kitty <u>is</u> thirsty,* far in advance of verbal inflections like past tense -*ed,* and the monolingual children with SLI acquired them in tandem; 2) English L2 learners were more likely to have "creative" errors in their attempts to use grammatical morphemes than the monolingual children with SLI, who tended only to omit them. Similarities between the morphosyntactic profiles of L2 children and children with SLI have also been documented in Hebrew, Dutch, and Swedish, (Armon-Lotem, 2010; de Jong, 2010; Håkansson, 2001). One unfortunate outcome of such overlap is that there are very few linguistic features that can be deemed unique to L2 learners or unique to children with SLI, although researchers seem to have found more of them in Dutch and Hebrew than we have found in English.

Paradis (2005, 2008) looked at the performance of English L2 children on a standardized test of morphosyntax developed to identify children with SLI and found that just 1 of 24 typical English L2 learners had age-appropriate scores after 1 year of exposure to English; after 3 years of exposure, still only about half of the children had age-appropriate scores on this test. Therefore, overlap in morphosyntactic characteristics between typical L2 development and impaired development could be a contributing factor to overidentification. Overlap between L2 and SLI has also been found for language processing. Windsor and Kohnert (2004) found that speed of processing and accuracy on a picture-naming task were similar in Spanish–English bilingual children and English monolingual children with SLI, but that both groups were different from monolingual children with typical language development. This means that differential diagnosis of language impairment among L2 learners might be difficult on the basis of tests and subtests probing either morphosyntactic or processing skills. Moreover, it is likely that many tests would probe these skills because, as noted earlier, children with language impairment have profound deficits—specific delays—in these two areas.

Bilingual Input Factors   As discussed in Chapter 4, simultaneous bilingual children sometimes take longer to master certain aspects of morphosytnax than monolingual children, and they also tend to have smaller vocabularies in each language than monolingual children—features likely related to their dual versus single language input. Recall also from Chapter 4 that simultaneous bilingual children are often dominant—or more proficient—in one of their languages. A bilingual child's dominant language is usually the language they hear and use more often. These features of typical bilingual development can have an impact on children's performance on monolingual norm-referenced tests. Studies of French–English bilingual children, from toddlers to school age, have found that they sometimes perform below age expectations on standardized tests of vocabulary and grammar (Paradis, 2009; 2010c; Thordardottir, Rothenberg, Rivard, & Naves, 2006, Thordardottir, 2008). However, these studies also found that when children's performance in their dominant language is considered, they usually perform according to age-expected norms.

More specifically, Thordardottir (2008) found that if 4-year-old bilingual children received 50% or more of their linguistic input in one of their languages, such as French, there was little risk of misidentification on the basis of a test given in French. Similarly, Paradis (2009, 2010c) found that balanced bilingual children, those who received roughly equal amounts of exposure to French and English at home, performed within age expectations on tests in both languages. In contrast, English-dominant bilingual children and French-dominant bilingual children often met age-based expectations on tests in their dominant language only. Studies with Spanish–English simultaneous bilingual children in the United States have also found that children can often perform within the normal range on vocabulary and grammar tests in the language they receive more exposure to, although this does not always mean they perform identically to monolingual children (Gutiérrez-Clellen & Simón-Cereijido, 2007; Oller & Eilers, 2002). In sum, even children who have been learning two languages from birth cannot be expected to perform according to monolingual norms on tests; however, they often do so if the language of testing is their dominant language.

Unique Bilingual Profiles Dual language children often display a unique profile of strengths and weakness in comparison with monolingual children across different domains of language and across different tasks. Assessment protocols typically consist of a test battery, or an omnibus test with numerous subtests, in order to generate a comprehensive view on a child's linguistic competence. In Chapter 6, we showed that L2 children can exhibit highly uneven performance across different tests, called *profile effects*. It is possible that L2 children could have scores two standard deviations below the normal range on one test or subtest, but well within the normal range on another. Profile effects are most likely the result of whether a test probes what could be called "language-general" versus "language-specific" abilities. Language-general abilities are basic processing mechanisms or linguistic–cognitive interface skills that do not depend entirely on accumulated language-specific knowledge, and could potentially be shared between the two languages of a bilingual (see Chapter 6). By contrast, language-specific abilities are, for example, vocabulary or morphosyntactic knowledge that is specific to one language. Furthermore, the task bilingual children are required to do on a test can make a difference in how well they can demonstrate their linguistic knowledge and processing abilities. Paradis (2010c) compared French–English bilingual children's performance on a production task for verbal morphology in English and on a grammaticality judgment task, where children had to indicate whether a sentence was correctly expressed—errors were with the same verbal morphology. The bilingual children were much more likely to perform according to monolingual age-based expectations on the grammaticality judgment task than on the production task. Paradis hypothesized that this discrepancy between language production and knowledge could be attributed to two factors: bilingual children might have enhanced metalinguistic awareness skills, giving them a relative advantage on a grammaticality judgment task, but at the same time, competition between their two linguistic systems makes accuracy in language production relatively more difficult for them.

Both profile effects and task effects can cause bilingual children's performance on the tests that constitute a test battery to have some unique characteristics, and furthermore, these characteristics can be present even in bilingual children's dominant language, and even in a second language after years of exposure. It is important to be aware that tests probing language specific abilities, or tasks demanding exact accuracy in production, could be more biased against dual language learners than other tests and tasks.

Cultural Issues in Testing   In Chapter 2, we discussed how child rearing and language socialization patterns could differ greatly across cultures. Standardized language assessment materials are typically designed for children from the mainstream or majority culture in a society and therefore contain many implicit assumptions in both content and procedure about what would be familiar to children. The mainstream cultural orientation of a test could make the results of that test biased against children who are not from that culture. We raise this issue here because it could pertain to many dual language children, but it is also important to keep in mind that cultural differences in child rearing and language socialization patterns can occur even when the language of the child and the test are the same.

How would cultural differences affect a child's performance on a test? First, cultural differences could influence how a child responds to individual words, to concepts being referred to, or to scenes that are depicted, due to the lack of experiences that would make them familiar. For example, test items might assume knowledge of foods, toys and toy play, and daily routines from the mainstream culture that are not familiar to children from a minority culture. Thus, children might not be able to provide the expected answers— not because they have vocabulary deficits or other language learning difficulties, but because they have had different experiences, at home in particular, than the children for whom the test was designed. Cultural differences could also influence whether a child is familiar with the testing procedures, or how a child views the appropriate way to respond to a question from an adult. For example, in many cultures, children are expected to not be talkative with adults, parents do not do a lot of book activities with their children, or engage them in question-and-answer routines to "check" the child's knowledge of color words, names of farm animals, and so on. If the Inuit child we profiled in Chapter 1, Pauloosie, were having his language skills evaluated using a task where he was asked to tell a story based on looking at a book, his language abilities might be underestimated simply because he was unfamiliar with how to do such a task, and because he kept his answers very brief when talking to an adult. In some cases, differences from mainstream children are not directly attributable to culture per se, but more to environmental factors. For example, the profiled child Faisal and his siblings spent time in a refugee camp and thus had no school experiences prior to migrating to Canada. Faisal and his siblings would be unfamiliar with the procedures used in most formal language and academic achievement tests, because they often mimic classroom-based routines or "school culture" more generally.

Limitations in Assessing a Minority Language   Obtaining information on both languages of a dual language child is essential for effective assessment, because children with SLI exhibit symptoms of a developmental language disorder in both languages, not just one. In addition, information on both languages would provide a more complete picture of a bilingual's linguistic abilities. However, when one of a bilingual's languages is a minority language, there can be many barriers to assessment of that language:

- The speech–language pathologist is not fluently bilingual in both languages spoken by the child.

- Interpreters and/or cultural brokers from the child's background cannot be found in the area.

- Very little information exists on the typical and atypical course of development of one of the child's languages.

- The child's current abilities in the minority language may be weak because she is in the process of losing that language and may thus perform poorly on formal or informal evaluations of that language, because they were developed for monolingual speakers of that language.

We would like to point out, in particular, that the use of translated tests from the majority language is problematic, even if interpreters or cultural brokers are available to administer them, for the following reasons:

- They may not be probing for the morphosyntactic structures known to be specifically delayed in children with language impairment. This is because such structures vary across languages (Leonard, 2000).

- Translations are not necessarily culturally adapted.

- The norm-referencing would not be valid.

- Attrition of the minority language could result in poor performance on the test, regardless of whether a child has language learning difficulties. (Even with a legitimately developed test in a child's minority language, a child's language learning abilities could be misrepresented because of minority language attrition.)

Specific Concerns for Internationally Adopted Children   In Chapter 7, we pointed out that some aspects of the language development of internationally adopted (IA) children are like the development of dual language children, but others are not. Therefore, it is worth considering which of the issues we have discussed should be considered when conducting assessments with IA children, and whether there are additional issues to be raised. The issue of input factors is a concern for IA children as well as for bilingual children. Although IA children typically cease to learn their first language when they begin to learn the language of their adopted family and community, they have still not had identical exposure time and experiences as monolingual children who have been learning that language from birth. Research indicates that IA children seem to become functionally monolingual rather rapidly, but this does not mean their proficiency in their adoptive language is necessarily on par with monolingual children in the early stages. IA children tend to score within or above the normal range of performance on language tests by 5 years of age, as long as they were adopted as infants or toddlers. Therefore, caution is recommended when interpreting the results of language tests with these children between the time of adoption and school entry. Interpreting IA children's performance, taking into account their exposure to the adoptive language, is necessary to avoid over-identification of language delay and impairment in IA children.

Another issue of particular concern in the case of IA children is preadoption adversity. Many IA children have spent time in orphanages, and these institutions are usually not optimal environments for child development; they also vary in the quality of care provided (see Chapter 7 for details). Some adopted children have had experiences in their early lives that could put them at risk for developmental delays, including delays in their language development. Although developmental language disorders like SLI are not caused by environmental factors, adverse environmental factors can have a negative impact on language development. Thus, if an IA child has experienced significant deprivation or difficulty prior to adoption, and especially if this adversity was experienced for more than 6 months, then intervention services might be considered, because they could help an individual IA child overcome the potential effects of prior adversity. Therefore, a good understanding of the preadoption circumstances of an IA child could be important for determining not only whether they show signs of language learning difficulties, but also what the source of those difficulties might be.

Strategies for Assessment and Identification of Dual Language Children

In this section, we discuss strategies for conducting assessment with dual language children that could address some of the issues raised in the previous section. Using one or more of these strategies might help to reduce the incidence of misidentification of dual language children. However, it is important to note that none of these strategies has been proven to eliminate the problem of misidentification entirely, so clinicians should be critical and cautious in their approach to assessment and identification of language impairment in dual language children, even when employing these strategies.

Obtain Information About Both Languages   Developmental language impairment affects both languages of a bilingual child; therefore, ascertaining that children show signs of language learning difficulties in both their languages, rather than in one language only, is imperative for accurate identification. There are different methods of obtaining information on both languages of dual language children, and for some of them, the clinician does not need to speak both languages.

Clearly, the most effective method of obtaining information on both languages of a bilingual child is to assess them using valid testing materials that have been developed for that population. In regions where there are large numbers of children learning the same language pair, dual language protocols and testing materials could be available. The Bilingual English Spanish Assessment (BESA), currently under development in the United States, is an example of this kind of testing material (Peña, Gutiérrez-Clellen, Iglesias, Goldstein, & Bedore, n.d.). However, as mentioned previously, the practical value and complexity of designing and norming tests for bilingual speakers of two particular languages make it unlikely that these kinds of tests will be available for many groups.

If no bilingual assessment measure is available, but there are tests available in each language (normed on monolingual speakers of those languages) and the resources to effectively administer them are in place, should they be used? As mentioned in the previous section, use of monolingual norm-referenced tests can lead to overidentification of language delay and impairment in bilingual children, and this could occur even if both languages were tested. However, researchers have investigated adaptations of scoring procedures that could reduce the problems associated with using such tests. Pearson, Fernandez, and Oller (1993) reported the results of an alternative scoring procedure for a parental checklist of early vocabulary and grammatical development in infants and toddlers, now the MacArthur-Bates Communicative Development Inventories™ (CDI; Fenson, Dale, Reznick, Bates, Thal, & Pethick 1994). More specifically, they combined the children's vocabularies in both languages, subtracted translation equivalent words, such as *mesa* and *table,* and then calculated a *total conceptual vocabulary* score across both languages. The rationale for using this alternative scoring system is that the purpose of such vocabulary checklists is to understand whether a child is acquiring word–concept associations at the expected pace. They found that, for total conceptual vocabulary, bilingual children showed similar progress to their monolingual peers (see Bedore, Peña, García, & Cortez, 2005, for more on conceptual scoring techniques).

If no formal tests in one of a bilingual child's two languages are available, informal examination of that language is a possible strategy. Spontaneous language samples from children that are analyzed for certain morphosyntactic structures known to be specifically delayed in children with language impairment can be very useful for assessment (Gutiérrez-Clellen et al., 2006; Restrepo, 1998). However, the clinician would need to be proficient enough in that language to record, transcribe, and analyze the language sample; also, time constraints might make this approach impractical. Alternatively, a clinician could work with a cultural broker or interpreter from that child's community to conduct an informal assessment of whether a child's language proficiency in the minority language appears to be age-appropriate for children growing up outside the home country. A final strategy we suggest is to use a structured parent questionnaire to obtain information on a child's abilities in the minority language. Paradis et al. (2010) examined how well scores from a parent questionnaire on the first language development of children learning English as an L2 discriminated between children with typical development and those with language impairment. The questionnaire had four sections: early milestones, current first-language abilities, behavior and activity preferences, and family history. The questionnaire was not designed for any particular minority language or cultural group and was administered with the assistance of a cultural broker or interpreter if the parents were not fluent in English. The questionnaire scores alone proved to be a moderate discriminator between the children with typical and impaired language development, but with superior specificity (identifying typically developing children as typically developing) to sensitivity (identifying SLI children as SLI). Thus, this questionnaire could be a useful addition to an assessment battery that included tests with good sensitivity.

Obtain Information about Language Exposure Dual language children can have very different input patterns in their two languages, such as simultaneous versus sequential bilingualism, minority versus majority language experiences, two languages at home versus one at home and one at school, and so on. Length of time learning a language, as well as quantity and quality of input, influence children's acquisition rates (see Chapters 4 and 6). It is essential for clinicians to obtain information on children's past and present language exposure patterns in order to set appropriate expectations for children's abilities in each language. The most common method of obtaining this information is through parent and/or teacher questionnaires, and there are several published questionnaires available (Gutiérrez-Clellen & Kreiter, 2003; Roseberry-McKibbin, 2008; Tabors, 2008). Questions for parents usually include the following topics: languages used among family members at home, languages of the child's books and other media, child's language use with peers, and whether the child's language exposure patterns have substantially changed over time. In some cases, parents can be asked to judge which language their child is more proficient in, as an indirect way of determining whether a child is a balanced bilingual or has a dominant language. Our research has shown that parent judgment of language dominance is generally consistent with our direct observation of children's abilities (see Chapter 4 for direct methods of determining language dominance).

For simultaneous bilingual children, knowing the language of greater exposure (i.e., the dominant language) would be useful for assessing the timing of early milestones and for deciding how to interpret a child's results on language tests. Simultaneous bilingual children can be expected to produce first words and first word combinations in at least their dominant language within the normal timeframe. For older bilingual children, assessment of children's abilities in their dominant language is crucial to knowing the upper limits of a child's competence. If testing has taken place in the nondominant language only, and results show a low score, this is a good reason for caution in the interpretation of those test results.

For L2 learners, knowing the length of exposure to the L2, and how much and what kind of L2 exposure a child is receiving outside the classroom, are vital to judging how reliable language assessment tests would be in the second language. In Chapter 6, we reviewed research showing that it takes from 3 to 5 years for L2 children to have oral language abilities close to their native-speaker peers, and in the previous section of this chapter, we showed that L2 children are at risk for overidentification as language impaired if monolingual norm-referenced tests are used uncritically with them early in their L2 development.

On one hand, lack of sufficient opportunity to learn the language of testing could be a legitimate exclusionary factor when diagnosing the presence of language impairment in dual language children. On the other hand, dual language children could perform poorly on a test in the L2/nondominant language because of *both* low exposure and inherent language learning difficulties. To strike a balance between avoiding overidentification and underidentification, we discuss a two-stage response-to-intervention approach in the next section.

Obtain Information about Cultural Background

For practical reasons, it is unlikely that culturally unbiased tests and testing procedures will be developed for dual language children from all backgrounds. However, clinicians can gain as much information as possible about the culturally determined childrearing and language socialization practices of the different groups whose children they encounter regularly, and they should always view test content and testing procedures through a cross-cultural lens. Roseberry-McKibbin (2008) provides detailed profiles of cultural values, beliefs, and practices for several cultural and religious minority communities in the United States with the purpose of assisting clinicians who work with families and children from these communities.

It is very important to remember that these profiles represent general trends within communities, and thus the behaviors, values, and beliefs that might apply to many individuals within a community do not necessarily apply to every member of that community.

Emphasize Language-General over Language-Specific Measures   One aspect of bilingual profile effects is that tests probing certain domains of language knowledge (i.e., language-specific capacities) could be more biased against dual language children than tests probing some language processing mechanisms or language–cognitive interface skills (i.e., language-general capacities). For example, researchers have been investigating the use of linguistic and nonlinguistic processing abilities, which are thought to be language-general in nature, to assess children's language learning capacities and, in so doing, identify whether a bilingual child has language impairment (Gutiérrez-Clellen & Simon-Cereijido, 2010; Kohnert, Windsor, & Ebert, 2009). For example, measuring nonword rather than real word repetition to identify language impairment reduces the importance of accumulated vocabulary knowledge, but still measures phonological short-term memory, which is specifically delayed in children with SLI. However it is important to bear in mind that nonword repetition is not a "language-free" task, because children's phonological abilities and vocabulary size in the language do play a role in their execution of such tasks. See Kohnert et al. (2009) for details on differential diagnosis of SLI among L2 learners using nonlinguistic processing tasks.

Language tasks that require a cognitive component might also be less biased against dual language children, because the cognitive component could be tapping into language-general capacities. For example, a child's ability to describe a picture story adequately to a naive listener requires some command of the target language grammar and vocabulary (microstructure), but also requires cognitive competence, such as understanding shared knowledge between speaker and listener and cohesive event sequencing (macrostructure). Because the cognitive–linguistic interface skills involved in narrative macrostructure can be shared between a bilingual child's languages, they might be a source of relative strength in dual language children's development, when compared with knowledge of target language specifics, such as vocabulary items or grammatical rules (Cardenas-Hagen, Carlson, & Pollard-Durodola, 2007; Cummins, 1991, 2000; Paradis & Schneider, 2008). In addition, delay in the acquisition of narrative abilities, both microstructure and macrostructure, is characteristic of impaired language development.

In sum, putting more emphasis on language-general over language-specific measures might enable a clinician to better understand a dual language child's language learning capacities.

Use Alternative Norm Referencing for Tests   Monolingual children are clearly not the most appropriate group for norm referencing dual language children's performance on a test. Development of entirely new testing materials for dual language children might not be possible or practical, except where populations warrant, as discussed earlier. However, the development of norms based on dual language children's performance for existing tests can be more feasible. In fact, some school districts might already have the data needed to develop such local norms using test results for dual children that have been conducted at regular intervals in the past according to ages/grades. Interpreting local test scores according to a set of local norms is not without its limitations. Such norms may not

meet all the stringent psychometric criteria used in developing published standardized test norms, and they may not be sensitive to variations in children's language exposure. Nevertheless, local norms are likely to be more informative than monolingual norms. Johanne Paradis is currently developing a set of local norms for a range of standardized tests administered to English L2 children that will be organized according to length of exposure to English, age, and L1 background (where relevant). These norms will be made publicly accessible online (see http://www.ualberta.ca/~jparadis/ for more information). In the absence of local norms, clinicians could, as much as possible, compare an individual dual language child suspected of having language impairment with dual language peers from a similar background, even informally. Consultation with teachers and other professionals who have long-standing experience with dual language children could be useful in determining if a child shows a slower or otherwise different developmental path from his peers.

Use Dynamic Assessment   *Dynamic assessment* refers to a variety of assessment procedures that depart from the traditional procedure of giving a standardized test once as a basis for diagnosis. The logic behind dynamic assessment is that children may perform poorly on tests for reasons that might not signal the presence of language impairment, but instead are the result of barriers (cultural, linguistic or experiential) that might negatively affect children's performance on a formal test. Gutiérrez-Clellen and Peña (2008) recommend adopting a *test-teach-retest* approach for dynamic assessment with dual language children. In such an approach, standardized tests are first administered and scores recorded. Then, children participate in what these researchers call *mediated learning experiences*, which are designed to enable them to better understand the principles of the test and how to respond. The children are not taught answers to specific items on the test, but are taught strategies for how best to access their linguistic knowledge and demonstrate what they know in response to test questions so that they can perform to their full potential on the test. After the teaching phase, the same tests are readministered and scored, and children's "modifiability"—that is, responsiveness and changes that emerged as a result of the teaching—is also observed and recorded. Interpretation of children's performance is based on retest scores and modifiability. Research using these dynamic assessment procedures with culturally and linguistically diverse children has shown that children with typical language development display higher levels of modifiability and score change as a result of the teaching phase when compared to children with language impairment (Gutiérrez-Clellen & Peña, 2008).

Approaches to Intervention with Dual Language Children

Even though there has been a recent increase in research on the characteristics of dual language learners with developmental disorders and on assessment with dual language children, there is still a paucity of research on intervention with dual language children. What we present in this section is based on the research evidence available to us, as well as on information we have already presented in this book on the nature of dual language learning and the broader social–emotional, cognitive, and academic needs of dual language children.

One of the most frequently debated questions concerning intervention for dual language children with language impairment is whether intervention should take place in one or both languages. Consideration of this question is an extension of our discussion in the earlier section, "Should children with language delay/impairment learn two languages?". All the reasons we have brought forward in this book about the importance of supporting the development of both languages in bilingual children, with or without language impairment, also apply to intervention practices. As Kohnert and Derr (2004) point out, if the broad goal of intervention is to effect positive change in a child's ability to communicate and if a child lives in a bilingual environment, then intervention that supports one language only is not meeting this broad goal. The reasons for the importance of supporting both languages through intervention are summarized in Box 9.5; these reasons are based on our discussions throughout this book and on Kohnert and Derr (2004) and Kohnert, Yim, Nett, Kan, and Duran (2005). There is limited research available comparing single versus dual language intervention, but one study we are aware of has examined this question directly. Thordardottir, Ellis Weismer, and Smith (1997) reported a study based on alternating single language (English) and dual language (English–Icelandic) intervention with an English–Icelandic child residing in the United States. The target of the intervention was vocabulary, and in the dual language condition, words were presented and

---

BOX 9.5

Reasons for Supporting Both Languages in Intervention

- There is no evidence that bilingualism exacerbates language impairment, so there is no reason to believe that it would impede the effectiveness of intervention.

- In the case of minority L1 children learning a majority L2, maintaining the home language can be important for children's social and emotional well-being and family relationships.

- Supporting both languages can benefit both languages academically and the child's cognitive development generally; more specifically, supporting the L1 early on can have long-term benefits for L2 development and academic success in the L2.

- Interdependence between two languages means that some aspects of intervention in one language will carry over to the other language; not all aspects of intervention need to take place twice.

- Bilingual children's dominant language can shift gradually over time, and often from the language spoken most at home to the majority language/language of schooling; dominant language shift makes it difficult to justify selecting one language for intervention.

- A sudden shift from a dual to a single language environment for a bilingual child with language impairment could be detrimental. This is because the child could lose the ability to rely on cross-language interdependence or to engage in natural bilingual behaviors, such as code-mixing, and also could receive less rich and complex linguistic input at home from parents if they have made a switch to their less-proficient language.

discussed in the language the child chose to speak, and translations were given and discussed. These researchers reported that the use of dual language intervention was as effective as single language intervention with respect to the child's gains in English vocabulary, and there was some evidence for the superiority of dual language intervention.

Approaches to Dual Language Intervention

There are different strategies that speech-language pathologists can use to support the development of both languages of a bilingual child. Some of these require fluency in both languages, but others do not. Let us first discuss possible approaches to intervention when the clinician can function professionally in both languages, and then turn to alternative strategies.

Kohnert and Derr (2004) make a distinction between bilingual and cross-linguistic approaches in intervention, and recommend combining them for an effective overall intervention program. The bilingual approach entails focusing on skills and linguistic elements that can be shared across the two languages, for example: 1) cognitive-processing mechanisms for language learning; 2) metacognitive and metalinguistic strategies for enhancing language leaning, perception of the content–form relationships, and cross-language awareness; and (3) linguistic elements that overlap between the two languages (such as overlapping sounds, grammar rules, and cognate words). In contrast, cross-linguistic approaches focus on separate training in the phonological, lexical, and grammatical features that are unique to each language and may be uniquely problematic for learners of each language. For example, direct-object pronouns follow different morphosyntactic rules in the Romance languages, like French, Spanish, and Italian, than they do in English. French-, Spanish-, and Italian-speaking children with SLI have difficulty learning direct object pronouns, but not English-speaking children with SLI. French–English bilingual children with SLI also display this cross-linguistic contrast: Children use direct object pronouns with ease and accuracy in English at the same time as they omit them frequently in French (Paradis, Crago, & Genesee, 2005/2006). Therefore, direct-object pronouns would be a more important target for intervention in French than in English for English–French bilingual children with SLI.

When a speech-language pathologist does not speak one of the child's two languages, or cannot provide professional services in that language, what can she do? Kohnert et al. (2005) suggest using team approaches to intervention that involve partners like cultural brokers or interpreters, paraprofessionals, and parents, as well as using peer-mediated strategies. Team approaches can take several configurations, but all include the speech-language pathologist acting as a trainer for partners who speak the child's home language so that they can deliver effective intervention in that language. In addition, the speech-language pathologist would need to work closely with partners who are also fluent in the majority language to plan appropriate linguistic intervention targets in the home language.

Some professionals may wonder if parents are able to provide appropriate and effective intervention programming for their children. In a meta-analysis of the outcomes of interventions with phonology, vocabulary, and syntax, Law, Garret, and Nye (2004) reported that no differences were found in outcomes when the interventions were delivered by trained parents or by clinicians. This meta-analysis was not based on studies of dual language children, but nevertheless suggests that parents can be effective partners in an intervention team. Another issue regarding the use of parents in intervention concerns the culturally determined language use patterns with children in the home; specifically, whether parents would be comfortable or able to engage in the kinds of communicative behaviors with their children that a clinician might suggest they use. Kohnert et al. (2005) recommend adapting programming to suit the language use patterns particular to a family, as well as encouraging siblings and peers to be actively engaged as communication partners with the affected child, if this fits better with their cultural norms. Adaptations should be built through open dialogue with parents about how and when they speak with their children, followed by a mutually agreed-upon plan for adaptations.

Kohnert et al. (2005) also discuss the use of peer-mediated intervention strategies in a classroom context. These strategies consist of structured language activities, such as reading tasks, that are done in pairs instead of individually. Although there has been no research on these strategies conducted with dual language children in particular, Kohnert and colleagues point out that research using these methods with African American children shows this approach holds promise for other children.

Response-to-Intervention Approaches for Identifying Dual Language Children with Language Impairment

Although we have discussed strategies that could lead to more accurate identification of language impairment in bilingual populations, over- and underidentification will continue to be ongoing problems. In particular, there will be many L2 children who have very low abilities in their L2, but who cannot be identified as having language impairment with confidence, due to factors such as insufficient exposure to the L2. These children could be more properly classified as "at risk" for language impairment. In this section, we discuss a process of identification and intervention for L2 children who are at risk for language impairment that uses a response-to-intervention approach. We emphasize that "at risk" does not pertain to all L2 children. Some L2 children clearly have typical language development, and some L2 children can confidently be diagnosed with language delay/impairment. It is L2 children who are performing poorly in their L2 for reasons that are not entirely clear whom we consider at risk and are most likely to benefit from this approach.

In Chapter 10, a two-stage response-to-intervention model is proposed for the process of identification and intervention for children with L2 reading impairment. We outline a version of this model for oral language impairment. Although the process of identification and intervention is not necessarily parallel for language and reading impairment, the rationale underlying this two-stage model has merits in both circumstances; moreover, we have encountered versions of this model that are currently being implemented for speech and language services in school districts we work with. We give a brief description of a two-stage model here; more details on this model are given in Chapter 10.

Stage I: Referrals and language assessments. Dual language children classified as "at risk" receive language-enriched programming in a preschool or school classroom setting.

Stage II: Second assessment of dual language children in the at-risk group, following experience with language enriched programming in a classroom. Children who demonstrate poor response to classroom intervention are then referred for one-on-one intervention with a speech-language pathologist.

Stage I   Referrals for language assessments are often made through health care or educational professionals, such as pediatricians, early childhood educators, or elementary
school teachers, and often stem from parent concern as well. Dual language children
should be assessed following the assessment procedures and strategies for interpretation
we have suggested previously, including obtaining information on children's first language
abilities. In some cases, assessment will reveal that some dual language children can be
confidently identified as language delayed or impaired and such children should receive
appropriate intervention from a speech-language pathologist. In other cases, some dual
language children might be considered as at risk only for language impairment, such as
those who show poor performance in the L2, but for whom exclusionary factors, like
insufficient opportunity to learn the L2, cannot be completely ruled out. A common
approach to making this distinction involves using cutoff points on the normal curve. For
example, children below the 16th percentile could be considered at risk, but those in the
2nd percentile might be more confidently identified as having a language impairment. It
is important to keep in mind that such cutoff points are essentially arbitrary, even if they
are widely used. Some of the at-risk children would be children with typical language
development, but others could have language impairment; thus, the negative consequences of underidentification are a concern for this group at this stage. As part of Stage I,
all children who are at risk should receive language-enriched programming in a classroom setting. Providing language-enriched programming for these children has several
advantages: 1) at-risk children's progress in their L2 can be more easily monitored if they
receive special programming; 2) regardless of whether the at-risk L2 children prove to
have language impairment, language-enriched programming could be beneficial for
them, because it would assist them in making progress in their L2 development; and 3)
insufficient exposure to the L2 can more easily be ruled out as an exclusionary factor
once the programming is finished.

What does language-enriched programming for L2 children consist of? There are a
variety of strategies for providing language enrichment within the context of an early
education or elementary school classroom. Some strategies incorporate pedagogical techniques that are used in L2 education. Other strategies would be informed by the intervention techniques used by speech-language pathologists. Though these strategies would
be aimed primarily at L2 learners with language learning difficulties, some could also be
used with monolingual children in need of language-learning assistance in the majority
language. Whether informed by L2 pedagogy or language intervention, language-
enriched programming usually entails modifications to how teachers use language in the
classroom and how they incorporate language into classroom activities so as to promote
the language development of children with language-learning difficulties. Some individualized educational programming can also play a role. See Tabors (2008) and Roseberry-
McKibbin (2008) for practical details.

Stage II   The at-risk children are tested a second time and their response to the Stage I
intervention is evaluated. There are no exact time intervals between Stage I and Stage II
that we can recommend, because research evidence is limited, but in practice, at-risk children are often in a classroom with language-enriched programming for an entire school
year before they are retested. Even at Stage II, appropriate assessment strategies for dual
language children need to be considered carefully, taking into account the content and

length of the language-enriched programming, and input from the classroom teacher could be important to obtain. Children who can be confidently identified as having language impairment at Stage II can then be referred for further intervention with a speech-language pathologist.

One advantage of this two-stage model is that the language abilities of L2 children who are at risk are assessed more than once. This is important because children's *language growth* over time can be evaluated. Children might be in the lower percentiles for their age at both time 1 and time 2 for a certain measure, but the growth curve between the times shows that adequate gains are being made. In contrast, children may be in the lower percentiles at time 1 and time 2, but the growth curve is rather flat, indicating that adequate gains are not being made (see Hadley & Holt, 2006). Assessing children's language abilities at one time only does not yield such detailed information about growth. A second advantage of this model is that it avoids a "wait and see" approach with at-risk children, but instead begins to provide additional assistance early on. This would be beneficial for children who are underidentified. A third advantage is that children who are typically developing but are classified as "at risk" can participate in programming that will assist them in developing their language skills in a general classroom environment; thus, they would avoid some of the negative consequences of overidentification. Despite the evident merits of this approach, in fact, there is no systematic research evidence for the efficacy of this kind of model of identification and intervention for at-risk dual language children. We recommend this model, but with caution, based on parallels drawn from research with reading impairment and because it represents a logical approach informed by a consideration of issues we have reviewed up to this point.

SUMMARY OF RECOMMENDATIONS FOR PRACTICE AND POLICY

* Expect dual language children with language delay and impairment to have similar patterns in their language development as monolingual children with language impairment; that is, their profiles of general and specific language delay are similar overall.

* Expect dual language children with language delay or impairment to exhibit normal bilingual language use patterns, such as code-mixing.

* Expect children with language or cognitive disabilities to have the capacity to become bilingual, unless there is compelling evidence to the contrary.

* Avoid counseling parents to raise their children with developmental disorders monolingually instead of bilingually, because it can have negative consequences for the children and their families and, equally importantly, because there is no scientific evidence that it benefits these children's language development.

* Consider the following issues when conducting and interpreting assessments with dual language children:

    o The linguistic characteristics of typically developing L2 learners overlap to some extent with those of monolingual children with language impairment who are the same age.
    o Dual language children are likely to have unequal exposure to their languages; this can be a reason for low performance on a language assessment.

○ Dual language children can display a highly uneven profile of performance across language tests, depending on whether tests are measuring domains of relative strength or weakness for them. As a general rule, the more language specific the content of a test, the more likely it is that dual language children could appear weak in that domain.

○ Due to cultural differences, dual language children might not perform to their full potential on a test because they lack familiarity with some of the test content and testing procedures; in particular, they may have a different understanding of how they should use language with an adult than children from the mainstream culture.

○ Assessing children's abilities in both their languages is important for accurate identification of language impairment; however, there are many challenges to obtaining reliable information about children's abilities in a minority language.

○ Translated versions of tests in the majority language are problematic for many reasons and should be avoided.

• The following strategies can help to address some of these issues in assessment with dual language children:

○ Obtain information on children's past and current development in both languages. For the minority language, language sampling, informal observation together with a cultural broker or interpreter or parent questionnaires can provide useful information.

○ Obtain information on children's language exposure patterns in both languages in order to set appropriate expectations. This information can be gathered through questionnaires.

○ Obtain information about cultural differences such as language use patterns in the home. Cultural brokers or other members of an ethnolinguistic community can assist with this.

○ Put greater emphasis on the results of tests probing more language-general skills, like processing and cognitive–linguistic skills, than on tests probing highly language-specific knowledge.

○ Consult alternative norm referencing instead of or in addition to monolingual norm referencing; compare a dual language child with his peers as much as possible.

○ Use dynamic instead of static assessment techniques.

• Support both languages of bilingual children in intervention; this can be achieved even if you do not speak both languages.

• Whenever possible, adopt a two stage, response-to-intervention approach with dual language children at risk for language impairment.

REFERENCES

Armon-Lotem, S. (2010). Instructive bilingualism: Can bilingual children with SLI rely on one language in learning a second one? *Applied Psycholinguistics, 31,* 253–260.

Bedore, L., Peña, E., García, M., & Cortez, C. (2005). Conceptual versus monolingual scoring: When does it make a difference? *Language, Speech and Hearing Services in Schools, 36,* 188–200.

Caesar, L., & Kohler, P. (2007). The state of school-based bilingual assessment: Actual practice versus recommended guidelines. *Language, Speech and Hearing Services in Schools, 38,* 190–200.

Cardenas-Hagan, E., Carlson, C., & Pollard-Durodola, S. (2007). The cross-linguistic transfer of early literacy skills: The role of initial L1 and L2 skills and language of instruction. *Language, Speech and Hearing Services in Schools, 38,* 249–259.

Crutchley, A., Conti-Ramsden, G., & Botting, N. (1997). Bilingual children with specific language impairment and standardized assessments: Preliminary findings from a study of children in language units. *International Journal of Bilingualism, 1,* 117–134.

Cummins, J. (1991). Interdependence of first- and second-language proficiency in bilingual children. In E. Bialystok (Ed.), *Language processing in bilingual children* (pp. 70–89). Cambridge, England: Cambridge University Press.

Cummins, J. (2000). *Language, power and pedagogy: bilingual children in the crossfire.* Clevedon, England: Multilingual Matters.

de Jong, J. (2010). Notes on the nature of bilingual SLI. *Applied Psycholinguistics, 31,* 273–277.

Donovan, S., & Cross, C.T. (Eds.). (2002). *Minority students in special and gifted education.* Washington, DC: National Academies Press.

Fenson, L., Dale, P.A., Reznick, J.S., Bates, E., Thal, D., & Pethick, S.J. (1994). Variability in early communicative development. *Monographs of the Society for Research in Child Development, 59*(5, Serial No. 231).

Goldstein, B. (Ed.). (2004). *Bilingual language development and disorders in Spanish–English speakers.* Baltimore: Paul H. Brookes Publishing Co.

Gutiérrez-Clellen, V., & Kreiter, J. (2003). Understanding child bilingual acquisition using parent and teacher reports. *Applied Psycholinguistics, 24,* 267–288.

Gutiérrez-Clellen, V., & Peña, E. (2008). Dynamic assessment of diverse children: A tutorial. *Language, Speech, and Hearing Services in Schools, 32,* 212–224.

Gutiérrez-Clellen, V., Restrepo, A., & Simon-Cereijido, G. (2006). Evaluating the discriminant accuracy of a grammatical measure with Spanish-speaking children. *Journal of Speech, Language and Hearing Research, 49,* 1209–1223.

Gutiérrez-Clellen, V., & Simón-Cereijido, G. (2007). The discriminant accuracy of a grammatical measure with Latino English-speaking children. *Journal of Speech, Language and Hearing Research, 50,* 968–981.

Gutiérrez-Clellen, V., Simon-Cereijido, G., & Wagner, C. (2008). Bilingual children with language impairment: A comparison with monolinguals and second language learners. *Applied Psycholinguistics, 29,* 3–20.

Gutiérrez-Clellen, Simon-Cereijido, G., & Erickson Leone, A. (2009). Code-switching in bilingual children with specific language impairment. *International Journal of Bilingualism, 13,* 91–109.

Gutiérrez-Clellen, V., & Simon-Cereijido, G. (2010). Using nonword repetition tasks for the identification of language impairment in Spanish-English speaking children: Does the language of assessment matter? *Learning Disabilities Research & Practice, 25,* 48–58.

Hadley, P., & Holt, J. (2006). Individual differences in the onset of tense marking: A growth-curve analysis. *Journal of Speech, Language and Hearing Research, 49,* 984–1000.

Håkansson, G. (2001). Tense morphology and verb-second in Swedish L1 children, L2 children and children with SLI. *Bilingualism: Language and Cognition, 4,* 85–99.

Jacobson, P.F., & Schwartz, R.G. (2005). Elicited production of English past tense by bilingual children with language impairment. *American Journal of Speech-Language Pathology, 4,* 313–323.

Kay-Raining Bird, E., Cleave, P., Trudeau, N., Thodardottir, E., Sutton, A., & Thorpe, A. (2005). The language abilities of bilingual children with Down Syndrome. *American Journal of Speech-Language Pathology, 14,* 187–199.

Kohnert, K., & Derr, A. (2004). Language intervention with bilingual children. In B. Goldstein (Ed.), *Bilingual language development and disorders in Spanish–English speakers* (pp. 311–338). Baltimore: Paul H. Brookes Publishing Co.

Kohnert, K., Windsor, J., & Ebert, K.D. (2009). Primary or "specific" language impairment and children learning a second language. *Brain and Language, 109,* 101–111.

Kohnert, K., Yim, D.S, Nett, K., Kan P.F., & Duran, L. (2005). Intervention with linguistically diverse preschool children: a focus on developing home language(s). *Language, Speech and Hearing Services in Schools, 36,* 251–263.

Kremer-Sadlik, T. (2005). To be or not to be bilingual: Autistic children from multilingual families. In J. Cohen, K.T. McAlister, K. Rostad, & J. MacSwan (Eds.), *Proceedings of the 4th International Symposium on Bilingualism* (pp. 1225–1234). Somerville, MA: Cascadilla Press.

Law, J., Garrett, Z., & Nye, C. (2004). The efficacy of treatment for children with developmental speech and language delay/disorder: A meta-analysis. *Journal of Speech, Language, and Hearing Research, 47,* 924–943.

Leonard, L. (1998). *Children with specific language impairment.* Cambridge, MA: The MIT Press.

Leonard, L. (2000). Specific language impairment across languages. In D. Bishop & L. Leonard (Eds.), *Speech and language impairments in children: Causes, characteristics, intervention and outcome* (pp. 115–129). Philadelphia, PA: Psychology Press.

Oller, K.D., & Eilers, R. (Eds.). (2002). *Language and literacy in bilingual children.* Clevedon, England: Multilingual Matters.

Orgassa, A., & Weerman, F. (2008). Dutch gender in specific language impairment and second language acquisition. *Second Language Research, 24,* 333–364.

Paradis, J. (2004). On the relevance of specific language impairment to understanding the role of transfer in second language acquisition. *Applied Psycholinguistics, 25,* 67–82.

Paradis, J. (2005). Grammatical morphology in children learning English as a second language: Implications of similarities with specific language impairment. *Language, Speech and Hearing Services in the Schools, 36,* 172–187.

Paradis, J. (2007). Bilingual children with SLI: Theoretical and applied issues. *Applied Psycholinguistics, 28,* 551–564.

Paradis, J. (2008). Tense as a clinical marker in English L2 acquisition with language delay/impairment. In E. Gavruseva & B. Haznedar (Eds.), *Current trends in child second language acquisition: A generative perspective* (pp. 337–356). Amsterdam: John Benjamins.

Paradis, J. (2009). *Oral language development in French and English and the role of home input factors.* Report for the Conseil Scolarie Centre-Nord, Edmonton, Alberta, Canada. Available at http://www.ualberta.ca/~jparadis/

Paradis, J. (2010a). The interface between bilingual development and specific language impairment. Keynote article for special issue with peer commentaries. *Applied Psycholinguistics, 31,* 3–28.

Paradis, J. (2010b). The interface between bilingual development and specific language impairment: Response to commentaries. *Applied Psycholinguistics, 31,* 119–136.

Paradis, J. (2010c). Bilingual children's acquisition of English verb morphology: Effects of language dominance, structure difficulty, and task type. *Language Learning, 60.*

Paradis, J., & Crago, M. (2000). Tense and temporality: Similarities and differences between language-impaired and second-language children. *Journal of Speech, Language, and Hearing Research, 43*(4), 834–848.

Paradis, J., Crago, M., Genesee, F., & Rice, M. (2003). Bilingual children with specific language impairment: How do they compare with their monolingual peers? *Journal of Speech, Language, and Hearing Research, 46,* 1–15.

Paradis, J., & Crago, M. (2004). Comparing L2 and SLI grammars in French: Focus on DP. In P. Prévost & J. Paradis (Eds.), *The acquisition of French in different contexts: Focus on functional categories* (pp. 89–108). Amsterdam: John Benjamins.

Paradis, J., Crago, M., & Genesee, F. (2005/2006). Domain-specific versus domain-general theories of the deficit in SLI: Object pronoun acquisition by French-English bilingual children. *Language Acquisition, 13,* 33–62.

Paradis, J., Emmerzael, K., & Sorenson Duncan, T. (2010). Assessment of English language learners: Using parent report on first language development. *Journal of Communication Disorders,* XX.doi:10.1016/j.jcomdis.2010.01.002

Paradis, J., Rice, M., Crago, M., & Marquis, J. (2008). The acquisition of tense in English: Distinguishing child L2 from L1 and SLI. *Applied Psycholinguistics, 29,* 1–34.

Paradis, J., & Schneider, P. (2008). Distinguishing bilingual children form monolinguals with SLI: Profile effects on the Edmonton narrative Norms Instrument. Poster presented at the Symposium on Research in Child language Disorders, University of Wisconsin, Madison.

Paradis, J., & Sorenson Duncan, T. (2009). Differentiating between English L2 children with typical and impaired language development. Paper presented at the Boston University Conference on Language Development, Boston University, Boston.

Pearson, B.Z., Fernández, S.C., & Oller, D.K. (1993). Lexical development in bilingual infants and toddlers: Comparison to monolingual norms. *Language Learning, 43,* 93–120.

Peña, E., Gutiérrez-Clellen, V., Iglesias, A., Goldstein, B., & Bedore, L. (n.d.). *Bilingual English Spanish Assessment* (BESA).

Restrepo, M.-A. (1998). Identifiers of predominantly Spanish-speaking children with language impairment. *Journal of Speech, Language, and Hearing Research, 41,* 1398–1411.

Rice, M.L. (2007). Children with specific language impairment: Bridging the genetic and developmental perspectives. In E. Hoff & M. Shatz (Eds.), *Handbook of language development* (pp. 411–431). Oxford, England: Blackwell.

Rice, M.L., Tomblin, B., Hoffman, L., Richman, W.A., & Marquis, J. (2004). Grammatical tense deficits in children with SLI and nonspecific language impairment: Relationships with nonverbal IQ overtime. *Journal of Speech, Language, and Hearing Research. 47,* 816–834.

Rice, M.L., Warren, S., & Betz, S. (2005). Language symptoms of developmental language disorders: An overview of autism, Down syndrome, fragile X, specific language impairment, and Williams syndrome. *Applied Psycholinguistics, 26,* 7–27.

Roseberry-McKibbin, C. (1995). Distinguishing language differences. *Multicultural Education, 4,* 12–16.

Roseberry-McKibbin, C. (2008). *Multicultural students with special language needs: Practical strategies for assessment and intervention.* Oceanside, CA: Academic Communication Associates.

Rothweiler, M., Chilla, S., & Clahsen, H. (2009). *Agreement and complex syntax in specific language impairment: A study of monolingual and bilingual German-speaking children.* Paper presented at Bilingualism and Specific Language Impairment Conference, The Hebrew University of Jerusalem, Israel.

Schwartz, R. (Ed.) (2009). *Handbook of child language disorders*. New York: Psychology Press.

Steenge, J. (2006). *Bilingual children with specific language impairment: Additionally disadvantaged?* Doctoral dissertation, Research Centre on Atypical Communication, Nijmegen, The Netherlands.

Swisher, L., Plante, E., & Lowell, S. (1994). Nonlinguistic deficits of children with language disorders complicate the interpretation of their nonverbal IQ scores. *Language, Speech and Hearing Services in Schools, 25,* 235–240.

Tabors, P. O. (2008). *One child, two languages: A guide of early childhood educators of children learning English as a second language* (2nd ed.). Baltimore: Paul H. Brookes Publishing Co.

Thordardottir, E. (2008). Relationship between amount of language exposure and language scores in older preschool children acquiring French and English simultaneously. Paper presented at the Congress of the International Association for the Study of Child Language, University of Edinburgh, Scotland.

Thordardottir, E., Ellis Wesimer, S., & Smith, M.E. (1997). Vocabulary learning in monolingual and bilingual clinical intervention. *Child Language Teaching and Therapy, 13,* 215–227.

Thordardottir, E., Rothenberg, A., Rivard, M.E., & Naves, R. (2006). Bilingual assessment: Can overall proficiency be estimated from separate measurement of two languages? *Journal of Multilingual Communication Disorders, 4,* 1–21.

Windsor, J., & Kohnert, K. (2004). The search for common ground: Part I. Lexical performance by linguistically diverse learners. *Journal of Speech, Language, and Hearing Research, 47,* 877–890.

APPENDIX

The Normal Curve and Related Concepts

We make reference in this chapter to concepts that are important for the measurement of children's performance using standardized tests, such as **normal curve, normal range, percentile,** and **standard deviation.** Because some readers may not be familiar with these concepts, we have included a brief explanation here. Imagine that all kindergarten students in a predominantly English-speaking city in the United States took a comprehensive oral language test that included subtests on vocabulary, grammar, and so forth. In all likelihood, if one were to look at a distribution of these children's scores, they would conform to a normal or bell-shaped curve, like that in Figure 9.1. The horizontal or *x*-axis of this figure represents score level, with children who got high scores represented on the right-hand side of the curve and children who got low scores represented on the left-hand side. Children who obtained scores in the average range are represented in the middle of the curve. The number of children who obtained every possible score on the test, from low to average to high, is represented by the height of the curve; the higher the curve, the more frequent the score. The greater the area under sections of the curve, the more children got scores in that range. As one would expect, most children scored in the middle, or average, range, and thus this portion of the curve is the highest; fewer children obtained very high or very low scores, as represented by the dips in the curve on the right- and left-hand sides.

The mean, or average score, on the test would be a score near the middle of the horizontal axis. An individual child's performance on such a test is often described in terms of how close his score was to the mean, whether above or below, of the larger group—the **norming sample** of children. When described this way, the position of a child's score with respect to the group is often expressed in standard deviation units. A standard deviation is the average distance from the mean of all the scores in the group. Positive standard deviations indicate that scores are above the mean, and negative standard deviations indicate they are below the mean. The distance of −1 to +1 standard deviations is the *normal,* or average, range, where roughly 68% of all the children who took the test scored. This normal range is marked by the central shaded area in Figure 9.1. The other 32% of the children are divided between the upper right-hand side and lower left-hand side of the curve. Thus, in a large group of children, roughly 16% of children's scores would fall below 1 standard deviation from the mean.

Another method of describing the distribution of scores on a test so that it is possible to better understand an individual score is using percentiles. The 50th percentile score is the mean and represents the score above which 50% of the children scored and below which 50% scored; with respect to our normal curve, it refers to the peak of the curve. The 16th percentile to the 84th percentile range is analogous to the −1 to +1 standard deviation range. Thus, lower scores on a test are those that fall below the 16th percentile.

If an individual child's score is described as −2 standard deviations from the mean, or at the 2nd percentile, this means that the score was quite low and compares with a very small number of children in the norming sample; specifically, this child scored better than only 2% of the norming sample and lower than 98%. Such a low score on a comprehensive

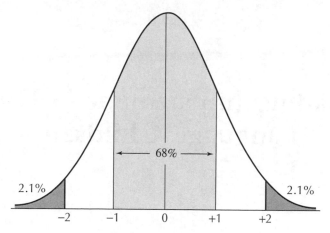

Figure 9.1. Normal curve.

language test could signal that a child has a developmental language disorder, but it could also be the result of environmental factors, such as the child not having slept well the night before or not having had enough exposure to the language to perform well on the test. It is important to consider alternative explanations when interpreting test results for dual language children. Normative comparison methods, like standard deviation units or percentiles, are optimal when the individual child being compared with the norming group has all the characteristics of that group. In the case of dual language children being compared with monolingual norming samples, there is clearly a mismatch.

CHAPTER 10

Reading Impairment in Dual Language Children

It has been estimated that as many as 20% of the school-age population in the United States may be affected by a reading impairment. Considering the downstream consequences of poor reading ability on student achievement in school and on later life opportunities, this statistic is alarming. It is no wonder that Sally and Bennett Shaywitz, two very prominent researchers in the field of dyslexia, see reading impairment as "perhaps the most common neurobehavioral disorder affecting children" (2005, p. 514). It is because of the critical importance of reading for schooling and for later life success that we have included a chapter in this book on reading impairment. This chapter is organized into two main sections, one ("Reading Acquisition and Impairment") that reviews what we know about reading acquisition and impairment in second language (L2) as well as first language (L1) readers, and one ("Identification and Intervention") that discusses how this information can be used for identification and intervention with L2 learners who have or are at risk for a reading impairment.

READING ACQUISITION AND IMPAIRMENT

The primary goal of this section is to review what we know about learning to read in an L2 for both typical learners and learners who are at risk for or have reading impairment. We focus on L2 learners, not simultaneous bilingual children, because virtually all research on L2 reading acquisition and impairment is based on L2 learners, although in studies conducted in the United States, the distinction between these learner groups is often not made. Even in the case of L2 learners, there is very little research on children with reading impairment per se. Most research on L2 learners has examined individual variation in L2 reading acquisition and the factors (instructional, student related, linguistic) that influence L2 reading development. However, there is a growing body of research on "struggling" L2 learners (or English language learners) in the United States (e.g., Mathes, Pollard-Durodola, Cardenas-Hagan, Linan-Thompson, & Vaughn, 2007). Even research findings from studies of typically developing L2 learners are nevertheless useful for understanding impairment because they allow us to better understand variations in the normal patterns of L2 reading acquisition and factors that can affect reading acquisition in L2 learners. This, in turn, is important for identifying exclusionary factors that must be considered when identifying reading impairment in L2 learners—a topic we return to later. After defining reading impairment, we discuss reading acquisition and impairment in children learning to read in their L1 in order to broaden our understanding of L2 learners and, as you will see, to determine whether we can fill gaps in our understanding of L2 reading by referring to research on L1 readers.

The remainder of this section addresses the following questions:

1. What is reading impairment?
2. What does research tell us about reading acquisition and impairment in L1 students?
3. Are L2 reading acquisition and impairment the same as L1 reading acquisition and impairment?
4. Are there significant differences between L2 and L1 reading acquisition and impairment?

What Is Reading Impairment?

Reading impairment is a distinct learning disability that manifests itself in great difficulty learning to read despite normal intelligence and perceptual abilities (vision, hearing), adequate learning opportunities, and the absence of psychological problems. Our concern is with reading impairments that are developmental and not acquired; that is, we are interested in reading difficulties that are not due to neurocognitive, perceptual-motor, social, or educational inadequacies. It has been customary to define reading impairment in terms of word decoding difficulties, or dyslexia. We also consider reading impairments that are evident in comprehension, for reasons that we discussed in Chapter 1. Broadening the discussion to include impairment related to reading comprehension implicates language impairment because some students with difficulty comprehending written text are thought to have language-related difficulties along with, or rather than, decoding difficulties. We consider the extent of overlap in language and reading impairment, the nature of the overlap, and what this might mean for identification and intervention. A list of some common behavioral manifestations of reading impairment are presented in Box 10.1.

Reading impairment is estimated to affect from 5% to 20% of the school-age population in the United States (Miles, 2004; Shaywitz, 2003) and in some other countries (e.g., Roongpraiwan, Ruanqdaraganon, Visudhiphan, & Santikul, 2002, for Thailand). Estimates vary greatly, due at least in part to different methods of calculating prevalence rates and different criteria for classifying children as having reading impairment. Lower prevalence rates usually arise from estimates based on the number of children receiving specialized services, whereas higher prevalence rates usually result from assessing unselected samples of children, be it a whole classroom or an entire school or school district. Although it is widely thought that reading impairment is more prevalent among boys than girls, this statistic too depends on the

---

BOX 10.1

Common Behavioral Manifestations of Reading Impairment

- Poor knowledge of the sounds and names of the letters of the alphabet
- Difficulty mapping sounds onto letters when reading, and letters onto sounds when writing
- Slow progress in learning to read words
- Slow and labored reading of words, sentences, and text
- Low levels of accuracy when reading common and uncommon words, sentences, and text-length text
- Reliance on context (including pictures) to figure out the meaning of words or text
- Lack of strategies for figuring out how to read and understand new words
- Poor understanding of what is read, literally as well as interpretively—that is, determining what are the causes, consequences, and implications of what is read
- Poor ability to relate what is read to one's own experiences
- Related problems in spelling and writing

---

method of estimation. The Connecticut Longitudinal Study (Shaywitz et al., 1999), for example, found that dyslexia affected as many boys as girls when all children in the district were tested individually, but four to five times as many boys as girls were identified as having dyslexia by schools. Teachers tend to refer more boys than girls for clinical assessment and support because boys tend to engage in more disruptive and off-focus behavior than girls who are often perceived to be behaving properly. Boys' disruptive behaviors are often misattributed to reading difficulties. In terms of the impact of reading impairment on school-age children, estimates based on unselected samples of students are alarming because they indicate that as many as 20% or more of school children may be affected. It is not only students' reading skills that are of concern, but also their academic achievement and intellectual development, because these are intimately linked to how well students can use reading as a tool for learning in school.

Estimates of prevalence rates can also vary depending on the actual tests or criteria used to classify individual children as having impairments. Tests of reading accuracy versus comprehension, for example, could result in different rates of impairment. Variation can also result from the use of different criteria to diagnose reading impairment (see Bishop & Snowling, 2004, for a discussion). One of the most common methods is based on the "discrepancy" between students' reading ability and their general intelligence (APA, 1994). Using this method, students are considered to have impairments if their reading scores are significantly lower than their general intelligence and their intelligence is within the normal range for their age. This approach has been used to try to ensure that children diagnosed as having impairments have an impairment that is specific to reading and not general intelligence. There are problems with this approach. Chief among these is that a child's general intelligence, as measured by an IQ test, could decline in the higher grades as a result of poor reading skills, making the use of general intelligence as a basis for estimating expected reading levels problematic. A serious side effect of this method is that intervention can be delayed, sometimes until as late as third grade, until students demonstrate a severe and persistent discrepancy between reading performance and intelligence. Yet evidence indicates that early identification and intervention can curtail long-term reading problems in many students who struggle during the primary grades (Scanlon, Gelzheiser, Vellutino, Schatschneider, & Sweeney, 2008). Thus, a method of identification of reading impairment that delays intervention is often not in the best interest of students who need early additional support.

More recently, reading impairment has often been operationally defined as normal intelligence, broadly defined, and performance on a reading test that falls significantly below age or grade norms. Sometimes "below normal" is defined as one or more standard deviations below the mean for the child's age/grade level, and sometimes it is defined in percentile terms. Lesaux et al. (2008) note that the most common criterion for identifying reading disability in studies of English language learners in the United States is a score on a standardized reading test at or below the 25th percentile. All of these variations can result in different estimates of prevalence (for details on the use of statistical concepts such as standard deviation and percentiles when assessing children's performance, see Chapter 9 and the Glossary).

There are no statistics that we know of that estimate the prevalence of reading impairment in L2 readers, although it has been estimated that as many as two of every three fourth-grade Spanish-speaking English language learners in the United States is unable to read English at a level that is sufficient to support their success in school (August & Hakuta, 1998; Sanchez, Bledsoe, Sumabat, & Ye, 2004). A number of studies reviewed by the National Literacy Panel found that English language learners in the United States were often able to attain levels of word reading that were equivalent to those of native speakers, but they tended to achieve significantly lower levels of ability on tests of reading comprehension (Lesaux et al., 2008; Snow, 2008). Similar patterns have been reported by Dutch researchers (e.g., Aarts & Verhoeven, 1999).

Despite these statistics, there is no reason to believe that rates of reading impairment should be higher in L2 learners, or simultaneous bilingual children, than in the monolingual population of school-age children. That many L2 learners in the United States do not achieve levels of reading proficiency that are adequate for success in school is likely due to multiple factors that go beyond reading impairment as defined clinically; for example, interrupted or inappropriate schooling and poverty. That L2 status alone is not a risk factor for reading impairment comes from studies in Canada which have not shown such elevated rates of reading difficulty among L2 immigrant learners. In fact, immigrant L2 learners in that country usually score as well or better than native-born Canadian students on tests of reading achievement in secondary school and have equal or better rates of secondary school graduation (Garnett, 2006; Organisation for Economic Co-operation and Development, 2006). The discrepancy between the U.S. and Canadian patterns can be explained, at least in part, by different immigration policies in these two countries, with Canada's policy favoring immigrant families whose parents are relatively well-educated, professional, and middle class in comparison with immigrants accepted into the United States. In any case, taken together, these results reinforce the conclusion that L2 or bilingual status alone is not a risk for poor reading outcomes. As we saw in Chapter 8, both minority language and majority language students who participate in bilingual school programs score as well as their peers in monolingual programs on a variety of reading tests, also indicating that bilingualism itself is insufficient to explain the elevated rates of poor reading ability among some groups of L2 learners. Despite all this evidence, majority language parents whose children are in bilingual programs and are struggling learning to read in their L2 often believe that they would be better off being taught in their L1; this kind of concern is expressed by a mother in Box 10.2.

BOX 10.2

Second Language/Bilingual Education for Children with Reading Difficulties

We are often asked by parents whose children show some difficulties in learning to read whether they should continue in second language or bilingual education programs, such as French immersion. Research discussed in Chapter 8 suggests that continuing in second language/bilingual programs does not result in negative academic consequences for children who display reading difficulties. The research discussed in this chapter also suggests that many aspects of reading skills transfer easily from one language to another, and that learning to read in two languages thus does not require learning all aspects of reading twice. The aspects that many children, including the boy referred to in the second letter, have most difficulty with—phonics and letter–sound correspondences—are the aspects of learning to read and write that show the most consistent transfer from one language to another. It is widely thought that there is so much transfer with respect to these skills because they depend on underlying abilities, related to phonological awareness and phonological memory, that affect learning in any language. In other words, changing the language of instruction is not likely to substantially change a child's underlying phonological processing abilities. However, each individual child's case must be considered in light of factors such as the availability of support for reading difficulties at the school, the willingness on the part of the child for continuing immersion education, the importance of bilingualism within the community and for future opportunities, and the commitment on the part of the parents to provide whatever extra effort it might take to help their child succeed in that educational environment.

LETTER FROM A MOTHER:

Hello Professor Genesee,

Our son has been in a French immersion program for the years of kindergarten and Grade 1. We recently learned that he has a reading and writing learning disability. He struggled during first grade, but as a result of extra support and motivation on his part, he made great gains in French reading and writing by the end of the year. We are having difficulty deciding whether to have him continue in French immersion or if this will put him at risk for further delay in mastering reading and writing skills. Do you have any feedback regarding this or any suggestions of articles or references we could consult?

Sincerely,
A mother

LETTER FROM A FATHER:

Dear Dr. Genesee:

Our 9-year-old son has a learning disability affecting his acquisition of reading and writing skills. Our first language is English, but he attends a French language school. He completed psychoeducational assessments in both English and French. Both assessments gave essentially the same results: difficulty in acquisition of writing and reading skills, specifically with phonics and sound–symbol association. In both evaluations, his baseline intelligence was found to be high and he has been identified by the school board as being gifted as well as having a learning disability. His comprehension of spoken French and English was found to be above average for his age. We live in a small town in central Canada that is mixed anglophone and francophone. Most of the children at his school have English as their first language. We are unsure of how much impact the addition of a second language will have on his learning. His school has been supportive and are trying to find adaptations and assistive technology to help him. We can't help but wonder if transferring him to an English school would make it easier for him to progress. We would appreciate any information or contacts you could supply.

Thank you,
A father

We refer to both students with reading impairment and those who might be at risk for reading impairment in the remainder of this chapter in order to take account of the uncertainty related to clear criteria for identifying reading impairment. Moreover, considering students who might be at risk for reading impairment before a firm identification makes it possible to identify L2 students who could benefit from additional support learning to read before their difficulties become entrenched and start to affect their academic achievement. Waiting until students display unequivocal signs of impairment can delay providing them with additional support and this, in turn, could put them at general educational risk.

What Does Research Tell Us About Reading Acquisition and Impairment in L1 Students?

We consider reading acquisition in L1 students without impairment in order to put L2 reading acquisition and impairment in L2 learners in a broader context. There is a much broader and deeper research base and, therefore, understanding of reading acquisition and impairment in L1 learners than in L2 learners. Our understanding of L2 reading acquisition and impairment is still evolving. Knowledge from L1 research could be used to fill in gaps in our understanding of L2 reading acquisition if there is evidence of substantive overlap between L1 and L2 reading acquisition and impairment, the topic of the next section. Although this is not an optimal strategy, decisions about and support for L2 students with reading impairment cannot wait until researchers fill all the gaps in our understanding. Of course, applying current research-based understandings about L1 reading and impairment to L2 learners must be done with caution and sensitivity to differences.

The extensive and ever-expanding body of research on L1 reading acquisition paints a picture of a process that is complex, hierarchical, and developmental in nature. What exactly does this mean? To start, reading acquisition is complex. It involves several interrelated skills and the use of diverse kinds of knowledge; this is especially true when reading text-length material. For example, take a student who is asked to read a story about a visit to the dentist, such as the following (adapted from Cloud, Genesee, & Hamayan, 2009):

> *Jason had a toothache so his father took him to see the dentist. When they got to the dentist's office, the dentist was busy with another patient. The dentist's assistant gave Jason a coloring book to keep him busy. After playing with the coloring book in the waiting room for a few minutes, Jason was called in to see the dentist.*

In order to understand this story, the student must know key words that are used to tell the story; words such as the following, which are not commonly used outside the context of visiting a dentist: *dentist, toothache, patient, and waiting room,* and he must also be able to decode the written versions of these words ((i.e., map sounds onto the letters that make up the written words) so that their meaning can be retrieved from memory. In addition, the student needs to know how adverbs, verb tenses, and pronouns are used in English to create coherence in text and to establish a timeline of events. Just as important, the reader must be motivated to read and must have certain background knowledge: what a dentist is, what she does, and why children go to dentists. Some of the skills and knowledge required to read and understand this story are specific to reading, such as knowing how to decode written words; some are related to language more generally speaking, such as deriving a timeline from a story using knowledge of verb tenses, pronouns, and connectors such as *then* and *after;* and some entail what is referred to as *general* or *world knowledge* and are thus not language-related at all. See Figure 10.1 for a schematic representation of reading acquisition and the kinds of skills and knowledge that are associated with different stages of reading development.

Although some of the components of learning to read—such as motivation and background knowledge—are critically important at all stages of acquisition, others—such as phonological awareness, phonics (learning to map sounds onto letters), and decoding—are building blocks for acquiring higher-order, more complex reading skills, in particular reading comprehension skills. In other words, some component skills of reading (i.e., decoding) need to be acquired before others can be acquired (i.e., comprehension), and they need to be acquired to a high level of competence so that cognitive resources can be devoted to higher-level reading skills, such as comprehending what is being read. For this reason, reading acquisition can be characterized as hierarchical and developmental in nature, with so-called *small-unit skills* that are linked to word-level reading being preliminary or developmental precursors to acquiring so-called *large-unit skills* of reading comprehension. Viewed from the perspective of reading impairment, difficulty acquiring efficient word-level reading skills can impede students from achieving fluent and accurate reading comprehension skills when text is involved.

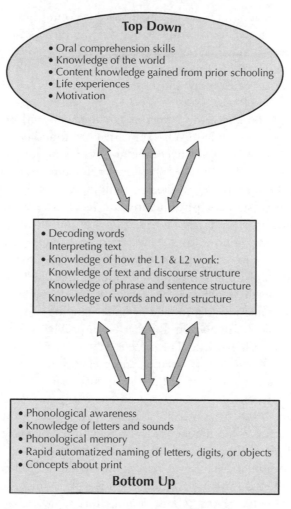

Figure 10.1. Schema of reading acquisition. (*Sources:* Birch 1998; National Early Literacy Panel, 2009.)

An extensive body of research has identified knowledge of the names and sounds of letters and **phonological awareness**, especially **phonemic awareness**, as critical for learning to decode single words. Phonological awareness is the knowledge that words are made up of individual sounds (be it syllables, phonemes, or other units of sound) that can be manipulated independently; that is, they can be added together, deleted, or inverted. *Phonemic awareness* (PA) refers specifically to knowledge of how individual phonemes make up words—for example, that the sounds /c/, /a/, and /t/ make up the word "cat." It can be assessed in a number of ways; for example, by asking children to delete a sound from a word and saying what is left (e.g., What is left if I say "stop" without the /s/ sound?), or by asking children to blend separate sounds/phonemes to form a whole word (e.g., What word do the sounds /b/, /a/, and /t/ make?). According to the National Reading Panel, "studies have identified PA and letter knowledge as the two best school-entry predictors of how well children will learn to read during the first 2 years of instruction" in English (2000, p. 7). Individual differences in PA are highly correlated with individual differences in single-word decoding ability in alphabetic languages, like English. Of particular importance for our discussion, L1 students with dyslexia have poor decoding skills. Moreover, the decoding abilities of children with dyslexia improve significantly following systematic and explicit phonological awareness training, arguing that PA is causally and not just statistically related to word reading ability (National Reading Panel, 2000).

Knowledge of the sounds of the letters of the alphabet (and how to represent the sounds that make up words with letters) has similarly been found to correlate significantly with individual differences in word decoding ability, as one might expect, given that knowledge of the sounds of letters is essential for transforming written words into verbal codes that can then be used to access word meanings. As was found for instruction in phonological awareness, systematic **phonics instruction** has been shown to result in significant gains for students in kindergarten to sixth grade and in students having difficulty learning to read. Together, phonological awareness and letter–sound knowledge can account for up to, and in some cases more than, 40% of the variation in word reading test scores of native speakers of English (National Reading Panel, 2000).

In comparison with the extensive research on word decoding, research on reading comprehension is in its infancy. As a result, our understanding of what underlies accurate and fluent comprehension and, conversely, what poses problems for students with comprehension difficulties is still evolving. The present evidence suggests that the picture with respect to individual differences in L1 reading comprehension is more complex than that for decoding. Specifically, it appears that the factors that correlate with individual differences in reading comprehension may differ at different stages of development (Johnston, Barnes, & Desrochers, 2008). Storch and Whitehurst (2002), for example, found that the most significant predictors of comprehension accuracy in the primary grades were word-related reading skills (i.e., phonological awareness, letter knowledge), but that oral language skills (i.e., vocabulary, narrative recall, and syntactic ability) were significant predictors of comprehension in Grades 3 and 4. Studies of reading comprehension in students in higher elementary grades (Grade 5 and later) suggest that even higher-order skills, such as inference-making ability, comprehension monitoring, and sensitivity to story structure, may play a significant role in comprehension of advanced-level texts (Muter, Hulme, Snowling, & Stevenson, 2004; Oakhill, Cain, & Bryant, 2003). That different constellations of component skills are related to reading comprehension at different grade levels may reflect differences in the demands on reading at different levels, with more literal meaning being the focus in lower grades and interpretation and inferencing required in higher grades.

Of particular relevance to our discussion of reading impairment, there is growing evidence that students with reading impairment that is reflected in comprehension difficulties may have different risk profiles. In particular, some students with reading comprehension difficulties have poor word decoding skills and, it is argued, it is their poor decoding skills that create their comprehension problems. More specifically, it is thought that poor decoders devote so many cognitive resources to decoding individual words that the additional resources needed to read and comprehend sentence- and text-length text are not available and, thus, comprehension is compromised. There are yet other students with reading comprehension difficulties who do not have difficulty with word decoding; these students are sometimes referred to as "poor comprehenders"

(Bishop & Snowling, 2004; see Catts, Adlof, Hogan, & Ellis Weismer, 2005, for an alternative view). It has been estimated that 5%–10% of children display this reading problem (Catts et al., 2005; Nation, 2005). Although the precise difficulties of poor comprehenders are not yet well understood, it is thought that their comprehension problems are linked to deficits in language, including semantic and syntactic aspects of language. In fact, it could be that these readers have a language impairment, although one that is perhaps not sufficiently severe to fall within clinically defined definitions, or one that has gone undetected and untreated, and it is their language impairment that is responsible for their reading comprehension difficulties (Bishop & Snowling, 2004; Catts et al., 2005). It is not difficult to imagine that language impairment could impair comprehension of written text because, as we noted in our example of the story about the dentist, making sense of this story requires some of the lexical and morphosyntactic skills that can be limited in children with language impairment.

The question arises of how frequently reading and language impairment co-occur. This is an important clinical as well as theoretical question because if the evidence indicates high rates of overlap, this would imply that reading and language impairment are different manifestations of the same underlying disorder. In contrast, if the evidence indicates low rates of overlap, this would imply that reading and language impairment are distinct disorders. In a large-scale study of more than 500 monolingual English-speaking children who were examined longitudinally from kindergarten to eighth grade, Catts and his colleagues estimated that about 20% of the children who met their criterion for specific language impairment in kindergarten also met their criterion for reading impairment subsequently, in Grades 2, 4, and 8 (Catts et al., 2005). Viewed from the opposite perspective, they also found that among the same large sample of students, of those who met the criteria for reading impairment in Grades 2, 4, and 8, about 15% also met their criteria for specific language impairment earlier, in kindergarten. Both of these estimates, prospective and retrospective, indicate some degree of overlap between language and reading impairment, but by no means is the overlap total. Thus, although some children in this study who met the criteria for language impairment also met criteria for dyslexia, the majority did not exhibit such overlap. These estimates of overlap are probably underestimates, as the criteria used by Catts et al. for reading impairment included performance on tests of word and pseudoword reading that assess classic or pure dyslexia. Greater overlap might have resulted had they used reading tests that called for reading comprehension and, thus, some of the kinds of language skills implicated in SLI. The percent overlap between children with reading difficulties and SLI varies across studies, most likely due to methodological differences in the criteria used (see Chapter 1), but importantly, some overlap is usually found. In any case, Catts et al. conclude that reading and language impairment are distinct disabilities with some overlap (or comorbidity). Bishop and Snowling (2004) also argue that they are distinct.

This is a controversial issue of ongoing interest among researchers, and there is no consensus yet on the precise relationship between language and reading impairment. Whether reading and language impairment are distinct disabilities awaits further investigation. In the meantime, these studies indicate that it is important when identifying children with reading impairment that is related to comprehension to examine their language skills as well as their word decoding skills in order to have a complete picture of their strengths and weaknesses. Poor comprehenders with and without dyslexia would benefit from different intervention strategies—strategies that focus on their specific weaknesses.

Are L2 Reading Acquisition and Impairment the Same as L1 Reading Acquisition and Impairment?

In this section, we draw on the findings of three large-scale systematic reviews of research on reading acquisition; one focused on native English speakers who were learning to read in English (National Reading Panel, 2000), and two focused on reading in L2 learners, most of whom were from minority language backgrounds and living in the United States, but not exclusively (August & Shanahan, 2006; see August & Shanahan, 2008, for an abbreviated version of the 2006 volume; Genesee, Lindholm-Leary, Saunders, & Christian, 2006). We also draw on a review of research on the L2 reading development of majority-language English-speaking students in French immersion programs in Canada prepared by Genesee and Jared (2008). This review is much smaller in scale than the others because there was far less research to review. Readers are referred to the full reports of these reviews for more details.

Taken together, the results from these reviews, as well as evidence from other recent studies (e.g., Erdos, Genesee, Savage, & Haigh, in press), indicate that learning to read in an L2 is similar to learning to read in an L1 in some fundamental and important ways. Here are the main ways in which L2 and L1 reading acquisition appear to be similar. First, predictors of word decoding ability in L1 readers, as discussed in the preceding section, are also significant predictors of L2 word decoding ability. To be more specific, phonological awareness and knowledge of letter–sound relationships in English are significant predictors of word decoding skills in English as a second language as they are in English as a first language. This is true whether the students are members of a minority-language group, such as Pauloosie, Bonnie, Luis, and Faisal (Riches & Genesee, 2006; Lesaux et al., 2008) or whether they are members of a majority-language group, such as Samantha and Trevor (Erdos et al., in press; Genesee & Jared, 2008). Of additional importance, these predictors are significant cross-linguistically as well as intralinguistically. In other words, individual variation in phonological awareness and letter–sound knowledge in the L1 of L2 learners is correlated with individual variation in their L2 word decoding skills. This means, for example, that in a group of native Spanish-speaking students who are learning to read in English as a second language, students with relatively good phonological awareness skills and letter–sound knowledge in Spanish will also have better decoding skills in English than their Spanish-speaking peers with relatively poor phonological awareness skills and letter–sound knowledge in the L1. These cross-linguistic relationships in language- and literacy-building skills are the main components in Cummins's model of interdependence and common underlying proficiencies between L1 and L2, as discussed in Chapter 6. We will see shortly that this has important implications for the early assessment of risk for reading difficulties in L2 learners.

Another way in which L2 and L1 reading acquisition are similar can be found in the results of research that has examined reading comprehension. These findings reveal similarities between L2 and L1 reading comprehension at a very general level, insofar as both can be influenced by a variety of individual difference and contextual factors. Similarities are also evident when the findings are examined more closely for the specific factors that are important in L2 and L1 reading comprehension. Here there is evidence that many of the same language and non–language-related factors that influence the development of L1 reading comprehension also influence the development of L2 reading comprehension. More specifically, and most importantly for our purposes, language-related factors that influence L2 reading comprehension include word decoding skills, vocabulary, oral proficiency in the L2, and listening comprehension skills in the L2 (Lesaux et al., 2008; Riches & Genesee, 2006). The precise aspects of these language-related skills that influence comprehension and how they influence comprehension is still a matter of empirical investigation. Factors of a non language nature that influence both L2 and L1 reading comprehension include: motivation, background knowledge, socioeconomic status, knowledge of text genres, and the nature and quality of reading instruction. These latter factors should be considered as exclusionary factors when identifying L2 learners with comprehension- or word-related reading difficulties because although they can depress some L2 students' reading performance, they do not signal reading difficulties as a clinical disorder.

L2 and L1 readers who are at risk for or have reading difficulties demonstrate similar weaknesses. It is important to recall here that there is little research that has examined L2 learners with reading impairments directly. As a result, for the most part, we can only infer from findings about individual differences in reading comprehension what the results for students with impairment would be like. This research shows that minority- and majority-language L2 readers who experience difficulty learning to decode demonstrate weaknesses in phonological awareness and in their knowledge of letter–sound relationships (Erdos et al., 2010; Lesaux et al., 2008). L2 students—again, both majority and minority groups—with poor reading comprehension skills, like their L1 counterparts, often have poor decoding skills and/or poor oral language skills related to listening comprehension, vocabulary, and morphosyntax. Research by Erdos, Genesee, Savage and Haigh (2010) has found that although reading and language impairment are distinct, some L2 learners exhibit risk for both. Although the precise implications of this were not examined in this research, these findings indicate that some L2 learners with reading impairment need intervention that addresses both their language and their reading difficulties and that the presence of overlap between these two disorders parallels findings from the L1 research.

Finally, evidence that L2 and L1 reading acquisition are the same in some fundamental ways comes from another recent study by Erdos et al. (in press). They examined whether the simple view of reading (SVR) applies to L2 readers in the same way that it applies to L1 readers (Gough & Tunmer, 1986). The SVR is one of the earliest theories and still one of the most popular explanations of reading comprehension. This theory is important for our purposes because it integrates word-level and language-level components of reading in a coherent framework. Briefly, and with some oversimplifications, according to the SVR, reading comprehension (RC) is related to decoding ability plus the product of decoding (D) and listening comprehension (LC); that is, $RC = D + (D \times LC)$. Erdos and her colleagues found that the SVR also applies to L2 reading comprehension. In fact, they found that it could account for up to 60% of the variance in the reading comprehension scores in French of a large group of English-L1 students who were learning to read in French.

In summary, there is considerable evidence that reading acquisition and impairment in L2 and L1 readers are similar in some important and fundamental ways. Although our understanding of L2 reading acquisition and impairment is still evolving, the current evidence indicates that a lot that we know about L1 reading also applies to L2 reading; similarly, a lot that we know about reading impairment in L1 learners also seems to apply to L2 learners. At the same time, there are important differences. This is the topic of the next section.

In What Ways Are L2 Reading Acquisition and L1 Reading Acquisition Different?

Despite similarities between L2 and L1 acquisition in both typical learners and those with impairments, there is also evidence that L2 reading acquisition is different from L1 reading acquisition in important ways. Three important ways in which they differ are: 1) students learning to read in an L2 usually come from different sociocultural backgrounds, 2) they know and use another language, and 3) they are still learning the L2. All three factors can influence the rate at which L2 students learn to read and also the speed, fluency, and accuracy with which they read, and these factors can in turn result in test performance that could be interpreted as evidence of reading impairment, as described earlier.

With respect to sociocultural background, it is widely recognized that students' reading and understanding of written language, be it a single word, a sentence, or longer text, can be influenced by their background knowledge, or what Moll has referred to as **"funds of knowledge"** (Gonzalez, Moll, & Amanti, 2005). Students with minority cultural backgrounds will find it more, or less, difficult to interpret written forms of English the way the author intended, depending on their familiarity with the content of what is being read. Let us return to our story about the dentist and take the case of Faisal, a non-native speaker of English who recently immigrated to Canada from Somalia and is now being educated in English in Edmonton. Although most, but not all, majority language students in the United States will know what dentists are and will probably have visited a dentist, many minority language students, especially recent immigrants, such as Faisal, might not. Thus, they will not have a ready-made schema that they can use to interpret the dentist story. Lacking a culturally appropriate schema for interpreting this story, Faisal might try to relate what he is reading to experiences he has had "back home." Failing to find an appropriate frame of reference in his personal experiences back home, he will necessarily have to interpret what he is reading solely on what he is reading. As a result, he is likely to read the story slowly, with many hesitations and false starts, and with flat affect. Moreover, when questioned about the story afterwards, Faisal is likely to demonstrate poor and inaccurate comprehension of what he read. Educational materials and instructional approaches in school are based on the cultural backgrounds of majority language students and, as a result, it is usually relatively easy for most majority language students to understand and relate to the content of what they are reading and being taught. This is not always the case, however. For example, African American students, who speak a nonstandard variety of English, and often have had very different cultural experiences from mainstream students, might have difficulty understanding some of the instructional materials used in mainstream schools. In other words, they may have different funds of knowledge than what has been assumed by creators of educational materials for mainstream students. Cultural background differences of these sorts can make it difficult for language-minority L2 learners to perform well on standardized reading tests used to screen for reading impairment.

L2 reading acquisition also differs from L1 reading acquisition because L2 students often draw on knowledge about the L1 when learning to read the L2 (August & Shanahan,

2006; Riches & Genesee, 2006). In effect, L2 learners use the L1 as a scaffold for learning to read the L2 (Riches & Genesee, 2006). Using the L1 to scaffold reading in the L2 is most useful during early stages of reading acquisition, when L2 learners have not fully acquired the L2. However, it can also be useful even later, when L2 students are confronted by difficult text. At this stage, they are likely to transfer strategies for figuring out the meaning of unfamiliar words or for monitoring comprehension of what they are reading (Riches & Genesee, 2006). These kinds of cross-linguistic influences are often referred to as *transfer*. We use this term in this chapter for convenience and because it parallels transfer in oral language, as discussed in Chapter 6. However, there is considerable controversy whether transfer is the actual cognitive mechanism by which these influences operate (see, for example, Genesee & Geva, 2006; Snow, 2008). The more similar the L1 to the L2 (as is the case for Spanish and English in comparison with Mandarin and English, for example), the greater the transfer. For example, the Spanish–English bilingual child we profiled, Gabriela, might read the word "have" as "av-ey" because the *h* is silent in Spanish and all vowels are pronounced, or she might pronounce the English word "jumper" as "humper" because the letter *j* is pronounced "h" in Spanish. As well as transferring knowledge about the sounds of letters from the L1 to the L2, L2 learners might also look for words that sound the same to figure out their meanings; that is, they might look for cognates to figure out the meaning of a new word (Langer, Bartolome, Vasquez, & Lucas, 1990). Again, how closely related, both historically and geographically, the two languages are will determine the number of cognates and borrowed words they have. Because English and Mandarin have separate writing systems based on separate principles and do not have shared vocabulary, apart from a few very recent borrowings into Mandarin, Bonnie would be less able to use this kind of transfer from her L1 when learning to read in English.

When students transfer specific skills and strategies from the L1 to the L2 that produce the correct response in the L2, the influence of the L1 is invisible; we simply think that they "got it right." It is transfer from the L1 that results in errors in the L2 that are noticed. Because most transfer effects that we notice are linked to errors in the target language, we often think that L2 learners should keep their L1 and L2 separate; in some cases, L2 learners have even been punished in school for using the L1 on this assumption. However, rather than interpreting transfer errors as signs of incompetence, it is more appropriate to interpret them as student's active attempts to fill in gaps in their L2 by drawing on corresponding skills and knowledge from the L1; a kind of linguistic bootstrapping (Genesee et al., 2006). For example, when Gabriela mispronounces "jumper" as "humper," she is demonstrating that she has phonological awareness and knows that sounds map onto letters in a systematic way; she simply has not acquired the letter–sound correspondences that are appropriate for English. Interpretation of transfer errors as deficiencies in L2 learners' reading abilities can contribute to overestimates of reading impairment in L2 learners. The possibility that L2 learners are transferring knowledge from the L1 when reading the L2 must be considered as an exclusionary factor when identifying L2 learners with reading impairment. Errors that are due to transfer of this type are not signs of impairment.

Finally, L2 learners obviously differ from students learning to read in their L1 because they are still learning important aspects of oral language and, in particular, they are still acquiring advanced-level morphosyntactic and discourse skills of the type that underpin academic language and reading comprehension. Evidence for this comes from studies reviewed by the National Literacy Panel (2006) showing that the effects of reading instruction are less likely to be significant and are less pronounced when reading comprehension is assessed than when word decoding is assessed and that the effects of instruction on comprehension are less pronounced in studies of English language learners than in studies on native English speakers (August & Shanahan, 2008) arguably because the effects of reading instruction alone on L2 readers is limited by their L2 oral language abilities. It makes sense that acquiring reading comprehension skills in a second language depends on learners' levels of oral competence because they are, by definition, L2 learners. It is also the case that the reading comprehension abilities of even native speakers of English will depend on their level of sophistication in oral English for academic purposes, but clearly not to the same extent as for L2 learners. This in turn means that effective reading instruction for L2 learners should be comprehensive and include systematic and sustained instruction in oral academic language skills. It also means that L2 oral competence should be taken into account when understanding the reasons why L2 learners might be having trouble learning to read; difficulties related to incomplete acquisition of the L2 is an exclusionary factor when determining specific reading impairment.

IDENTIFICATION AND INTERVENTION

The identification of L2 learners with reading impairment is complex, in part because of the complexity of the disability, as we noted in the preceding sections, and in part because it is a process. By this, we mean that identifying whether a student has a reading impairment cannot be done on the basis of a single test administered at one point in time. A more dynamic process is required to ensure that a student's poor reading abilities are indeed due to an underlying impairment and thus require the attention of a reading specialist. Struggling L2 readers whose reading difficulties are due to other factors, such as inadequate prior reading instruction or visual problems, do not require the attention of a specialist; their reading difficulties can be addressed by appropriate classroom instruction or by treatment by other professionals, in many cases. In light of these complexities, we provide recommendations and guidelines for identifying L2 learners with or at risk for reading impairment that are part of a broad approach to prevent reading failure among all struggling L2 readers. Key to the success of this approach is early identification and intervention. Early identification and intervention are major weaknesses of standard identification approaches because L2 learners are often not diagnosed as having a reading impairment early on and are thus not given additional support for several years. The approach we recommend provides additional support to all struggling L2 readers through supplemental classroom instruction, or what is sometimes called *Tier 2 instruction* (see Mathes et al., 2007, for details of one such intervention for ELLs in the United States), and it does so early in their education. Struggling L2 readers who demonstrate poor response to supplemental classroom intervention can be more confidently identified as being at risk for reading impairment because their difficulties do not reflect inadequate opportunity to learn the L2 or to learn to read. They are then referred for follow-up by a reading specialist. In effect, we recommend a two-stage process of identification and intervention:

Stage I: Identification of all struggling L2 readers and the provision of supplemental classroom instruction in the acquisition of foundational reading skills.

Stage II: Identification of struggling L2 readers from Stage I who demonstrate poor response to intervention (RTI) in the classroom and referral to a reading or special education teacher for follow-up assessment and support, if appropriate.

There are several reasons why this approach is recommended. First, and as noted before, research indicates that the difficulties of students with reading impairment are not fundamentally different from those of struggling readers, although the difficulties of the former are more intractable and thus require more intensive, extended, and specialized remediation. This means that the same kinds of early interventions can benefit all L2 students who are struggling learning to read while recognizing that L2 students with specific reading impairment will require more extended support by specialists (Denton & Mathes, 2003).

Second, because L2 learners are by definition still in the process of acquiring the L2, it can be difficult to disentangle issues of opportunity to learn the L2 from issues related to reading impairment, especially when L2 learners first begin schooling in the L2. Similarly, to the extent that many minority language L2 learners, such as the profiled children Faisal and Luis in particular, have had inadequate, interrupted, or no previous literacy instruction, it can be difficult to know whether their current reading difficulties reflect previous inadequacies in their education or an underlying impairment. A preventive approach of the type suggested here, as also recommended by others (e.g., Vaughn et al., 2009), incorporates an RTI component for all struggling readers, regardless of the cause of their difficulties.

Third, there is growing evidence that L2 learners who struggle learning to read in an L2, including those with reading impairment, benefit from early systematic in-class intervention that focuses on the foundational skills that research has identified are critical for reading acquisition (Gersten & Geva, 2003; Lesaux & Siegel, 2003; Mathes et al., 2007; Vaughn, Linan-Thompson, Pollar-Durodola, Mathes, & Cardenas-Hagan, 2006). When a standard approach to identifying reading impairment is used, additional support is often not provided to L2 learners with reading impairment until later grades, when a more definitive identification of their status can be made. Educators often take a "wait-and-see" approach to the difficulties of struggling L2 readers, on the assumption that their difficulties will resolve once they have been in school longer and have advanced in the L2 proficiency—also see discussion of underidentification in Chapter 9. Although this may be true for some L2 learners, it is not likely for many, and especially not for L2 learners with reading impairment. The problems that result from delaying intervention can be avoided, or at least minimized, if a preventive classroom-based approach is used because intervention can begin early (Al Otaiba et al., 2009).

Finally, the preventive approach we recommend can be implemented within the context of classroom instruction and is based on what is currently regarded as the most promising method for identifying students with reading impairment: RTI. The advantage of this approach is that it can serve the needs of all struggling readers while also contributing to the identification of L2 learners who have a specific reading impairment. This will be explained in the next section. In short, a preventive two-stage approach to identification and intervention for L2 learners with reading impairment accomplishes a number of goals at the same time. Let us briefly consider what each stage of this process looks like.

Stage I

An important feature of this stage is that screening for reading impairment begins as soon as possible. For L2 learners, such as Trevor and Bonnie, the process could begin when they start school, at around 5 years of age, or kindergarten, the usual age for beginning school in North America. For L2 learners, such as Faisal's older brothers and sisters, who immigrate from another country after the typical age for starting school, formal reading instruction in the L2 begins in higher grades. The screening process that is part of Stage I will necessarily begin later for these students, but it should nevertheless begin as early as possible after they begin schooling in the L2. Screening that takes place in the primary grades should focus on word-level skills; screening in higher grades should include reading comprehension as well as word-level skills because students in these grades are expected to be reading text as part of their general education. By including reading comprehension measures with older learners, it is possible to begin the process of identifying L2 learners in these grades whose reading difficulties entail comprehension problems, with or without decoding problems.

Many schools require testing of all new students, whatever their grade level, and many classroom teachers conduct informal reading assessments of new students in order to better devise differentiated reading instruction. These assessment activities can be the basis for identifying "struggling readers." The definition of a struggling reader is open to interpretation, but much research on reading acquisition in L2 learners has used performance at or below the 25th percentile on a standardized test (e.g., Lesaux & Siegel, 2003). School or school districts may have their own criteria for identifying students with reading difficulties, in which case these should be used. The goal in this stage is to identify students who are significantly below grade-level expectation for reading and could benefit from supplemental reading support. Thus, variation in cut off scores from region to region is not necessarily problematic. In line with findings of research on early reading outcomes, assessment at this stage should focus on foundational skills, including letter-name knowledge, phonological awareness, and phonics, and should also include reading comprehension in the case of older L2 learners.

Research on what constitutes the most effective form of supplemental instruction is ongoing; thus, our understanding of best practices for such instruction is still evolving. Evidence from a number of studies suggests that the features listed in Box 10.3 are probably important (see Gersten & Geva, 2003, Mathes et al., 2005, and Vaughn et al., 2006, for more detailed discussions of effective interventions for struggling L2 readers).

As just noted, it would appear that for supplemental reading instruction to be effective for struggling readers, considerable time commitment is required (Mathes et al., 2007). This requires daily allocations of time during a school year as well as extended time over more than one grade, if necessary and possible (Vaughn et al., 2008). Depending on the resources available, different arrangements will be required to make this investment in time in different schools. Some school districts may be able to provide additional personnel, such as teachers' aides, to assist with supplemental instruction or to free up classroom teachers so that they can do supplemental instruction. Alternatively, classroom teachers can build supplemental instruction for struggling readers into their differentiated instructional plans. The same time allocation is probably not necessary for all struggling readers. It is likely that less time is required for more advanced L2 learners and those with less severe difficulties.

BOX 10.3

Features of Effective Reading Intervention

- It should provide explicit, systematic, and focused instruction of foundation skills: letter–sound knowledge, phonological awareness, and decoding.

- It should also be comprehensive and include supplemental instruction in vocabulary, listening comprehension, and language development in order to support reading comprehension and the development of academic language skills.

- It should be provided in small (3–5 students), relatively homogenous groups.

- Interactive instruction that encourages student engagement and language use is recommended (e.g., cooperative learning, peer pairing).

- It should be provided on a daily basis, during significant blocks of time, and for extended periods of time, preferably for one or more grades (Vaughn et al., 2008).

- It should incorporate adaptations that have been shown to be appropriate and effective for L2 learners: use of gestures and visuals to support meaning making; scaffolding through the use of preview-review methods; and repetition and routines to reinforce acquisition and to provide opportunities for practice.

- If possible, it should build on knowledge and skills students already have, including those related to the native language.

- It should include regular monitoring of individual student progress in acquiring the targeted skills in order to adapt instruction to individual student needs as they change.

Teachers are critical during Stage I because their support and involvement is necessary for implementing and sustaining supplemental instruction. In some cases, they may be providing supplemental instruction; in other cases, they will be collaborating with other personnel who are providing it. Because L2 learners can begin schooling in an L2 at any grade level and, thus, begin learning to read in an L2 at any grade level, all teachers in schools with L2 learners need to be prepared to begin the process of screening for reading impairment and possibly even providing supplemental instruction. As we noted in the beginning of this chapter, estimates of reading impairment in some school-age populations run as high as 20%. This is not an isolated problem. It has serious consequences for a large percentage of school-age children and thus requires the collective resources of all teachers who are involved in the reading development of L2 learners.

Stage II

Students who fail to demonstrate significant growth in response to supplemental instruction during Stage I should be referred to a reading specialist or special education professional for follow-up assessment. There is currently no agreement as to what constitutes adequate growth in response to intervention to differentiate students at risk for reading impairment from those who are simply struggling readers. Results from two studies with first-grade English language learners in the United States suggest that monitoring change in L2 readers' oral reading fluency in response to intervention can differentiate students with a learning/reading disability from typically developing L2 learners (see Al Otaiba et al., 2009; Vaughn, Linan-Thompson, & Hickman-Davis, 2003). Fluency was measured in terms of number of words read accurately in one minute, and growth in fluency was measured in terms of number of additional words read accurately per minute per week over the course of intervention. These studies suggest that adequate response to intervention among primary-grade L2 learners would be growth of one additional word read correctly per minute for each week of intervention. We are not aware of similar studies of response to intervention in higher grades. In the absence of definitive criteria for defining adequate response to intervention, each school or district will need to carry out its own action research to develop criteria that distinguish struggling readers who are able to catch up to grade-level expectations as a result of classroom instruction and those who cannot and need the support of a reading/learning specialist.

Failure to respond to intervention, however defined, does not by itself determine that a student has a reading impairment. Although Stage I serves to rule out inadequate instruction and insufficient opportunity to learn the L2 as explanations for poor reading performance, it is still necessary to rule out additional exclusionary factors that might explain their difficulties (see the list in Box 10.4). Collecting information on some of these exclusionary factors could begin during Stage I. In fact, some of this information may be collected as a matter of routine in many schools—for example, on hearing and vision impairment. Information about other exclusionary factors, such as medical history, prior educational experiences, and circumstances of immigration, may be collected when students register for school attendance. In these cases, school records should be consulted. It may be necessary to collect information about some exclusionary factors specifically for purposes of identifying reading impairment, such as information about family and sociocultural issues.

BOX 10.4

Exclusionary Factors When Identifying Reading Impairment

- Prior education, and especially reading instruction
- Access to and engagement in literacy activities outside school
- Vision or hearing problems
- Neurocognitive disabilities
- Health or medical conditions, such as malnutrition
- Cognitive or socioemotional problems, such as attention-deficit/hyperactivity disorder, or autism spectrum disorder
- Family or home-related circumstances
- Sociocultural factors

Students for whom the primary explanation for their difficulties appears to be one or more of these factors would not be considered further for reading impairment because the cause(s) of their reading difficulties do not require the services of a reading or learning specialist. They should nevertheless, in some cases, be referred to appropriate professionals for assistance. Indeed, in some jurisdictions, law requires that they be referred to appropriate specialists. Educators and other school personnel should familiarize themselves with their local and state/provincial guidelines and legislation, where such exist. Moreover, even L2 learners who do not qualify for specialist services because they do not meet formal criteria for reading impairment should continue to receive individualized reading support in class. The point here is that L2 learners whose reading difficulties can reasonably be explained by any of these factors do not meet clinical criteria for reading impairment and, thus, do not qualify for the services of reading/learning specialists. Moreover, children who are identified clinically as having a reading-related disability vary with respect to the severity of their disability, with some children facing much greater challenges than others, as illustrated in the email we received from a father (see Box 10.2).

L2 learners for whom exclusionary factors are inadequate to explain their reading difficulties meet the criteria for reading impairment and would continue to be supported by a reading or learning specialist. The following guidelines are intended to help guide reading or other learning specialists identify the specific strengths and weaknesses of L2 learners who are deemed to have a reading impairment so that individualized interventions can be prepared. Research indicates that intervention that focuses on individual needs is most effective in remediating the difficulties of students with reading impairment (Healy, Vanderwood, & Edelson, 2005). These guidelines reflect our interpretation of findings on studies on reading acquisition and impairment in both L1 and L2 readers and have not been examined directly in research. Thus, each should be considered critically with a view to modifying them to better serve L2 learners with impairment.

Examine Reading Skills in the L1   There are two very important reasons for examining L2 students in their L1 as well as their L2, if possible. Dual language students' knowledge and skills in language are distributed across both languages (e.g., Oller, Pearson, & Cobo-Lewis, 2007). Thus, taking a careful look at what they know and can do in both provides a comprehensive picture of their language competencies that is not possible if only the majority language is examined. Moreover, and as noted in Chapters 6 and 8, there is considerable evidence from research on both majority language L2 learners (Erdos et al., in press, 2009; Genesee & Jared, 2008) and minority language L2 learners (August & Shanahan, 2006; Durgunoglu, 2002; Genesee et al., 2006; Gerber & Durgunoglu, 2004) of positive cross-linguistic correlations in certain skills and knowledge related to reading acquisition. To be more specific, there are significant and positive correlations between the L1 and L2 in the following areas of language and literacy: word decoding, phonological awareness, higher-order vocabulary knowledge, reading comprehension, and use of reading comprehension strategies. This means that the results of L2 learners on tests of these skills and knowledge in the L1 can be used as predictors of their likely levels of competence in these domains in their L2. We focus here on those predictors that can be influenced by educators. There are yet other predictors of reading acquisition, such a **rapid automatized naming,** that we do not consider in detail because they are not easily manipulated through instruction. Cross-linguistic effects have been noted most consistently and significantly for word-level skills. For example, minority language L2 students, such as Bonnie, who have already acquired phonological awareness skills in their L1 are likely to acquire phonological awareness skills easily and relatively rapidly in their L2; phonological awareness skills even transfer from a language such as Mandarin to English because they operate on the oral renditions of words, not their written forms. To give another example, a majority language student such as Samantha, who has acquired decoding skills in English, is likely to acquire decoding skills relatively quickly and easily in her L2 in comparison with students who have not acquired these skills in the L1.

As a result of these cross-linguistic effects, it is possible to determine indirectly whether an L2 learner's reading difficulties are related to reading impairment even if his or her proficiency in the L2 is minimal or still developing. This can be done by examining the child's abilities in decoding and foundation reading skills (e.g., phonological awareness) in the L1 (see Erdos et al., in press, for evidence that supports this approach). Students who demonstrate that they have acquired reading-related (e.g., word decoding) or reading-readiness (knowledge of the alphabet) skills in their L1 are demonstrating that they do not have reading impairments; otherwise they could not have acquired these skills in their L1. Evidence that they have acquired some literacy skills in the L1 augurs well for the student's acquisition of them in the L2. These students are not likely to have a reading impairment and could probably be supported through individualized instruction by the classroom teacher.

In the case of L2 students who do not demonstrate L1 reading-related competencies, it is important to keep in mind that this may reflect influences that do implicate reading impairment; for example, inadequate opportunity to acquire reading-related skills in the L1 or even loss of the L1. With respect to the latter possibility, many minority language L2 learners begin to lose competencies in their L1 as exposure to and competence in the majority group language grows. This must be considered when interpreting students' performance on L1 tests. In any case, students who do not give evidence of having acquired foundational skills in reading in the L1 should continue to be considered for additional reading support by a specialist, provided that other exclusionary factors do not apply. For ways in which L1 reading-related skills can be assessed by educators who lack competence in the student's L1, see Chapter 3 in Cloud et al. (2009).

Assess within Learners' L2 Proficiency Limits   The accuracy and fluency with which L2 learners read necessarily depends on the level of their competence in the L2. This is especially true when it comes to reading for comprehension, a point we turn to shortly. A reading test is supposed to assess reading ability, not oral language ability. Thus, when using tests to ascertain the specific strengths and weaknesses of individual learners who are at risk for or have reading impairment, always assess within the limits of the student's current oral language abilities and always interpret their performance on reading tests while taking their current L2 oral language abilities into account. This means that a reading test that is appropriate for the grade level of the student is not necessarily the most appropriate level for testing his or her reading skills. L2 learners who begin schooling in English beyond the normal starting grade, such as Faisal's older brothers and sisters, may lack not only oral language skills expected of students at that grade level, but also literacy and academic knowledge more generally; therefore, giving them a reading test at grade level could be inappropriate. It may be necessary to step back a level, or more, in order to identify a test that is at the appropriate level of difficulty for an individual learner. It is important to keep in mind that testing at this stage is not intended to show whether students are at grade level, but rather to identify what they know and can do and, conversely, what they have not yet acquired and need to be taught with the assistance of a reading specialist.

An assessment of an L2 learner's current oral language abilities may be necessary. Often, teachers' observations are satisfactory for establishing level of oral proficiency in the L2 if they have had the opportunity to interact with and observe the student in class. Alternatively, there are a number of tests available in English for assessing expressive or receptive vocabulary and oral language skills, such as the Peabody Picture Vocabulary Test (Dunn & Dunn, 2007) and the One-Word Expressive Vocabulary Test (Brownwell, 2000), which assess receptive and expressive vocabulary skills, respectively, if formal testing is undertaken. Such tests also exist in other languages, most notably Spanish, but they are not readily available in all languages. The norms of tests standardized on native speakers of English should not be used to interpret the performance of English L2 learners, unless one can confidently assume that the learner is at a fairly advanced level in his or her oral language proficiency. Such tests can, nevertheless, be useful because they can provide a general indication of students' level of oral language proficiency that in turn can be used to gauge the appropriateness of reading tests. See Chapter 9 for more information on using standardized tests of oral language with dual language children.

Assess Decoding Skills

We recommend that assessment of L2 learners' strengths and weaknesses begin with decoding and the foundational skills of phonological awareness, phonics (i.e., letter–sound correspondences), and knowledge of the alphabet. There are two reasons for this. First, research shows that L2 learners are relatively successful in acquiring these skills, even in the absence of advanced levels of oral proficiency in the L2 (e.g., Snow, 2008). Thus, starting with these skills makes it possible to examine critical components of reading acquisition without the confounding effects of general L2 competence. Moreover, because these skills are transferable across languages, as noted earlier, even L2 learners with limited L2 competence can often demonstrate whether they have acquired these skills by virtue of transfer from the L1. Although some reading comprehension skills are also transferable, the evidence for this is much less robust and clear. Second, competency in these skills is critical for acquiring high levels of competency in reading, and, thus, a detailed understanding of the specific competencies that students with reading impairment have in decoding and related foundational skills is essential for planning appropriate intervention.

Assess Reading Comprehension

At the same time, in the case of older L2 learners, assessing reading comprehension skills in detail is also important. L2 learners beyond the primary grades must be able to read and comprehend academic texts efficiently and accurately if they are to succeed in school. Moreover, and as noted earlier, there is growing evidence of reading comprehension problems without dyslexia. It is important to determine the nature of the underlying problems of students who perform significantly below grade level on tests of reading comprehension. If a student's comprehension problems are linked to word decoding (i.e., dyslexia), this would call for different intervention than what is needed in the case of a student whose reading comprehension problems are linked to language impairment. It is also possible that a student's comprehension problems are linked to language, but differ from those of students with language impairment. Thus, assessment of L2 learners with significant reading comprehension difficulties should consider three possible sources of difficulty: inadequate decoding skills, language impairment, or other language-related difficulties, such as inadequate vocabulary skills and knowledge, poor comprehension monitoring skills, and so on. In most cases, L2 students whose comprehension difficulties are not linked to dyslexia or to language impairment, but appear to be linked to more general language issues, can be supported effectively through supplemental individualized instruction in class. In particular, they probably need additional support in acquiring oral academic language skills. Whether these students continue to be served by reading/learning specialists may be a matter of school policy and/or the availability of specialist resources.

As was true for decoding, it is important to assess reading comprehension skills in ways that are commensurate with the learners' level of oral competence in the L2. It is also important to use methods of assessment that include content that is familiar to the student. A test that includes content that is unfamiliar to an L2 learner is assessing not only reading comprehension, but also knowledge of text content. Again, if using a standardized test, it is inappropriate to use test norms if the student's oral language skills are not at the intermediate or advanced level. The goal of testing reading comprehension at this stage is to determine L2 learners' strengths and weaknesses with a view to planning intervention.

Effective Intervention

As is true for so many other aspects of L2 students with disabilities, the research base for implementing effective intervention is still meager, but growing (Mathes et al., 2007; Rivera, Moughamian, Lesaux, & Francis, 2009). Some studies show that, generally speaking, what is good intervention with native L1 speakers with reading impairment or struggling L1 readers appears to be effective, with modifications, for students who are struggling learning to read in an L2 (e.g., Denton, Fletcher, Anthony, & Francis, 2006). Synthesizing across studies, the following features appear to be important in clinical interventions for L2 students with reading impairment (see Rivera et al., 2009, for more details). Effective intervention is

- In the language of instruction in order to maximize impact (see Box 10.5)

- Differentiated, to take into account individual student's profile of strengths and weaknesses

- Adapted to be appropriate for each student's level of L2 oral language development in particular

- Intensive, preferably with daily sessions or at least three sessions per week

- Sustained until assessment indicates that intervention is no longer needed (in most cases, L2 students will need extended support)

- Explicit with respect to individual students' specific needs

- One on one, if possible, or in small groups including students with similar needs and skill levels

BOX 10.5

Language of Intervention for Reading Impairment

In Chapter 9, we provided many reasons why supporting both languages in intervention for oral language impairment is considered the best practice with dual language children. Is our recommendation the same for intervention for reading impairment? The following letter from a special educator typifies the kinds of questions such professionals have about the language of intervention. In the following case, the educator has chosen to provide intervention in the child's dominant language, English. As we have mentioned in this chapter, there is considerable transfer of phonics, phonological awareness, and word decoding skills from one language to another in dual language learners; there is even some evidence for the transfer of skills related to reading comprehension. Therefore, there is reason to believe that intervention in English will help this child's development of reading skills in French. However, there are other reasons why intervention in both French and English would benefit this child. Because this child is actually getting formal reading and writing instruction in French, it might be advisable to provide additional support in French, as this will provide him with assistance that should have an immediate impact on his schooling. This course of action might also be best because the French letter–sound system is more regular than the English one, and by focusing on French, some of the many irregularities in English can be avoided. It might also be advisable to focus on those aspects of letter–sound and spelling–sound correspondence in French that are the same or similar in English, to enhance cross-linguistic transfer of skills.

Dear Dr. Genesee:

I hope you don't mind me contacting you with a clinical question. I've just evaluated an 11-year-old with ADHD. He is from a bilingual family, and is considerably more dominant in English (according to his parents), but has attended a French school since kindergarten. He is struggling immensely in school, and I've diagnosed him with a severe written language disorder. I did the evaluation in English, given that everyone reports it to be his stronger language. I'm struggling though with whether it makes sense to do therapy in English. I'll be working with him a lot on grapheme–phoneme correspondences, reading syllabically, phonological awareness, and so on, and I don't know how much I can expect that to transfer to French, the language in which he is receiving formal reading/writing instruction. Do you have any recommendations as to which language I should provide therapy in? I tend to always pick the stronger language, as the weaker one usually bootstraps onto skills learned in the stronger language, but I'm not sure if this is the case for written language since the sound correspondences are different. However, at the same time, it seems logical to me that once he learns how to separate words into syllables/sounds, he may figure out how to do so in French as well.

A special educator

- Organized to provide lots of guided practice with feedback from a teacher or peer
- Interactive, providing for dialogue and cooperative learning
- Comprehensive; that is, it should include a focus on the range of skills/knowledge that are needed for progress, including language intervention in the case of students who also have a language learning impairment (see Chapter 9)
- Inclusive of regular and individualized assessment to monitor progress and adapt intervention, as needed

SUMMARY OF RECOMMENDATIONS FOR PRACTICE AND POLICY

- Bilingualism and L2 acquisition are not risk factors for reading impairment; thus, there is no reason to expect dual language students to be at higher risk for, or display higher rates of, reading impairment than monolingual students.

- Expect dual language students who are struggling readers to have difficulties in the same areas as monolingual students. Monolingual students can struggle learning to read because of difficulties acquiring small-unit skills related to word decoding or large-unit skills, such as grammar and semantics, related to reading comprehension. Small-unit skills are particularly important because they are essential for mastering skills related to reading comprehension and are often associated with reading impairment in an L1 or an L2.

- Testing letter–sound knowledge and phonological awareness can fairly accurately predict students' risk for reading impairment. In the case of dual language students, this can be done in the L1 or L2 because there is significant cross-linguistic transfer of these skills.
  - Testing beginner L2 students' knowledge of sound–letter correspondences and their phonological awareness in the L1 is useful for early identification of at-risk L2 readers who can then be given early additional individualized support.

- Be aware that a minority of students has serious comprehension difficulties without word reading difficulty (or dyslexia). Some of these students may have underlying language impairment, or they may have other difficulties, such as poor mastery of the grammatical or semantic systems of the language.

- In order to make a clinical identification of reading impairment, it is necessary to rule out the effects of exclusionary factors, such as inadequate or no prior reading instruction, inadequate opportunity to learn the target language, sociocultural factors, visual or sensorimotor problems, serious intellectual impairment, and trauma.

- When dual language students make errors reading in their L2 that can be traced to their L1, this should not be viewed as a sign of difficulty, but rather as a sign of L1 bootstrapping because students draw on all of their linguistic resources to break into the new language.

- Effective early individualized classroom-based support for struggling readers should
  - Be explicit, focused, and systematic
  - Be focused on individual students' reading-related weaknesses
  - Be provided on a frequent and regular basis for an extended period of time

o Take place in individual or small-group sessions that elicit active student engagement and provide lots of opportunities for feedback

o Include adaptations that are effective for L2 learners, such as extensive use of gestures and visual support, increased wait time, repetition, and redundancy

- Refer struggling L2 readers who demonstrate poor response to classroom intervention to a learning specialist. The following guidelines are suggested to help reading or other learning specialists identify the specific strengths and weaknesses of L2 learners who are deemed to have a reading impairment so that individualized interventions can be prepared:

o Examine reading skills in the L1.

o Assess within individual learner's L2 proficiency limits.

o Assess decoding skills and the small-unit skills that underlie decoding; that is, phonological awareness and letter–sound knowledge.

o Assess reading comprehension skills and large-unit skills that are linked to comprehension, such as comprehension of complex oral language, breadth and depth of vocabulary, ability to monitor comprehension, and so forth.

- Research evidence, although limited at present, suggests that effective clinical intervention for individual L2 students with reading impairment should be

o Differentiated to take into account individual student's profile of strengths and weaknesses

o Adapted to be appropriate for each student's level of L2 oral language development

o Intensive, preferably with daily sessions or at least three sessions per week

o Sustained until assessment indicates that intervention is not longer needed (in most cases, L2 students will need extended support)

o Explicit with respect to individual students' specific needs

o One on one, if possible, or in small groups including students with similar needs and skill levels

o Interactive, providing lots of guided practice with feedback from a teacher or peers

REFERENCES

Aarts, R., & Verhoeven, L. (1999). Literacy attainment in a second language submersion context. *Applied Psycholinguistics, 20*(3), 377–393.

Al Otaiba, S., Petscher, Y., Pappamiheil, N.E., Williams, R.S., Dyrlund, A.K., & Connor, C. (2009). Modeling oral reading fluency development in Latino students: A longitudinal study across second and third grade. *Journal of Educational Psychology, 101*(3), 315–329.

American Psychiatric Association. (1994). *Diagnostic and statistical manual of mental disorders (DSM-IV)* (4th ed.). Washington, DC: American Psychiatric Association.

August, D., & Hakuta, K. (1998). *Improving schooling for language minority children: A research agenda.* Washington, DC: National Academies Press.

August, D., & Shanahan, T. (2006). *Developing literacy in second language learners. Report of the National Literacy Panel on Minority-Language Children and Youth.* Mahwah, NJ: Lawrence Erlbaum Associates.

August, D., & Shanahan, T. (Eds.). (2008). *Developing reading and writing in second language learners.* New York: Routledge, Center for Applied Linguistics, and International Reading Association.

Bishop, D.V.M., & Snowling, M.J. (2004). Developmental dyslexia and specific language: Same or different? *Psychological Bulletin 130,* 858–888.

Brownell, R. (2000). *Expressive one-word picture vocabulary test* (3rd ed.). Novato, CA: Academic Therapy Publications.

Catts, H.W., Adlof, S.M., Hogan, T.P., & Weismer, S.E. (2005). Are specific language impairment and dyslexia distinct disorders? *Journal of Speech, Language, and Hearing Research, 48,* 1378–1396.

Cloud, N., Genesee, F., & Hamayan, E. (2009). *Literacy instruction for English language learners: A teacher's guide to research-based practices.* Portsmouth, NH: Heinemann.

Denton, C.A., Fletcher, J.M, Anthony, J.L., & Francis, D.J. (2006). An evaluation of intensive intervention for students with persistent reading difficulties. *Journal of Learning Disabilities, 39,* 447–466.

Denton, C.A., & Mathes, P.G. (2003). Intervention for struggling readers: Possibilities and challenges. In B.R. Foorman (Ed.), *Preventing and remediating reading difficulties. Bringing science to scale* (pp. 229–251). Baltimore: York Press.

Dunn, L.M., & Dunn, D.M. (2007). *Peabody Picture Vocabulary Test* (4th ed.). San Antonio, TX: Pearson.

Durgunoglu, A.Y. (2002). Cross-linguistic transfer in literacy development and implications for language learners. *Annals of Dyslexia, 52,* 189–206.

Erdos, C., Genesee, F., Savage, R., & Haigh, C. (2010). *Predicting risk for oral and written language learning difficulties in students educated in a second language.* Unpublished manuscript, Department of Psychology, McGill University, Toronto.

Erdos, C., Genesee, F., Savage, R., & Haigh, C. (in press). Individual differences in second language reading outcomes. *International Journal of Bilingualism.*

Garnett, B. (2006, October). *An introductory look at the academic trajectories of ESL students.* Paper presented at the Immigration, Integration and Language Conference, University of Calgary.

Genesee, F., & Geva, E. 2006. Cross-linguistic relationships in working memory, phonological processes, and oral language. In D. August & T. Shanahan (Eds.), *Developing literacy in second language learners. Report of the National Literacy Panel on Minority-Language Children and Youth* (pp. 175–184). Mahwah, NJ: Lawrence Erlbaum Associates.

Genesee, F., & Jared, D. (2008). Literacy development in early French immersion programs. *Canadian Psychology, 49,* 140–147.

Genesee, F., Lindholm-Leary, K., Saunders, W., & Christian, D. (2006). *Educating English language learners: A synthesis of research evidence.* New York: Cambridge University Press.

Gerber, M., & Durgunoglu, A.Y. (2004). Reading risk and intervention for young English learners. *Learning Disabilities Research & Practice, 19,* 199–201.

Gersten, R., & Geva, E. (2003). Teaching reading to early language learners. *Educational Leadership, 60*(7), 44–49.

Gonzalez, N., Moll, L.C., & Amanti, C. (2005). *Funds of knowledge: Theorizing practices in household, communities and classrooms.* Mahwah, NJ: Lawrence Erlbaum Associates.

Gough, P.B., & Tunmer, W.E., (1986). Decoding, reading and reading disability. *Remedial and Special Education, 77,* 6–10.

Healy, K., Vanderwood, M., & Edelston, D. (2005). Early literacy interventions for English language learners: Support for an RTI Model. *The California School Psychologist, 10,* 55–63.

Johnston, A.M., Barnes, M.A., & Desrochers, A. (2008). Reading comprehension: Developmental processes, individual differences, and interventions. *Canadian Psychology/Psychologie canadienne, 49*(2), 125–132.

Langer, J.A., Bartolome, L., Vasquez, O., & Lucas, T. (1990). Meaning construction in school literacy tasks: A study of bilingual students. *American Educational Research Journal, 27*(3), 427–471.

Lesaux, N., & Geva, E., with Koda, K., Siegel, L., & Shanahan, T. (2008). Development of literacy in second-language learners. In D. August & T. Shanhan (Eds.), *Developing reading and writing in second language learners* (pp. 27–60). New York: Routledge, Center for Applied Linguistics, and International Reading Association.

Lesaux, N.K., & Siegel, L.S. (2003). The development of reading in children who speak English as a second language. *Developmental Psychology, 3*(6), 1005–1019.

Mathes, P.G., Denton, C.A., Fletcher, J.M., Anthony, J., Francis, D.J., & Schatschneider, C. (2005). The effects of theoretically different instruction and student characteristics on the skills of struggling readers. *Reading Research Quarterly, 40*(2), 148–182.

Mathes, P.G., Pollard-Durodola, S.D., Cardenas-Hagan, E., Linan-Thompson, S., & Vaughn, S. (2007). Teaching struggling readers who are native Spanish speakers: What do we know? *Language, Speech, and Hearing Services in Schools, 38,* 260–271.

Miles, T.R. (2004). Some problems in determining the prevalence of dyslexia. *Electronic Journal of Research in Educational Psychology, 2,* 5–12.

Muter, V., Hulme, C., Snowling, M.J., & Stevenson, J. (2004). Phonemes, rimes and language skills as foundations of early reading development: Evidence from a longitudinal study. *Developmental Psychology, 40,* 663–681.

Nation, K. (2005). Children's reading comprehension difficulties. In M.J. Snowling & C. Hulme (Eds.), *The science of reading: A handbook* (pp. 248–265). Oxford, England: Blackwell.

National Early Literacy Panel. (2009). *Developing early literacy report.* Retrieved July 26, 2010, from http://www.nifl.gov/earlychildhood/NELP/NELPreport.html

National Reading Panel. (2000). *Teaching children to read: An evidence-based assessment of the scientific research literature on reading and its implications for reading instruction.* Washington, DC: U.S. Department of Health and Human Services.

Oakhill, J., Cain, K., & Bryant, P. E. (2003). The dissociation of word reading and text comprehension: evidence from component skills. *Language and Cognitive Processes, 18,* 443–468.

Organisation for Economic Co-operation and Development. (2006). *Where immigrant students succeed: A comparative review of performance and engagement in PISA 2003.* Available online at http//www.oecd.org

Oller, D.K., Pearson, B.Z., & Cobo-Lewis, A.B. (2007). Profile effects in early bilingual language and literacy. *Applied Psycholinguistics, 28,* 191–230.

Riches, C., & Genesee, F. (2006). Cross-linguistic and cross-modal aspects of literacy development. In F. Genesee, K. Lindholm-Leary, W. Saunders, & D. Christian (Eds.), *Educating English language learners: A synthesis of research evidence* (pp. 64–108). New York: Cambridge University Press.

Rivera, M., Moughamian, A., Lesaux, N.K., & Francis, D. (2009). *Language and reading interventions for English language learners and English language learners with disabilities.* Houston, TX: Center for Instruction, Texas Institute for Measurement, Evaluation and Statistics.

Roongpraiwan, R., Ruanqdaraganon, N., Visudhiphan, P., & Santikul, K. (2002). Prevalence and clinical characteristics of dyslexia in primary school students. *Journal of the Medical Association of Thailand, 85*(4), 1097–1103.

Sanchez, K.S., Bledsoe, L.M., Sumabat, C., & Ye, R. (2004). Hispanic students' reading situations and problems. *Journal of Hispanic Higher Education, 3*(1), 50–63.

Scanlon, D.M., Gelzheiser, L.M., Vellutino, F.R., Schatschneider, C., & Sweeney, J.M. (2008). Reducing the incidence of early reading difficulties: Professional development for classroom teachers vs. direct interventions for children. *Learning and Individual Differences, 18,* 346–359.

Shaywitz, S.E. (2003). *Overcoming dyslexia.* New York: Random House.

Shaywitz, S.E., Fletcher, J.M., Holahan, J.M., Shneider, A.E., Marchione, K.E., Stuebing, K.K., et al. (1999, December). Persistence of dyslexia: The Connecticut longitudinal study at adolescence. *Pediatrics, 104*(6), 1351–1359.

Shaywitz, S.E., & Shaywitz, B.A. (2005). Neurobiological indices of dyslexia. In H.L. Swanson, K.R. Harris, & S. Graham (Eds.), *Handbook of learning disabilities* (pp. 514–531). New York: Guilford Press.

Snow, C. (2008). Cross-cutting themes and future research directions. In D. August & T. Shanahan (Eds.), *Developing reading and writing in second language learners* (pp. 275–300). New York: Routledge, Center for Applied Linguistics, and International Reading Association.

Storch, S.A., & Whitehurst, G.J. (2002). Oral language and code-related precursors to reading: Evidence from a longitudinal structural model. *Developmental Psychology, 38,* 934–947.

Vaughn, S., Cirino, P.T., Tolar, T., Fletcher, J.M., Cardenas-Hagan, E., Carlson, C.D., et al. (2008). Long-term follow-up for Spanish and English interventions for 1st grade English language learners at risk for reading problems. *Journal of Research on Educational Effectiveness, 1*(4), 179–214.

Vaughn, S., Linan-Thompson, S., & Hickman-Davis, P. (2003). Response to instruction as a means of identifying students with reading/learning disabilities. *Exceptional Children, 69,* 391–410.

Vaughn, S., Linan-Thompson, S., Pollar-Durodola, S.D., Mathes, P.G., & Cardenas-Hagan, E. (2006). Effective intervention for English language learners (Spanish-English) at risk for reading difficulties. In D.K. Dickinson & S.B. Neuman (Eds.), *Handbook of early literacy research* (Vol. 2, pp. 185–197). New York, Guilford Press.

Vaughn, S., Wanzek, J., Murray, C.S., Scammacca, N., Linan-Thompson, S., & Woodruff, A.L. (2009, Winter). Response to early reading intervention: Examining higher and lower responders. *Exceptional Children, 75*(2), 165–183.

Glossary

additive bilingual environments   Language learning environments (including family, community, and/or school settings) that encourage the acquisition of children's native or home language at the same time that they acquire an additional language. Acquisition of a second language in an additive bilingual environment does not occur at the expense of maintenance and development of the native language. Such environments also usually embrace dual cultural identity; this is characteristic of the language learning environments of children from majority ethnolinguistic groups who learn more than one language. This environment usually fosters high levels of bilingual proficiency in a child, and is also sometimes referred to as "additive bilingualism."

adopted children   *See* internationally adopted (IA) children.

Anglo-Western culture   Culture that is based on or is derived from English-speaking cultures and/or broader Western cultural values and traditions; for example, Canada, the United States, Australia, and New Zealand have distinct mainstream cultures but share values and beliefs that are similar because they are derived from their common historical links to England and other Western cultural traditions.

bell curve   *See* normal curve.

bilingual bootstrapping   Refers to the idea that a bilingual child's development in one language can be advanced by the other, dominant language, and/or that the two languages can be mutually advanced by virtue of sharing some linguistic–conceptual knowledge. This means that development might proceed more rapidly than one might expect if a bilingual child were acquiring two language systems in absolute isolation from each other. *See also* interdependence hypothesis/common underlying proficiency hypothesis.

bilingual children   *See* simultaneous bilingual children, sequential bilingual children, and second language learners.

bilingual education/programs   K–12 programs for language minority students in the United States in which both English and the students' native language are used for academic and literacy instruction during several grades.

bound morphemes/morphology   *See* grammatical morphology and morphosyntax.

child-directed talk   Adult talk that is directed to children who have not yet mastered language. In certain cultures, the adult will attend to or share in children's activities and talk directly to them about such activities. Child-centered talk can include modifications, such as lexical and grammatical simplifications, that make the words different from the way adults would typically talk to older children or other adults. This form of talk is typical of the white middle-class culture in North America and is also referred to as child-directed speech or language or "motherese."

code-mixing   Use of elements from two or more languages of a bilingual in the same utterance or stretch of conversation. The mixed elements may be phonological, lexical, or morphosyntactic. Mixing that occurs in a single sentence or utterance is called *intrautterance code-mixing.* Mixing that involves a switch from one language to another from one turn to another in the same conversation is called *interutterance code-mixing.* Examples of each are provided in Chapter 5. Code-mixing is a common form of language use in both bilingual adults and children. It is grammatically and socioculturally constrained; that is, it does not occur randomly. It is also sometimes referred to as *code-switching.*

common underlying proficiency hypothesis   *See* interdependence hypothesis.

contingent query   Conversational activity in which someone asks a question that elicits a direct or contingent response. It is a frequent pattern in the conversational interactions of adults and children in certain cultures (e.g., white, middle-class North American culture).

cross-linguistic influence   Interactions between a bilingual child's two languages during development. These interactions result in grammatical structures in one language that reflect grammatical properties of the other language. Cross-linguistic influence is distinct from the concept of a Unitary Language System, because these cross-linguistic structures do not result from across-the-board blending of the two languages but instead are limited in scope. The structures that result from cross-linguistic influence are not pervasive, and many researchers have found that they are not permanent in a bilingual child's language but occur as part of the typical bilingual developmental process. This concept is also called *cross-linguistic transfer* or *cross-linguistic interference.*

delayed immersion   Educational program for majority language students in which use of the second language for academic instruction is delayed until the middle elementary grades (e.g., Grade 4 or 5). At that time, usually about 50% of academic instruction is presented through the second language and the remainder through the students' first language.

developmental bilingual programs   Bilingual programs for language minority students that aim for full bilingual proficiency and grade-appropriate standards in academic subjects. The majority second language and the student's native language are both used to teach literacy and academic subjects throughout the elementary grades and sometimes through the secondary grades.

developmental errors   Omission or substitution of morphemes, wrong word order, or other errors produced by second language learners in their *interlanguage*. Developmental errors are those that are typical of all learners of a certain language regardless of their first language background. In other words, the source of these errors cannot be traced to the first language of the second language learner; *see also* transfer errors.

dominance/dominant language   The condition of bilingual people having one language in which they possess greater grammatical proficiency, more vocabulary, and greater fluency than the other language. This language may also be used more often than the other language. Most, if not all, bilingual children and adults have a *dominant language*. The dominant language can change throughout the life span, and a bilingual person can be slightly or highly dominant in one language. In bilingual children, dominance can affect language choice (choosing to use the dominant language more than the *nondominant language*) and rate of language development (the bilingual child's competence in the dominant language more closely resembles that of monolingual children who speak that language).

Down syndrome   Neurodevelopmental disorder caused by a chromosomal abnormality, the presence of an extra 21st chromosome. This condition results in a distinctive physical appearance and moderate to severe intellectual disability. It also affects language development.

dual language learners/children   *Simultaneous bilingual children* and *second language learners* of preschool or school age.

Dual Language System Hypothesis   Theory about early bilingual development that claims that when an infant is presented with dual language input, he or she constructs two separate linguistic representations from the outset, such as two vocabularies and grammars. According to this view, there is no period in development in which a child exposed to two languages cannot be considered bilingual, and there is no discernable stage in development in which the child's language system has to differentiate or separate into two. This view has been the majority view among researchers since the 1990s and contrasts with the *Unitary Language System Hypothesis*.

dyslexia   *See* reading impairment.

early immersion   Educational program for majority language students in which use of the second language for academic instruction begins in kindergarten. The percentage of instruction in the first language varies among programs.

English language learners (ELLs)   Language minority students in the United States who are learning English, the majority language, for social integration and educational purposes (e.g., Spanish-speaking, Vietnamese-speaking, and Korean-speaking children residing and being educated in the United States). These children were previously referred to as *limited English proficient (LEP)* students; this term continues to prevail in federal and state legislation but is not widely used by educators and researchers because of the pejorative connotations of the term *limited*. Similar terms are *English as a second language (ESL)* learners, *English as an additional language (EAL)* learners, or simply *English learners (EL)*. The term ELL is also used in Canada.

English-only programs   K–12 programs for language minority students in the United States in which all instruction is provided in English. Language minority students may be provided with some English as a second language instruction by trained specialists; otherwise, all instruction is provided by general classroom teachers.

errors of omission/commission   Terms referring to two kinds of *errors* that appear in the *interlanguage* of second language learners. An omission error is one in which an obligatory element, such as a grammatical morpheme, has been deleted (e.g., *Robin Ø going there* instead of *Robin* is *going there*). A commission error is one in which the learner has supplied a morpheme but chosen the wrong one (e.g., *Robin* am *going there* instead of *Robin* is *going there*) or mispronounced the right one. In the second language acquisition of English, omission errors are more common than commission errors.

family bilingualism   Situation in which the immediate family is bilingual (e.g., the parents speak two languages to their children), but one of the two languages is not used in the community. Many children being raised in *one parent–one language* families experience family bilingualism.

first language (L1) attrition   Process whereby proficiency in the native language declines as the second language becomes dominant. This process can result in restricted communicative competence in the first language compared with the second language and/or complete loss of the first language. Attrition can take many forms: decay or stagnation in size of the first language vocabulary, reduction in fluency/spontaneity in the first language, transfer of grammatical rules from the second language into the first language, borrowing vocabulary from the second language into the first language, or erosion of details in grammatical structures in the first language. When the first language is a minority language, whether a child is a simultaneous bilingual or a second language learner, there is a risk of first language attrition.

formulaic language   Type of language children produce when they begin speaking the second language after the nonverbal stage. Children's utterances in the second language at this stage are often short—one word responses to questions—or consist of mainly memorized phrases with little original content. For example, children might produce sentences that for them, do not really consist of separate words: *I don't know, Excuse me, So what?* and *What's happening?*

function words   *See* grammatical morphology and morphosyntax.

funds of knowledge   Knowledge and competencies that individuals acquire in their day-to-day lives as they grow up and live in families and communities. It is knowledge and skills that are acquired informally during everyday experiences and that allow individuals to function appropriate and effectively in their families and communities, make sense of the world around them, and fit in socially. Funds of knowledge contrast with the knowledge and skills that children acquire formally in school, but are nevertheless important, because they shape the way young learners interpret what goes on in school and they can influence how successful they are in school. Students from minority cultural backgrounds often have funds of knowledge based on their specific cultural experiences that differ from those of students from the majority cultural group.

grammatical morphology   Morphemes that mark grammatical functions such as, past or present tense, and contrast with content morphemes like nouns, verbs, and adjectives. Grammatical morphemes can be inflectional or bound morphemes (e.g., the plural -*s*, or past tense -*ed*), which are attached to words, or freestanding words such as articles (*the, a*) or auxiliary verbs (*is* in *she is eating*). *See also* morphosyntax.

heritage language   The minority language spoken by members of a minority ethnolinguistic group or the language associated with that group. This term is often used when describing immigrants, refugees, and their children and may refer to a language that is no longer spoken by members of the group in the community in which they are currently living. Examples include Italian in the case of Italian adults and children living outside Italy; Spanish in the case of Mexican American children who have migrated to the United States; and Turkish in the case of children living in Germany or The Netherlands.

immersion programs K–12 bilingual programs for students who are members of the majority ethnolinguistic group in which at least 50% of curriculum instruction is provided through the medium of a second or foreign language for one grade or more. The grade level when instruction through the medium of the second language begins varies from the primary grades (kindergarten or first grade) to the middle grades of elementary school (around fourth grade) to middle or early high school grades (Grade 7 or 8). As well, the duration of immersion instruction can vary from 1 to several years. These types of program are also referred to as "second language" or "foreign language" immersion programs.

inflectional morphology *See* grammatical morphology and morphosyntax.

interdependence hypothesis/common underlying proficiency hypothesis Two closely related concepts that characterize the relationship between the first and second language of second language learners. Because there are many aspects of language structure, language learning skills, and literacy skills whose fundamental components can be shared between two languages of a bilingual—that is, common underlying proficiency, interdependence in development between the two languages can be expected. Such interdependence is viewed as faciliatory to dual language children. See also *bilingual bootstrapping*.

interlanguage Intermediate language of second language learners that does not correspond entirely with the second language and appears errorful from the perspective of the second language. Interlanguage is thought to be a viable language system, even if it is not exactly like the target language (i.e., the second language). In other words, interlanguage is a rule-governed systematic language that is dynamic in nature because it is continually developing toward the second language.

internationally adopted (IA) children Children who are adopted into a family residing in another country. Most commonly, these children stop hearing and learning their first language when they are adopted, because that language is not spoken by their adopted families. What sets these children apart from other dual language children is that they are usually transitional bilinguals who will become functionally monolingual during the childhood years. What these children have in common with other dual language children is that they have had exposure to more than one language early in life, and they experience a delay in the onset of exposure to one of their languages.

interutterance code-mixing *See* code-mixing.

intrautterance code-mixing *See* code-mixing.

L1 attrition *See* first language (L1) attrition.

L2-only/English-only programs *See* second language (L2)-only/English-only programs.

language aptitude Ability or potential that an individual has for learning language. Language aptitude is distinct from general intelligence and includes skills such as the ability to rapidly and accurately decode unfamiliar speech into phonetic units and parts of speech (e.g., nouns, verbs, adjectives). *Phonological memory* is also associated with language aptitude. Language aptitude predicts success in second language learning better than personality, social, or attitudinal factors. It is considered to be an intrinsic ability and not a learned skill.

language crossing   Term used to describe the language use practices of adolescents in multiethnic schools in England. These young people would borrow certain phrases and expressions from each other's first languages and integrate them into their own first language. This kind of intentional language mixing created and represented a kind of social bond between them.

language impairment   *See* specific language impairment (SLI).

language socialization   The process by which children are socialized into their culture through language, and, in turn, the process by which cultural patterning socializes children in how and with whom to use the language or languages they are learning.

late immersion   Educational programs for language majority students that provide at least 50% of instruction, including reading, writing, and academic subjects, through the medium of a second/foreign language beginning in middle or high school.

lexical gap hypothesis   Theory that children and adults mix words from one language into an utterance in another language when they do not know or cannot easily access the word in the appropriate language (e.g., if a Spanish speaker is trying to say, "I lost my wallet," but does not know or cannot remember the word for *wallet* in English, he may insert the Spanish word *cartera*).

limited capacity hypothesis   Theory that infants and children have the ability to acquire one language completely, but the acquisition of two or more languages exceeds their innate ability. As a result, it is argued, acquisition of two languages simultaneously during infancy and early childhood or the acquisition of a second language during early childhood (after a first language has been established) will result in reduced levels of first and/or second language proficiency. The parents of children who are suspected of having a language disorder are often counseled to limit the child to one language on the assumption that the child's disorder is related to (and perhaps even caused by) excessive demands on the child's language learning ability. Much evidence is presented in this book against the limited capacity hypothesis.

majority ethnolinguistic community   A community of individuals who speak the language spoken by most of the members of the community and/or are members of the ethnic/cultural group of most members of the community. The community may be as large as a country, or it may be a state or province within a country or some smaller unit. The majority language and culture usually have special recognition as the official language and culture of the community. In other cases, they are regarded unofficially as the high status language and culture in the community. The majority language is the language used in most newspapers and other media, in the courts, and by political bodies in the community. Examples are Anglo-Americans in the United States; English Canadians in Canada; and native German speakers in Germany. We also use the term *majority group*.

majority group   *See* majority ethnolinguistic community.

majority language   Language spoken by members of a *majority ethnolinguistic community*.

majority language students   K–12 students who speak a majority language and/or are members of a majority ethnolinguistic group (e.g., English-speaking students from mainstream sociocultural backgrounds in the United States, or in English-speaking regions of Canada).

mean length of utterance (MLU) Common measure of language development that is often considered to reflect overall grammatical development. It is the average length of utterances produced by a child spontaneously. MLU may be based on average number of words (including bound morphemes) or average number of separate morphemes, bound and free (see *morphosyntax*). The former is a more conservative estimate of development, because it does not count bound morphemes separately; this estimate is often more appropriate when comparing development of languages with different morphological complexity.

metalinguistic awareness Conscious awareness of and the ability to manipulate the elements of language, including sounds, words, and grammatical structures (e.g., ability to count the number of sounds in a word or to remove, add, or otherwise manipulate the sounds of words; ability to identify words and the characteristics of words). Some metalinguistic skills, especially *phonological awareness,* have been shown to be highly correlated with reading and writing ability.

middle immersion *See* delayed immersion.

minimal pairs *See* phonemic.

minority ethnolinguistic community A community made up of individuals who speak a minority language and belong to a minority culture. The language and culture may be in the demographic minority or may be in a minority status by virtue of their relatively low social, economic, and political power. Examples include Spanish speakers or individuals of Hispanic background in the United States, speakers of Inuktitut or Cantonese languages in Canada, speakers of Navajo in the United States, and Turkish speakers in The Netherlands and Germany. We also use the term *minority group.*

minority group *See* minority ethnolinguistic community.

minority language Language spoken by members of a *minority ethnolinguistic community.*

minority language students K–12 students who speak a minority language and/or are members of a minority ethnolinguistic group (e.g., Spanish-speaking students with central or south American sociocultural backgrounds in the United States, or Chinese-speaking Canadian students with Chinese sociocultural backgrounds).

MLU *See* mean length of utterance.

morphemes/morphology *See* grammatical morphology and morphosyntax.

morphosyntax A more technical term for grammar. Morphosyntax refers to two elements of language that combine to form grammar: morphology and syntax. Morphology refers to free-standing function words like articles (*the, a*), auxiliary verbs (*she is going, does she like milk?*), prepositions (*to, at, in, on*), or negative markers (*she does not like milk*), and to inflections that attach to words like nouns and verbs in the form of suffixes or prefixes, for example, *-s* in *he walk-s* or *the cat-s* or *Mommy's sock,* or *-ed* for the past tense, *walked, helped.* Freestanding function words are also known as *free morphemes,* and inflections are also known as *bound morphemes.* Syntax mainly refers to the rules for the order of the words in a clause or sentence, and the relationships between them.

nondominant language The language for many bilingual children and adults that is less proficient than the other. Children usually have smaller vocabularies, are less fluent, and have less advanced grammatical skills in the nondominant language. Children may also code-mix more when trying to use their nondominant language because they have less well-developed proficiency in that language and thus draw on the skills of the dominant language to fill gaps in their proficiency. Dominance is often related to the child's exposure to each language, and the nondominant language is typically the language to which the child has had less exposure. It is important to assess dual language children who are suspected of having language impairments in the dominant language to get an estimate of the child's maximum ability with language.

nonverbal period   Stage children go through early in their acquisition of a second language when they do not speak or speak very little in the presence of speakers of the second language. Children accumulate receptive knowledge of the second language in a school or preschool setting, and communicate mainly with nonverbal gestures, but they produce very few or no words in that language. The nonverbal period can last a few weeks to a few months; in general, younger children stay longer in this stage than older ones.

normal curve   Distribution of measurement or ability scores from a group of individuals. The distribution usually follows a bell shape, with most scores falling in the middle level of performance—meaning that most individuals have mid-level scores. Fewer individuals have low and high scores. See also *standard deviation* and *percentile*. See also Chapter 9 for a detailed discussion.

normal range   Scores that fall from +1 to −1 standard deviation around the mean in a normal distribution of scores. Scores below the normal range, that is, below −1 standard deviation, on a measurement of language or reading ability could signal the presence of disorder.

norming sample   Group of individuals who have contributed scores on a measure such that a normal distribution can be determined. The norming sample constitutes the group against which an individual child's score on the same measure can be compared, and thus interpreted.

one parent–one language rule   Pattern of parental language use in bilingual families in which each parent uses only, or primarily, one language (usually his or her native language) with the child.

partial immersion   Educational programs for majority language students in which 50% of academic instruction is presented through the medium of the students' first language and 50% through the medium of the second language. These programs often begin in kindergarten or first grade and continue until the end of elementary school.

percentile   Method of dividing scores on the *normal curve*. The 50th percentile represents the mid-level performance, and the 25th percentile and 75th percentile represent lower and higher performance, respectively.

phonemic   Acoustic/articulatory differences in *segments* (speech sounds) that signal a difference in meaning in *minimal pairs*. Minimal pairs are pairs of words in which all of the segments are the same except for two segments that contrast (e.g., *bat* and *pat*). Which segments contrast phonemically differs cross-linguistically. For example, the acoustic/articulatory difference between /l/ and /r/ makes a difference in meaning when these sounds are used in minimal pairs in English (e.g., *rice* and *lice*). This difference is not phonemic in Japanese; thus, Japanese speakers often have trouble hearing and producing this contrast when they listen to or speak English.

phonetic segments   Individual speech sounds, or phones, that make up the phonetic/phonemic inventory of a language. For example, [b], [p], [g], [I], and [u] are all segments in the phonetic/phonemic inventory of English. The International Phonetic Alphabet is used to transcribe the sound segments used in the world's languages because there are many more sound segments than can be written with the Roman alphabet.

phonics instruction   A method for teaching learners how to read and write individual words. It involves teaching how to connect the sounds of spoken words with letters or groups of letters (e.g., the sound /k/ can be represented by *c, k, ck,* or *ch* spellings in English) and teaching learners to blend the sounds of letters together to produce approximate pronunciations of new or unknown words.

phonemic awareness   Refers to knowledge of how individual phonemes make up words—for example, that the sounds /c/, /a/, and /t/ make up the word "cat." Phonemic awareness is part of the more general ability, *phonological awareness.*

phonological awareness   The knowledge that words are made up of individual sounds (be it syllables, phonemes, or other units of sound) that can be manipulated independently; that is, they can be added together, deleted, or inverted. Phonological awareness is part of the more general ability, *metalinguistic awareness.*

phonological memory   (Related terms are *verbal working memory* and *short-term memory*) An individual's ability to retain phonological information in short-term memory; that is, for a very brief time. It is often measured using digit span or pseudoword repetition tasks; for example, children are presented with a list of pseudowords and asked to repeat them as accurately as they can. If the task requires that the individual simply repeat the numbers or pseudowords as presented, then it is seen as measuring short-term memory capacity. If the individual must manipulate the material to be remembered in some way, such as repeating the digits or pseudowords in reverse order, then it is seen as measuring working memory capacity.

poor comprehenders   *See* reading impairment.

primary language impairment   *See* specific language impairment (SLI).

prosody   Intonation contour of speech, including pauses and changes in stress and pitch.

rapid automatized naming   (Also referred to as *phonological recoding*) The ability to access or produce verbal labels or names for nonphonological stimuli, such as pictures of objects, color patches, or a list of numbers. It is usually assessed using tasks such as rapid naming of pictures, numbers, or colors under timed conditions; for example, how many objects can be named in 30 seconds.

reading impairment   A distinct learning disability that manifests itself in great difficulty learning to read despite normal intelligence, adequate learning opportunities, and the absence of neurological and psychological problems. It can be evident in different aspects of learning to read and reading ability, including word decoding, reading comprehension, and fluency. *Dyslexia* is a more specific term that denotes a kind of reading impairment that pertains primarily to word decoding. *Poor comprehenders* refers to children who do not appear to have word decoding problems but nevertheless show difficulty understanding written text. It is possible that poor comprehenders have deficits in oral language, semantics, and syntax especially, and these deficits impede their ability to understand written text.

second language (L2)-only programs   *See* English-only programs.

second language learners/children   Children who begin to learn an additional language after 3 years of age; that is, after the first language is established. There is no definitive demarcation at 3 years of age, but this is the most widely used cutoff between *simultaneous bilinguals* and second language learners. Second language learners are often exposed to their additional language through schooling.

semilingualism   Label for the state of linguistic knowledge of a second language learner whose first-language abilities have significantly eroded and whose second-language abilities have not yet reached a proficient level. These individuals are sometimes labeled *semilingual,* meaning they do not possess reasonable levels of competence in either language. The existence of semilingualism has been challenged on both conceptual and empirical grounds, and it has become a controversial label, for second language children in particular.

sequential bilingual children   *See* second language learners.

simultaneous bilingual children   Children who learn two or more languages from birth or begin learning both languages sometime before 3 years of age. In effect, simultaneous bilinguals have two first languages. Simultaneous bilinguals can be exposed to languages in different ways—from their parents or siblings in the home, from child care workers in the home or in child care centers, or from grandparents or relatives. There is no definitive demarcation at 3 years of age, but this is the most widely used cutoff between simultaneous bilinguals and *second language learners.*

successive bilinguals   *See* second language learners.

sink-or-swim programs   *See* submersion programs.

specific language impairment (SLI)   A developmental disorder that causes children to have a delayed onset and protracted difficulties in language development through the preschool and school-age years. Despite their linguistic disabilities, children with SLI have nonverbal intelligence within or above the normal limits, no hearing impairment, no autism spectrum disorder, no clinically significant oromotor limitations, and no frank neurological damage. Effectively, these children's primary disorder is in language itself, rather than being a consequence of disorders/deficits in other domains. *Language impairment* is a more general term covering similar language learning disabilities in children that are a consequence of other disorders/deficits in other domains, such as intellectual disability, autism, or hearing impairment.

standard deviation   The average distance of a score, in a group of scores, from the mean score. The distance of scores from the mean score is often expressed in standard deviation units. Two thirds or 68% of all individuals within a *norming sample* have scores that fall within the range of −1 to +1 standard deviations. Scores below −1 standard deviation are below the *normal range,* and scores above 1 standard deviation are above the normal range.

submersion programs   K–12 programs for language minority students in which the majority language is used for all instruction (including literacy and academic subjects); typically, no or limited adjustments are made to instruction to accommodate L2 students' special language and cultural characteristics. This type of program is also referred to as *sink-or-swim.*

subtractive bilingual environments   Language-learning environments (including family, community, and school settings) that are associated with stagnation, erosion, or loss of the native language as a result of acquisition of a second language. Dual language children in these environments usually lose identification with the culture associated with the native language and family. This process is referred to as *subtractive bilingualism* and occurs in children from minority ethnolinguistic groups, such as immigrant, refugee, or indigenous group children, when they acquire a majority group language. In the long run, subtractive bilingualism often results in monolingual proficiency in the majority language.

telegraphic language   Type of language children use when they begin to speak the second language productively, after or concurrent with the formulaic stage. Children's utterances in the second language at this stage are more original than in the formulaic stage, but they often seem stripped of anything but the core content words (like a telegram). For example, children may say *he no like play car* instead of *he doesn't like to play cars,* thus omitting most of the *grammatical morphology.*

threshold hypothesis Theory proposed to explain different cognitive and linguistic consequences of bilingualism. According to this hypothesis, children who acquire relatively high levels of competence in two languages are likely to exhibit higher than average levels of general cognitive and language ability, whereas children who acquire relatively low levels of ability in their two languages are likely to experience lower than average levels of general cognitive and language ability. No significant positive or negative cognitive or linguistic consequences are likely to result from the acquisition of levels of bilingual competence that fall intermediary between the upper and lower thresholds.

total immersion Educational program for majority language students that often begins in kindergarten and provides 90%–100% of instruction through the medium of a second/foreign language for a minimum of 2 years. Instruction through the first language of the students is introduced in Grade 2 or higher. The percentage of instruction in the first language varies among programs.

transfer errors Mispronunciations, wrong word order, or other errors in a second language learner's interlanguage that are due to influence from the first language. For example, a second language speaker of English whose first language is Spanish may put an *e* before *sp* in words (e.g., *Spanish* becomes *Espanish*; *stop* becomes *estop*). In this example, second language speakers appear to have transferred a phonological rule from their native language to their second language; see also *developmental errors.*

transitional bilingual/immersion programs Programs for language minority students that use the students' native language to teach literacy and some academic subjects during the primary grades for at most 3 years, at which time the students are transitioned into mainstream classes in which all instruction is provided in English. These programs aim for full proficiency in English only and grade-appropriate academic standards.

translation equivalents Words in a bilingual speaker's vocabulary in one language that have a corresponding word in the other language that means virtually the same thing (e.g., *zapatos* in Spanish corresponds to *shoes* in English).

two-way bilingual/immersion programs Bilingual programs in the United States in which half the students are from a minority language group (e.g., Spanish) and half are from the majority language group (i.e., English). Both English and the minority language are used to teach literacy and academic subjects throughout the elementary grades and sometimes through the high school grades. These programs aim for full bilingual proficiency and grade-appropriate standards in academic subjects. The most common forms of two-way immersion are referred to as the *90/10* and the *50/50* models, because they provide 90% and 50%, respectively, of instruction through the medium of a minority language and the remaining instruction through English.

Unitary Language System Hypothesis Theory about early simultaneous bilingual development that claims that when an infant is presented with dual language input, he does not construct two separate linguistic representations at first, but instead melds the dual language input into a single system that must undergo a process of differentiation. After differentiation, which is thought to occur around 3 years of age, the child is considered to be bilingual. This hypothesis contrasts with the *Dual Language System Hypothesis.*

Index

Academic language, 167, 168
Academic success, language proficiency and, 167–170
Acquisition
  reading, 239–244
  second language, 129–130
Additive bilingualism, 50
Adopted children, *see* Internationally adopted (IA) children, language development in
Adults, bilingual code-mixing and, 90–92
Age, second language acquisition and, 129–130
Anglo-Western culture, 170–171
Assessment, *see* Specific language impairment, assessment
Attrition, language, 134–139

Babbling, 44, 45
Behavioral manifestations of reading impairment, 236
Bilingual bootstrapping, 79–80, 119
Bilingual code-mixing (BCM)
  adults and, 90–92
  defined, 12, 88–90
  examples of, 89
  flagging, 91–92, 101–103
  gap-filling hypothesis, 97–99
  grammatical deviance, 103–105
  grammatical errors, 91
  intra-versus interutterance, 88–89
  key points and implications, 105–108
  pragmatic explanations, 99
  reasons for, in children, 92–103
  social norms, 99–101
  unitary language system and, 92, 93–97, 95f, 96f
Bilingual education/programs, 166
  acquisition of majority language and effects of, 175–178
  developmental, 174–175
  for majority-language students, 178–190
  success of minority language students and, 174–178
  transitional, 174, 175
  two-way, 174–175
Bilingual English Spanish Assessment (BESA), 218

CDIs, *see* MacArthur-Bates Communicative Development Inventories
Child-directed talk, 30, 33
Chinese Canadian, 30
Code-mixing, *see* Bilingual code-mixing (BCM)
Cognition
  defined, 39
  see also Language-cognition connection
Common underlying proficiency, 119
Communication and Symbolic Behavior Scales Developmental Profile™ (CSBS-DP™), 154
Contingent queries, 30
Cross-language adopted children, 146
Cross-linguistic influence, 67–69
Cultural factors, minority language students and, 170–172
Cultures
  changing patterns, 34–36
  in contact, 30–34
  language socialization across, 28–30
  see also Language-culture connection

Developmental bilingual programs, 174–175
Developmental errors, 113
Development language impairment, 18
Dominance, 71
Dominant language, determining, 70, 71–72
Down syndrome (DS), learning of second language and, 47–49
Dual language children/learners
  subgroups, 7, 8f
  use of term, 5, 200
Dual language learning
  burdens of, 40–49
  influence on cognitive development, 49–53, 52f
  intelligence and, 45–49
  limitations to simultaneous, 41–45
  milestones, 44–45
  speech perception in preverbal infants, 41–44
Dual language programs, 165
Dual Language System Hypothesis, 62–63
DUFDE project, 66
Dynamic assessment, 222
Dyslexia, defined, 22

English language learners (ELLs), 110
English-only programs, 176
Errors of commission, 115
Errors of omission, 115
Ethnolinguistic vitality, 137
Executive control functions, 51, 80

Family background factors, success of minority
    language students and, 172
Family bilingualism, 80–81
Family history, 35–36
First language
    immersion programs and ability in, 190
    second language acquisition and what happens
        to, 133–134
    structure and second language acquisition,
        130–131
Flagging, 91–92, 101–103
Formulaic language, 112
Funds of knowledge, 246

Gap-filling hypothesis, 97–99
General all-purpose (GAP) words, 114
Grammatical deviance, 103–105
Grammatical errors, 91
Grammatical morphemes, 112

Heritage language, 10–11
Hispanic children, teaching strategies and, 32

IA, *see* Internationally adopted children
Immersion programs, 9, 165, 174–175
    academic ability, 187–189
    academic achievement, 185–186
    delayed, 185
    development of, 180
    early, 180–181
    effectiveness of, 183–187
    English, 182
    first language ability and, 190
    late, 180–181
    middle, 180–181
    models of, 181f
    objectives, 182
    partial, 181
    questions from parents about, 179
    second language development, 185
    socioeconomic status, 189–190
    submersion programs, 166, 182
    total, 181
Infants, speech perception in, 41–44,
        63–64
Intelligence, relationship between dual language
    learning and, 45–49, 52f

Interdependence between first and second
        language, 119–120
Interlanguage, use of term, 113
Internationally adopted (IA) children, 7–9
Internationally adopted (IA) children, language
        development in
    age at adoption and, 151–153
    assessment issues, 217–218
    birth language, affects on, 146–147
    country of origin and, 153
    during preschool years, 148–156
    institutional care, affects of, 147–148
    key points and implications, 160–161
    language or academic difficulties, 156–159
    methodological considerations, 155–156
    outcomes in general, 149–151
    risk for difficulties, 154–155
Internationally adopted (IA) children, profile of
        Kristina, 17–18
Interutterance, 88–89
Interventions, *see* Specific language impairment,
        interventions
Intrautterance, 88–89
Inuit, 29, 31–32, 34, 35, 171

Language aptitude, second language acquisition
        and, 128–129
Language attrition and shift, 134–139
Language cognition connection
    burdens of, 40–49
    children with severe cognitive challenges, 47–49
    importance of, 39–40
    influence of dual language learning on cognitive
        development, 49–53
    intelligence and dual language learning,
        relationship between, 45–49, 52f
    limitations to simultaneous, 41–45
    milestones, 44–45
    speech perception in preverbal infants,
        41–44
Language crossing, 35
Language culture connection
    changing patterns, 34–36
    cultures in contact, 30–34
    language socialization, 27, 28–30
Language delay, defined, 200–201
Language development, *see* Internationally adopted
        (IA) children, language development in;
        Second language development;
        Simultaneous bilingual children, language
        development in
Language Development Survey (LDS), 149
Language dominance, determination, 70,
        71–72

Language impairment
    characteristics of, 201, 202–207
    defined, 19, 200–201
    see also Reading impairment; Specific language
        impairment (SLI)
Language proficiency and academic success,
    167–170
Language socialization, 27, 28–30
Language systems
    bilingual code-mixing and unitary, 92, 93–97, 95*f*
    interaction of, 67–69
    one versus two, 62–67, 62f, 63*f*
Lexical Gap Hypothesis, 97–99
Limited capacity hypothesis, 41, 203
    limitations to simultaneous dual language
        learning, 41–45
Literacy and language experiences, success of
        minority language students and prior,
        172–174
L1 attrition, 134

MacArthur-Bates Communicative Development
        Inventories (CDIs), 149, 150, 152, 154,
        155, 219
Majority ethnolinguistic community, 5
Majority group, 6
Majority language, 5–6
Majority language students
    defined, 165
    immersion programs for, 178–190
    key points and implications, 190–194
Mean length of utterance (MLU), 75–79, 149
Mediated learning experiences, 222
Memory, phonological working, 129
Meta-analysis, 158–159
Metalinguistic awareness, 51
Mexicano homes, 30, 34
Minimal pairs, 73
Minority ethnolinguistic community, 6
Minority group, 6
Minority language, 6
    development, 80–81
Minority language students
    in bilingual programs, 174–178
    cultural factors, 170–172
    defined, 165–166
    exposure versus acquisition of language, 178
    family background factors, 172
    key points and implications, 190–194
    language proficiency and academic success,
        167–170
    prior literacy and language experiences, 172–174
    in second language only school programs,
        166–174

MLU, *see* Mean length of utterance
Monolingual children
    language developmental rates in bilingual
        children versus, 69–81
    mean length of utterance, 77
Montreal McGill University project, 66, 72, 76
Morphosyntactic development, 123
    in second language learners, 123
Morphosyntax, 65–67, 75–79
    in simultaneous bilingual children, 65–67,
        75–79
Motivation, second language acquisition and,
    127–128
Multilingual development, 81–83

Nondominant language, 71
Nonverbal period, 111–112
Normal curve, 201, 232
Normal range, 201, 232
Norming sample, 232
Norm-referencing tests, 221–222

One parent-one language method/rule, 61,
    93, 94
One-Word Expressive Vocabulary Test, 255

Parents, questions from
    about bilingualism, 61
    about dual language learning appropriateness for
        children with developmental speech and
        language disorders, 209–210
    about immersion programs, 179
    about reading impairments, 238–239
Peabody Picture Vocabulary Test., 46, 255
Percentile, 201, 232
Personality, second language acquisition and, 128
Phonemic
    awareness, 241–242
    defined, 43
Phonetic segments, 43
Phonics instruction, 242
Phonological awareness, 241
Phonological development, 122–123
Phonological memory, 129, 238
Phonology, 64
    in simultaneous bilingual children, 64
Piaget, J., 38
Power differentials, 31–32
Pragmatic effects, bilingual code-mixing and, 99
Preschool children, dominant language,
        determination, 70, 71–72
Profile effects, 125–126, 127*f*, 215–216
Prosody, 42
Puerto Ricans, 34

Rapid automatized naming, 253–254
Raven's Coloured Progressive Matrices Test, 46
Reading acquisition, 239–244, 241f
Reading impairment
  behavioral manifestations of, 236
  defined, 21–23, 235–239
  differences and similarities between L1 and L2,
    244–248
  identifying, 248–249, 252
  interventions, 250–256
  interventions, effectiveness of, 256–258
  other terms for, 22
  questions from parents, 238–239
  reading acquisition and, 239–244
  recommendations, 258–259
  statistics, 234, 235, 237
Response-to-intervention two-stage model,
    225–227, 250–256

School-age children, dominant language,
    determination, 70, 71–72
Second language development
  characteristics of, 113–120
  developmental patterns, 113–117
  first language of minority children, what
    happens to, 133–134
  how long before native-speaker proficiency
    occurs, 120–126
  interdependence between first and second
    language, 119–120
  key points and implications, 139–142
  language shift and attrition, 134–139
  morphosyntactic development, 123
  phonological development, 122–123
  profile effects, 125–126, 127f
  stages of, 111–113
  transfer in, 117–119
  vocabulary development, 124–125
Second language development, factors affecting
    individual differences
  age of acquisition, 129–130
  language aptitude, 128–129
  motivation, 127–128
  personality and social interaction, 128
  quantity and quality of second language
    exposure, 131–133
  structure of first language, 130–131
Second language learners, 6
  specific language impairment and, 205–207
Second language learners, profiles of
  Bonnie, 15
  Faisal, 15–16, 32
  Luis, 14–15
  Pauloosie, 16–17, 32

Samantha, 12–13
  Trevor, 13–14
Second language-only school programs, 166–174
Semilingualism, 136
Sequential bilinguals, 6
SES, see Socioeconomic status
Shift, language, 134–139
Simple View of Reading, 22, 245
Simultaneous bilingual children, 6
Simultaneous bilingual children, language
    development in
  bilingual bootstrapping, 79–80
  developmental rates in bilingual versus
    monolingual children, 69–81
  dominant language, determining, 70, 71–72
  interaction of language systems, 67–69
  key points and implications, 83–85
  mean length of utterance, 75–79
  minority language development, 80–81
  morphosyntax, 65–67, 75–79
  multilingual development, 81–83
  one versus two language systems, 62–67
  phonology, 64
  questions from parents, 61
  specific language impairment and, 203–205
  speech perception, 63–64
  vocabulary, 64–65, 72–75
Simultaneous bilingual children, profiles of
  Bistra, 9–11
  Gabriela, 11–12
  James, 9
Sink-or-swim programs, 166
Social interaction, second language acquisition
    and, 128
Social norms, bilingual code-mixing and, 99–101
Socioeconomic status (SES), 132
  immersion programs and success of majority
    language students and, 189–190
  success of minority language students and, 172
Specific language impairment (SLI)
  characteristics of, 201, 202–207
  defined, 18–21
  learning two languages and, 208–211
  other terms for, 18
  recommendations, 227–228
  second language learners and, 205–207
  simultaneous bilingual children and, 203–205
  tests for identifying, 201–202
  see also Language impairment
Specific language impairment, assessment
  bilingual input factors, 214–215
  cultural backgrounds, obtain information about,
    220–221
  cultural differences in testing, 216

Specific language impairment (*continued*)
  dynamic assessment, 222
  internationally adopted children and, 217–218
  language exposure, obtain information about, 219–220
  language-general versus language-specific measures, 221
  limitations in, 217
  norm-referencing tests, 221–222
  obtain information about both languages, 218–219
  overlapping, 214
  strategies for, 218–222
  unique profiles, 215–216
Specific language impairment, interventions
  bilingual and cross-linguistic approaches, 224–225
  lack of research on, 222–223
  response-to-intervention two-stage model, 225–227
  supporting both languages in, 223–224
Speech perception, 41–44, 63–64
Standard deviation, 201, 232–233

Submersion programs, 166, 182
Subtractive bilingualism, 49–50
Successive bilinguals, 6

Telegraphic, 112
Test-teach-retest approach, 222
Threshold hypothesis, 52
Tier 2 instruction, 248
Time-on-task argument, 176
Tipping points, 33
Transfer errors, 113
Transitional bilingual programs, 174, 175
Translation equivalents, 64–65
Two-way bilingual/immersion programs, 174–175

Unitary Language System Hypothesis
  bilingual code-mixing and, 92, 93–97, 95*f*, 96*f*
  description of, 62–63, 62*f*, 63*f*

Vocabulary, 64–65, 72–75
  development in L2, 124–125
Vygotsky, L., 38